RECKLESSLY ALIVE

Mental Health Journal

A 10-Week Companion to
Smash Your Goals, Plan Your Self-Care,
and Conquer Your Emotions

Sam Eaton

Copyright © 2022 by Sam Eaton
All rights reserved.

No part of this journal may be reproduced or used without the prior written permission of the copyright owner. To request permission, contact sam@recklesslyalive.com
Published Minneapolis, MN

ISBN-978-1-7355854-0-6
First Edition: June 2022
Design Assistance: Jill Gregory

recklesslyalive.com

Printed in the United States of America

CONTENTS

Plan Your Adventures...1

Crush Your Goals..9

Plan Your Self-Care..17

Week 1..25
Week 2..57
Week 3..89
Week 4..121
Week 5..153
Week 6..185
Week 7..217
Week 8..249
Week 9..281
Week 10..313

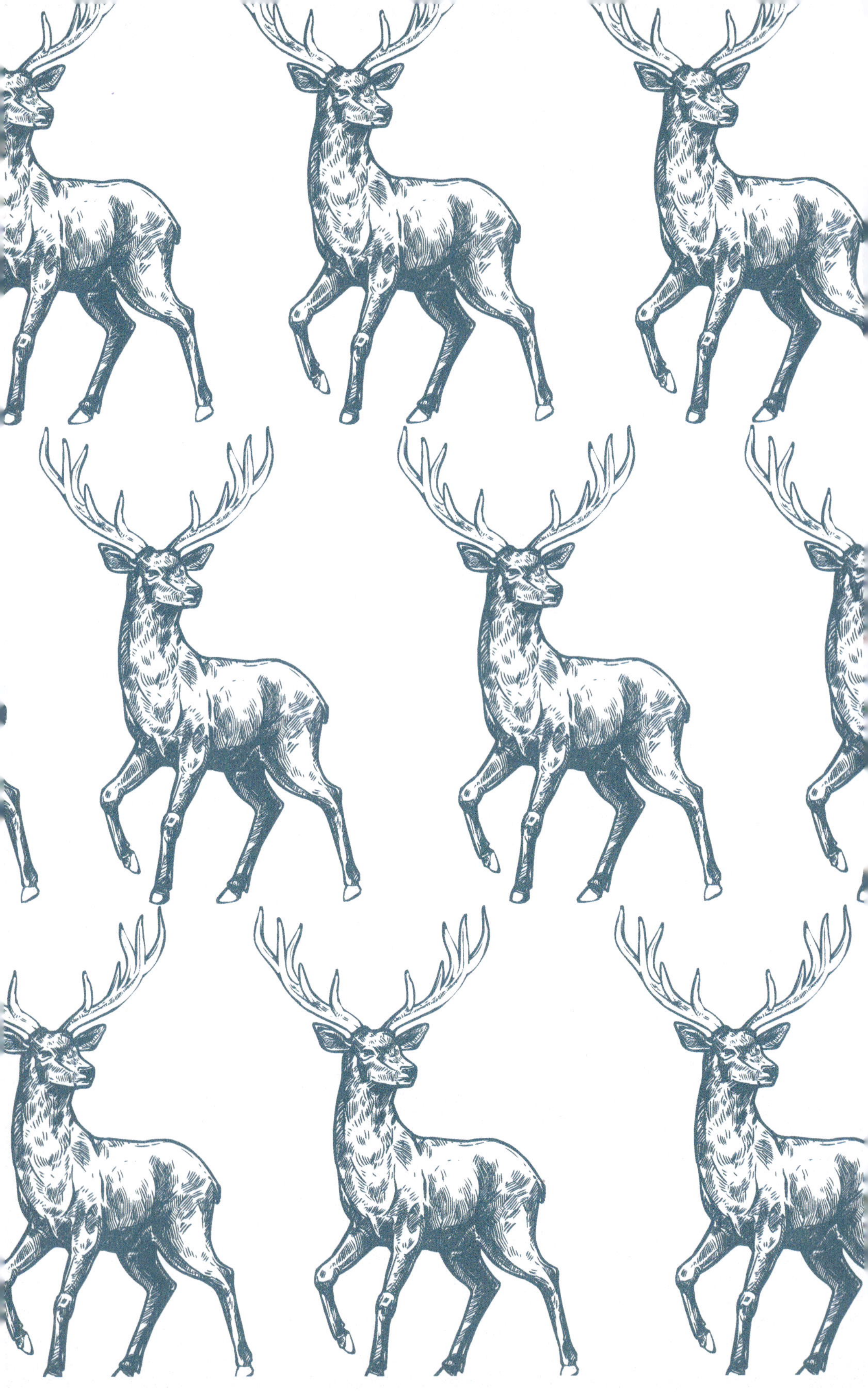

AUTHOR'S NOTE

Dear friend,

My brain can be a scary place. Maybe you know what that's like? I've been battling depression and suicidal thoughts for nearly twenty years with varying degrees of progress and Oreo-fueled regressions.

While therapy and exercise have been two of my greatest weapons, finding a few minutes each day to ground myself is a close third. Since I've never found a journal that completely meets my mental-health needs, I designed this to help all of us.

The pages ahead include daily check-in questions to improve self-talk, spaces to set goals and celebrate wins, reflection pauses to increase self-awareness, and pages to dream about the future you want to create. By purchasing this journal, you are also supporting my work to create a world with zero deaths from suicide. Thank you for joining me in this fight.

May this journal move you closer to the person you want to be while finding some happiness now. Never forget you are worthy of a life that is fully and recklessly alive.

Love,
Sam

P.S. Make sure to post and share your progress on Instagram, Facebook, or TikTok @RecklesslyAlive so I can cheer you on.

Plan Your Adventures

Following my suicide attempt at age twenty-three, this question changed my future:

Have you really given life everything you've got?

Nevertheless, most of the time I would choose a very indoor life with lots of blankets and *Law & Order SVU* reruns. I must push myself to live life to the fullest.

Since the day I decided to stay, I have served in Zimbabwe, Haiti, and Puerto Rico. I finished a marathon, a triathlon, and several CrossFit competitions. I paid off over $90,000 in student loans, completed my master's degree, and flipped a house.

During the hard seasons, chasing adventures helps me fight back against the voice that whispers my life is meaningless and disposable.

I challenge you to take and think about the life you want to live. Nobody else gets to tell you what dreams you have tucked away in your heart. You get to decide what makes you happy and be courageous enough to go for it.

BUCKET

Things I'd Like to Do:

- [ ] _____
- [ ] _____
- [ ] _____
- [ ] _____
- [ ] _____
- [ ] _____
- [ ] _____
- [ ] _____
- [ ] _____
- [ ] _____
- [ ] _____
- [ ] _____
- [ ] _____
- [ ] _____
- [ ] _____
- [ ] _____
- [ ] _____
- [ ] _____
- [ ] _____
- [ ] _____
- [ ] _____
- [ ] _____
- [ ] _____
- [ ] _____
- [ ] _____
- [ ] _____
- [ ] _____
- [ ] _____
- [ ] _____
- [ ] _____

Notes & Doodles

LISTS

Things I'd Like to Learn:

- [ ] _____
- [ ] _____
- [ ] _____
- [ ] _____
- [ ] _____
- [ ] _____
- [ ] _____
- [ ] _____
- [ ] _____
- [ ] _____
- [ ] _____
- [ ] _____
- [ ] _____
- [ ] _____
- [ ] _____
- [ ] _____
- [ ] _____

- [ ] _____
- [ ] _____
- [ ] _____
- [ ] _____
- [ ] _____
- [ ] _____
- [ ] _____
- [ ] _____
- [ ] _____
- [ ] _____
- [ ] _____
- [ ] _____
- [ ] _____
- [ ] _____
- [ ] _____
- [ ] _____
- [ ] _____

Notes & Doodles

BUCKET

Places I'd Like to Explore:

- [ ] _____
- [ ] _____
- [ ] _____
- [ ] _____
- [ ] _____
- [ ] _____
- [ ] _____
- [ ] _____
- [ ] _____
- [ ] _____
- [ ] _____
- [ ] _____
- [ ] _____
- [ ] _____
- [ ] _____
- [ ] _____

- [ ] _____
- [ ] _____
- [ ] _____
- [ ] _____
- [ ] _____
- [ ] _____
- [ ] _____
- [ ] _____
- [ ] _____
- [ ] _____
- [ ] _____
- [ ] _____
- [ ] _____
- [ ] _____
- [ ] _____
- [ ] _____

Notes & Doodles

LISTS

CHOOSE

If money weren't an issue, where would I go?

What local places would I love to explore?

What stops me from living a life of adventure? How can I overcome that?

ADVENTURE

What brings me the most joy in life?

What photos or videos have I seen that make me say, "I want to try that!"?

When I am nearing the end of my life, what will I wish I had done?

Crush Your Goals

Don't get me wrong, I think you're God's gift to humanity just the way you are. Still, it seems most of us continue to work on ourselves. (Or at least you do, or you wouldn't have bought this journal in the first place.)

I highly recommend you choose one to three goals to focus on for the next ten weeks. Take time to envision where you want to be, make a plan, and get after it.

Many researchers suggest small, measurable goals. Sometimes, however, a huge undertaking—like the time I spontaneously signed up for a marathon—can be the spark your soul needs.

Wherever you are, I hope you listen to what your heart is saying and quiet the noise of whom everyone else thinks you should be. Only you know what will make you truly happy. You've got this, my friend.

GOALS

MAIN GOAL:

ACTION STEPS

1.
2.
3.

SECOND GOAL:

ACTION STEPS

1.
2.
3.

THIRD GOAL:

ACTION STEPS

1.
2.
3.

GOAL #1:

How will the result of this goal improve my life?

ACTION STEPS + TASKS
-
-
-
-
-
-
-
-

Who will support me in achieving this goal?

What actions will I take when I feel like giving up?

GOAL #2:

How will the result of this goal improve my life?

ACTION STEPS + TASKS
•
•
•
•
•
•
•
•

Who will support me in achieving this goal?

What actions will I take when I feel like giving up?

GOAL #3:

How will the result of this goal improve my life?

ACTION STEPS + TASKS

-
-
-
-
-
-
-

Who will support me in achieving this goal?

What actions will I take when I feel like giving up?

Monthly Planner

MON	TUES	WED	THU	FRI	SAT	SUN

Monthly Planner

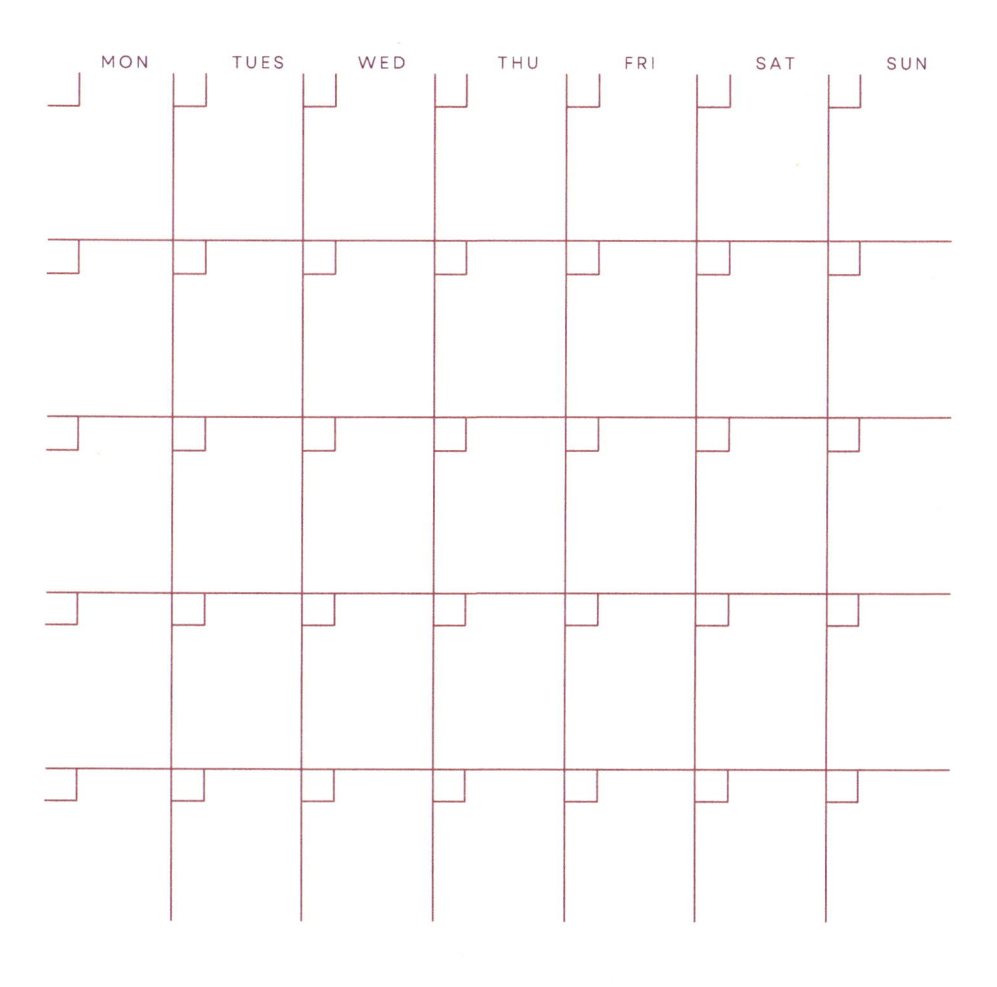

MON	TUES	WED	THU	FRI	SAT	SUN

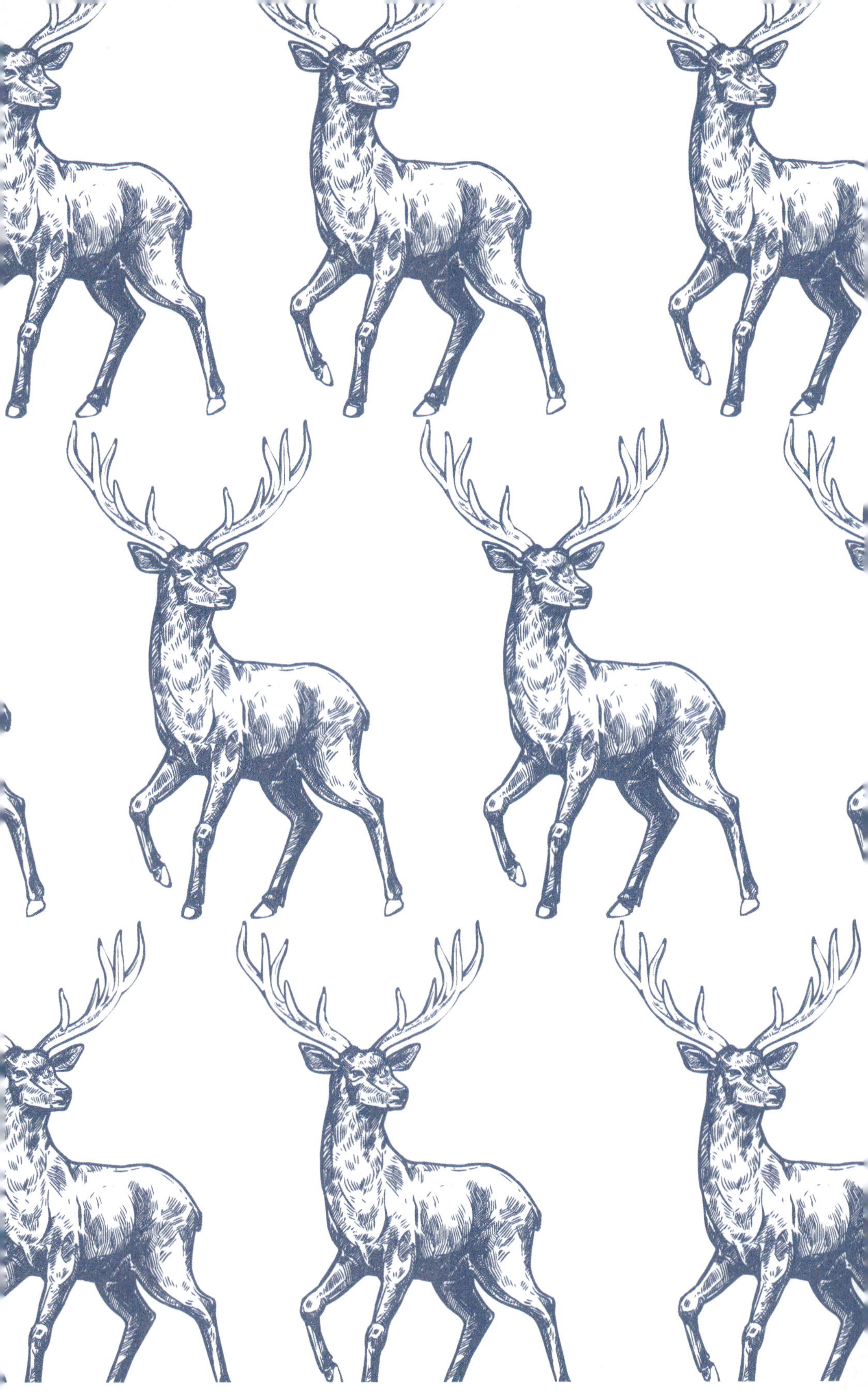

Plan Your Self-Care

Most of what you have been told about self-care is wrong. For whatever reason, self-care has become synonymous with bubble baths.

However, there are six different categories of self-care:
- emotional
- practical
- physical
- mental
- social
- spiritual

Sometimes lying around is the exact opposite of self-care because it isn't what you need most. One of the most important tips to be recklessly alive is to listen to your body. Then ask the question, "What do I need to do to feel like my best self?"

The following pages contain information and exercises to plan your self-care, so you have the capacity to be the best version of who you are.

TYPES OF SELF-CARE

EMOTIONAL SELF-CARE

Activities that help you connect, process, and reflect on what you are feeling.

Examples: Seeing a therapist, writing in a journal, creating art, playing music

PRACTICAL SELF-CARE

Tasks you complete to negate future stressful situations.

Examples: Creating a budget, organizing your closet, sticking to a schedule, making needed appointments

PHYSICAL SELF-CARE

Activities you do that improve the well-being of your physical health.

Examples: Going for a walk, getting quality sleep, staying hydrated, eating nutritious foods

MENTAL SELF-CARE

Activities that stimulate your brain.

Examples: Reading a book, solving a puzzle, playing chess, going to a museum, learning a new skill, taking a class

SOCIAL SELF-CARE

Activities that nurture and deepen the relationships with the people in your life.

Examples: Eating with friends, going on a date, calling your loved ones, meeting new people

SPIRITUAL SELF-CARE

Activities that nurture your spirit and allow you to connect with the world. Spiritual self-care does not have to be religious.

Examples: Meditation, yoga, going to a place of worship, being in nature, dedicating time for self-reflection

SELF-CARE IDEAS

○ Stretch for 10 minutes	○ Drink 64 oz of water	○ Go for a walk in nature	○ Take a social media break	○ Go to bed early
○ Listen to favorite song	○ Complete one nagging task	○ Take a long bath or shower	○ Cook or order your favorite meal	○ Call a friend or family member
○ Go on an adventure	○ Journal	○ Do something creative	○ Write a thank you note	○ Try a DIY project
○ Watch the sunrise or sunset	○ Read a book	○ Explore a new place	○ Watch your favorite movie	○ Volunteer
○ Get some sunlight	○ Start a new hobby	○ Plan an event or trip	○ Organize something	○ Work on a bucket list
○ _____	○ _____	○ _____	○ _____	○ _____

SELF-CARE

How will I put myself first without feeling guilty?

What helps me slow down and be present?

What are some ways I recharge?

When was a time in my life I felt more balanced?

What practices were in place during that time?

REFLECTION

How do I remind myself that I'm enough?

How will I set and protect my boundaries?

How will I notice when I'm nearing burnout?

What are some activities I do out of guilt that drain my happiness?

MY SELF-CARE IDEAS

EMOTIONAL

-
-
-
-
-
-

-
-
-
-
-
-

PRACTICAL

-
-
-
-
-
-

-
-
-
-
-
-

PHYSICAL

-
-
-
-
-

-
-
-
-
-

MY SELF-CARE IDEAS

MENTAL

-
-
-
-
-
-

SOCIAL

-
-
-
-
-
-

SPIRITUAL

-
-
-
-
-

BREATHE

Week 1

EXCERPT FROM
Recklessly Alive

I'm sorry your mind can be a scary place.
I'm sorry your brain loops the trauma.
I'm sorry that sleep can be the only relief.
I'm sorry the pills didn't help at first.
I'm sorry you feel completely alone.
I'm sorry a good day can be just staying alive.
I'm sorry ignorant dirtbags call you weak.
I'm sorry you're told to "be more positive."
I'm sorry people have abandoned you.
I'm sorry you stay in when you can't fake it.

I'm sorry for all of it.

I wish I could wave a magic wand and heal you, but, much to my chagrin, I am not an all-powerful supergod of the universe. (I was shocked, too.)

There is, however, more help available than ever before. There is better research and an army of us dropkicking the crap out of the stigma. There are opportunities to participate in talk therapy, support groups, and online communities. There are more mental health coaches and better-informed doctors. There is a world full of people waiting to help you, but you have to ask—and keep asking.

Please don't spend another second locked in your stupid dark room. Life won't always be this unbearable. If you want to be recklessly alive, stop suffering in silence. You don't have to fight this alone. You can ask for the help you deserve.

Recklessly Alive: What My Suicide Attempt Taught Me About God and Living Life to the Fullest by Sam Eaton (26-27)

HABIT TRACKER

WEEK OF :

HABIT	MON	TUE	WED	THU	FRI	SAT	SUN
	☐	☐	☐	☐	☐	☐	☐
	☐	☐	☐	☐	☐	☐	☐
	☐	☐	☐	☐	☐	☐	☐
	☐	☐	☐	☐	☐	☐	☐
	☐	☐	☐	☐	☐	☐	☐
	☐	☐	☐	☐	☐	☐	☐
	☐	☐	☐	☐	☐	☐	☐
	☐	☐	☐	☐	☐	☐	☐
	☐	☐	☐	☐	☐	☐	☐
	☐	☐	☐	☐	☐	☐	☐

DAILY CHECK-IN

DATE:

WHAT ARE THE FEELINGS OR EMOTIONS I AM CURRENTLY EXPERIENCING?

WHAT LIMITING BELIEFS OR NEGATIVE THOUGHTS AM I HAVING TODAY?

WHAT DO I NEED TO HEAR TO COMBAT THOSE THOUGHTS?

WHAT ARE THREE THINGS I AM THANKFUL FOR TODAY?
-
-
-

WHAT IS THE ONE DAILY TASK I WILL COMPLETE TODAY?

MY FIELD NOTES:

MY DAY

WAKE TIME

TODAY'S MANTRA

SCHEDULE

TOP PRIORITIES

7:00
8:00
9:00
10:00
11:00
12:00
1:00
2:00
3:00
4:00
5:00
6:00
7:00
8:00
9:00
10:00

WEEKLY GOALS

TODAY'S SELF-CARE

What is one thing I am looking forward to?

Be the reason someone believes in good people.

RECKLESSLY ALIVE

JOURNAL

DAILY CHECK-IN

DATE:

WHAT ARE THE FEELINGS OR EMOTIONS I AM CURRENTLY EXPERIENCING?

WHAT LIMITING BELIEFS OR NEGATIVE THOUGHTS AM I HAVING TODAY?

WHAT DO I NEED TO HEAR TO COMBAT THOSE THOUGHTS?

WHAT ARE THREE THINGS I AM THANKFUL FOR TODAY?
-
-
-

WHAT IS THE ONE DAILY TASK I WILL COMPLETE TODAY?

MY FIELD NOTES:

MY DAY

WAKE TIME

TODAY'S MANTRA

SCHEDULE

7:00
8:00
9:00
10:00
11:00
12:00
1:00
2:00
3:00
4:00
5:00
6:00
7:00
8:00
9:00
10:00

TOP PRIORITIES

- [ ]
- [ ]
- [ ]

WEEKLY GOALS

- [ ]
- [ ]
- [ ]
- [ ]
- [ ]

TODAY'S SELF-CARE

- [ ]
- [ ]
- [ ]
- [ ]
- [ ]

What is one thing I need to let go?

Not getting what you want can be the greatest blessing in disguise.

RECKLESSLY ALIVE

JOURNAL

DAILY CHECK-IN

DATE:

WHAT ARE THE FEELINGS OR EMOTIONS I AM CURRENTLY EXPERIENCING?

WHAT LIMITING BELIEFS OR NEGATIVE THOUGHTS AM I HAVING TODAY?

WHAT DO I NEED TO HEAR TO COMBAT THOSE THOUGHTS?

WHAT ARE THREE THINGS I AM THANKFUL FOR TODAY?
-
-
-

WHAT IS THE ONE DAILY TASK I WILL COMPLETE TODAY?

MY FIELD NOTES:

MY DAY

WAKE TIME

TODAY'S MANTRA

SCHEDULE

7:00
8:00
9:00
10:00
11:00
12:00
1:00
2:00
3:00
4:00
5:00
6:00
7:00
8:00
9:00
10:00

TOP PRIORITIES

- [ ]
- [ ]
- [ ]

WEEKLY GOALS

- [ ]
- [ ]
- [ ]
- [ ]
- [ ]

TODAY'S SELF-CARE

- [ ]
- [ ]
- [ ]
- [ ]
- [ ]

> Who has had the greatest impact on my life? How can I be more like them?

If it won't matter in five years, let it go.

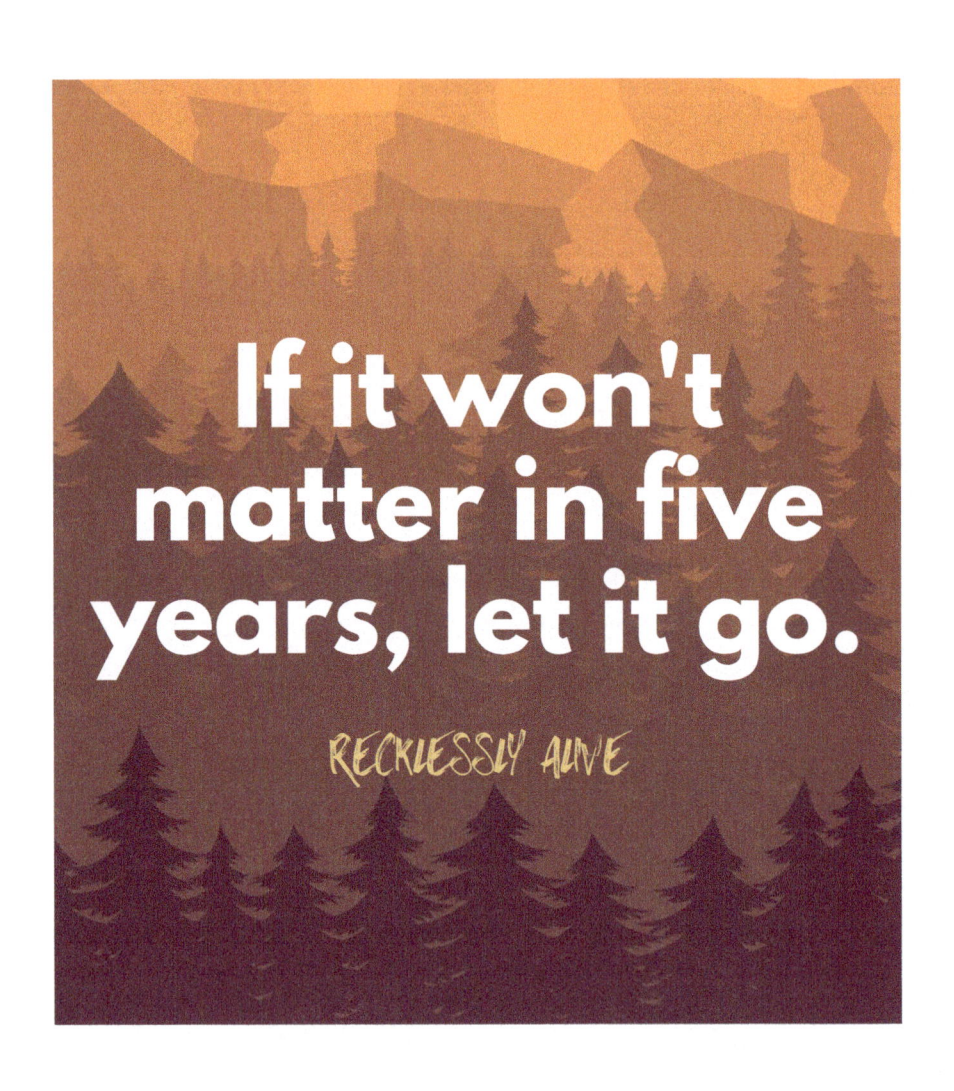

RECKLESSLY ALIVE

JOURNAL

DAILY CHECK-IN

DATE:

WHAT ARE THE FEELINGS OR EMOTIONS I AM CURRENTLY EXPERIENCING?

WHAT LIMITING BELIEFS OR NEGATIVE THOUGHTS AM I HAVING TODAY?

WHAT DO I NEED TO HEAR TO COMBAT THOSE THOUGHTS?

WHAT ARE THREE THINGS I AM THANKFUL FOR TODAY?
-
-
-

WHAT IS THE ONE DAILY TASK I WILL COMPLETE TODAY?

MY FIELD NOTES:

MY DAY

WAKE TIME

TODAY'S MANTRA

SCHEDULE

7:00
8:00
9:00
10:00
11:00
12:00
1:00
2:00
3:00
4:00
5:00
6:00
7:00
8:00
9:00
10:00

TOP PRIORITIES

- [ ]
- [ ]
- [ ]

WEEKLY GOALS

- [ ]
- [ ]
- [ ]
- [ ]
- [ ]

TODAY'S SELF-CARE

- [ ]
- [ ]
- [ ]
- [ ]
- [ ]

How can I make someone smile today?

Let go of the things you can't change.

RECKLESSLY ALIVE

JOURNAL

DAILY CHECK-IN

DATE:

WHAT ARE THE FEELINGS OR EMOTIONS I AM CURRENTLY EXPERIENCING?

WHAT LIMITING BELIEFS OR NEGATIVE THOUGHTS AM I HAVING TODAY?

WHAT DO I NEED TO HEAR TO COMBAT THOSE THOUGHTS?

WHAT ARE THREE THINGS I AM THANKFUL FOR TODAY?
-
-
-

WHAT IS THE ONE DAILY TASK I WILL COMPLETE TODAY?

MY FIELD NOTES:

MY DAY

WAKE TIME

TODAY'S MANTRA

SCHEDULE

7:00
8:00
9:00
10:00
11:00
12:00
1:00
2:00
3:00
4:00
5:00
6:00
7:00
8:00
9:00
10:00

TOP PRIORITIES

- [ ]
- [ ]
- [ ]

WEEKLY GOALS

- [ ]
- [ ]
- [ ]
- [ ]

TODAY'S SELF-CARE

- [ ]
- [ ]
- [ ]
- [ ]
- [ ]

When I reach the end of my life, what would I like others to remember about me?

Impossible is just an opinion.

RECKLESSLY ALIVE

JOURNAL

DAILY CHECK-IN

DATE:

WHAT ARE THE FEELINGS OR EMOTIONS I AM CURRENTLY EXPERIENCING?

WHAT LIMITING BELIEFS OR NEGATIVE THOUGHTS AM I HAVING TODAY?

WHAT DO I NEED TO HEAR TO COMBAT THOSE THOUGHTS?

WHAT ARE THREE THINGS I AM THANKFUL FOR TODAY?
-
-
-

WHAT IS THE ONE DAILY TASK I WILL COMPLETE TODAY?

MY FIELD NOTES:

MY DAY

WAKE TIME

TODAY'S MANTRA

SCHEDULE

7:00
8:00
9:00
10:00
11:00
12:00
1:00
2:00
3:00
4:00
5:00
6:00
7:00
8:00
9:00
10:00

TOP PRIORITIES

- [ ]
- [ ]
- [ ]

WEEKLY GOALS

- [ ]
- [ ]
- [ ]
- [ ]
- [ ]

TODAY'S SELF-CARE

- [ ]
- [ ]
- [ ]
- [ ]
- [ ]

What do I want most? What actions am I taking to get there?

You are too full of life to be half loved.

RECKLESSLY ALIVE

JOURNAL

DAILY CHECK-IN

DATE:

WHAT ARE THE FEELINGS OR EMOTIONS I AM CURRENTLY EXPERIENCING?

WHAT LIMITING BELIEFS OR NEGATIVE THOUGHTS AM I HAVING TODAY?

WHAT DO I NEED TO HEAR TO COMBAT THOSE THOUGHTS?

WHAT ARE THREE THINGS I AM THANKFUL FOR TODAY?
-
-
-

WHAT IS THE ONE DAILY TASK I WILL COMPLETE TODAY?

MY FIELD NOTES:

MY DAY

WAKE TIME

TODAY'S MANTRA

SCHEDULE

7:00
8:00
9:00
10:00
11:00
12:00
1:00
2:00
3:00
4:00
5:00
6:00
7:00
8:00
9:00
10:00

TOP PRIORITIES

- [ ]
- [ ]
- [ ]

WEEKLY GOALS

- [ ]
- [ ]
- [ ]
- [ ]

TODAY'S SELF-CARE

- [ ]
- [ ]
- [ ]
- [ ]
- [ ]

What matters most in my life?

Done is better than perfect.

RECKLESSLY ALIVE

JOURNAL

WEEKLY REFLECTION

RATING MY WEEK: 1   2   3   4   5   6   7   8   9   10

I CHOSE THIS RATING BECAUSE:

....
....
....

I AM PROUD OF MYSELF FOR:

-
-
-
-
-

MY WINS FOR THE WEEK:

....
....
....
....
....

I WOULD LIKE TO IMPROVE:

....
....
....
....
....

LESSONS I LEARNED:

....
....
....
....
....

I AM LETTING GO OF GUILT ABOUT:

....
....
....
....
....

Week 2

EXCERPT FROM
Recklessly Alive

Some people who have been hurt spend their whole lives trying to hurt the world back. And some of us bury that pain deep within.

We sabotage relationships before the other person can leave us. We lose touch with friends because we can't tell them we're barely hanging on. We don't trust a God who would give us a story filled with hurt and despair. We never chase our wildest dreams because we're always waiting for someone to break down the front door and drag us back into a past nightmare.

But that's no way to live, my friend. In fact, that's not living at all. You weren't created to spend your nights beating yourself up and cowering in fear. If you want to be recklessly alive, you have to get out of bed and fight back. Pick up the metaphorical bat and say, "Enough! I will not spend the next thirty years hating myself. I will not let trauma rob another second of the precious days I have left. I will not be silenced about my pain ever again. I will not sit here and let anyone stop me from taking my life back."

You have the power to get help, escape the abuse, and change your life. You are strong enough to overcome anyone trying to hold you down. You can pick yourself up and dust off the past. You can pick up your baseball bat and fight back.

(Eaton 32-33)

HABIT TRACKER

WEEK OF :

HABIT	MON	TUE	WED	THU	FRI	SAT	SUN
	☐	☐	☐	☐	☐	☐	☐
	☐	☐	☐	☐	☐	☐	☐
	☐	☐	☐	☐	☐	☐	☐
	☐	☐	☐	☐	☐	☐	☐
	☐	☐	☐	☐	☐	☐	☐
	☐	☐	☐	☐	☐	☐	☐
	☐	☐	☐	☐	☐	☐	☐
	☐	☐	☐	☐	☐	☐	☐
	☐	☐	☐	☐	☐	☐	☐
	☐	☐	☐	☐	☐	☐	☐

DAILY CHECK-IN

DATE:

WHAT ARE THE FEELINGS OR EMOTIONS I AM CURRENTLY EXPERIENCING?

WHAT LIMITING BELIEFS OR NEGATIVE THOUGHTS AM I HAVING TODAY?

WHAT DO I NEED TO HEAR TO COMBAT THOSE THOUGHTS?

WHAT ARE THREE THINGS I AM THANKFUL FOR TODAY?
-
-
-

WHAT IS THE ONE DAILY TASK I WILL COMPLETE TODAY?

MY FIELD NOTES:

MY DAY

WAKE TIME _____

TODAY'S MANTRA _____

SCHEDULE

7:00 _____
8:00 _____
9:00 _____
10:00 _____
11:00 _____
12:00 _____
1:00 _____
2:00 _____
3:00 _____
4:00 _____
5:00 _____
6:00 _____
7:00 _____
8:00 _____
9:00 _____
10:00 _____

TOP PRIORITIES

☐ _____
☐ _____
☐ _____

ONGOING WEEKLY GOALS

☐ _____
☐ _____
☐ _____
☐ _____
☐ _____

TODAY'S SELF-CARE

☐ _____
☐ _____
☐ _____
☐ _____
☐ _____

What are some difficulties I have had to overcome in my life?

What if it all goes right?

RECKLESSLY ALIVE

JOURNAL

DAILY CHECK-IN

DATE:

WHAT ARE THE FEELINGS OR EMOTIONS I AM CURRENTLY EXPERIENCING?

WHAT LIMITING BELIEFS OR NEGATIVE THOUGHTS AM I HAVING TODAY?

WHAT DO I NEED TO HEAR TO COMBAT THOSE THOUGHTS?

WHAT ARE THREE THINGS I AM THANKFUL FOR TODAY?
-
-
-

WHAT IS THE ONE DAILY TASK I WILL COMPLETE TODAY?

MY FIELD NOTES:

MY DAY

WAKE TIME

TODAY'S MANTRA

SCHEDULE

7:00
8:00
9:00
10:00
11:00
12:00
1:00
2:00
3:00
4:00
5:00
6:00
7:00
8:00
9:00
10:00

TOP PRIORITIES

☐
☐
☐

ONGOING WEEKLY GOALS

☐
☐
☐
☐
☐

TODAY'S SELF-CARE

☐
☐
☐
☐
☐

What is the bravest thing I have ever done?

Let your struggles teach you to be more kind and loving.

RECKLESSLY ALIVE

JOURNAL

DAILY CHECK-IN

DATE:

WHAT ARE THE FEELINGS OR EMOTIONS I AM CURRENTLY EXPERIENCING?

WHAT LIMITING BELIEFS OR NEGATIVE THOUGHTS AM I HAVING TODAY?

WHAT DO I NEED TO HEAR TO COMBAT THOSE THOUGHTS?

WHAT ARE THREE THINGS I AM THANKFUL FOR TODAY?
-
-
-

WHAT IS THE ONE DAILY TASK I WILL COMPLETE TODAY?

MY FIELD NOTES:

MY DAY

WAKE TIME

TODAY'S MANTRA

SCHEDULE

TOP PRIORITIES

- 7:00
- 8:00
- 9:00
- 10:00
- 11:00

ONGOING WEEKLY GOALS

- 12:00
- 1:00
- 2:00
- 3:00
- 4:00
- 5:00

TODAY'S SELF-CARE

- 6:00
- 7:00
- 8:00
- 9:00
- 10:00

What is one accomplishment I am proud of?

One day your story will save someone else.
RECKLESSLY ALIVE

JOURNAL

DAILY CHECK-IN

DATE:

WHAT ARE THE FEELINGS OR EMOTIONS I AM CURRENTLY EXPERIENCING?

WHAT LIMITING BELIEFS OR NEGATIVE THOUGHTS AM I HAVING TODAY?

WHAT DO I NEED TO HEAR TO COMBAT THOSE THOUGHTS?

WHAT ARE THREE THINGS I AM THANKFUL FOR TODAY?
-
-
-

WHAT IS THE ONE DAILY TASK I WILL COMPLETE TODAY?

MY FIELD NOTES:

MY DAY

WAKE TIME

TODAY'S MANTRA

SCHEDULE

7:00
8:00
9:00
10:00
11:00
12:00
1:00
2:00
3:00
4:00
5:00
6:00
7:00
8:00
9:00
10:00

TOP PRIORITIES

- [ ]
- [ ]
- [ ]

ONGOING WEEKLY GOALS

- [ ]
- [ ]
- [ ]
- [ ]
- [ ]

TODAY'S SELF-CARE

- [ ]
- [ ]
- [ ]
- [ ]
- [ ]

Which past experiences am I most thankful for?

You are worthy of a life you love.

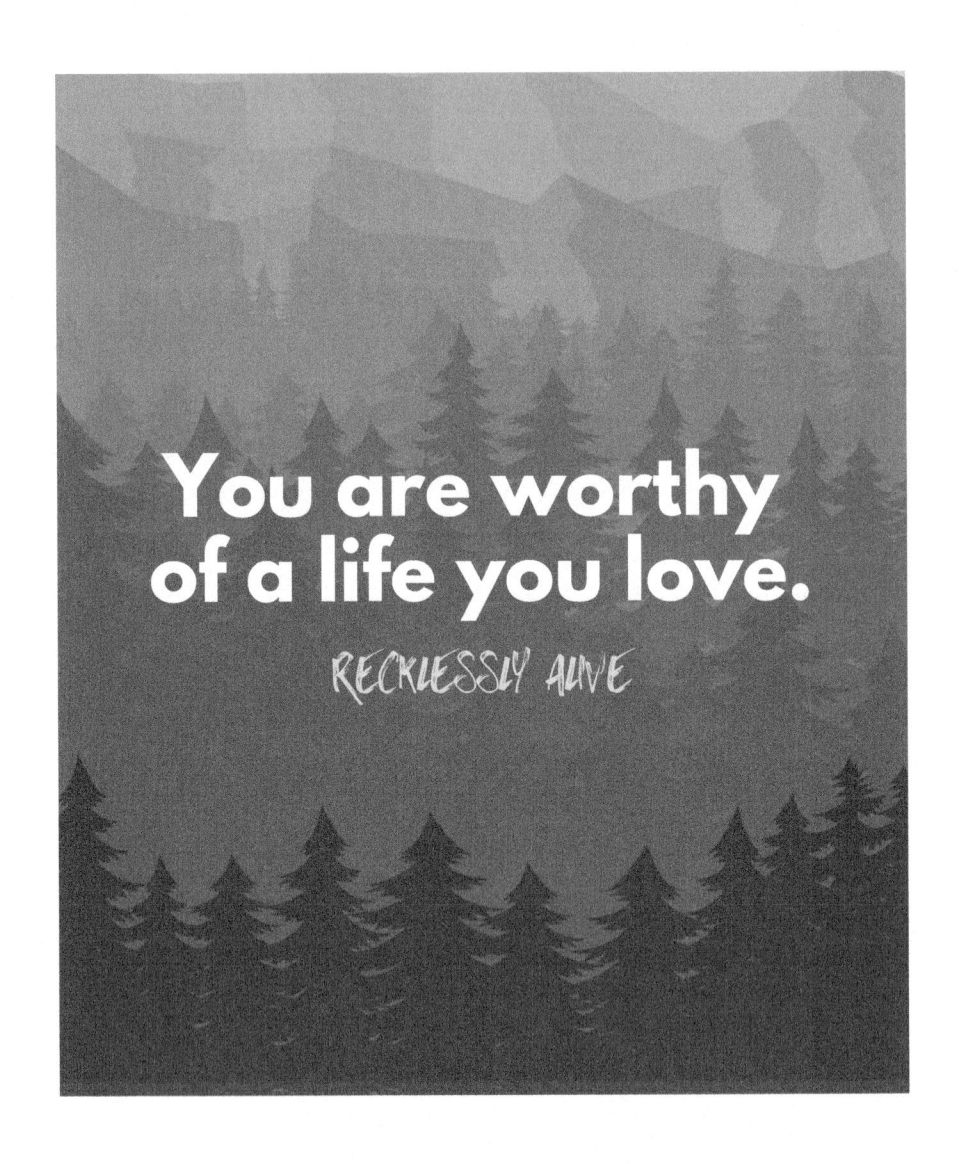

RECKLESSLY ALIVE

JOURNAL

DAILY CHECK-IN

DATE:

WHAT ARE THE FEELINGS OR EMOTIONS I AM CURRENTLY EXPERIENCING?

WHAT LIMITING BELIEFS OR NEGATIVE THOUGHTS AM I HAVING TODAY?

WHAT DO I NEED TO HEAR TO COMBAT THOSE THOUGHTS?

WHAT ARE THREE THINGS I AM THANKFUL FOR TODAY?
-
-
-

WHAT IS THE ONE DAILY TASK I WILL COMPLETE TODAY?

MY FIELD NOTES:

MY DAY

WAKE TIME

TODAY'S MANTRA

SCHEDULE

7:00
8:00
9:00
10:00
11:00
12:00
1:00
2:00
3:00
4:00
5:00
6:00
7:00
8:00
9:00
10:00

TOP PRIORITIES

☐
☐
☐

ONGOING WEEKLY GOALS

☐
☐
☐
☐
☐

TODAY'S SELF-CARE

☐
☐
☐
☐
☐

If I had the opportunity, what would I tell my childhood self?

Sometimes courage sounds like asking for help.

RECKLESSLY ALIVE

JOURNAL

DAILY CHECK-IN

DATE:

WHAT ARE THE FEELINGS OR EMOTIONS I AM CURRENTLY EXPERIENCING?

WHAT LIMITING BELIEFS OR NEGATIVE THOUGHTS AM I HAVING TODAY?

WHAT DO I NEED TO HEAR TO COMBAT THOSE THOUGHTS?

WHAT ARE THREE THINGS I AM THANKFUL FOR TODAY?
-
-
-

WHAT IS THE ONE DAILY TASK I WILL COMPLETE TODAY?

MY FIELD NOTES:

MY DAY

WAKE TIME   **TODAY'S MANTRA**

SCHEDULE   TOP PRIORITIES

7:00
8:00
9:00
10:00
11:00   **ONGOING WEEKLY GOALS**
12:00
1:00
2:00
3:00
4:00
5:00   **TODAY'S SELF-CARE**
6:00
7:00
8:00
9:00
10:00

When was a time I felt good about my mental health? What self-care did I have in place?

It's okay to rest.
RECKLESSLY ALIVE

JOURNAL

DAILY CHECK-IN

DATE:

WHAT ARE THE FEELINGS OR EMOTIONS I AM CURRENTLY EXPERIENCING?

WHAT LIMITING BELIEFS OR NEGATIVE THOUGHTS AM I HAVING TODAY?

WHAT DO I NEED TO HEAR TO COMBAT THOSE THOUGHTS?

WHAT ARE THREE THINGS I AM THANKFUL FOR TODAY?
-
-
-

WHAT IS THE ONE DAILY TASK I WILL COMPLETE TODAY?

MY FIELD NOTES:

MY DAY

WAKE TIME

TODAY'S MANTRA

SCHEDULE

7:00
8:00
9:00
10:00
11:00
12:00
1:00
2:00
3:00
4:00
5:00
6:00
7:00
8:00
9:00
10:00

TOP PRIORITIES

ONGOING WEEKLY GOALS

TODAY'S SELF-CARE

What is a little thing that brings me joy?

You've survived 100% of your worst days.

RECKLESSLY ALIVE

JOURNAL

WEEKLY REFLECTION

RATING MY WEEK: 1 2 3 4 5 6 7 8 9 10

I CHOSE THAT RATING BECAUSE:
....
....
....

I AM PROUD OF MYSELF FOR:

-
-
-
-
-

MY WINS FOR THE WEEK:
....
....
....
....
....

I WOULD LIKE TO IMPROVE:
....
....
....
....
....

LESSONS I LEARNED:
....
....
....
....
....

I AM LETTING GO OF GUILT ABOUT:
....
....
....
....
....

Week 3

EXCERPT FROM
Recklessly Alive

"Aren't you tired of hiding, my friend? Tired of wondering if someone will ever love you for who you really are? Tired of feeling empty and numb because it's been so long since you allowed yourself to hope and dream? Tired of believing the lie that things will never get better?

On my long healing journey, I learned if you want to be recklessly alive, you have to freaking own your story.

You have to let go of anyone who tries to shame you for what you've endured. You have to stop worrying so stinkin' much about what anybody else thinks and start being true to the person you were made to be. You have to let people in and talk to someone who can help heal the wounds you never allow anyone to see.

(Eaton 18)

HABIT TRACKER

WEEK OF :

HABIT	MON	TUE	WED	THU	FRI	SAT	SUN
	☐	☐	☐	☐	☐	☐	☐
	☐	☐	☐	☐	☐	☐	☐
	☐	☐	☐	☐	☐	☐	☐
	☐	☐	☐	☐	☐	☐	☐
	☐	☐	☐	☐	☐	☐	☐
	☐	☐	☐	☐	☐	☐	☐
	☐	☐	☐	☐	☐	☐	☐
	☐	☐	☐	☐	☐	☐	☐
	☐	☐	☐	☐	☐	☐	☐
	☐	☐	☐	☐	☐	☐	☐

DAILY CHECK-IN

DATE:

WHAT ARE THE FEELINGS OR EMOTIONS I AM CURRENTLY EXPERIENCING?

WHAT LIMITING BELIEFS OR NEGATIVE THOUGHTS AM I HAVING TODAY?

WHAT DO I NEED TO HEAR TO COMBAT THOSE THOUGHTS?

WHAT ARE THREE THINGS I AM THANKFUL FOR TODAY?
-
-
-

WHAT IS THE ONE DAILY TASK I WILL COMPLETE TODAY?

MY FIELD NOTES:

MY DAY

WAKE TIME

TODAY'S MANTRA

SCHEDULE

7:00
8:00
9:00
10:00
11:00
12:00
1:00
2:00
3:00
4:00
5:00
6:00
7:00
8:00
9:00
10:00

TOP PRIORITIES

- [ ]
- [ ]
- [ ]

WEEKLY GOALS

- [ ]
- [ ]
- [ ]
- [ ]

TODAY'S SELF-CARE

- [ ]
- [ ]
- [ ]
- [ ]
- [ ]

What encouragement would I give to my past self?

Be the hero you needed when you were younger.

RECKLESSLY ALIVE

JOURNAL

DAILY CHECK-IN   DATE:

WHAT ARE THE FEELINGS OR EMOTIONS I AM CURRENTLY EXPERIENCING?

WHAT LIMITING BELIEFS OR NEGATIVE THOUGHTS AM I HAVING TODAY?

WHAT DO I NEED TO HEAR TO COMBAT THOSE THOUGHTS?

WHAT ARE THREE THINGS I AM THANKFUL FOR TODAY?
-
-
-

WHAT IS THE ONE DAILY TASK I WILL COMPLETE TODAY?

MY FIELD NOTES:

MY DAY

WAKE TIME

TODAY'S MANTRA

SCHEDULE

7:00
8:00
9:00
10:00
11:00
12:00
1:00
2:00
3:00
4:00
5:00
6:00
7:00
8:00
9:00
10:00

TOP PRIORITIES

- [ ]
- [ ]
- [ ]

WEEKLY GOALS

- [ ]
- [ ]
- [ ]
- [ ]
- [ ]

TODAY'S SELF-CARE

- [ ]
- [ ]
- [ ]
- [ ]
- [ ]

How have I stepped out of my comfort zone this week/month/ year?

Never apologize for how you survived.

RECKLESSLY ALIVE

JOURNAL

DAILY CHECK-IN

DATE:

WHAT ARE THE FEELINGS OR EMOTIONS I AM CURRENTLY EXPERIENCING?

WHAT LIMITING BELIEFS OR NEGATIVE THOUGHTS AM I HAVING TODAY?

WHAT DO I NEED TO HEAR TO COMBAT THOSE THOUGHTS?

WHAT ARE THREE THINGS I AM THANKFUL FOR TODAY?
-
-
-

WHAT IS THE ONE DAILY TASK I WILL COMPLETE TODAY?

MY FIELD NOTES:

MY DAY

WAKE TIME   **TODAY'S MANTRA**

_____   _____

SCHEDULE   TOP PRIORITIES

- 7:00 _____ ☐ _____
- 8:00 _____ ☐ _____
- 9:00 _____ ☐ _____
- 10:00 _____
- 11:00 _____ **WEEKLY GOALS**
- 12:00 _____ ☐ _____
- 1:00 _____ ☐ _____
- 2:00 _____ ☐ _____
- 3:00 _____ ☐ _____
- 4:00 _____ ☐ _____
- 5:00 _____ **TODAY'S SELF-CARE**
- 6:00 _____ ☐ _____
- 7:00 _____ ☐ _____
- 8:00 _____ ☐ _____
- 9:00 _____ ☐ _____
- 10:00 _____ ☐ _____

What does my dream life look like?

Today I will do what's best for me.

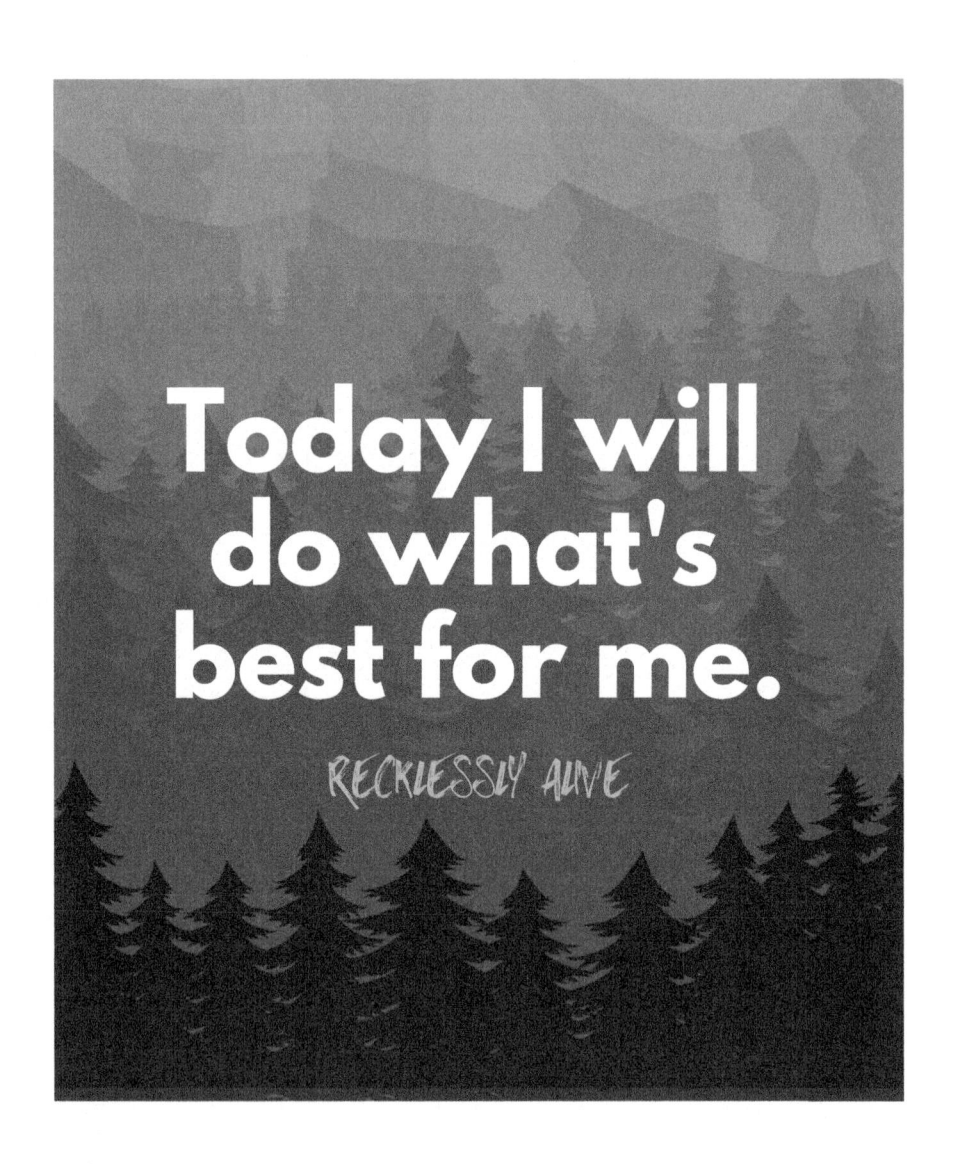

RECKLESSLY ALIVE

JOURNAL

DAILY CHECK-IN

DATE:

WHAT ARE THE FEELINGS OR EMOTIONS I AM CURRENTLY EXPERIENCING?

WHAT LIMITING BELIEFS OR NEGATIVE THOUGHTS AM I HAVING TODAY?

WHAT DO I NEED TO HEAR TO COMBAT THOSE THOUGHTS?

WHAT ARE THREE THINGS I AM THANKFUL FOR TODAY?
-
-
-

WHAT IS THE ONE DAILY TASK I WILL COMPLETE TODAY?

MY FIELD NOTES:

MY DAY

WAKE TIME

TODAY'S MANTRA

SCHEDULE

7:00
8:00
9:00
10:00
11:00
12:00
1:00
2:00
3:00
4:00
5:00
6:00
7:00
8:00
9:00
10:00

TOP PRIORITIES

- [ ]
- [ ]
- [ ]

WEEKLY GOALS

- [ ]
- [ ]
- [ ]
- [ ]
- [ ]

TODAY'S SELF-CARE

- [ ]
- [ ]
- [ ]
- [ ]
- [ ]

If I had the chance, what would I tell my future self?

You're the one who has to love your decisions.

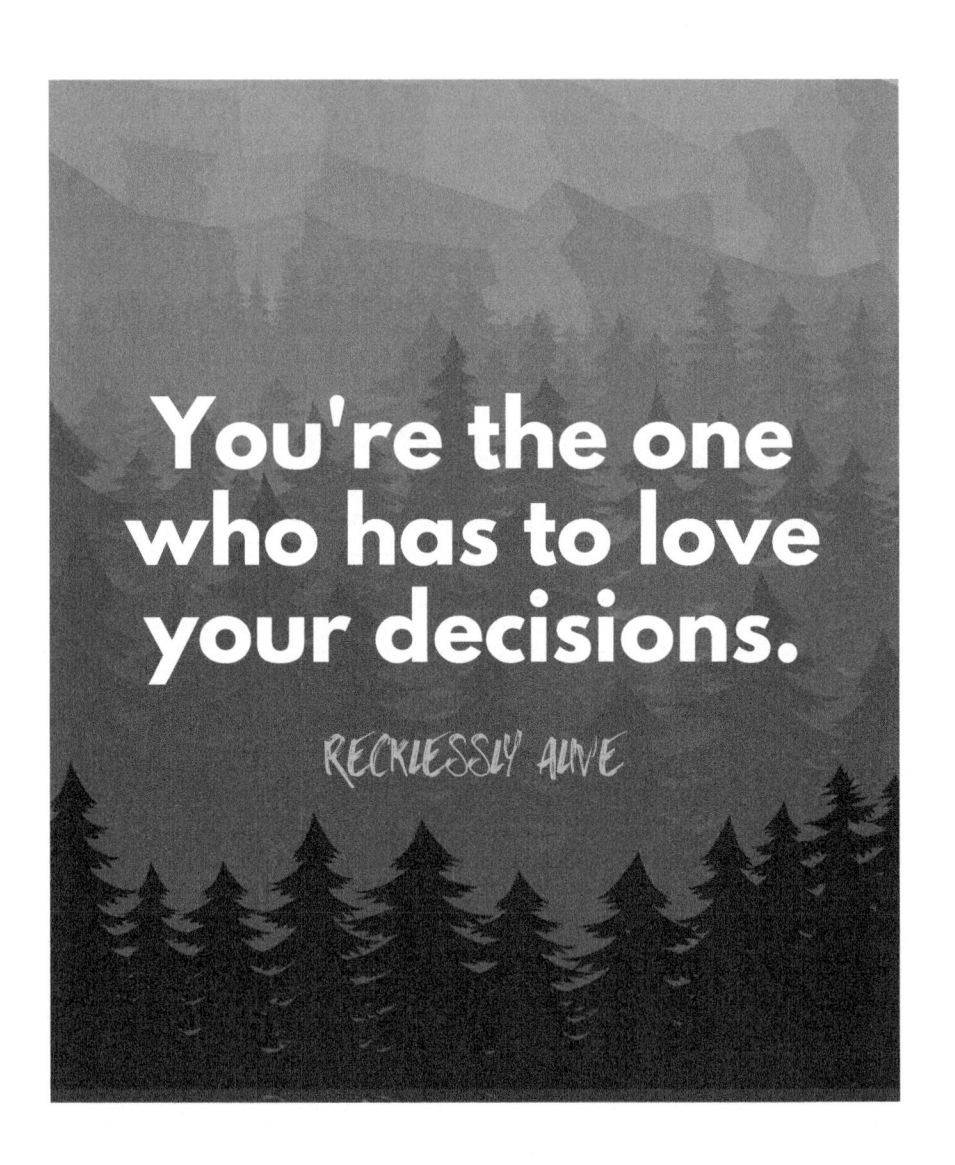

RECKLESSLY ALIVE

JOURNAL

DAILY CHECK-IN

DATE:

WHAT ARE THE FEELINGS OR EMOTIONS I AM CURRENTLY EXPERIENCING?

WHAT LIMITING BELIEFS OR NEGATIVE THOUGHTS AM I HAVING TODAY?

WHAT DO I NEED TO HEAR TO COMBAT THOSE THOUGHTS?

WHAT ARE THREE THINGS I AM THANKFUL FOR TODAY?
-
-
-

WHAT IS THE ONE DAILY TASK I WILL COMPLETE TODAY?

MY FIELD NOTES:

MY DAY

WAKE TIME   TODAY'S MANTRA

SCHEDULE   TOP PRIORITIES

7:00   ☐
8:00   ☐
9:00   ☐
10:00
11:00   WEEKLY GOALS
12:00   ☐
1:00   ☐
2:00   ☐
3:00   ☐
4:00
5:00   TODAY'S SELF-CARE
6:00   ☐
7:00   ☐
8:00   ☐
9:00   ☐
10:00   ☐

If I had more time to do what I love, what would I do?

Hope is believing that tomorrow can be better than today.

RECKLESSLY ALIVE

JOURNAL

DAILY CHECK-IN

DATE:

WHAT ARE THE FEELINGS OR EMOTIONS I AM CURRENTLY EXPERIENCING?

WHAT LIMITING BELIEFS OR NEGATIVE THOUGHTS AM I HAVING TODAY?

WHAT DO I NEED TO HEAR TO COMBAT THOSE THOUGHTS?

WHAT ARE THREE THINGS I AM THANKFUL FOR TODAY?
-
-
-

WHAT IS THE ONE DAILY TASK I WILL COMPLETE TODAY?

MY FIELD NOTES:

MY DAY

WAKE TIME   TODAY'S MANTRA

SCHEDULE   TOP PRIORITIES

7:00
8:00
9:00
10:00
11:00   ### WEEKLY GOALS
12:00
1:00
2:00
3:00
4:00
5:00   ### TODAY'S SELF-CARE
6:00
7:00
8:00
9:00
10:00

What are five positive words I would use to describe myself?

Love them fully while they're here.

RECKLESSLY ALIVE

JOURNAL

DAILY CHECK-IN

DATE:

WHAT ARE THE FEELINGS OR EMOTIONS I AM CURRENTLY EXPERIENCING?

WHAT LIMITING BELIEFS OR NEGATIVE THOUGHTS AM I HAVING TODAY?

WHAT DO I NEED TO HEAR TO COMBAT THOSE THOUGHTS?

WHAT ARE THREE THINGS I AM THANKFUL FOR TODAY?
-
-
-

WHAT IS THE ONE DAILY TASK I WILL COMPLETE TODAY?

MY FIELD NOTES:

MY DAY

WAKE TIME

TODAY'S MANTRA

SCHEDULE

7:00
8:00
9:00
10:00
11:00
12:00
1:00
2:00
3:00
4:00
5:00
6:00
7:00
8:00
9:00
10:00

TOP PRIORITIES

- [ ]
- [ ]
- [ ]

WEEKLY GOALS

- [ ]
- [ ]
- [ ]
- [ ]

TODAY'S SELF-CARE

- [ ]
- [ ]
- [ ]
- [ ]
- [ ]

What did I say yes to this week/month/year that I probably should have said no to?

Happiness is a gift you give yourself.

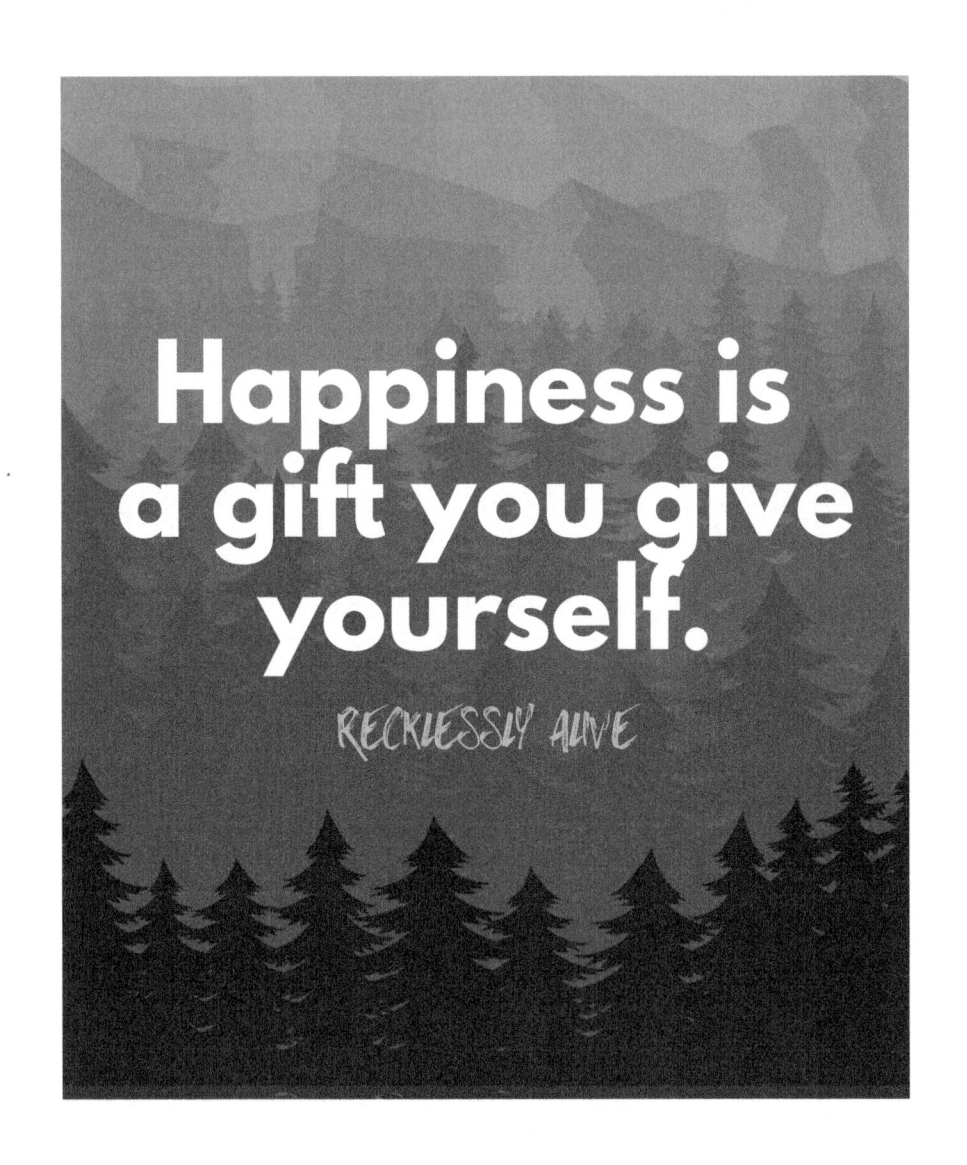

RECKLESSLY ALIVE

JOURNAL

WEEKLY REFLECTION

RATING MY WEEK: 1   2   3   4   5   6   7   8   9   10

I CHOSE THAT RATING BECAUSE:

....
....
....

I AM PROUD OF MYSELF FOR:

-
-
-
-
-

MY WINS FOR THE WEEK:

....
....
....
....
....

I WOULD LIKE TO IMPROVE:

....
....
....
....
....

LESSONS I LEARNED:

....
....
....
....
....

I AM LETTING GO OF GUILT ABOUT:

....
....
....
....
....

Week 4

EXCERPT FROM
Recklessly Alive

"I know your mind can be a scary place when agonizing words and painful memories loop out of control until you're a sobbing mess. I'm sorry a few hateful people hijacked your confidence and self-worth. I'm sorry your brain has been conditioned to self-destruct.

But how many more years are you going to spend hating yourself? How many more years are you going to suffer without giving healing everything you've got?"

(Eaton 48-49)

HABIT TRACKER

WEEK OF:

HABIT	MON	TUE	WED	THU	FRI	SAT	SUN
	☐	☐	☐	☐	☐	☐	☐
	☐	☐	☐	☐	☐	☐	☐
	☐	☐	☐	☐	☐	☐	☐
	☐	☐	☐	☐	☐	☐	☐
	☐	☐	☐	☐	☐	☐	☐
	☐	☐	☐	☐	☐	☐	☐
	☐	☐	☐	☐	☐	☐	☐
	☐	☐	☐	☐	☐	☐	☐
	☐	☐	☐	☐	☐	☐	☐
	☐	☐	☐	☐	☐	☐	☐

DAILY CHECK-IN

DATE:

WHAT ARE THE FEELINGS OR EMOTIONS I AM CURRENTLY EXPERIENCING?

WHAT LIMITING BELIEFS OR NEGATIVE THOUGHTS AM I HAVING TODAY?

WHAT DO I NEED TO HEAR TO COMBAT THOSE THOUGHTS?

WHAT ARE THREE THINGS I AM THANKFUL FOR TODAY?
-
-
-

WHAT IS THE ONE DAILY TASK I WILL COMPLETE TODAY?

MY FIELD NOTES:

MY DAY

WAKE TIME

TODAY'S MANTRA

SCHEDULE

7:00
8:00
9:00
10:00
11:00
12:00
1:00
2:00
3:00
4:00
5:00
6:00
7:00
8:00
9:00
10:00

TOP PRIORITIES

- [ ]
- [ ]
- [ ]

WEEKLY GOALS

- [ ]
- [ ]
- [ ]
- [ ]
- [ ]

TODAY'S SELF-CARE

- [ ]
- [ ]
- [ ]
- [ ]
- [ ]

How can I take better care of myself? How will I make that happen?

You are worthy of a happy & peaceful life.

RECKLESSLY ALIVE

JOURNAL

DAILY CHECK-IN

DATE:

WHAT ARE THE FEELINGS OR EMOTIONS I AM CURRENTLY EXPERIENCING?

WHAT LIMITING BELIEFS OR NEGATIVE THOUGHTS AM I HAVING TODAY?

WHAT DO I NEED TO HEAR TO COMBAT THOSE THOUGHTS?

WHAT ARE THREE THINGS I AM THANKFUL FOR TODAY?
-
-
-

WHAT IS THE ONE DAILY TASK I WILL COMPLETE TODAY?

MY FIELD NOTES:

MY DAY

WAKE TIME

TODAY'S MANTRA

SCHEDULE

7:00
8:00
9:00
10:00
11:00
12:00
1:00
2:00
3:00
4:00
5:00
6:00
7:00
8:00
9:00
10:00

TOP PRIORITIES

- [ ]
- [ ]
- [ ]

WEEKLY GOALS

- [ ]
- [ ]
- [ ]
- [ ]
- [ ]

TODAY'S SELF-CARE

- [ ]
- [ ]
- [ ]
- [ ]
- [ ]

What are some things I am passionate about? How can I make more time for things I love?

I am worthy of love and belonging.

RECKLESSLY ALIVE

JOURNAL

DAILY CHECK-IN

DATE:

WHAT ARE THE FEELINGS OR EMOTIONS I AM CURRENTLY EXPERIENCING?

WHAT LIMITING BELIEFS OR NEGATIVE THOUGHTS AM I HAVING TODAY?

WHAT DO I NEED TO HEAR TO COMBAT THOSE THOUGHTS?

WHAT ARE THREE THINGS I AM THANKFUL FOR TODAY?
-
-
-

WHAT IS THE ONE DAILY TASK I WILL COMPLETE TODAY?

MY FIELD NOTES:

MY DAY

WAKE TIME   **TODAY'S MANTRA**

SCHEDULE

TOP PRIORITIES

7:00
8:00
9:00
10:00
11:00

WEEKLY GOALS

12:00
1:00
2:00
3:00
4:00

TODAY'S SELF-CARE

5:00
6:00
7:00
8:00
9:00
10:00

What is one time I didn't get what I wanted and it turned out for the better?

I am creating
the life of
my dreams.

RECKLESSLY ALIVE

JOURNAL

DAILY CHECK-IN

DATE:

WHAT ARE THE FEELINGS OR EMOTIONS I AM CURRENTLY EXPERIENCING?

WHAT LIMITING BELIEFS OR NEGATIVE THOUGHTS AM I HAVING TODAY?

WHAT DO I NEED TO HEAR TO COMBAT THOSE THOUGHTS?

WHAT ARE THREE THINGS I AM THANKFUL FOR TODAY?
-
-
-

WHAT IS THE ONE DAILY TASK I WILL COMPLETE TODAY?

MY FIELD NOTES:

MY DAY

WAKE TIME

TODAY'S MANTRA

SCHEDULE

7:00
8:00
9:00
10:00
11:00
12:00
1:00
2:00
3:00
4:00
5:00
6:00
7:00
8:00
9:00
10:00

TOP PRIORITIES

- [ ]
- [ ]
- [ ]

WEEKLY GOALS

- [ ]
- [ ]
- [ ]
- [ ]
- [ ]

TODAY'S SELF-CARE

- [ ]
- [ ]
- [ ]
- [ ]
- [ ]

What is something I am working to improve in my life?

I know it feels impossible.
Try once more.

RECKLESSLY ALIVE

JOURNAL

DAILY CHECK-IN

DATE:

WHAT ARE THE FEELINGS OR EMOTIONS I AM CURRENTLY EXPERIENCING?

WHAT LIMITING BELIEFS OR NEGATIVE THOUGHTS AM I HAVING TODAY?

WHAT DO I NEED TO HEAR TO COMBAT THOSE THOUGHTS?

WHAT ARE THREE THINGS I AM THANKFUL FOR TODAY?
-
-
-

WHAT IS THE ONE DAILY TASK I WILL COMPLETE TODAY?

MY FIELD NOTES:

MY DAY

WAKE TIME

TODAY'S MANTRA

SCHEDULE

7:00
8:00
9:00
10:00
11:00
12:00
1:00
2:00
3:00
4:00
5:00
6:00
7:00
8:00
9:00
10:00

TOP PRIORITIES

- [ ]
- [ ]
- [ ]

WEEKLY GOALS

- [ ]
- [ ]
- [ ]
- [ ]
- [ ]

TODAY'S SELF-CARE

- [ ]
- [ ]
- [ ]
- [ ]
- [ ]

What do I find myself complaining about the most? How can I work to change that circumstance?

Your happiness doesn't have to make sense to anyone else.

RECKLESSLY ALIVE

JOURNAL

DAILY CHECK-IN

DATE:

WHAT ARE THE FEELINGS OR EMOTIONS I AM CURRENTLY EXPERIENCING?

WHAT LIMITING BELIEFS OR NEGATIVE THOUGHTS AM I HAVING TODAY?

WHAT DO I NEED TO HEAR TO COMBAT THOSE THOUGHTS?

WHAT ARE THREE THINGS I AM THANKFUL FOR TODAY?
-
-
-

WHAT IS THE ONE DAILY TASK I WILL COMPLETE TODAY?

MY FIELD NOTES:

MY DAY

WAKE TIME

TODAY'S MANTRA

SCHEDULE

7:00
8:00
9:00
10:00
11:00
12:00
1:00
2:00
3:00
4:00
5:00
6:00
7:00
8:00
9:00
10:00

TOP PRIORITIES

- [ ]
- [ ]
- [ ]

WEEKLY GOALS

- [ ]
- [ ]
- [ ]
- [ ]

TODAY'S SELF-CARE

- [ ]
- [ ]
- [ ]
- [ ]

What good habits do I have? Are there any new habits I want to adopt?

Get out of your own way.

RECKLESSLY ALIVE

JOURNAL

DAILY CHECK-IN

DATE:

WHAT ARE THE FEELINGS OR EMOTIONS I AM CURRENTLY EXPERIENCING?

WHAT LIMITING BELIEFS OR NEGATIVE THOUGHTS AM I HAVING TODAY?

WHAT DO I NEED TO HEAR TO COMBAT THOSE THOUGHTS?

WHAT ARE THREE THINGS I AM THANKFUL FOR TODAY?
-
-
-

WHAT IS THE ONE DAILY TASK I WILL COMPLETE TODAY?

MY FIELD NOTES:

MY DAY

WAKE TIME

TODAY'S MANTRA

SCHEDULE

7:00
8:00
9:00
10:00
11:00
12:00
1:00
2:00
3:00
4:00
5:00
6:00
7:00
8:00
9:00
10:00

TOP PRIORITIES

☐
☐
☐

WEEKLY GOALS

☐
☐
☐
☐
☐

TODAY'S SELF-CARE

☐
☐
☐
☐
☐

What bad habits would I like to get rid of? What steps do I need to take to make that happen?

Happiness is an emotion, not a destination.

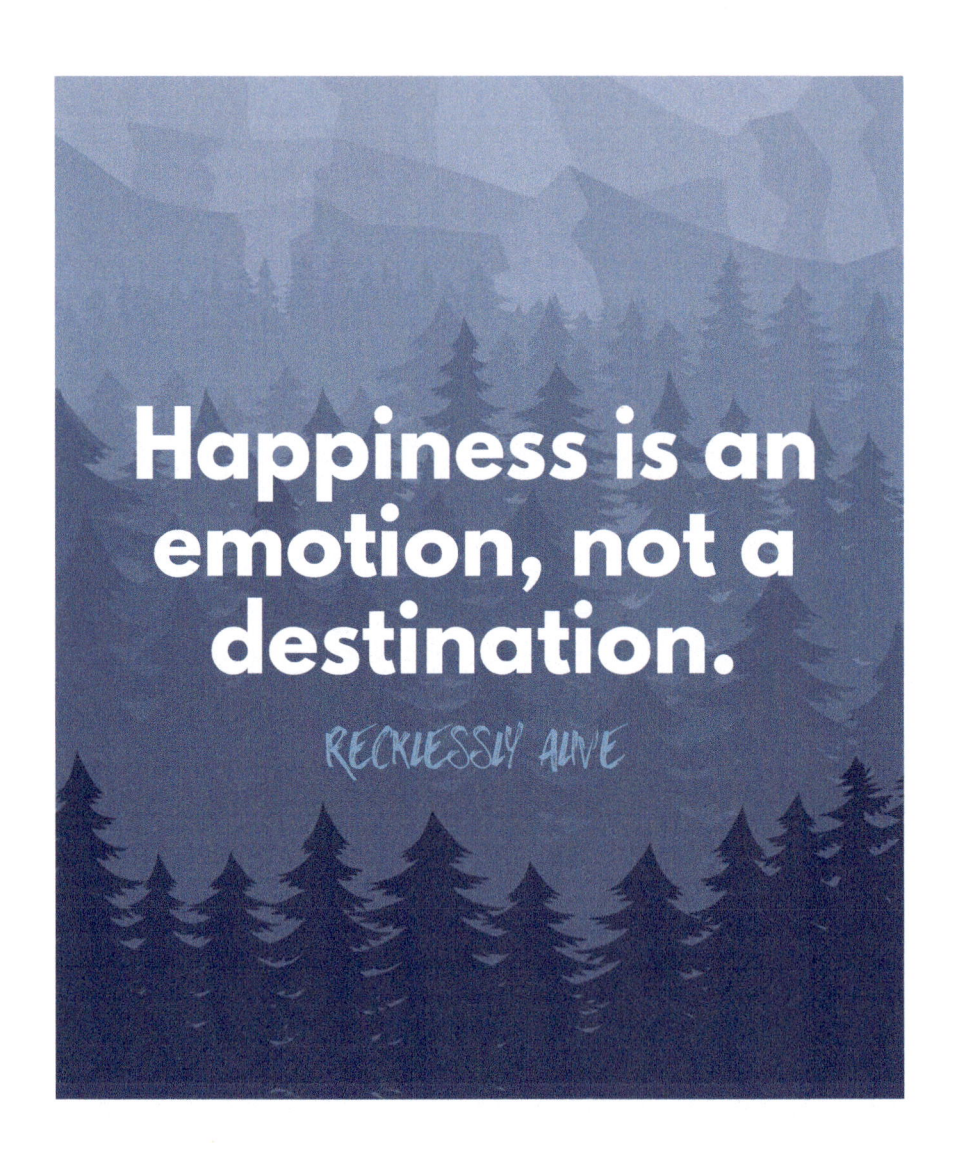

RECKLESSLY ALIVE

JOURNAL

WEEKLY REFLECTION

RATING MY WEEK: 1   2   3   4   5   6   7   8   9   10

I CHOSE THAT RATING BECAUSE:

....
....
....

I AM PROUD OF MYSELF FOR:

-
-
-
-
-

MY WINS FOR THE WEEK:

....
....
....
....
....

I WOULD LIKE TO IMPROVE:

....
....
....
....
....

LESSONS I LEARNED:

....
....
....
....
....

I AM LETTING GO OF GUILT ABOUT:

....
....
....
....
....

Week 5

EXCERPT FROM
Recklessly Alive

"I hope you're brave enough to change the areas of your world that feel dark and destructive. I hope you're bold enough to create a life you don't want to forget. I hope you're courageous enough to chase I-can't-believe-that- just-happened stories.

I hope you're strong enough to allow yourself to fully feel your emotions and fight for healing. I hope you never give up on a life that is fully and recklessly alive.

But most of all, if you've lost your way, I hope you never forget you can always choose a different path."

(Eaton 64-65)

HABIT TRACKER

WEEK OF :

HABIT	MON	TUE	WED	THU	FRI	SAT	SUN
	☐	☐	☐	☐	☐	☐	☐
	☐	☐	☐	☐	☐	☐	☐
	☐	☐	☐	☐	☐	☐	☐
	☐	☐	☐	☐	☐	☐	☐
	☐	☐	☐	☐	☐	☐	☐
	☐	☐	☐	☐	☐	☐	☐
	☐	☐	☐	☐	☐	☐	☐
	☐	☐	☐	☐	☐	☐	☐
	☐	☐	☐	☐	☐	☐	☐
	☐	☐	☐	☐	☐	☐	☐

DAILY CHECK-IN

DATE:

WHAT ARE THE FEELINGS OR EMOTIONS I AM CURRENTLY EXPERIENCING?

WHAT LIMITING BELIEFS OR NEGATIVE THOUGHTS AM I HAVING TODAY?

WHAT DO I NEED TO HEAR TO COMBAT THOSE THOUGHTS?

WHAT ARE THREE THINGS I AM THANKFUL FOR TODAY?
-
-
-

WHAT IS THE ONE DAILY TASK I WILL COMPLETE TODAY?

MY FIELD NOTES:

MY DAY

WAKE TIME

TODAY'S MANTRA

SCHEDULE

7:00
8:00
9:00
10:00
11:00
12:00
1:00
2:00
3:00
4:00
5:00
6:00
7:00
8:00
9:00
10:00

TOP PRIORITIES

- [ ]
- [ ]
- [ ]

WEEKLY GOALS

- [ ]
- [ ]
- [ ]
- [ ]
- [ ]

TODAY'S SELF-CARE

- [ ]
- [ ]
- [ ]
- [ ]
- [ ]

When do I feel best about myself?

Celebrate who you are and who you didn't become.

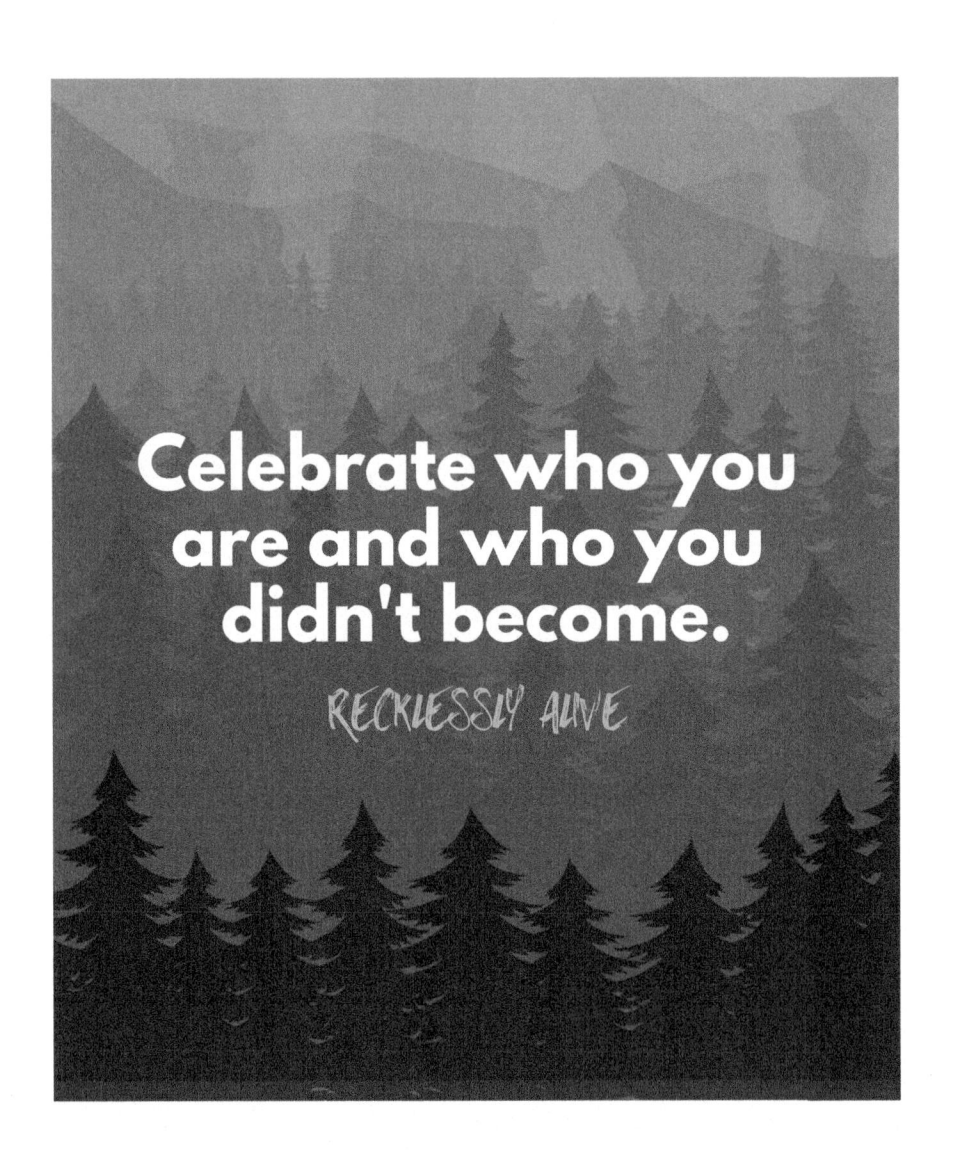

RECKLESSLY ALIVE

JOURNAL

DAILY CHECK-IN

DATE:

WHAT ARE THE FEELINGS OR EMOTIONS I AM CURRENTLY EXPERIENCING?

WHAT LIMITING BELIEFS OR NEGATIVE THOUGHTS AM I HAVING TODAY?

WHAT DO I NEED TO HEAR TO COMBAT THOSE THOUGHTS?

WHAT ARE THREE THINGS I AM THANKFUL FOR TODAY?
-
-
-

WHAT IS THE ONE DAILY TASK I WILL COMPLETE TODAY?

MY FIELD NOTES:

MY DAY

WAKE TIME

TODAY'S MANTRA

SCHEDULE

7:00
8:00
9:00
10:00
11:00
12:00
1:00
2:00
3:00
4:00
5:00
6:00
7:00
8:00
9:00
10:00

TOP PRIORITIES

- [ ]
- [ ]
- [ ]

WEEKLY GOALS

- [ ]
- [ ]
- [ ]
- [ ]
- [ ]

TODAY'S SELF-CARE

- [ ]
- [ ]
- [ ]
- [ ]
- [ ]

What helps me feel energized and refreshed?

You're not too old. It's not too late.

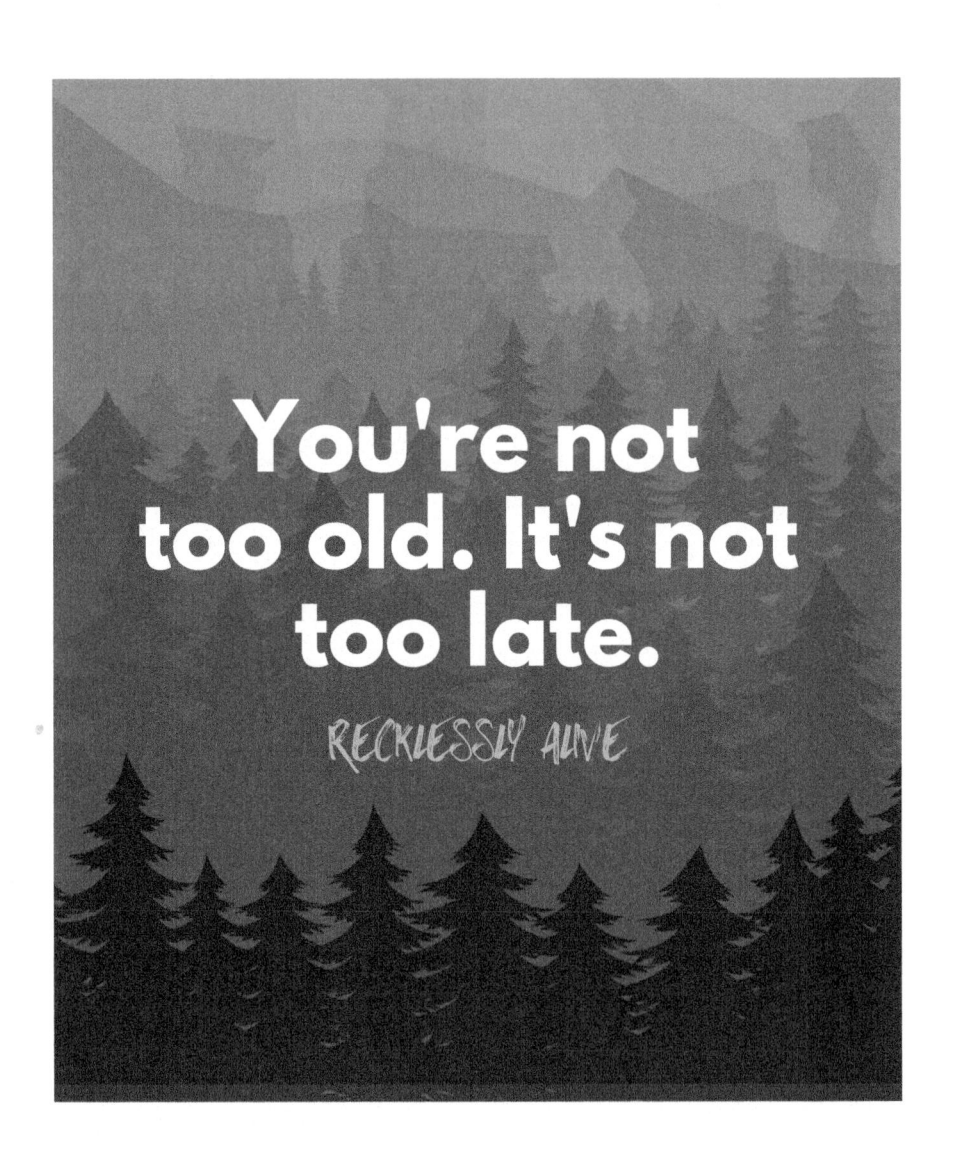

RECKLESSLY ALIVE

JOURNAL

DAILY CHECK-IN   DATE:

WHAT ARE THE FEELINGS OR EMOTIONS I AM CURRENTLY EXPERIENCING?

WHAT LIMITING BELIEFS OR NEGATIVE THOUGHTS AM I HAVING TODAY?

WHAT DO I NEED TO HEAR TO COMBAT THOSE THOUGHTS?

WHAT ARE THREE THINGS I AM THANKFUL FOR TODAY?
-
-
-

WHAT IS THE ONE DAILY TASK I WILL COMPLETE TODAY?

MY FIELD NOTES:

MY DAY

WAKE TIME
_____

TODAY'S MANTRA
_____

SCHEDULE

7:00 _____
8:00 _____
9:00 _____
10:00 _____
11:00 _____
12:00 _____
1:00 _____
2:00 _____
3:00 _____
4:00 _____
5:00 _____
6:00 _____
7:00 _____
8:00 _____
9:00 _____
10:00 _____

TOP PRIORITIES

☐ _____
☐ _____
☐ _____

WEEKLY GOALS

☐ _____
☐ _____
☐ _____
☐ _____
☐ _____

TODAY'S SELF-CARE

☐ _____
☐ _____
☐ _____
☐ _____
☐ _____

What do I worry about the most? How can I work on relieving that stress?

True strength is forgiving someone who isn't sorry.

RECKLESSLY ALIVE

JOURNAL

DAILY CHECK-IN

DATE:

WHAT ARE THE FEELINGS OR EMOTIONS I AM CURRENTLY EXPERIENCING?

WHAT LIMITING BELIEFS OR NEGATIVE THOUGHTS AM I HAVING TODAY?

WHAT DO I NEED TO HEAR TO COMBAT THOSE THOUGHTS?

WHAT ARE THREE THINGS I AM THANKFUL FOR TODAY?
-
-
-

WHAT IS THE ONE DAILY TASK I WILL COMPLETE TODAY?

MY FIELD NOTES:

MY DAY

WAKE TIME
_____

TODAY'S MANTRA
_____

SCHEDULE

7:00	_____
8:00	_____
9:00	_____
10:00	_____
11:00	_____
12:00	_____
1:00	_____
2:00	_____
3:00	_____
4:00	_____
5:00	_____
6:00	_____
7:00	_____
8:00	_____
9:00	_____
10:00	_____

TOP PRIORITIES

- [ ] _____
- [ ] _____
- [ ] _____

WEEKLY GOALS

- [ ] _____
- [ ] _____
- [ ] _____
- [ ] _____
- [ ] _____

TODAY'S SELF-CARE

- [ ] _____
- [ ] _____
- [ ] _____
- [ ] _____
- [ ] _____

Am I my own best friend or my own worst enemy?

We repeat what we don't repair.

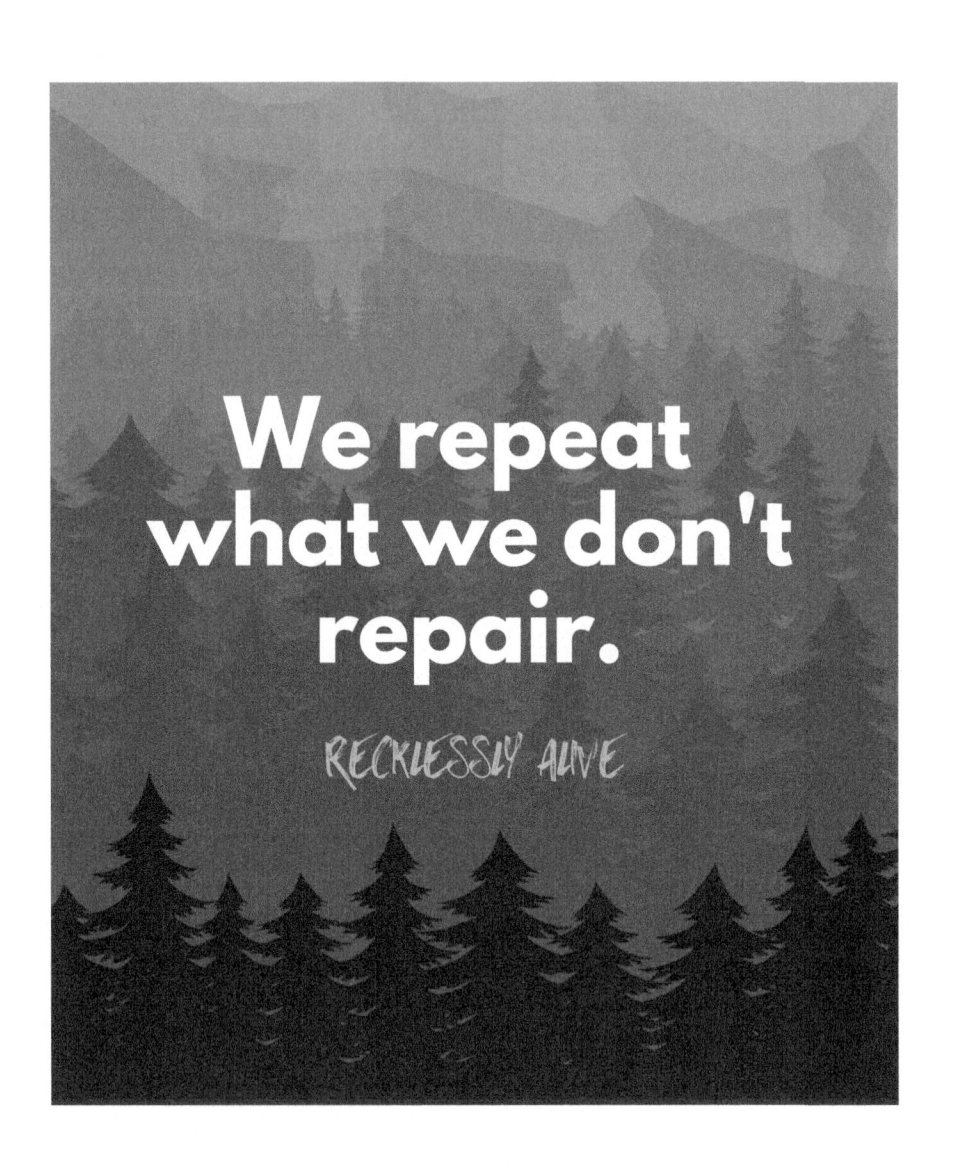

RECKLESSLY ALIVE

JOURNAL

DAILY CHECK-IN

DATE:

WHAT ARE THE FEELINGS OR EMOTIONS I AM CURRENTLY EXPERIENCING?

WHAT LIMITING BELIEFS OR NEGATIVE THOUGHTS AM I HAVING TODAY?

WHAT DO I NEED TO HEAR TO COMBAT THOSE THOUGHTS?

WHAT ARE THREE THINGS I AM THANKFUL FOR TODAY?
-
-
-

WHAT IS THE ONE DAILY TASK I WILL COMPLETE TODAY?

MY FIELD NOTES:

MY DAY

WAKE TIME

TODAY'S MANTRA

SCHEDULE

7:00
8:00
9:00
10:00
11:00
12:00
1:00
2:00
3:00
4:00
5:00
6:00
7:00
8:00
9:00
10:00

TOP PRIORITIES

- [ ]
- [ ]
- [ ]

WEEKLY GOALS

- [ ]
- [ ]
- [ ]
- [ ]
- [ ]

TODAY'S SELF-CARE

- [ ]
- [ ]
- [ ]
- [ ]
- [ ]

What does self-love mean to me?

Yesterday is heavy.
Put it down.

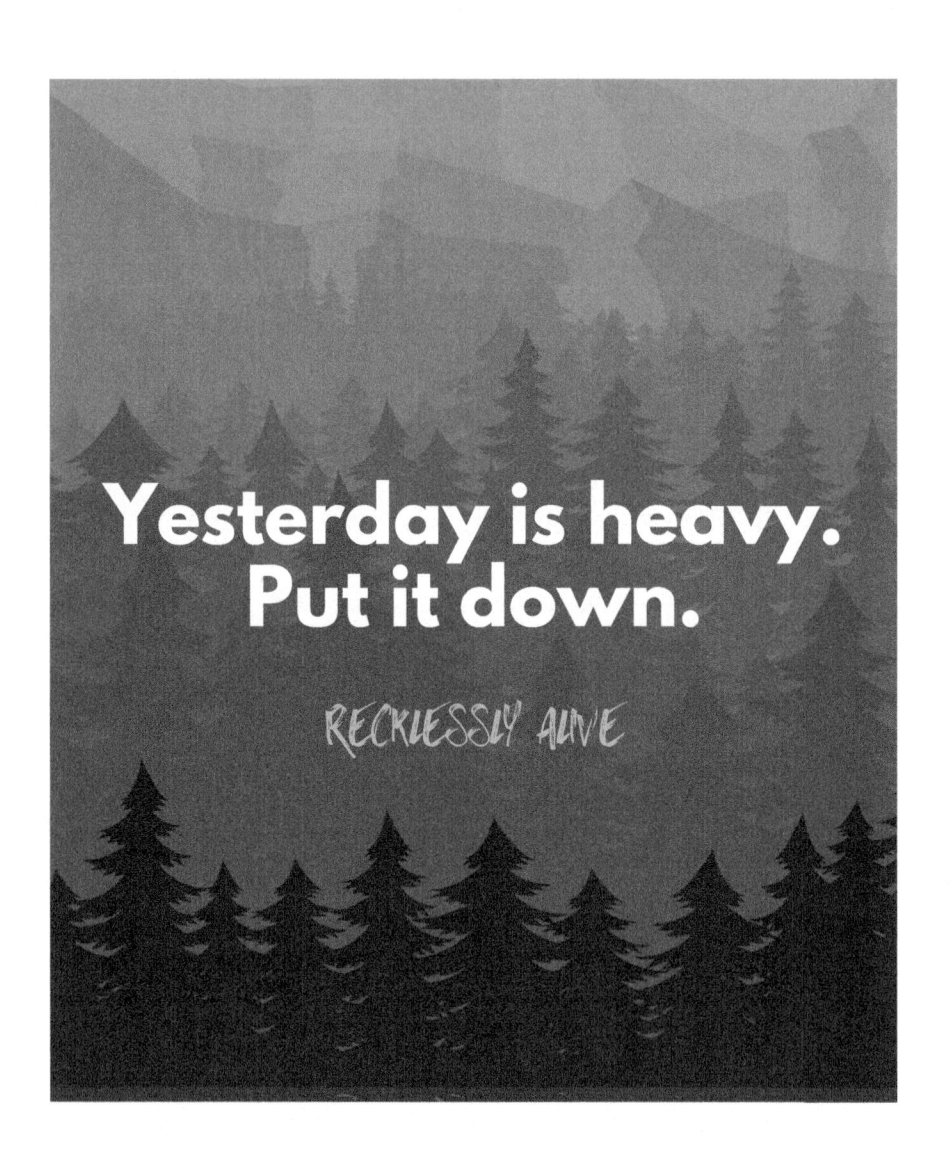

RECKLESSLY ALIVE

JOURNAL

DAILY CHECK-IN

DATE:

WHAT ARE THE FEELINGS OR EMOTIONS I AM CURRENTLY EXPERIENCING?

WHAT LIMITING BELIEFS OR NEGATIVE THOUGHTS AM I HAVING TODAY?

WHAT DO I NEED TO HEAR TO COMBAT THOSE THOUGHTS?

WHAT ARE THREE THINGS I AM THANKFUL FOR TODAY?
-
-
-

WHAT IS THE ONE DAILY TASK I WILL COMPLETE TODAY?

MY FIELD NOTES:

MY DAY

WAKE TIME

TODAY'S MANTRA

_____

_____

SCHEDULE

TOP PRIORITIES

7:00 _____
8:00 _____
9:00 _____
10:00 _____
11:00 _____
12:00 _____
1:00 _____
2:00 _____
3:00 _____
4:00 _____

☐ _____
☐ _____
☐ _____

WEEKLY GOALS

☐ _____
☐ _____
☐ _____
☐ _____

TODAY'S SELF-CARE

5:00 _____
6:00 _____
7:00 _____
8:00 _____
9:00 _____
10:00 _____

☐ _____
☐ _____
☐ _____
☐ _____
☐ _____

How can I show myself more love?

Go where life is beautiful.

RECKLESSLY ALIVE

JOURNAL

DAILY CHECK-IN

DATE:

WHAT ARE THE FEELINGS OR EMOTIONS I AM CURRENTLY EXPERIENCING?

WHAT LIMITING BELIEFS OR NEGATIVE THOUGHTS AM I HAVING TODAY?

WHAT DO I NEED TO HEAR TO COMBAT THOSE THOUGHTS?

WHAT ARE THREE THINGS I AM THANKFUL FOR TODAY?
-
-
-

WHAT IS THE ONE DAILY TASK I WILL COMPLETE TODAY?

MY FIELD NOTES:

MY DAY

WAKE TIME

TODAY'S MANTRA

SCHEDULE

7:00
8:00
9:00
10:00
11:00
12:00
1:00
2:00
3:00
4:00
5:00
6:00
7:00
8:00
9:00
10:00

TOP PRIORITIES

☐
☐
☐

WEEKLY GOALS

☐
☐
☐
☐
☐

TODAY'S SELF-CARE

☐
☐
☐
☐
☐

How can I improve my health and well-being this week/month/year?

Be afraid and do it anyway.

RECKLESSLY ALIVE

JOURNAL

WEEKLY REFLECTION

RATING MY WEEK: 1 2 3 4 5 6 7 8 9 10

I CHOSE THAT RATING BECAUSE:
....
....
....

I AM PROUD OF MYSELF FOR:

-
-
-
-
-

MY WINS FOR THE WEEK:
....
....
....
....
....
....

I WOULD LIKE TO IMPROVE:
....
....
....
....
....
....

LESSONS I LEARNED:
....
....
....
....
....
....

I AM LETTING GO OF GUILT ABOUT:
....
....
....
....
....
....

Week 6

EXCERPT FROM
Recklessly Alive

"If you woke up today believing that suicide is your best option, you are wrong. You have a million other options. You can choose:

To ask for help.
To fight for the healing and wholeness you deserve.
To call your doctor and talk about what you're going through.
To learn how nutrition, sleep, and exercise can improve your mental health.
To make an appointment with a counselor and open up.
To let go of toxic people.
To set boundaries around anyone who makes you want to die.
To fight back against the endless automatic thoughts that scream you are worthless.
To believe, against all odds, that tomorrow will be better than today.

Do not spend another hour suffering in silence. Do not spend another minute being a victim in your own life. Do not spend another second believing the God of the universe has abandoned you. Depression is not a choice. Suicidal thoughts are not a choice. The abuse, trauma, and struggle you have been through were not a choice. But death is not your only way out.

I promise you can find another way.

(Eaton 70-71)

HABIT TRACKER

WEEK OF :

HABIT	MON	TUE	WED	THU	FRI	SAT	SUN
	☐	☐	☐	☐	☐	☐	☐
	☐	☐	☐	☐	☐	☐	☐
	☐	☐	☐	☐	☐	☐	☐
	☐	☐	☐	☐	☐	☐	☐
	☐	☐	☐	☐	☐	☐	☐
	☐	☐	☐	☐	☐	☐	☐
	☐	☐	☐	☐	☐	☐	☐
	☐	☐	☐	☐	☐	☐	☐
	☐	☐	☐	☐	☐	☐	☐
	☐	☐	☐	☐	☐	☐	☐

DAILY CHECK-IN

DATE:

WHAT ARE THE FEELINGS OR EMOTIONS I AM CURRENTLY EXPERIENCING?

WHAT LIMITING BELIEFS OR NEGATIVE THOUGHTS AM I HAVING TODAY?

WHAT DO I NEED TO HEAR TO COMBAT THOSE THOUGHTS?

WHAT ARE THREE THINGS I AM THANKFUL FOR TODAY?
-
-
-

WHAT IS THE ONE DAILY TASK I WILL COMPLETE TODAY?

MY FIELD NOTES:

MY DAY

WAKE TIME

TODAY'S MANTRA

SCHEDULE

TOP PRIORITIES

7:00
8:00
9:00
10:00
11:00

WEEKLY GOALS

12:00
1:00
2:00
3:00
4:00
5:00

TODAY'S SELF-CARE

6:00
7:00
8:00
9:00
10:00

What does success look like to me?

You are enough.
It is crazy how
enough you are.

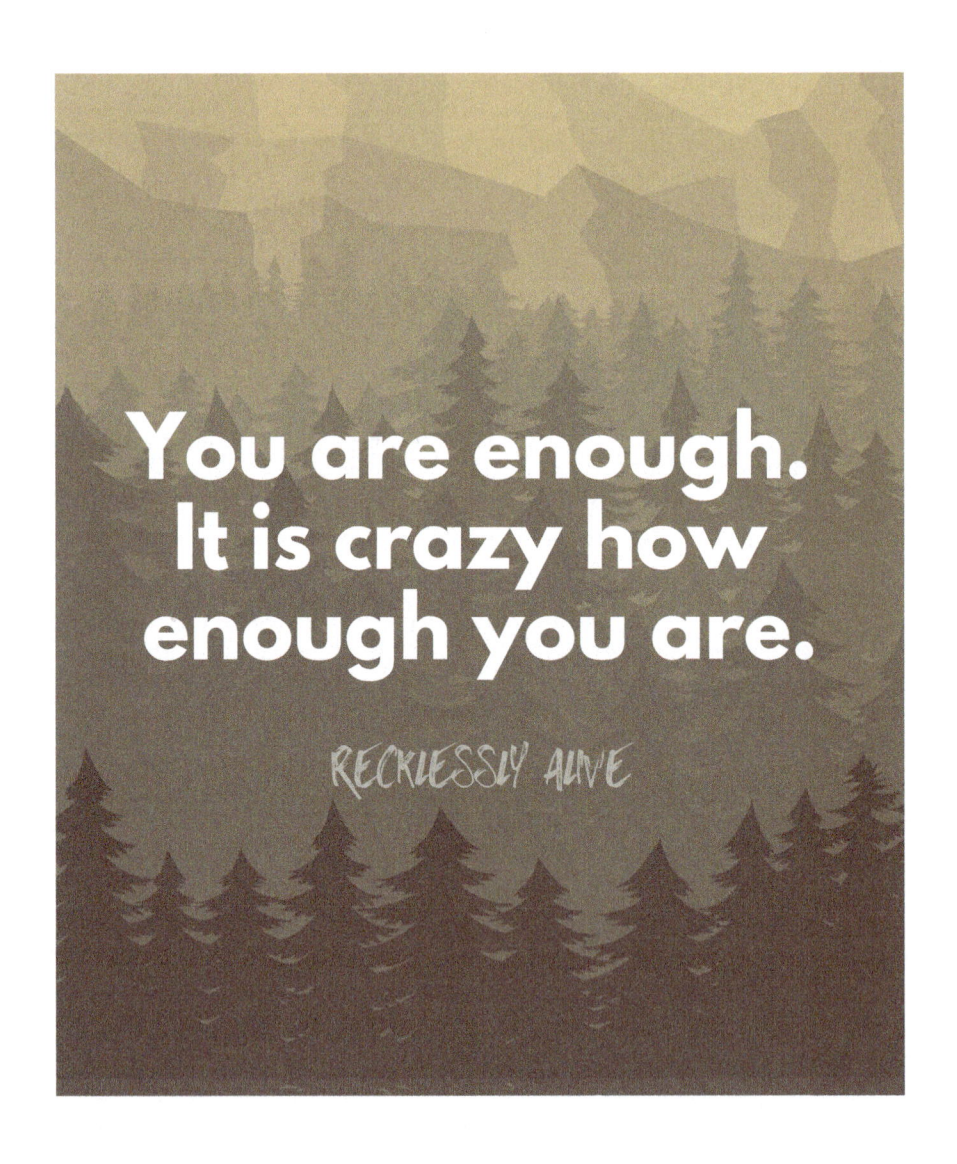

RECKLESSLY ALIVE

JOURNAL

DAILY CHECK-IN

DATE:

WHAT ARE THE FEELINGS OR EMOTIONS I AM CURRENTLY EXPERIENCING?

WHAT LIMITING BELIEFS OR NEGATIVE THOUGHTS AM I HAVING TODAY?

WHAT DO I NEED TO HEAR TO COMBAT THOSE THOUGHTS?

WHAT ARE THREE THINGS I AM THANKFUL FOR TODAY?
-
-
-

WHAT IS THE ONE DAILY TASK I WILL COMPLETE TODAY?

MY FIELD NOTES:

MY DAY

WAKE TIME _____

TODAY'S MANTRA _____

SCHEDULE

7:00 _____
8:00 _____
9:00 _____
10:00 _____
11:00 _____
12:00 _____
1:00 _____
2:00 _____
3:00 _____
4:00 _____
5:00 _____
6:00 _____
7:00 _____
8:00 _____
9:00 _____
10:00 _____

TOP PRIORITIES

☐ _____
☐ _____
☐ _____

WEEKLY GOALS

☐ _____
☐ _____
☐ _____
☐ _____
☐ _____

TODAY'S SELF-CARE

☐ _____
☐ _____
☐ _____
☐ _____
☐ _____

Who inspires me the most? What makes them so inspiring?

Don't let one bad interaction ruin your entire day.

RECKLESSLY ALIVE

JOURNAL

DAILY CHECK-IN

DATE:

WHAT ARE THE FEELINGS OR EMOTIONS I AM CURRENTLY EXPERIENCING?

WHAT LIMITING BELIEFS OR NEGATIVE THOUGHTS AM I HAVING TODAY?

WHAT DO I NEED TO HEAR TO COMBAT THOSE THOUGHTS?

WHAT ARE THREE THINGS I AM THANKFUL FOR TODAY?
-
-
-

WHAT IS THE ONE DAILY TASK I WILL COMPLETE TODAY?

MY FIELD NOTES:

MY DAY

WAKE TIME

TODAY'S MANTRA

SCHEDULE

7:00
8:00
9:00
10:00
11:00
12:00
1:00
2:00
3:00
4:00
5:00
6:00
7:00
8:00
9:00
10:00

TOP PRIORITIES

-
-
-

WEEKLY GOALS

-
-
-
-
-

TODAY'S SELF-CARE

-
-
-
-
-

Who do I hope to become in the next three months?

Be stronger than your excuses.

RECKLESSLY ALIVE

JOURNAL

DAILY CHECK-IN

DATE:

WHAT ARE THE FEELINGS OR EMOTIONS I AM CURRENTLY EXPERIENCING?

WHAT LIMITING BELIEFS OR NEGATIVE THOUGHTS AM I HAVING TODAY?

WHAT DO I NEED TO HEAR TO COMBAT THOSE THOUGHTS?

WHAT ARE THREE THINGS I AM THANKFUL FOR TODAY?
-
-
-

WHAT IS THE ONE DAILY TASK I WILL COMPLETE TODAY?

MY FIELD NOTES:

MY DAY

WAKE TIME

TODAY'S MANTRA

SCHEDULE

7:00
8:00
9:00
10:00
11:00
12:00
1:00
2:00
3:00
4:00
5:00
6:00
7:00
8:00
9:00
10:00

TOP PRIORITIES

- [ ]
- [ ]
- [ ]

WEEKLY GOALS

- [ ]
- [ ]
- [ ]
- [ ]

TODAY'S SELF-CARE

- [ ]
- [ ]
- [ ]
- [ ]
- [ ]

What do I want to have accomplished by this time next year?

In a world full of no's, make your own yes.

RECKLESSLY ALIVE

JOURNAL

DAILY CHECK-IN

DATE:

WHAT ARE THE FEELINGS OR EMOTIONS I AM CURRENTLY EXPERIENCING?

WHAT LIMITING BELIEFS OR NEGATIVE THOUGHTS AM I HAVING TODAY?

WHAT DO I NEED TO HEAR TO COMBAT THOSE THOUGHTS?

WHAT ARE THREE THINGS I AM THANKFUL FOR TODAY?
-
-
-

WHAT IS THE ONE DAILY TASK I WILL COMPLETE TODAY?

MY FIELD NOTES:

MY DAY

WAKE TIME

TODAY'S MANTRA

SCHEDULE

7:00
8:00
9:00
10:00
11:00
12:00
1:00
2:00
3:00
4:00
5:00
6:00
7:00
8:00
9:00
10:00

TOP PRIORITIES

- [ ]
- [ ]
- [ ]

WEEKLY GOALS

- [ ]
- [ ]
- [ ]
- [ ]

TODAY'S SELF-CARE

- [ ]
- [ ]
- [ ]
- [ ]
- [ ]

What demotivates me and what helps me regain motivation after I lose it?

What would you do if you knew you couldn't fail?

RECKLESSLY ALIVE

JOURNAL

DAILY CHECK-IN

DATE:

WHAT ARE THE FEELINGS OR EMOTIONS I AM CURRENTLY EXPERIENCING?

WHAT LIMITING BELIEFS OR NEGATIVE THOUGHTS AM I HAVING TODAY?

WHAT DO I NEED TO HEAR TO COMBAT THOSE THOUGHTS?

WHAT ARE THREE THINGS I AM THANKFUL FOR TODAY?
-
-
-

WHAT IS THE ONE DAILY TASK I WILL COMPLETE TODAY?

MY FIELD NOTES:

MY DAY

WAKE TIME

TODAY'S MANTRA

SCHEDULE

7:00
8:00
9:00
10:00
11:00
12:00
1:00
2:00
3:00
4:00
5:00
6:00
7:00
8:00
9:00
10:00

TOP PRIORITIES

☐
☐
☐

WEEKLY GOALS

☐
☐
☐
☐
☐

TODAY'S SELF-CARE

☐
☐
☐
☐
☐

In what ways do I get in the way of my own happiness?

Life is a rollercoaster. Stay.

RECKLESSLY ALIVE

JOURNAL

DAILY CHECK-IN

DATE:

WHAT ARE THE FEELINGS OR EMOTIONS I AM CURRENTLY EXPERIENCING?

WHAT LIMITING BELIEFS OR NEGATIVE THOUGHTS AM I HAVING TODAY?

WHAT DO I NEED TO HEAR TO COMBAT THOSE THOUGHTS?

WHAT ARE THREE THINGS I AM THANKFUL FOR TODAY?
-
-
-

WHAT IS THE ONE DAILY TASK I WILL COMPLETE TODAY?

MY FIELD NOTES:

MY DAY

WAKE TIME

TODAY'S MANTRA

SCHEDULE

7:00
8:00
9:00
10:00
11:00
12:00
1:00
2:00
3:00
4:00
5:00
6:00
7:00
8:00
9:00
10:00

TOP PRIORITIES

- [ ]
- [ ]
- [ ]

WEEKLY GOALS

- [ ]
- [ ]
- [ ]
- [ ]
- [ ]

TODAY'S SELF-CARE

- [ ]
- [ ]
- [ ]
- [ ]
- [ ]

Do I surround myself with people who lift me up or bring me down?

You absolutely have what it takes. Go for it.

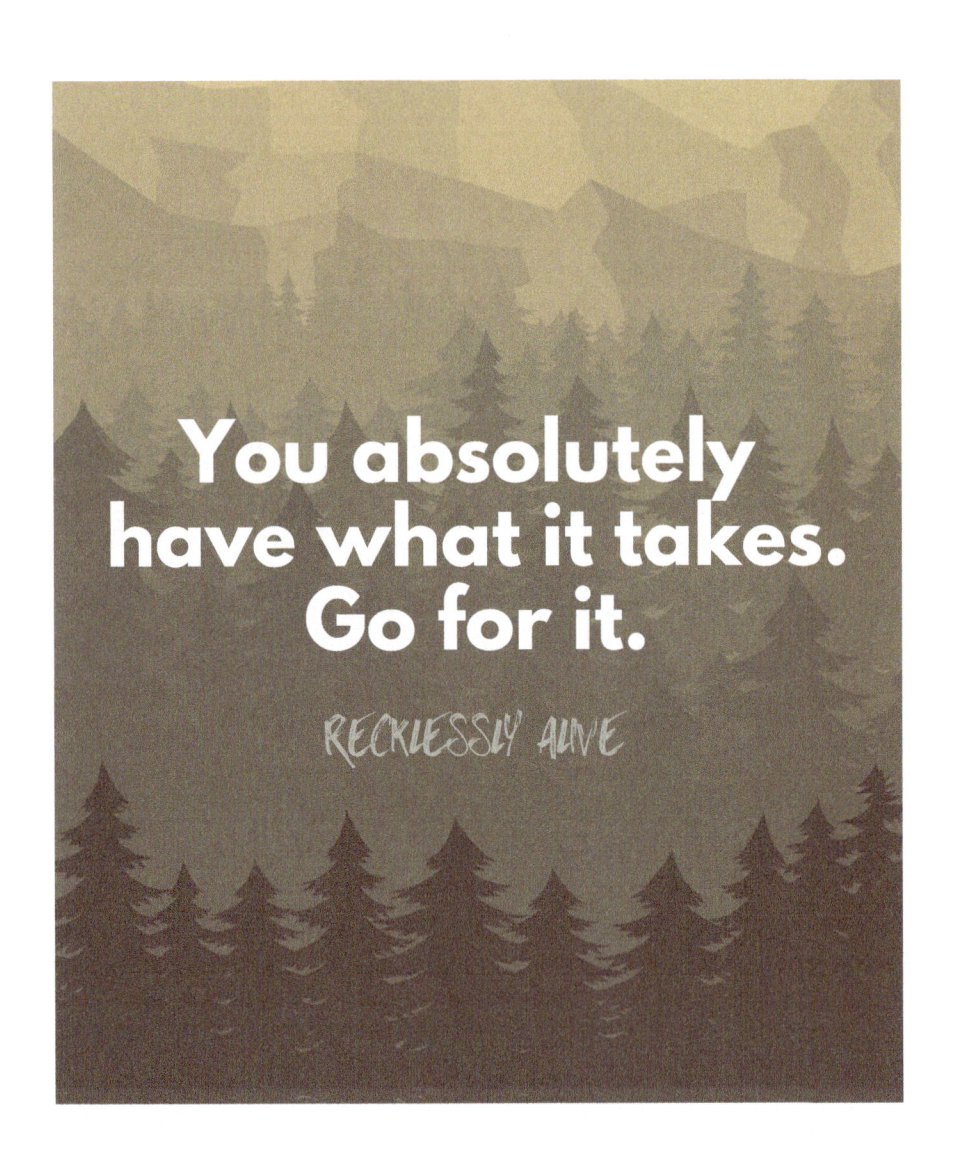

RECKLESSLY ALIVE

JOURNAL

WEEKLY REFLECTION

RATING MY WEEK: 1 2 3 4 5 6 7 8 9 10

I CHOSE THAT RATING BECAUSE:

....
....
....

I AM PROUD OF MYSELF FOR:

-
-
-
-
-

MY WINS FOR THE WEEK:

....
....
....
....
....

I WOULD LIKE TO IMPROVE:

....
....
....
....
....

LESSONS I LEARNED:

....
....
....
....
....

I AM LETTING GO OF GUILT ABOUT:

....
....
....
....
....

Week 7

EXCERPT FROM
Recklessly Alive

If you can't see that life is worth living, maybe it's time to change. Maybe it's time to explore the plethora of healing options available to you. Maybe it's time to stop caring what everyone thinks and instead care more about being the person you were created to be.

Please don't spend your whole life stuck inside the plane—bored and just trying to make it through the ride. If you feel lost and lifeless, it's because you weren't made to obsess about wealth, appearances, promotions, and popularity.

You weren't made to sit back and watch everyone else do great things. You were made to be recklessly alive. You were made to jump.

(Eaton 101)

HABIT TRACKER

WEEK OF :

HABIT	MON	TUE	WED	THU	FRI	SAT	SUN
	☐	☐	☐	☐	☐	☐	☐
	☐	☐	☐	☐	☐	☐	☐
	☐	☐	☐	☐	☐	☐	☐
	☐	☐	☐	☐	☐	☐	☐
	☐	☐	☐	☐	☐	☐	☐
	☐	☐	☐	☐	☐	☐	☐
	☐	☐	☐	☐	☐	☐	☐
	☐	☐	☐	☐	☐	☐	☐
	☐	☐	☐	☐	☐	☐	☐
	☐	☐	☐	☐	☐	☐	☐

DAILY CHECK-IN

DATE:

WHAT ARE THE FEELINGS OR EMOTIONS I AM CURRENTLY EXPERIENCING?

WHAT LIMITING BELIEFS OR NEGATIVE THOUGHTS AM I HAVING TODAY?

WHAT DO I NEED TO HEAR TO COMBAT THOSE THOUGHTS?

WHAT ARE THREE THINGS I AM THANKFUL FOR TODAY?
-
-
-

WHAT IS THE ONE DAILY TASK I WILL COMPLETE TODAY?

MY FIELD NOTES:

MY DAY

WAKE TIME

TODAY'S MANTRA

SCHEDULE

7:00
8:00
9:00
10:00
11:00
12:00
1:00
2:00
3:00
4:00
5:00
6:00
7:00
8:00
9:00
10:00

TOP PRIORITIES

- [ ]
- [ ]
- [ ]

WEEKLY GOALS

- [ ]
- [ ]
- [ ]
- [ ]
- [ ]

TODAY'S SELF-CARE

- [ ]
- [ ]
- [ ]
- [ ]
- [ ]

What is one thing that was extremely painful at the time that has healed?

What if it turns out better than you ever imagined?

RECKLESSLY ALIVE

JOURNAL

DAILY CHECK-IN

DATE:

WHAT ARE THE FEELINGS OR EMOTIONS I AM CURRENTLY EXPERIENCING?

WHAT LIMITING BELIEFS OR NEGATIVE THOUGHTS AM I HAVING TODAY?

WHAT DO I NEED TO HEAR TO COMBAT THOSE THOUGHTS?

WHAT ARE THREE THINGS I AM THANKFUL FOR TODAY?
-
-
-

WHAT IS THE ONE DAILY TASK I WILL COMPLETE TODAY?

MY FIELD NOTES:

MY DAY

WAKE TIME   **TODAY'S MANTRA**

SCHEDULE   TOP PRIORITIES

7:00
8:00
9:00
10:00
11:00

WEEKLY GOALS

12:00
1:00
2:00
3:00
4:00

TODAY'S SELF-CARE

5:00
6:00
7:00
8:00
9:00
10:00

How do you feel when you see yourself in the mirror? Does this support the person I am trying to become?

Be brave enough to fail at something new.

RECKLESSLY ALIVE

JOURNAL

DAILY CHECK-IN

DATE:

WHAT ARE THE FEELINGS OR EMOTIONS I AM CURRENTLY EXPERIENCING?

WHAT LIMITING BELIEFS OR NEGATIVE THOUGHTS AM I HAVING TODAY?

WHAT DO I NEED TO HEAR TO COMBAT THOSE THOUGHTS?

WHAT ARE THREE THINGS I AM THANKFUL FOR TODAY?
-
-
-

WHAT IS THE ONE DAILY TASK I WILL COMPLETE TODAY?

MY FIELD NOTES:

MY DAY

WAKE TIME

TODAY'S MANTRA

SCHEDULE

7:00
8:00
9:00
10:00
11:00
12:00
1:00
2:00
3:00
4:00
5:00
6:00
7:00
8:00
9:00
10:00

TOP PRIORITIES

☐
☐
☐

WEEKLY GOALS

☐
☐
☐
☐
☐

TODAY'S SELF-CARE

☐
☐
☐
☐
☐

What are some new skills I would love to develop?

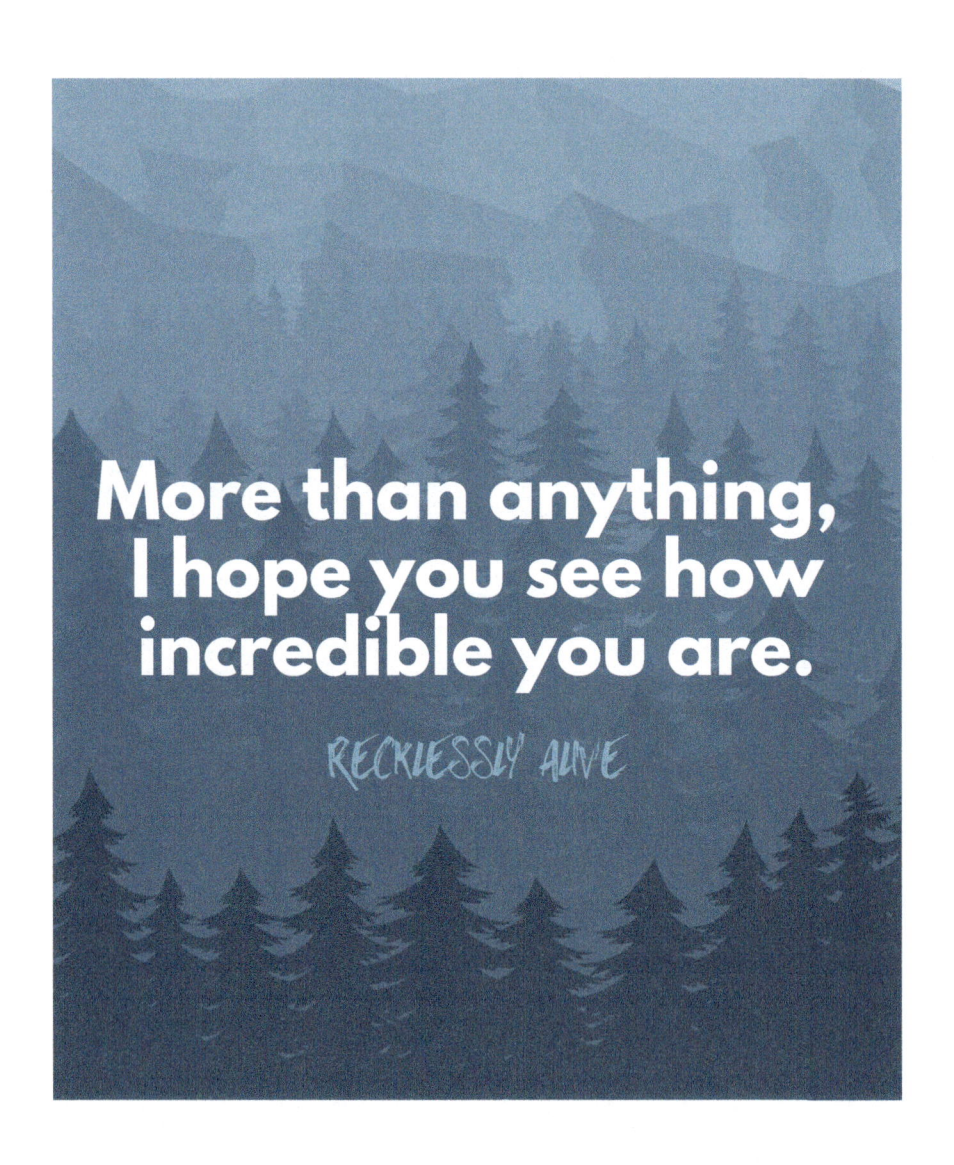

More than anything, I hope you see how incredible you are.

RECKLESSLY ALIVE

JOURNAL

DAILY CHECK-IN

DATE:

WHAT ARE THE FEELINGS OR EMOTIONS I AM CURRENTLY EXPERIENCING?

WHAT LIMITING BELIEFS OR NEGATIVE THOUGHTS AM I HAVING TODAY?

WHAT DO I NEED TO HEAR TO COMBAT THOSE THOUGHTS?

WHAT ARE THREE THINGS I AM THANKFUL FOR TODAY?
-
-
-

WHAT IS THE ONE DAILY TASK I WILL COMPLETE TODAY?

MY FIELD NOTES:

MY DAY

WAKE TIME

TODAY'S MANTRA

SCHEDULE

7:00
8:00
9:00
10:00
11:00
12:00
1:00
2:00
3:00
4:00
5:00
6:00
7:00
8:00
9:00
10:00

TOP PRIORITIES

☐
☐
☐

WEEKLY GOALS

☐
☐
☐
☐
☐

TODAY'S SELF-CARE

☐
☐
☐
☐
☐

What activities make me feel content, energized, and fulfilled?

What are you waiting for?

RECKLESSLY ALIVE

JOURNAL

DAILY CHECK-IN

DATE:

WHAT ARE THE FEELINGS OR EMOTIONS I AM CURRENTLY EXPERIENCING?

WHAT LIMITING BELIEFS OR NEGATIVE THOUGHTS AM I HAVING TODAY?

WHAT DO I NEED TO HEAR TO COMBAT THOSE THOUGHTS?

WHAT ARE THREE THINGS I AM THANKFUL FOR TODAY?
-
-
-

WHAT IS THE ONE DAILY TASK I WILL COMPLETE TODAY?

MY FIELD NOTES:

MY DAY

WAKE TIME
_____

TODAY'S MANTRA
_____

SCHEDULE

7:00 _____
8:00 _____
9:00 _____
10:00 _____
11:00 _____
12:00 _____
1:00 _____
2:00 _____
3:00 _____
4:00 _____
5:00 _____
6:00 _____
7:00 _____
8:00 _____
9:00 _____
10:00 _____

TOP PRIORITIES

☐ _____
☐ _____
☐ _____

WEEKLY GOALS

☐ _____
☐ _____
☐ _____
☐ _____
☐ _____

TODAY'S SELF-CARE

☐ _____
☐ _____
☐ _____
☐ _____
☐ _____

What are my strategies for bouncing back after a setback?

Give life everything you've got and never look back.

RECKLESSLY ALIVE

JOURNAL

DAILY CHECK-IN

DATE:

WHAT ARE THE FEELINGS OR EMOTIONS I AM CURRENTLY EXPERIENCING?

WHAT LIMITING BELIEFS OR NEGATIVE THOUGHTS AM I HAVING TODAY?

WHAT DO I NEED TO HEAR TO COMBAT THOSE THOUGHTS?

WHAT ARE THREE THINGS I AM THANKFUL FOR TODAY?
-
-
-

WHAT IS THE ONE DAILY TASK I WILL COMPLETE TODAY?

MY FIELD NOTES:

MY DAY

WAKE TIME

TODAY'S MANTRA

SCHEDULE

7:00
8:00
9:00
10:00
11:00
12:00
1:00
2:00
3:00
4:00
5:00
6:00
7:00
8:00
9:00
10:00

TOP PRIORITIES

- [ ]
- [ ]
- [ ]

WEEKLY GOALS

- [ ]
- [ ]
- [ ]
- [ ]
- [ ]

TODAY'S SELF-CARE

- [ ]
- [ ]
- [ ]
- [ ]
- [ ]

What do I spend too much time doing?

Be courageous enough to heal.

RECKLESSLY ALIVE

JOURNAL

DAILY CHECK-IN

DATE:

WHAT ARE THE FEELINGS OR EMOTIONS I AM CURRENTLY EXPERIENCING?

WHAT LIMITING BELIEFS OR NEGATIVE THOUGHTS AM I HAVING TODAY?

WHAT DO I NEED TO HEAR TO COMBAT THOSE THOUGHTS?

WHAT ARE THREE THINGS I AM THANKFUL FOR TODAY?
-
-
-

WHAT IS THE ONE DAILY TASK I WILL COMPLETE TODAY?

MY FIELD NOTES:

MY DAY

WAKE TIME

TODAY'S MANTRA

SCHEDULE

7:00
8:00
9:00
10:00
11:00
12:00
1:00
2:00
3:00
4:00
5:00
6:00
7:00
8:00
9:00
10:00

TOP PRIORITIES

- [ ]
- [ ]
- [ ]

WEEKLY GOALS

- [ ]
- [ ]
- [ ]
- [ ]

TODAY'S SELF-CARE

- [ ]
- [ ]
- [ ]
- [ ]

What do I not spend enough time doing?

You can overcome.

RECKLESSLY ALIVE

JOURNAL

WEEKLY REFLECTION

RATING MY WEEK:　　1　　2　　3　　4　　5　　6　　7　　8　　9　　10

I CHOSE THAT RATING BECAUSE:

....
....
....

I AM PROUD OF MYSELF FOR:

-
-
-
-
-

MY WINS FOR THE WEEK:

....
....
....
....
....

I WOULD LIKE TO IMPROVE:

....
....
....
....
....

LESSONS I LEARNED:

....
....
....
....
....

I AM LETTING GO OF GUILT ABOUT:

....
....
....
....
....

Week 8

EXCERPT FROM
Recklessly Alive

I don't know if there's anything more disheartening than sitting in a place where you used to—but no longer— belong. Part of me wanted to stuff my pain and small talk until the end of time, thankful anyone wanted to be around me at all. Yet the more I fought to be recklessly alive, the more I valued myself and recognized when others didn't.

With the help of my counselor and what I'd learned about who God had created me to be, I began to stand up for myself, set boundaries around toxic people, assert my voice in relationships, and, most importantly, believe I was worth more than being anyone's afterthought.

I could have spent my life sprinkling ill will like an evil fairy godfather.
I could have blamed others and never owned my part in the breakdown.
I could have let the past consume and destroy the beautiful future waiting for me.

But God says if anyone starts following Jesus, the old is gone and the new has come. I like that. At any point, we can choose to start over and find ways to be more fully alive. For some this is instantaneous. (I mean, I don't know anyone like that, but good for you if it was.) Others, like me, find a little more freedom from the past one day at a time.

I hope you walk away from any place that keeps you from becoming the best version of yourself. I hope you thank the people who have left and wish them well. I hope you work so hard on yourself that people notice how much you've changed.

You are worth so much more than sitting on the outside looking in. You are too full of life to be half-loved. You were made to belong.

(Eaton 150-151)

HABIT TRACKER

WEEK OF :

HABIT	MON	TUE	WED	THU	FRI	SAT	SUN
	☐	☐	☐	☐	☐	☐	☐
	☐	☐	☐	☐	☐	☐	☐
	☐	☐	☐	☐	☐	☐	☐
	☐	☐	☐	☐	☐	☐	☐
	☐	☐	☐	☐	☐	☐	☐
	☐	☐	☐	☐	☐	☐	☐
	☐	☐	☐	☐	☐	☐	☐
	☐	☐	☐	☐	☐	☐	☐
	☐	☐	☐	☐	☐	☐	☐
	☐	☐	☐	☐	☐	☐	☐

DAILY CHECK-IN

DATE:

WHAT ARE THE FEELINGS OR EMOTIONS I AM CURRENTLY EXPERIENCING?

WHAT LIMITING BELIEFS OR NEGATIVE THOUGHTS AM I HAVING TODAY?

WHAT DO I NEED TO HEAR TO COMBAT THOSE THOUGHTS?

WHAT ARE THREE THINGS I AM THANKFUL FOR TODAY?
-
-
-

WHAT IS THE ONE DAILY TASK I WILL COMPLETE TODAY?

MY FIELD NOTES:

MY DAY

WAKE TIME

TODAY'S MANTRA

SCHEDULE

7:00
8:00
9:00
10:00
11:00
12:00
1:00
2:00
3:00
4:00
5:00
6:00
7:00
8:00
9:00
10:00

TOP PRIORITIES

- [ ]
- [ ]
- [ ]

WEEKLY GOALS

- [ ]
- [ ]
- [ ]
- [ ]
- [ ]

TODAY'S SELF-CARE

- [ ]
- [ ]
- [ ]
- [ ]
- [ ]

Is there someone I still need to forgive?

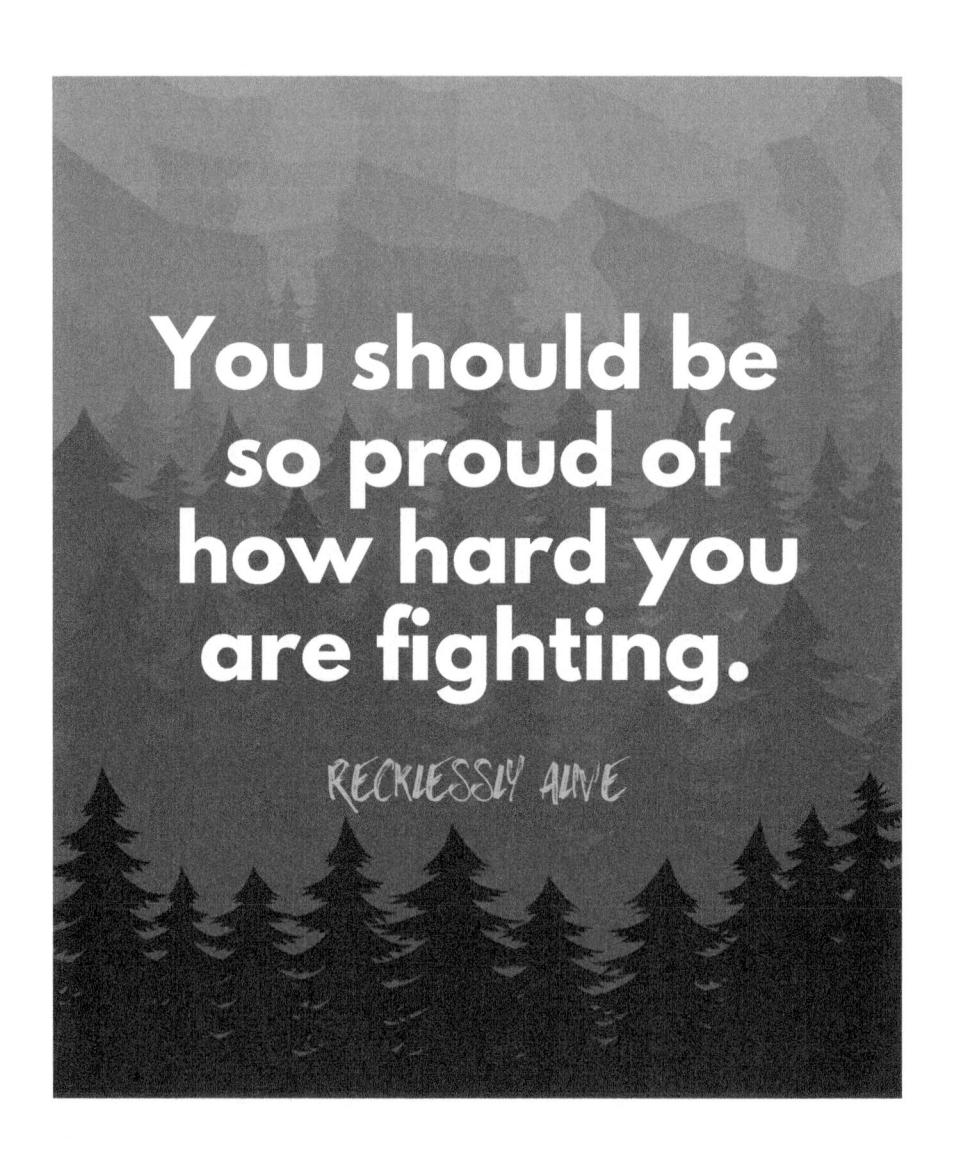

> You should be so proud of how hard you are fighting.
>
> RECKLESSLY ALIVE

JOURNAL

DAILY CHECK-IN

DATE:

WHAT ARE THE FEELINGS OR EMOTIONS I AM CURRENTLY EXPERIENCING?

WHAT LIMITING BELIEFS OR NEGATIVE THOUGHTS AM I HAVING TODAY?

WHAT DO I NEED TO HEAR TO COMBAT THOSE THOUGHTS?

WHAT ARE THREE THINGS I AM THANKFUL FOR TODAY?
-
-
-

WHAT IS THE ONE DAILY TASK I WILL COMPLETE TODAY?

MY FIELD NOTES:

MY DAY

WAKE TIME   **TODAY'S MANTRA**

SCHEDULE

- 7:00
- 8:00
- 9:00
- 10:00
- 11:00
- 12:00
- 1:00
- 2:00
- 3:00
- 4:00
- 5:00
- 6:00
- 7:00
- 8:00
- 9:00
- 10:00

TOP PRIORITIES

- ☐
- ☐
- ☐

WEEKLY GOALS

- ☐
- ☐
- ☐
- ☐
- ☐

TODAY'S SELF-CARE

- ☐
- ☐
- ☐
- ☐
- ☐

What positive qualities do I bring into my close relationships?

It's okay rockstar.
We all lose our
way sometimes.

RECKLESSLY ALIVE

JOURNAL

DAILY CHECK-IN

DATE:

WHAT ARE THE FEELINGS OR EMOTIONS I AM CURRENTLY EXPERIENCING?

WHAT LIMITING BELIEFS OR NEGATIVE THOUGHTS AM I HAVING TODAY?

WHAT DO I NEED TO HEAR TO COMBAT THOSE THOUGHTS?

WHAT ARE THREE THINGS I AM THANKFUL FOR TODAY?
-
-
-

WHAT IS THE ONE DAILY TASK I WILL COMPLETE TODAY?

MY FIELD NOTES:

MY DAY

WAKE TIME _____

TODAY'S MANTRA _____

SCHEDULE

7:00 _____
8:00 _____
9:00 _____
10:00 _____
11:00 _____
12:00 _____
1:00 _____
2:00 _____
3:00 _____
4:00 _____
5:00 _____
6:00 _____
7:00 _____
8:00 _____
9:00 _____
10:00 _____

TOP PRIORITIES

☐ _____
☐ _____
☐ _____

WEEKLY GOALS

☐ _____
☐ _____
☐ _____
☐ _____

TODAY'S SELF-CARE

☐ _____
☐ _____
☐ _____
☐ _____
☐ _____

What compliment do I like to hear the most and why?

Your future is created by your habits.

RECKLESSLY ALIVE

JOURNAL

DAILY CHECK-IN

DATE:

WHAT ARE THE FEELINGS OR EMOTIONS I AM CURRENTLY EXPERIENCING?

WHAT LIMITING BELIEFS OR NEGATIVE THOUGHTS AM I HAVING TODAY?

WHAT DO I NEED TO HEAR TO COMBAT THOSE THOUGHTS?

WHAT ARE THREE THINGS I AM THANKFUL FOR TODAY?
-
-
-

WHAT IS THE ONE DAILY TASK I WILL COMPLETE TODAY?

MY FIELD NOTES:

MY DAY

WAKE TIME _____

TODAY'S MANTRA _____

SCHEDULE

7:00 _____
8:00 _____
9:00 _____
10:00 _____
11:00 _____
12:00 _____
1:00 _____
2:00 _____
3:00 _____
4:00 _____
5:00 _____
6:00 _____
7:00 _____
8:00 _____
9:00 _____
10:00 _____

TOP PRIORITIES

☐ _____
☐ _____
☐ _____

WEEKLY GOALS

☐ _____
☐ _____
☐ _____
☐ _____
☐ _____

TODAY'S SELF-CARE

☐ _____
☐ _____
☐ _____
☐ _____
☐ _____

> When was the last time I pushed myself to do something I was afraid to do?

Put your mental health first.

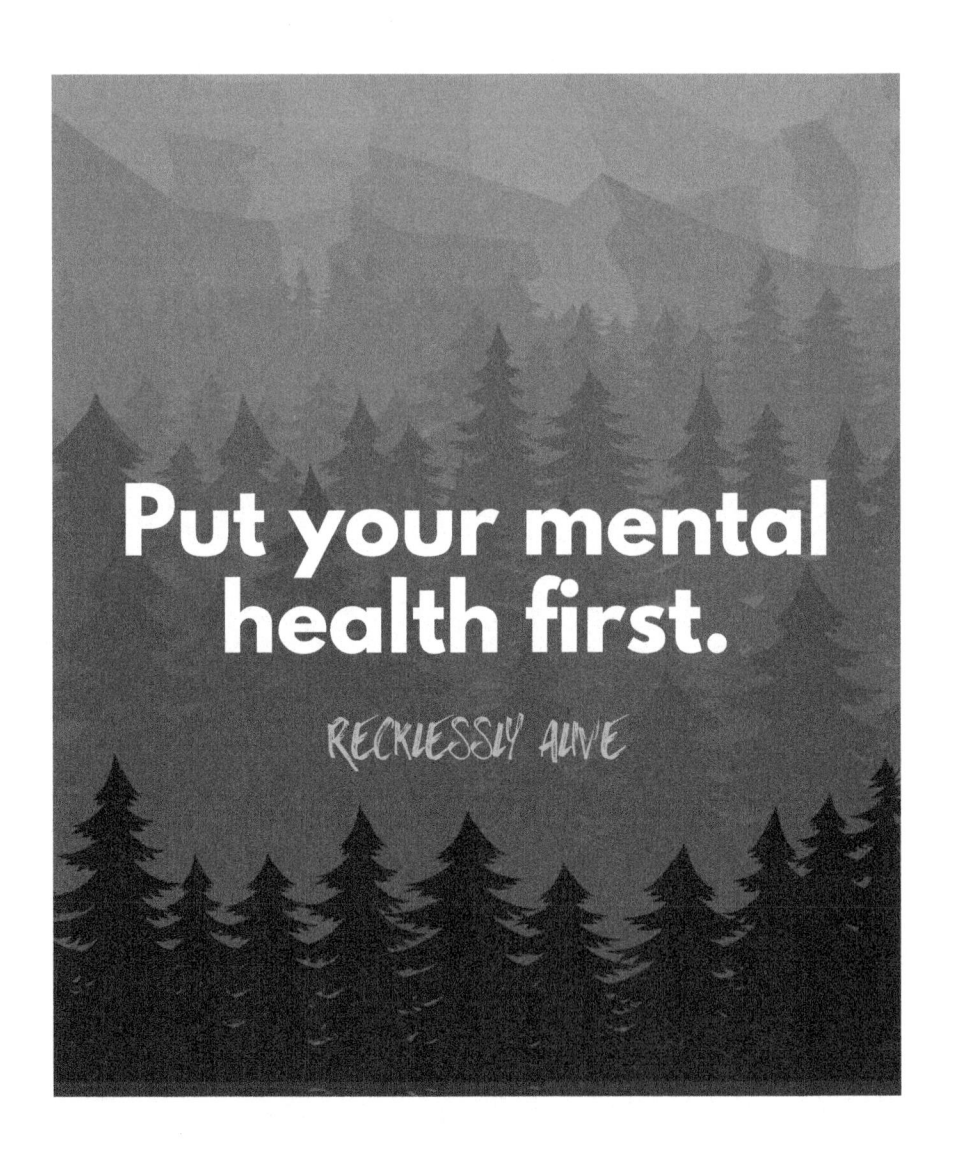

RECKLESSLY ALIVE

JOURNAL

DAILY CHECK-IN

DATE:

WHAT ARE THE FEELINGS OR EMOTIONS I AM CURRENTLY EXPERIENCING?

WHAT LIMITING BELIEFS OR NEGATIVE THOUGHTS AM I HAVING TODAY?

WHAT DO I NEED TO HEAR TO COMBAT THOSE THOUGHTS?

WHAT ARE THREE THINGS I AM THANKFUL FOR TODAY?
-
-
-

WHAT IS THE ONE DAILY TASK I WILL COMPLETE TODAY?

MY FIELD NOTES:

MY DAY

WAKE TIME

TODAY'S MANTRA

SCHEDULE

7:00
8:00
9:00
10:00
11:00
12:00
1:00
2:00
3:00
4:00
5:00
6:00
7:00
8:00
9:00
10:00

TOP PRIORITIES

- [ ]
- [ ]
- [ ]

WEEKLY GOALS

- [ ]
- [ ]
- [ ]
- [ ]

TODAY'S SELF-CARE

- [ ]
- [ ]
- [ ]
- [ ]
- [ ]

When was the last time I said "no" and felt good about it?

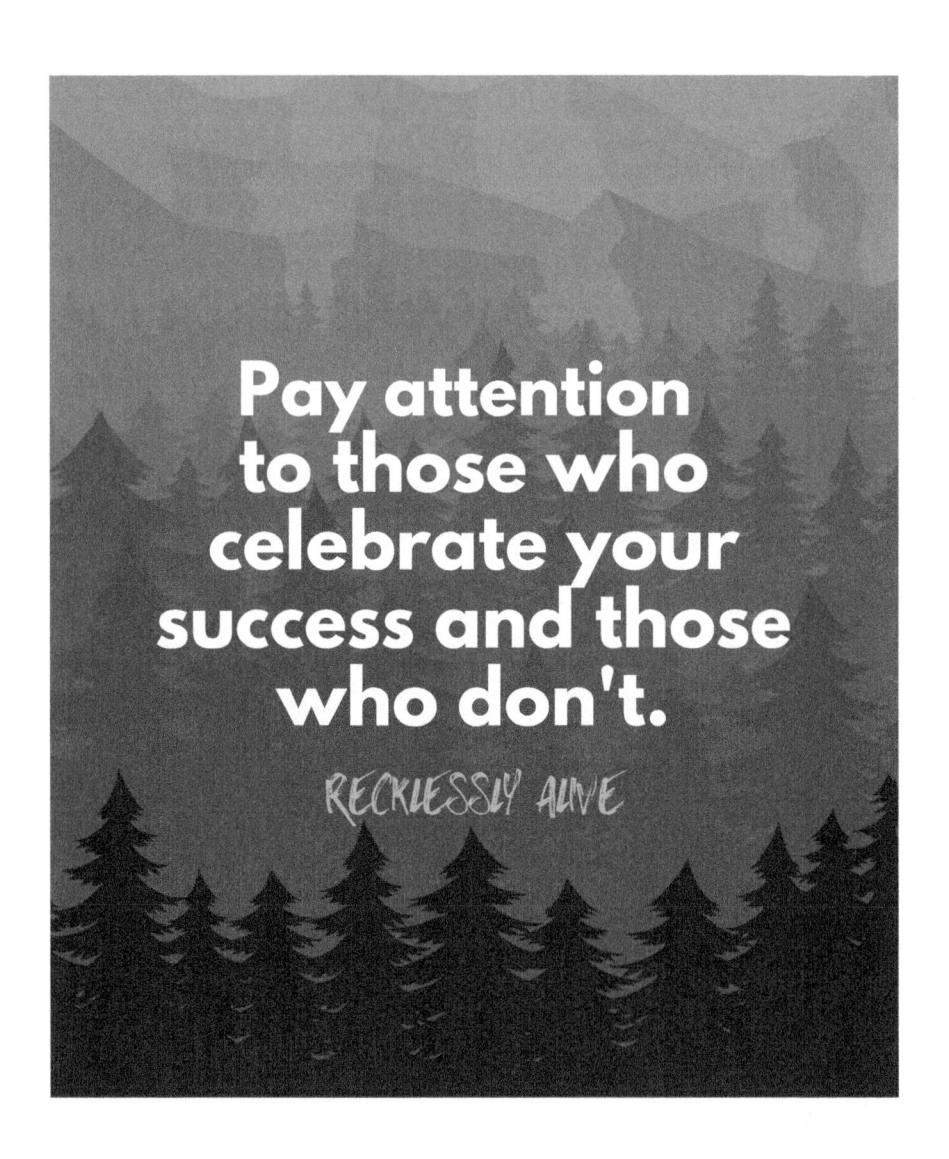

Pay attention to those who celebrate your success and those who don't.

RECKLESSLY ALIVE

JOURNAL

DAILY CHECK-IN

DATE:

WHAT ARE THE FEELINGS OR EMOTIONS I AM CURRENTLY EXPERIENCING?

WHAT LIMITING BELIEFS OR NEGATIVE THOUGHTS AM I HAVING TODAY?

WHAT DO I NEED TO HEAR TO COMBAT THOSE THOUGHTS?

WHAT ARE THREE THINGS I AM THANKFUL FOR TODAY?
-
-
-

WHAT IS THE ONE DAILY TASK I WILL COMPLETE TODAY?

MY FIELD NOTES:

MY DAY

WAKE TIME

TODAY'S MANTRA

SCHEDULE

7:00
8:00
9:00
10:00
11:00
12:00
1:00
2:00
3:00
4:00
5:00
6:00
7:00
8:00
9:00
10:00

TOP PRIORITIES

- [ ]
- [ ]
- [ ]

WEEKLY GOALS

- [ ]
- [ ]
- [ ]
- [ ]
- [ ]

TODAY'S SELF-CARE

- [ ]
- [ ]
- [ ]
- [ ]
- [ ]

What is one thing I would do if I knew I couldn't fail?

Stronger than yesterday.
RECKLESSLY ALIVE

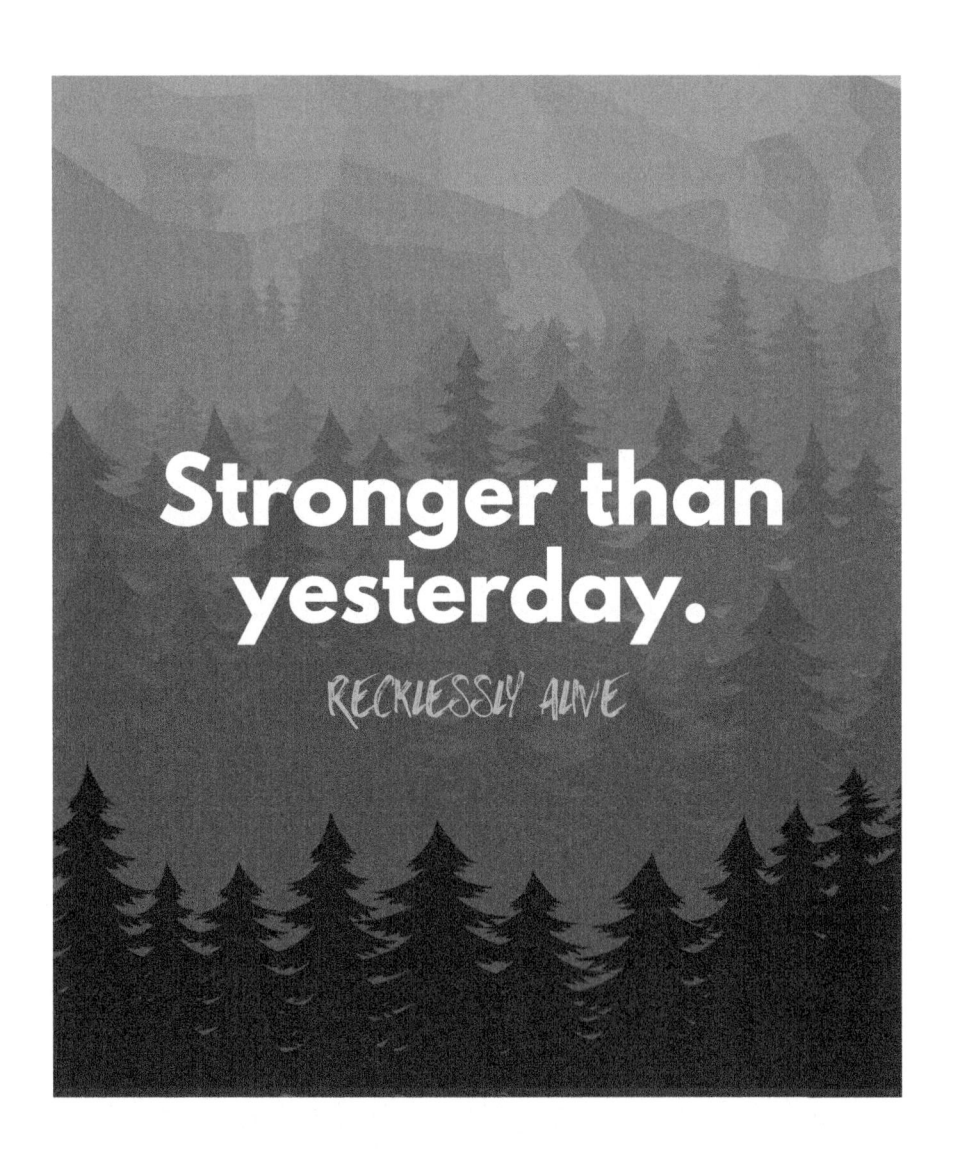

JOURNAL

DAILY CHECK-IN

DATE:

WHAT ARE THE FEELINGS OR EMOTIONS I AM CURRENTLY EXPERIENCING?

WHAT LIMITING BELIEFS OR NEGATIVE THOUGHTS AM I HAVING TODAY?

WHAT DO I NEED TO HEAR TO COMBAT THOSE THOUGHTS?

WHAT ARE THREE THINGS I AM THANKFUL FOR TODAY?
-
-
-

WHAT IS THE ONE DAILY TASK I WILL COMPLETE TODAY?

MY FIELD NOTES:

MY DAY

WAKE TIME

TODAY'S MANTRA

SCHEDULE

7:00
8:00
9:00
10:00
11:00
12:00
1:00
2:00
3:00
4:00
5:00
6:00
7:00
8:00
9:00
10:00

TOP PRIORITIES
-
-
-

WEEKLY GOALS
-
-
-
-
-

TODAY'S SELF-CARE
-
-
-
-
-

Do I feel like I am on the right path in life? How can I tell?

Change your thoughts to change your life.

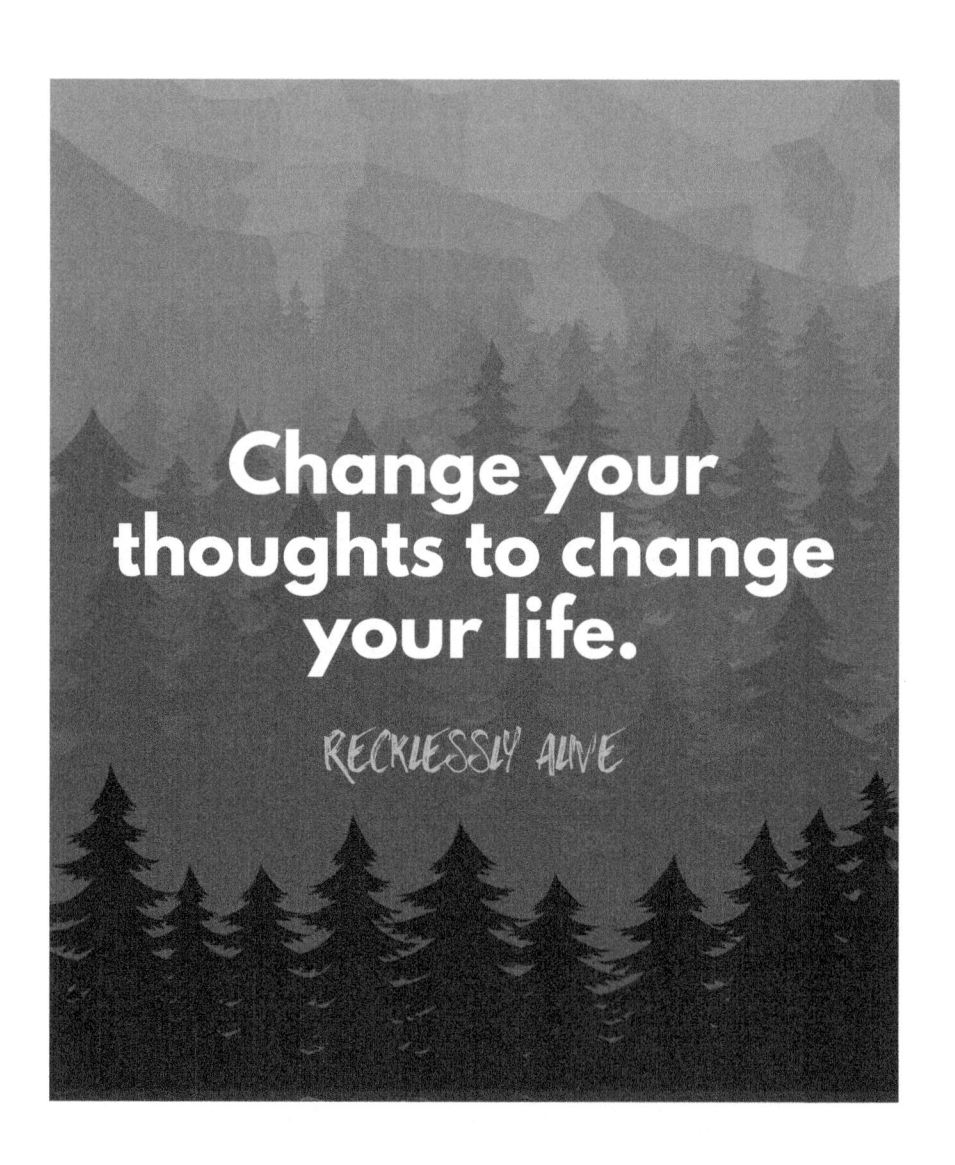

RECKLESSLY ALIVE

JOURNAL

WEEKLY REFLECTION

RATING MY WEEK: 1   2   3   4   5   6   7   8   9   10

I CHOSE THAT RATING BECAUSE:

....
....
....

I AM PROUD OF MYSELF FOR:

-
-
-
-
-

MY WINS FOR THE WEEK:	**I WOULD LIKE TO IMPROVE:**

LESSONS I LEARNED:	**I AM LETTING GO OF GUILT ABOUT:**

Week 9

EXCERPT FROM
Recklessly Alive

Maybe life has nothing to do with how happy you can make yourself, but how alive you can decide to become. There's a reason Jesus is the greatest example of how to be recklessly alive: He was relentless about making a difference and focusing on what matters most. He spent His time connecting with people, investing in others, taking care of Himself, listening to God, and choosing to love.

We are obsessed with stalking wealthy celebrities, lifting them up as the model everyone should aspire to be. I wonder if we lose so many famous people to addiction, crime, mental health, and suicide because they are burdened with our expectations to be the happiest people on earth.

Happiness, however, is an emotion that comes and goes—a mirage no one can ever infinitely sustain. You can spend your whole life focusing on yourself, or you can chase a life that is fully and recklessly alive. You can't have both.

I hope you're brave enough to focus on what matters most.
I hope you're courageous enough to fight complacency and get your hands dirty.
I hope you finally realize that your life was never about you.

You were made to make a difference.

(Eaton 158-159)

HABIT TRACKER

WEEK OF :

HABIT	MON	TUE	WED	THU	FRI	SAT	SUN
	☐	☐	☐	☐	☐	☐	☐
	☐	☐	☐	☐	☐	☐	☐
	☐	☐	☐	☐	☐	☐	☐
	☐	☐	☐	☐	☐	☐	☐
	☐	☐	☐	☐	☐	☐	☐
	☐	☐	☐	☐	☐	☐	☐
	☐	☐	☐	☐	☐	☐	☐
	☐	☐	☐	☐	☐	☐	☐
	☐	☐	☐	☐	☐	☐	☐
	☐	☐	☐	☐	☐	☐	☐

DAILY CHECK-IN

DATE:

WHAT ARE THE FEELINGS OR EMOTIONS I AM CURRENTLY EXPERIENCING?

WHAT LIMITING BELIEFS OR NEGATIVE THOUGHTS AM I HAVING TODAY?

WHAT DO I NEED TO HEAR TO COMBAT THOSE THOUGHTS?

WHAT ARE THREE THINGS I AM THANKFUL FOR TODAY?
-
-
-

WHAT IS THE ONE DAILY TASK I WILL COMPLETE TODAY?

MY FIELD NOTES:

MY DAY

WAKE TIME

TODAY'S MANTRA

SCHEDULE

7:00
8:00
9:00
10:00
11:00
12:00
1:00
2:00
3:00
4:00
5:00
6:00
7:00
8:00
9:00
10:00

TOP PRIORITIES

☐
☐
☐

WEEKLY GOALS

☐
☐
☐
☐
☐

TODAY'S SELF-CARE

☐
☐
☐
☐
☐

What will I never give up on?

Never stop believing that good things are on the way.

RECKLESSLY ALIVE

JOURNAL

DAILY CHECK-IN

DATE:

WHAT ARE THE FEELINGS OR EMOTIONS I AM CURRENTLY EXPERIENCING?

WHAT LIMITING BELIEFS OR NEGATIVE THOUGHTS AM I HAVING TODAY?

WHAT DO I NEED TO HEAR TO COMBAT THOSE THOUGHTS?

WHAT ARE THREE THINGS I AM THANKFUL FOR TODAY?
-
-
-

WHAT IS THE ONE DAILY TASK I WILL COMPLETE TODAY?

MY FIELD NOTES:

MY DAY

WAKE TIME _____

TODAY'S MANTRA _____

SCHEDULE

7:00 _____
8:00 _____
9:00 _____
10:00 _____
11:00 _____
12:00 _____
1:00 _____
2:00 _____
3:00 _____
4:00 _____
5:00 _____
6:00 _____
7:00 _____
8:00 _____
9:00 _____
10:00 _____

TOP PRIORITIES

☐ _____
☐ _____
☐ _____

WEEKLY GOALS

☐ _____
☐ _____
☐ _____
☐ _____

TODAY'S SELF-CARE

☐ _____
☐ _____
☐ _____
☐ _____
☐ _____

What is one of the best decisions I've ever made?

Be still and listen.

RECKLESSLY ALIVE

JOURNAL

DAILY CHECK-IN

DATE:

WHAT ARE THE FEELINGS OR EMOTIONS I AM CURRENTLY EXPERIENCING?

WHAT LIMITING BELIEFS OR NEGATIVE THOUGHTS AM I HAVING TODAY?

WHAT DO I NEED TO HEAR TO COMBAT THOSE THOUGHTS?

WHAT ARE THREE THINGS I AM THANKFUL FOR TODAY?
-
-
-

WHAT IS THE ONE DAILY TASK I WILL COMPLETE TODAY?

MY FIELD NOTES:

MY DAY

WAKE TIME

TODAY'S MANTRA

SCHEDULE

TOP PRIORITIES

- 7:00
- 8:00
- 9:00
- 10:00
- 11:00

WEEKLY GOALS

- 12:00
- 1:00
- 2:00
- 3:00
- 4:00
- 5:00

TODAY'S SELF-CARE

- 6:00
- 7:00
- 8:00
- 9:00
- 10:00

What is one way I can be kinder to myself?

Rejection is just redirection.
RECKLESSLY ALIVE

JOURNAL

DAILY CHECK-IN

DATE:

WHAT ARE THE FEELINGS OR EMOTIONS I AM CURRENTLY EXPERIENCING?

WHAT LIMITING BELIEFS OR NEGATIVE THOUGHTS AM I HAVING TODAY?

WHAT DO I NEED TO HEAR TO COMBAT THOSE THOUGHTS?

WHAT ARE THREE THINGS I AM THANKFUL FOR TODAY?
-
-
-

WHAT IS THE ONE DAILY TASK I WILL COMPLETE TODAY?

MY FIELD NOTES:

MY DAY

WAKE TIME

TODAY'S MANTRA

SCHEDULE

7:00
8:00
9:00
10:00
11:00
12:00
1:00
2:00
3:00
4:00
5:00
6:00
7:00
8:00
9:00
10:00

TOP PRIORITIES

☐
☐
☐

WEEKLY GOALS

☐
☐
☐
☐
☐

TODAY'S SELF-CARE

☐
☐
☐
☐
☐

When was the last time I surprised myself?

Be the person you always dreamed of becoming.

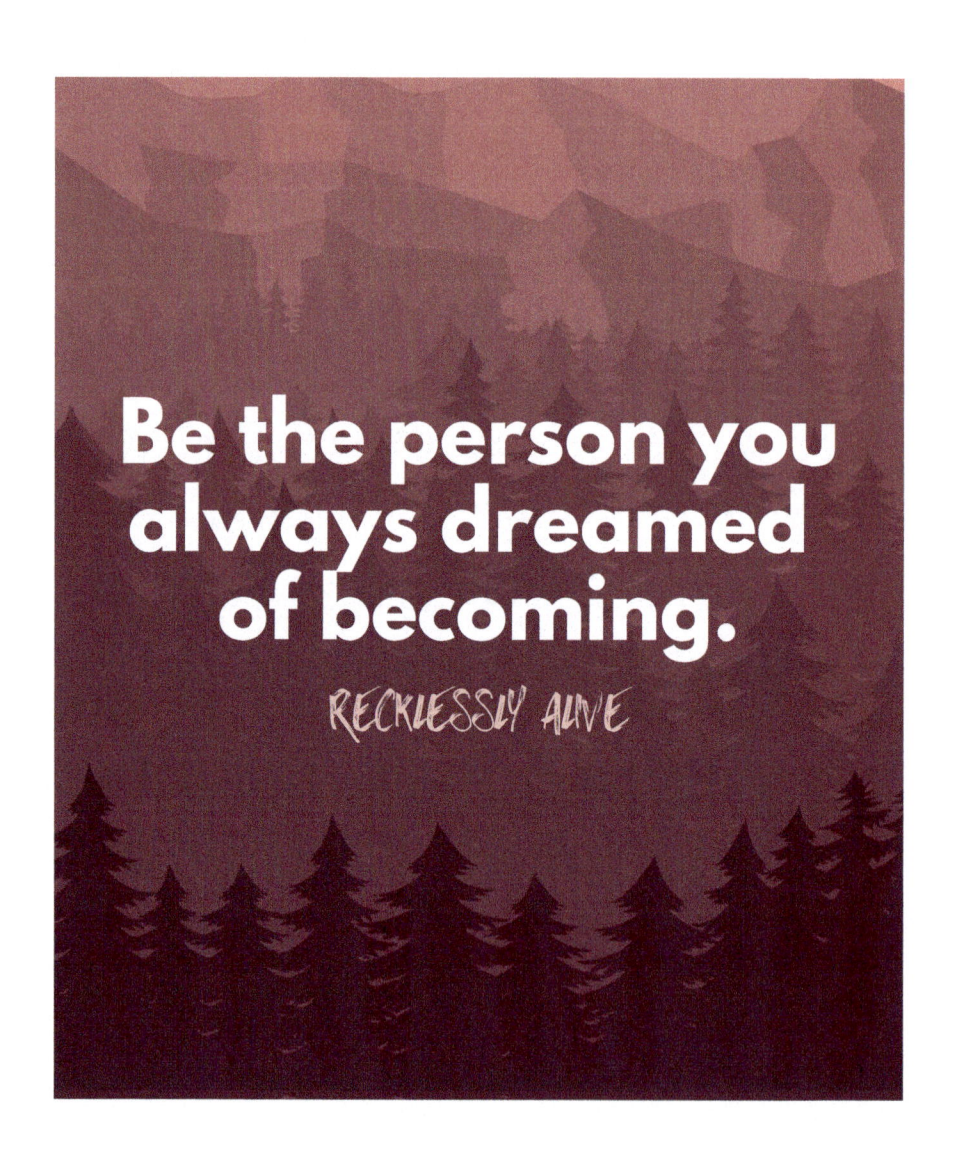

RECKLESSLY ALIVE

JOURNAL

DAILY CHECK-IN

DATE:

WHAT ARE THE FEELINGS OR EMOTIONS I AM CURRENTLY EXPERIENCING?

WHAT LIMITING BELIEFS OR NEGATIVE THOUGHTS AM I HAVING TODAY?

WHAT DO I NEED TO HEAR TO COMBAT THOSE THOUGHTS?

WHAT ARE THREE THINGS I AM THANKFUL FOR TODAY?
-
-
-

WHAT IS THE ONE DAILY TASK I WILL COMPLETE TODAY?

MY FIELD NOTES:

MY DAY

WAKE TIME

TODAY'S MANTRA

SCHEDULE

7:00
8:00
9:00
10:00
11:00
12:00
1:00
2:00
3:00
4:00
5:00
6:00
7:00
8:00
9:00
10:00

TOP PRIORITIES

- [ ]
- [ ]
- [ ]

WEEKLY GOALS

- [ ]
- [ ]
- [ ]
- [ ]
- [ ]

TODAY'S SELF-CARE

- [ ]
- [ ]
- [ ]
- [ ]
- [ ]

What is my theme for this upcoming season?

Life doesn't have to be perfect to be wonderful.

RECKLESSLY ALIVE

JOURNAL

DAILY CHECK-IN

DATE:

WHAT ARE THE FEELINGS OR EMOTIONS I AM CURRENTLY EXPERIENCING?

WHAT LIMITING BELIEFS OR NEGATIVE THOUGHTS AM I HAVING TODAY?

WHAT DO I NEED TO HEAR TO COMBAT THOSE THOUGHTS?

WHAT ARE THREE THINGS I AM THANKFUL FOR TODAY?
-
-
-

WHAT IS THE ONE DAILY TASK I WILL COMPLETE TODAY?

MY FIELD NOTES:

MY DAY

WAKE TIME

TODAY'S MANTRA

SCHEDULE

7:00
8:00
9:00
10:00
11:00
12:00
1:00
2:00
3:00
4:00
5:00
6:00
7:00
8:00
9:00
10:00

TOP PRIORITIES

- [ ]
- [ ]
- [ ]

WEEKLY GOALS

- [ ]
- [ ]
- [ ]
- [ ]

TODAY'S SELF-CARE

- [ ]
- [ ]
- [ ]
- [ ]
- [ ]

Do I trust my instincts? Why or why not?

If it's not a hell yes, it's a no.

RECKLESSLY ALIVE

JOURNAL

DAILY CHECK-IN

DATE:

WHAT ARE THE FEELINGS OR EMOTIONS I AM CURRENTLY EXPERIENCING?

WHAT LIMITING BELIEFS OR NEGATIVE THOUGHTS AM I HAVING TODAY?

WHAT DO I NEED TO HEAR TO COMBAT THOSE THOUGHTS?

WHAT ARE THREE THINGS I AM THANKFUL FOR TODAY?
-
-
-

WHAT IS THE ONE DAILY TASK I WILL COMPLETE TODAY?

MY FIELD NOTES:

MY DAY

WAKE TIME   **TODAY'S MANTRA**

SCHEDULE

- 7:00
- 8:00
- 9:00
- 10:00
- 11:00
- 12:00
- 1:00
- 2:00
- 3:00
- 4:00
- 5:00
- 6:00
- 7:00
- 8:00
- 9:00
- 10:00

TOP PRIORITIES

- [ ]
- [ ]
- [ ]

WEEKLY GOALS

- [ ]
- [ ]
- [ ]
- [ ]
- [ ]

TODAY'S SELF-CARE

- [ ]
- [ ]
- [ ]
- [ ]
- [ ]

What mistakes am I still holding onto from the past? How can I work to forgive myself?

Not everybody has the tools to love you the way you deserve.

RECKLESSLY ALIVE

JOURNAL

WEEKLY REFLECTION

RATING MY WEEK: 1   2   3   4   5   6   7   8   9   10

I CHOSE THAT RATING BECAUSE:
....
....
....

I AM PROUD OF MYSELF FOR:

-
-
-
-
-

MY WINS FOR THE WEEK:
....
....
....
....
....

I WOULD LIKE TO IMPROVE:
....
....
....
....
....

LESSONS I LEARNED:
....
....
....
....
....

I AM LETTING GO OF GUILT ABOUT:
....
....
....
....
....

Week 10

EXCERPT FROM
Recklessly Alive

Being recklessly alive isn't a nirvana-like state we achieve and enjoy until we take our last breath. Rather, it's a million little decisions we make.
To let life pass us by—or live it to the fullest.
To make ourselves happy—or discover true fulfillment in loving others.
To bury our deepest wounds—or get the help we deserve.
To hide all of our weaknesses—or use them to glorify God.

This is the craziest part of my story. When I tried to save my life through the comforts, wealth, and self-indulgence the world preaches, I wanted to die. But when I decided to lose my old way of life and try to live more like Jesus, I was finally saved.

Choosing to go all-in with God didn't instantly cure my mental illness. Fighting depression continues to be an ongoing mental, physical, and spiritual journey. Quite often, I'd rather hide than chase the waterfall moments God has planned for me. Some days I find myself trapped in the stupid dark room again, clawing at the door. Some days I still wake up thinking maybe I don't want to be alive. And that's real life. We fall and muster up enough strength to rise one more time.

If you're wondering if God is real, look at my story. Then look around. Living, breathing miracles are all around us. Becoming recklessly alive —after being two seconds away from completing suicide—is what He can do in anyone's life. He brings people back from the dead. It's His specialty.

(Eaton 164-165)

HABIT TRACKER

WEEK OF :

HABIT	MON	TUE	WED	THU	FRI	SAT	SUN
	☐	☐	☐	☐	☐	☐	☐
	☐	☐	☐	☐	☐	☐	☐
	☐	☐	☐	☐	☐	☐	☐
	☐	☐	☐	☐	☐	☐	☐
	☐	☐	☐	☐	☐	☐	☐
	☐	☐	☐	☐	☐	☐	☐
	☐	☐	☐	☐	☐	☐	☐
	☐	☐	☐	☐	☐	☐	☐
	☐	☐	☐	☐	☐	☐	☐
	☐	☐	☐	☐	☐	☐	☐

DAILY CHECK-IN

DATE:

WHAT ARE THE FEELINGS OR EMOTIONS I AM CURRENTLY EXPERIENCING?

WHAT LIMITING BELIEFS OR NEGATIVE THOUGHTS AM I HAVING TODAY?

WHAT DO I NEED TO HEAR TO COMBAT THOSE THOUGHTS?

WHAT ARE THREE THINGS I AM THANKFUL FOR TODAY?
-
-
-

WHAT IS THE ONE DAILY TASK I WILL COMPLETE TODAY?

MY FIELD NOTES:

MY DAY

WAKE TIME

TODAY'S MANTRA

SCHEDULE

7:00
8:00
9:00
10:00
11:00
12:00
1:00
2:00
3:00
4:00
5:00
6:00
7:00
8:00
9:00
10:00

TOP PRIORITIES

- [ ]
- [ ]
- [ ]

WEEKLY GOALS

- [ ]
- [ ]
- [ ]
- [ ]

TODAY'S SELF-CARE

- [ ]
- [ ]
- [ ]
- [ ]

What is something that has improved in my life over the past ten weeks?

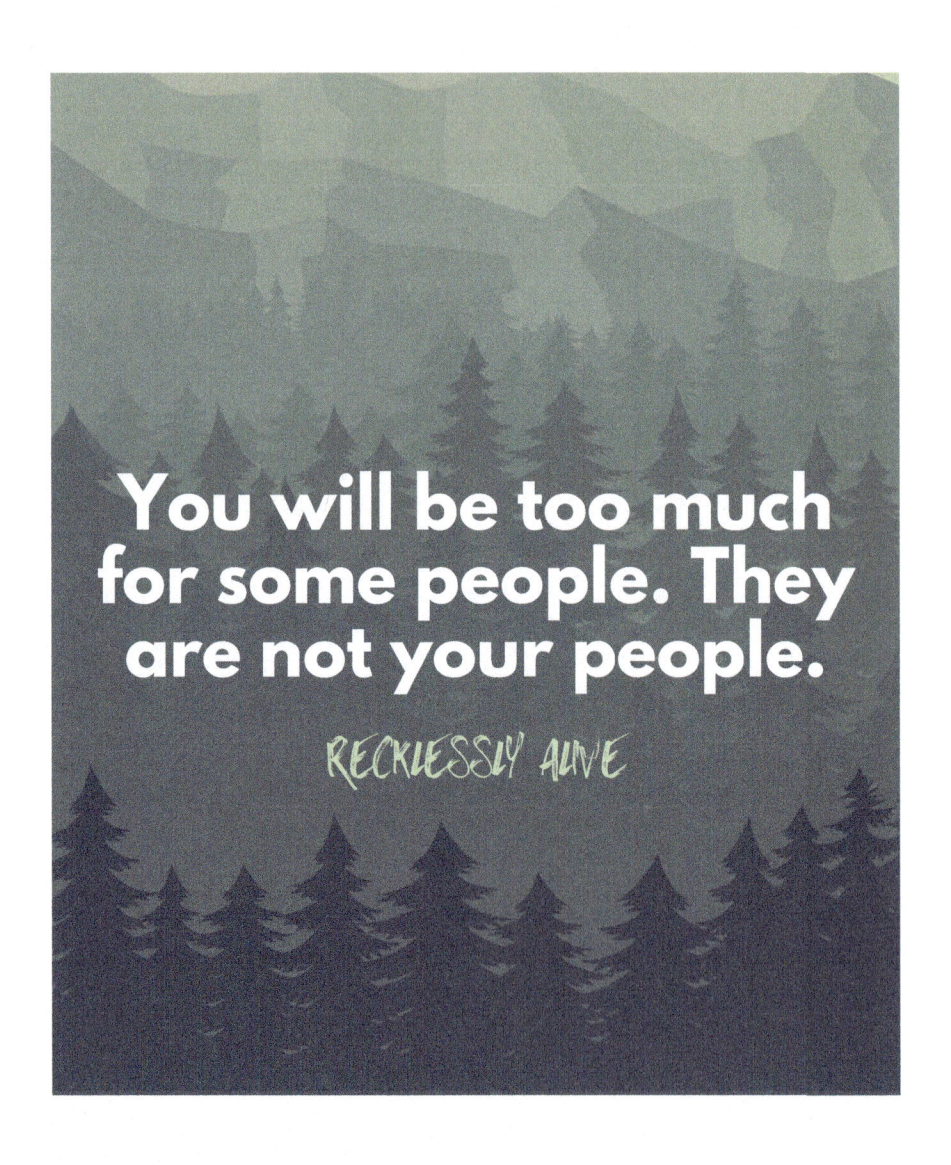

You will be too much for some people. They are not your people.

RECKLESSLY ALIVE

JOURNAL

DAILY CHECK-IN

DATE:

WHAT ARE THE FEELINGS OR EMOTIONS I AM CURRENTLY EXPERIENCING?

WHAT LIMITING BELIEFS OR NEGATIVE THOUGHTS AM I HAVING TODAY?

WHAT DO I NEED TO HEAR TO COMBAT THOSE THOUGHTS?

WHAT ARE THREE THINGS I AM THANKFUL FOR TODAY?
-
-
-

WHAT IS THE ONE DAILY TASK I WILL COMPLETE TODAY?

MY FIELD NOTES:

MY DAY

WAKE TIME   **TODAY'S MANTRA**

_____   _____

SCHEDULE   TOP PRIORITIES

7:00   _____   ☐ _____
8:00   _____   ☐ _____
9:00   _____   ☐ _____
10:00   _____
11:00   _____   **WEEKLY GOALS**
12:00   _____   ☐ _____
1:00   _____   ☐ _____
2:00   _____   ☐ _____
3:00   _____   ☐ _____
4:00   _____   ☐ _____
5:00   _____   **TODAY'S SELF-CARE**
6:00   _____   ☐ _____
7:00   _____   ☐ _____
8:00   _____   ☐ _____
9:00   _____   ☐ _____
10:00   _____   ☐ _____

What tools have I developed to improve my mental health?

Breathe and keep moving forward.

RECKLESSLY ALIVE

JOURNAL

DAILY CHECK-IN

DATE:

WHAT ARE THE FEELINGS OR EMOTIONS I AM CURRENTLY EXPERIENCING?

WHAT LIMITING BELIEFS OR NEGATIVE THOUGHTS AM I HAVING TODAY?

WHAT DO I NEED TO HEAR TO COMBAT THOSE THOUGHTS?

WHAT ARE THREE THINGS I AM THANKFUL FOR TODAY?
-
-
-

WHAT IS THE ONE DAILY TASK I WILL COMPLETE TODAY?

MY FIELD NOTES:

MY DAY

WAKE TIME

TODAY'S MANTRA

SCHEDULE

7:00
8:00
9:00
10:00
11:00
12:00
1:00
2:00
3:00
4:00
5:00
6:00
7:00
8:00
9:00
10:00

TOP PRIORITIES

- [ ]
- [ ]
- [ ]

WEEKLY GOALS

- [ ]
- [ ]
- [ ]
- [ ]
- [ ]

TODAY'S SELF-CARE

- [ ]
- [ ]
- [ ]
- [ ]
- [ ]

What is one lesson I have taken to heart over the past ten weeks?

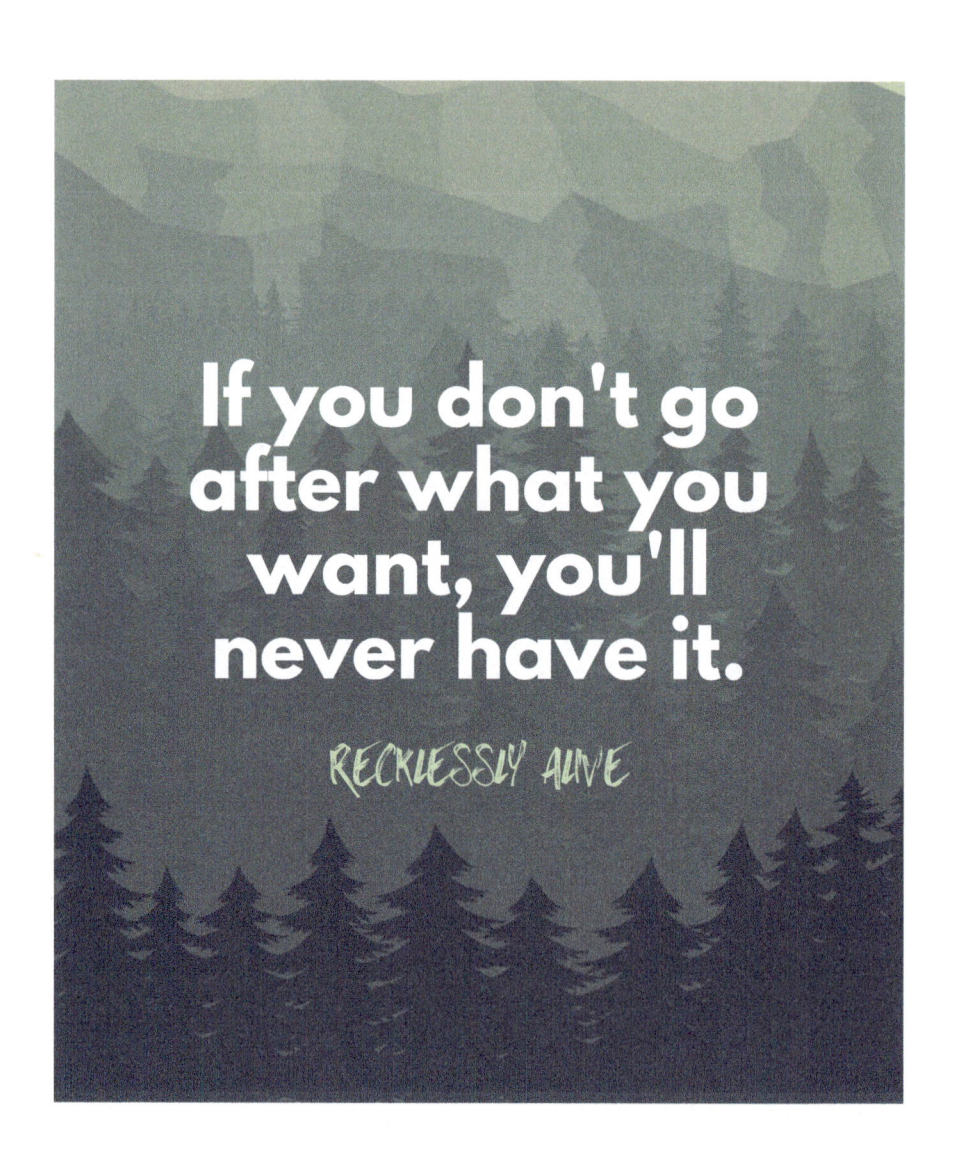

If you don't go after what you want, you'll never have it.

RECKLESSLY ALIVE

JOURNAL

DAILY CHECK-IN

DATE:

WHAT ARE THE FEELINGS OR EMOTIONS I AM CURRENTLY EXPERIENCING?

WHAT LIMITING BELIEFS OR NEGATIVE THOUGHTS AM I HAVING TODAY?

WHAT DO I NEED TO HEAR TO COMBAT THOSE THOUGHTS?

WHAT ARE THREE THINGS I AM THANKFUL FOR TODAY?
-
-
-

WHAT IS THE ONE DAILY TASK I WILL COMPLETE TODAY?

MY FIELD NOTES:

MY DAY

WAKE TIME
_____

TODAY'S MANTRA
_____

SCHEDULE

7:00 _____
8:00 _____
9:00 _____
10:00 _____
11:00 _____
12:00 _____
1:00 _____
2:00 _____
3:00 _____
4:00 _____
5:00 _____
6:00 _____
7:00 _____
8:00 _____
9:00 _____
10:00 _____

TOP PRIORITIES

☐ _____
☐ _____
☐ _____

WEEKLY GOALS

☐ _____
☐ _____
☐ _____
☐ _____
☐ _____

TODAY'S SELF-CARE

☐ _____
☐ _____
☐ _____
☐ _____
☐ _____

If I could go back and start these ten weeks over, what is one thing I would change?

Live so that you die with memories, not dreams.

RECKLESSLY ALIVE

JOURNAL

DAILY CHECK-IN

DATE:

WHAT ARE THE FEELINGS OR EMOTIONS I AM CURRENTLY EXPERIENCING?

WHAT LIMITING BELIEFS OR NEGATIVE THOUGHTS AM I HAVING TODAY?

WHAT DO I NEED TO HEAR TO COMBAT THOSE THOUGHTS?

WHAT ARE THREE THINGS I AM THANKFUL FOR TODAY?
-
-
-

WHAT IS THE ONE DAILY TASK I WILL COMPLETE TODAY?

MY FIELD NOTES:

MY DAY

WAKE TIME

TODAY'S MANTRA

SCHEDULE

7:00
8:00
9:00
10:00
11:00
12:00
1:00
2:00
3:00
4:00
5:00
6:00
7:00
8:00
9:00
10:00

TOP PRIORITIES

- [ ]
- [ ]
- [ ]

WEEKLY GOALS

- [ ]
- [ ]
- [ ]
- [ ]
- [ ]

TODAY'S SELF-CARE

- [ ]
- [ ]
- [ ]
- [ ]
- [ ]

Was I able to accomplish my goals over these ten weeks?
If yes, how do I feel? If no, what support will I need next time?

Don't ruin a good day by thinking about a bad yesterday.

RECKLESSLY ALIVE

JOURNAL

DAILY CHECK-IN

DATE:

WHAT ARE THE FEELINGS OR EMOTIONS I AM CURRENTLY EXPERIENCING?

WHAT LIMITING BELIEFS OR NEGATIVE THOUGHTS AM I HAVING TODAY?

WHAT DO I NEED TO HEAR TO COMBAT THOSE THOUGHTS?

WHAT ARE THREE THINGS I AM THANKFUL FOR TODAY?
-
-
-

WHAT IS THE ONE DAILY TASK I WILL COMPLETE TODAY?

MY FIELD NOTES:

MY DAY

WAKE TIME

TODAY'S MANTRA

SCHEDULE

TOP PRIORITIES

7:00
8:00
9:00
10:00
11:00
12:00
1:00
2:00
3:00
4:00
5:00
6:00
7:00
8:00
9:00
10:00

WEEKLY GOALS

TODAY'S SELF-CARE

What is one of my favorite adventures over the past ten weeks?

If the world was blind, how many people would you impress?

RECKLESSLY ALIVE

JOURNAL

DAILY CHECK-IN

DATE:

WHAT ARE THE FEELINGS OR EMOTIONS I AM CURRENTLY EXPERIENCING?

WHAT LIMITING BELIEFS OR NEGATIVE THOUGHTS AM I HAVING TODAY?

WHAT DO I NEED TO HEAR TO COMBAT THOSE THOUGHTS?

WHAT ARE THREE THINGS I AM THANKFUL FOR TODAY?
-
-
-

WHAT IS THE ONE DAILY TASK I WILL COMPLETE TODAY?

MY FIELD NOTES:

MY DAY

WAKE TIME

TODAY'S MANTRA

SCHEDULE

7:00
8:00
9:00
10:00
11:00
12:00
1:00
2:00
3:00
4:00
5:00
6:00
7:00
8:00
9:00
10:00

TOP PRIORITIES

☐
☐
☐

WEEKLY GOALS

☐
☐
☐
☐

TODAY'S SELF-CARE

☐
☐
☐
☐
☐

What am I most proud of myself for over these past ten weeks?

Very little is needed to make a happy life.

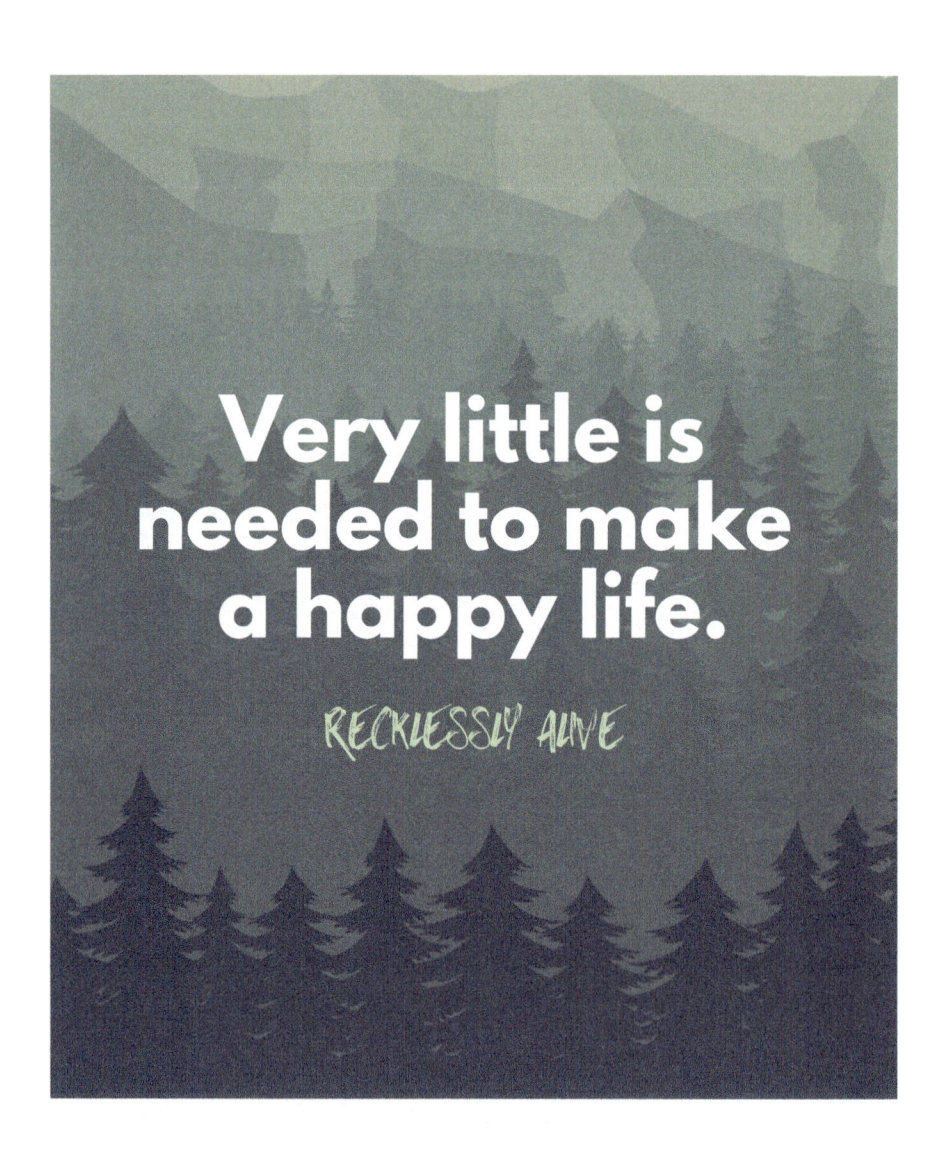

RECKLESSLY ALIVE

JOURNAL

WEEKLY REFLECTION

RATING MY WEEK: 1 2 3 4 5 6 7 8 9 10

I CHOSE THAT RATING BECAUSE:

....
....
....

I AM PROUD OF MYSELF FOR:

-
-
-
-
-

MY WINS FOR THE WEEK:

....
....
....
....

I WOULD LIKE TO IMPROVE:

....
....
....
....

LESSONS I LEARNED:

....
....
....
....

I AM LETTING GO OF GUILT ABOUT:

....
....
....
....

CONGRATS!

You did it! You deserve an aggressive high five, a giant bear hug, and a moderate-sized parade. I hope you carve out some time to reflect on your journaling and ruminate on your growth and celebrate your wins.

You've been intentional for the past ten weeks and I am proud of you. Whatever you do, don't stop now. Keep fighting for your recklessly alive life.

Ready to start again? Order your next Recklessly Alive Mental Health Journal now!

Make sure to connect with us on social media @RecklesslyAlive and at RecklesslyAlive.com.

Love, Sam

Acknowledgements:

Thank you all for supporting my dream of a world with zero deaths by suicide. An enormous thank you to Jill Gregory for your dear friendship and all of your design assistance. Thank you to Beth Saadati for continuing to tirelessly catch my adverbs and grammar mishaps.

About the Author

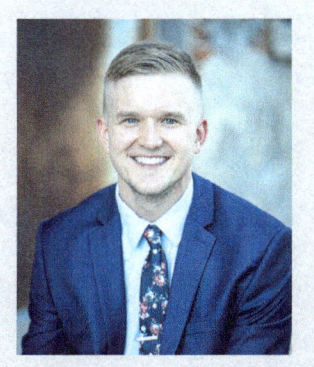

Sam Eaton is an author, speaker, and founder of Recklessly Alive, a suicide prevention organization sprinting toward a world with zero deaths by suicide. Sam has spoken at over one-hundred events throughout the U.S. sharing his story of battling depression and suicidal thoughts.

Sam's first book, Recklessly Alive: What My Suicide Attempt Taught Me About God and Living Life to the Fullest, was released in January 2021 and reached the top 200 best-selling books on Amazon. He currently resides in Minneapolis, MN where he enjoys collecting vinyl records, lifting moderately heavy weights, and trying every flavor of Oreos.

Printed in Great Britain
by Amazon

CW01316618

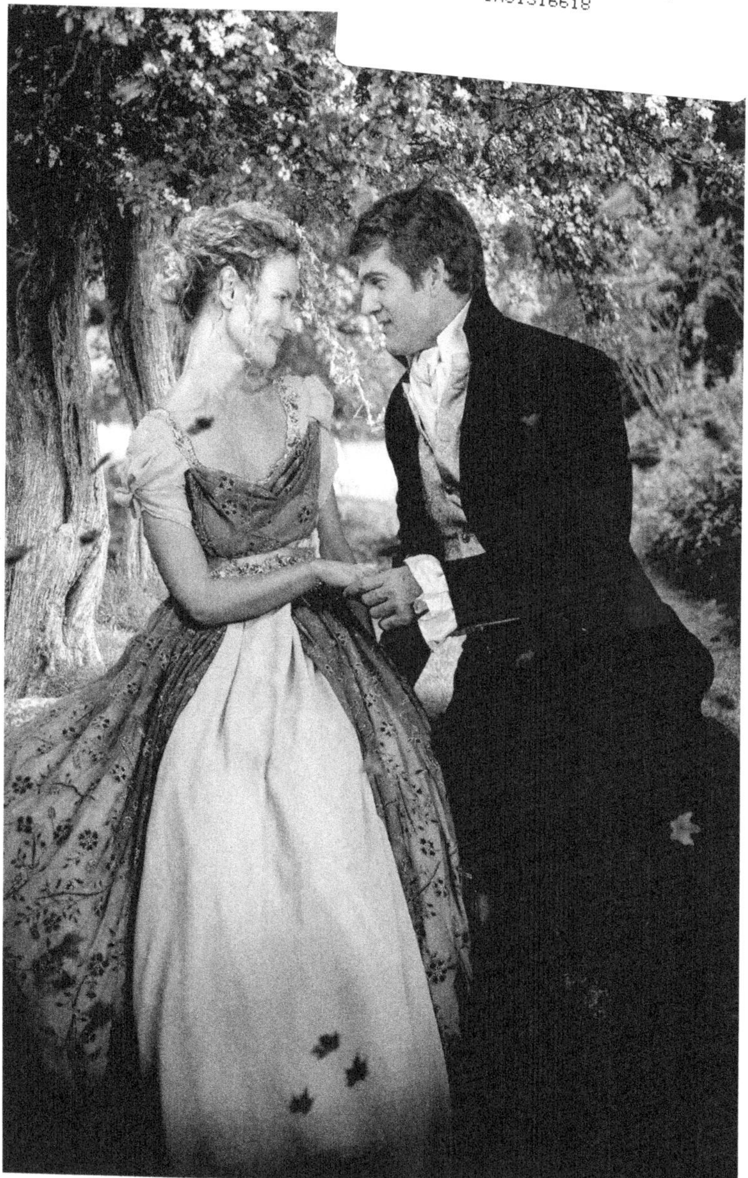

This Time Love

by

MARY ELLEN BOYD

Copyright © 2021 by Mary Ellen Boyd

All rights reserved.

No part of this book may be reproduced in any form or by any electronic or mechanical means, including information storage and retrieval systems, without written permission from the author, except for the use of brief quotations in a book review.

ISBN-13: 978-1-7376781-0-6

1

That annoying flash kept sparking on the edge of her vision. She had moved further down the line of tables out in the blazing sun, but that odd glint of light seemed to follow her. Either she was on the verge of a heatstroke, or something nearby reflected the sun.

She hadn't seen anything reflective enough to do that. In fact, everything she passed leaned more toward wood and rusty cast iron. Nothing that would catch the sun.

Grace lifted her ponytail off her sweaty neck, trying to pretend that would cool her. It didn't work. Open air flea markets were such fun, but not when the day was this brutal.

The flash came again, and she finally turned to find it.

There it was, right near the edge of the table she just passed. That was odd. She'd already looked at everything the seller had, and saw nothing worth more than a glance. Bent metal cups, an old comb, possibly celluloid, with several teeth missing—part of a set with brush in about the same condition, bristles sticking out every which way. A little further down sat several flour sifters clogged with spiderwebs and dust, and a few nice pieces of mismatched china.

If that shine was anything worth buying—and goodness knew, in this heat and humidity, it would be easy to overlook a treasure—she would never find out unless she went back.

Grace had a bit of splurge money in her purse. What a pity it would be to go home with it unspent.

She lifted the hair off her neck again, and hoped for a breeze while she tried to find the energy to decide whether it was worth retracing her steps. The wind didn't have to be cool, it just had to move the air.

The van was filled with her current client's requests. "Antique chairs. Queen Anne legs and carved oval backs, the older the better. Make sure there is one wing chair." They didn't look like much now, tattered upholstery and dull finishes, but they would be great when she finished them.

"Oh, why not?" She asked the question to the open air. Working alone tended to make her do that. Grace retraced her steps.

The table looked as unpromising on the second examination as it had on the first. The sparkle must have come from the next table over —although she didn't think her sense of perspective was *that* badly affected by the oppressive humidity and the broiling temperature. The sun reflected dully off old glass. Heavy carving framed a small oval of beveled glass. It fairly screamed of age.

Her hand reached for the useless but beautiful antique vanity mirror as if pulled by a string. She took it up and the handle fit perfectly, almost like she had held it before. Scallops etched the long, solid handle and curled up and around the clouded glass. Despite the heavy carvings, her fingers shifted automatically to compensate for the design, and tightened in possession. The handle was warm, as if someone just set it down, but that had to be from sitting in the sun.

A heavy layer of tarnish turned the entire mirror nearly black. Silver-plate or the real thing, only checking the hallmark would tell, but the weight made Grace suspect it was solid silver.

How could she have missed this her first time past?

"I thought that one was gone," a gravelly voice said from nearby. Grace gave a start and spun around toward the sound. Middle-aged and paunchy, wearing jeans and a t-shirt that probably started the day white, a man, obviously the seller, sat on a rickety stool behind the table.

She had not seen him before, but during slow times dealers often stepped over to visit with friends, and kept a watchful eye on their own display from a short distance.

A steaming cup of coffee sat next to his register, an antique nearly as old as the mirror she held. Grace looked at the vapor rising from the coffee and shuddered at the mere thought of pouring something hot down her throat. People believed Minnesota was cold? They should visit in August, she thought, as perspiration trickled down her back.

The man rose and came over, his eyes fixed on what she held. His face was shiny with sweat, either from the temperature or from that coffee.

"I just sold a whole collection of 'em," he said when he stopped across from her. "I told them to take whatever they wanted. I guess they left that one behind."

He raised his watery blue eyes to meet hers. The pale gaze held Grace in place, the blue seeming to deepen with his every word. She stared at those eyes, watching them change, darkening into a rich sapphire while he continued. "The glass is bad. I bet that's why those folks didn't buy it. Their loss. That glass is original. I suspect all the silvering on the back is gone, and that's probably why it doesn't reflect well." He scratched his head through his baseball cap, but his gaze still held Grace's.

It took effort, but she broke that odd hold from those mesmerizing eyes and looked down at the mirror again, nestled so comfortably in her grip. The metal seemed to lighten in the sun, the tarnish fading to hint at its original glow.

As she tilted it for one last look before she made herself put it back, she suddenly caught her reflection in it, but something was wrong, the hairstyle maybe. The image vanished, leaving her looking at the grimy glass. She tilted the mirror, hoping for another peek at that reflection, wondering if it had been there at all or if the sun played a trick on her.

The man interrupted her reverie. "I'll knock five bucks off the price if you want it. It's real old, or I'd take off even more. You pay for age."

She nodded before she gave herself a chance to change her mind. The mirror didn't want to be left behind. She sensed it, an urgency, like the mirror was pleading for rescue. She sometimes felt that way when she walked past a chair frame, as if the poor thing knew it was destined for the garbage burner.

Forty dollars poorer, she walked away, the mirror in a white paper bag clutched tightly in her hand, but satisfaction buoyed her all the way to the van.

Grace pulled into the driveway behind her house and turned off the engine. The heat pressed against the windows when the air conditioner stopped. She had the oddest sense that the bag holding the mirror might disappear at any moment unless she got it someplace safe—and soon.

The chairs could wait. She pushed the door open, clutching the bag against her chest and hurried for the house.

It was cooler inside than out, but stickiness pressed against the walls of her small home as if searching for a way in as the air conditioner struggled against the numbing humidity. After looking around for the best place, Grace stopped at the bedroom, leaned over and set her small package safely in the middle of her bed. Not that it could roll off, it wasn't a living thing, but she still felt better knowing it was far from the edge.

She went back out to the van to get the chair frames, carting them in one by one. Every trip outside made the hot air feel hotter, but once they were all lined up, she nodded, well satisfied. Refinished and with new upholstery, the designer should be pleased at her selections.

The mirror now, that was just for herself. She had no intention of selling it even if she could clean it up. What did the man say again? The silvering was gone? Maybe it was just dirty.

She closed her workshop door, and kicked off her shoes. No sense tracking any more dirt in than she already had. She felt cooler with her bare feet on the floor, where the air conditioning seemed to congregate.

That taken care of, she returned to the bedroom, sat down and pulled the mirror out of the bag. There had to be a silver hallmark somewhere, but under all the tarnish it would be hard to find. Flipping on her bedside table light, Grace tilted the mirror side to side—and there it was. Or rather, there *they* were. Small symbols had been pressed into the mirror's back, each one different. A rectangle with very worn letters. The "A" was clear, and after it an "O" or "D" or "P," then some man's head, and a letter "S," what might be a cat with a hat, and was that a lion?

It had to be genuine. No one would go through the trouble of putting all those symbols on a mirror unless they meant something.

She leaned back against the headboard and clutched her purchase to her chest. A real antique silver mirror. "If only you could talk," she said, and laughed. "What stories would you tell?"

A box of tissues sat by the bed. Grace pulled one out and started rubbing the dirt off the glass. The wind picked up from outside, predicting a storm, breaking the stifling heat of the past week.

Her hair stirred, caught by the currents of air, and she brushed the blonde strands out of her eyes as she kept rubbing. The breeze stirred again, wafting the hair back into her eyes with more force this time, and she had to hold it in place. Grace froze, her hand still holding her flailing hair.

Wind? Inside? All the windows were closed this morning when she turned the air conditioner on.

An angry gust whirled around her and in a blink whipped her off the bed, holding her suspended for a brief instant, not long enough for her to open her mouth to scream, and then she was sucked into the whirling maelstrom.

The mirror was still clenched in her hand; the carvings dug into her palm. Shapes flew past too quickly to see them, her hair ripped free from the ponytail and slapped curls against her cheeks, her mouth, blocking her vision, clearing it, only to come back again. There was nothing to grab onto as she spun round and round, just the mirror, the only solid object, and she held tighter, feeling it cut into her palm. She tried to scream, to release the cry trapped in her throat, but couldn't suck in any air. Her heart pounded in her chest, her hair flailed around and snapped against her face like sharp stings.

Before she could compose a prayer, Grace hit the floor with a thump that knocked the air out of her lungs. *Air*, she needed *air*, and fought for a breath. After a frightening moment when her lungs refused to relax, sweet oxygen rushed in. Her eyes were still squeezed shut, and she dared not open them yet, not until all the grit and remnants settled.

For such a violent storm, the air felt clear, smelled clear, no dust sifted past her cheeks or filled her mouth. After her breath steadied, Grace concentrated on any damage to her body before she dared open her eyes. Other than landing hard, nothing hurt, not even her bottom, despite how hard she hit. Her arms didn't hurt, her legs were fine, her shoes were even still on her feet.

At that realization, her eyes popped open. She hadn't been wearing shoes in her house.

Grace stared down past a peach-colored skirt, registering its presence but not ready to analyze that oddity yet, and looked at her feet, and the shoes there.

These were not her shoes. She knew every pair she owned—she didn't have that many—and none of them looked like this, soft flat shoes made from some richly embroidered fabric. She stared down at them as she sat there on the floor and angled her foot to see the underside as best she could. Bending was difficult. Grace craned her neck and peered at what she could see of the shoe bottom. Leather, carefully stitched to the top, and without a heel.

Now for the peach gown that draped her, with a skirt that—she had already discovered—blocked her view of her legs. Wow! A tumbled froth of ruffles and silk. And a frill of ivory lace around her very low neckline.

Very, *very* low neckline. She never knew she had cleavage like this.

Grace felt the blush rise up her cheeks. She took a surprised breath, only to find out that whatever kept her from bending was wrapped around her torso, cramping her lungs. She ran a hand around her middle, and discovered boning running vertically down her ribs. She had never worn one before, but she knew it was a corset.

So *that* explained why bending was difficult.

For the first time since the—dream? hallucination? Whatever this was—began, Grace shifted her attention from herself to her surroundings, and her mouth dropped open.

Instead of a tornado-ravaged house, she was in the most enormous room she had ever seen. The floor beneath her was wide planks of genuine hardwood, dark as opposed to the blonde oak laminate she had at home. Some kind of shimmery blue wallpaper glistened on the walls, a bright contrast to the heaviness of the floor.

A dark wood four-poster bed rested against the wall she faced and ran lengthwise along her left. A blue canopy hung from the tall frame. A matching blue comforter had been spread on the mattress with what appeared to be careful smoothness. A white bedskirt dusted the floor.

Visible beyond the bed, tall, narrow windows marked an outside wall. Heavy blue curtains that surely were velvet hung from nearly the ceiling to the floor.

She twisted around to see the wall behind her, an armoire, a real dark wood antique armoire almost as long as her bedroom at home, stood against the wall with room to spare. Beyond it, a small, elegant fireplace of a white stone carved with vines and vases had been built into the wall. From the smoke stains on the matching white mantle, it was well-used.

Between the fireplace and the windows, a folding screen of ruffled fabric on a wooden frame didn't quite cover an item she recognized. A strange shaped chair with a small footrest and no back. She didn't have to go over and look to know it was an antique commode. The top opened to become the missing back, and no doubt if she wanted to lift it, she would find a porcelain bowl inside. That object had come from her own mind, for she had seen items just like it in many a flea market and auction.

It was better than a bedpan, but not by much.

As she stared from the armoire to the fireplace to the commode to the windows and back to the bed at her side, something tugged on her scalp, an unexpected weight and tightness. Grace reached up to check her head, half expecting to find blood from whatever was pulling at her scalp, afraid there might be an injury that would help explain her fantasy presence in this lovely place.

As her fingers slid into her hair, she gave another start. What on earth? Unusual hairpins were stuck all over, holding an intricate style in place. Braids wove through the curls, and her fingertips slid along what felt like ribbons worked into the plaits.

This she *had* to see. Perhaps if she saw it, she would know whether it was real or a figment of her imagination, a hallucination caused by some injury her mind would not, dared not, recognize yet.

A whisper of fear crept through. Her body could be broken and covered with debris, her imagination the only defense it had. Searchers might not find her for days. When would the pain of her injuries seep through this lovely layer of protection?

She clung to the vision like a lifeline. The real world would break through soon enough, and what it would bring terrified her.

Where was the mirror? She remembered having it in her hand, and looked around the floor at her side, then patted through the disturbing layers of fabric on her legs. Nothing. Had she dropped it along the way?

It took a bit of a struggle to get to her feet, and fear crept through again, her heart thumping, chills prickling her arms. What was happening outside this hallucination? In this world, her legs wobbled but they held, and the gown settled in place.

That pinching around her chest wasn't just the corset, but the high-waisted style, with a ribbon that tied just under her breasts. The skirt went clear to the floor.

She was grateful the vision still held, holding bandages and broken bones, shattered walls and collapsed roof, at bay.

Her fingers slid along the fabric, enjoying the smooth silk. The gown wasn't as full as it had seemed, being narrow in front, but the weight of gathers in the back gave the gown the sense of being broader than it was. A ruffle that viewed from above looked a foot wide, noticeable but not overwhelming, ran around the bottom.

As she twisted from side to side, trying to take in this new fantasy as the rich fabric swished around her feet and the fuller back skirt tugged at her mid-back, Grace pulled her mind away from the gown and back to that missing mirror. It was the key, the last thing she touched before the world went mad. If she found it, her mind would know where everything else was, the door, the bed, the closet.

For now, before reality came crashing back in, bills and work and cleaning and cooking—and hospitals?—Grace intended to absorb all she could.

She looked to the right, the only wall she hadn't examined yet. A large, paneled dark wood door out of the same wood as the floor, the bed, and the armoire, more of that shimmering wallpaper, and a gilt dressing table with a large oval mirror hanging on a bracket. A large china pitcher in a bowl, something very familiar to anyone who prowled flea markets and antique sales, sat on a large dressing table, and next to that, a small pouch beside a little tin.

She didn't want to snoop, but after all, this was only a dream. Grace let the scene play out and picked up the pouch. It was oddly bulky. Opening it, Grace tugged at the cloth just inside. Other objects tumbled about at the movement. The fabric unfolded and unfolded with each pull on the edge until the last of it slid out. Nothing fancy, just a rough square of silk.

Why silk? Ah, well, she was never one to turn away silk in any form.

She set the silk aside and turned back to the pouch. A round-ish opaque ball clinked out onto the table, lumpy and strangely colored. She picked it up and rubbed her fingers across it, then took a whiff. It didn't smell like anything she recognized, but it felt like . . . soap?

Grace looked from the silk to the soap and back again, and said aloud, "A washcloth!" It had probably started out as a handkerchief and been relegated to this lowly job.

The only other item in the pouch confused her. A tiny sponge, not big enough for washing.

Next to those things a silver tray, and hiding behind the scalloped edge was—yes!—her vanity hand mirror. Together with a matching brush and comb. A matching set when she only bought the mirror.

They looked brand new, even the mirror. No missing teeth in the comb, or bristles heading every which direction in the brush, and most decidedly not made of plastic. No, these pieces were also of silver, and carved exactly like the mirror.

A chill of a different kind shivered up her spine, and goosebumps mottled her arms.

The room had been comfortable just a moment ago.

Was she cold? Was rain pummeling her broken self in that other world?

Grace leaned over and picked the mirror up, enjoying the weight of the gown with her movement, the faint pulling of the gathered fabric hanging down the back. It was in perfect condition, the glass clear, the handle clean and gleaming. She stared at the reflection in the oval glass and immediately recognized what she saw.

The same reflection she had seen at the flea market, the one she had wanted another look at—herself in the gown she now wore.

Her hand started to shake, and she set the vanity mirror back down, sank onto the chair in front of the dressing table and looked into the larger mirror.

The gown was in fact as low-cut as that partial look in the mirror indicated, and she clapped a hand over her billowing breasts so she could concentrate on the rest without embarrassing herself. Her hair drew her attention away from her cleavage, pinned into layers of curls and tiny braids. The ribbons in her hair matched the gown so perfectly it must be from the same bolt of fabric.

She had purchased several costume patterns thinking someday she would make them, even though she didn't know where she could wear anything so obviously from another era.

Whatever the cause of this world she found herself in, it was a lovely dream. Her lips curved and so did the ones in the mirror.

There was so much more to see in this world she had conjured. Grace slipped around the bed and over to the window, pulled back the curtain enough to see, and peeked outside. No cars. In fact, not only no cars, but no pavement. At least, not as asphalt.

It must have been all those antiques that set her brain on this path.

An unpaved driveway, marred with shallow, thin ruts, ran in a half-circle outside her window, edged on the far side with a tall white wooden fence, the bars running lengthwise. The fence abruptly ended in a pruned hedge that formed the other side of the fence and headed away from her out of her view. A path led on the outside of the hedge, going into a thin woods.

Off to the far right, inside the fence and hedge, she saw dark shapes, shifting and moving only to stop again. Horses grazing in a field?

"Binoculars would be helpful," she muttered, wondering if they would appear as soon as she mentioned the need. Things like that happened in a dream. This fantasy did not cooperate.

A very human whistle cut the air. Instead of rescuers breaking through her lovely escape, one of the dark shapes she stared at, identifiable now as a magnificent horse, turned and galloped, coming closer until it disappeared behind what was visible from the window's edge.

She shifted and tried from another angle. Carriages lined the packed dirt drive, all pulled close to a building that was a sort of garage. Inside the building, hiding in shadows, she thought she saw more carriages. *Carriages!* Grace giggled with a bit of hysteria, imagining them dropped into a parking lot in Minneapolis.

A man came around the side of one of the carriages, and Grace ducked further behind the curtain, leaving the slimmest gap to peek. The man carried a bucket with a rag draped over the edge. Grace watched as he began washing the near side of the carriage, such a normal activity with such a bizarre twist. Carriage washing? His clothes were unlike anything she was used to, breeches that fastened under the knee and wooden clogs that even from this distance had seen plenty of use. He didn't pull out a cell phone, there was no radio nearby, no music coming from anywhere.

Another man dressed much the same led a horse into view and eased the big animal into place between two bars coming out of the next carriage in line. The two men appeared to be bantering back and forth. The new man harnessed the animal with the skill of one who did this on a regular basis.

No wires, no poles, no car exhaust. In fact, the air smelled wonderful—except for the tang of manure, but even that had a freshness to it, untainted by anything else lying over it. Ruts in the drive, yes, but no wider than a bike tire would leave.

Grace let the curtain fall closed, backed up, and sank down on the bed. Any moment now she would wake up and chalk this whole scenario down to that tornado on top of too much heat. But the dress was silky beneath her fingers, the corset snug around her middle, and she could feel the pull of the fancy curls pinned on her head.

She pinched herself, just out of curiosity. The pinch hurt. Did that mean this was real, that her senses weren't lying?

Nearby, and close, much too close, a door opened. Grace froze, still touching the pinched spot. This was *her* dream. Nobody else was supposed to be in it. She turned to face the door that led . . . where?

2

Voices seeped through the heavy wood. Young voices, feminine, full of zest and laughter. Happy sounds, out of place in a broken world.

Maybe the world wasn't as smashed as she feared, if the sounds seeping into her consciousness were so bright. Grace crept closer to the door and pressed her ear against the wood. Words finally started to become clear.

"I am so glad I came! It is much more relaxing out here in the country. My mother hopes I might catch someone's eye with less competition," a woman said in a young voice with what sounded like a British accent, and giggled.

"That's all very well, but most of the men stayed in London. Less competition means fewer men to choose from, you know." This one sounded practical and a bit of a spoilsport. One would think she could at least have said, *You are just fine the way you are, you need not worry about competition,* or something equally kind.

"My mother says I must be careful," the first speaker said, her voice still so bright Grace doubted she knew what 'careful' meant.

"Fortune hunters are everywhere in Town. I hardly think Fairfax would let just anyone through, so I think I can safely enjoy myself."

Fairfax? Grace didn't know anyone by that name, didn't know how it got into her dream.

"Enjoy yourself? What are you planning on doing?" It was the spoilsport again. "Just remember, indiscretions make it back to Town, and a ruined reputation will destroy you. How would you like to be sent home in disgrace?"

A pair of gasps just beyond the door made Grace jump back. "Susan!" She could hear the rustling of their gowns.

It all felt so realistic. The clothes, the sound of gasps and rustles, the whistles from the men outside, even the brief sound of horses' hooves.

The invisible scene continued, just voices behind the heavy door in front of her eyes, the weave of the rich gown under her fingers, and the tugging weight of the hair on her head.

"How could you say that about me?" The young voice had lost all its familiar laughing brightness. *Maybe I judged her too quickly*, Grace thought. "I have done nothing to hurt my reputation, and I never said I would. Why do you always put the worst face on what I say?"

"You don't have to attack me," Susan of the spoilsport attitude retorted. "I am only trying to warn you to be cautious."

"Come, now," a rich young voice, almost like a singer's, said. "We are here to enjoy ourselves, not to argue. I for one never thought I would be invited to a house party, and I intend to be happy. I don't enjoy fighting, especially not with my closest friends." More rustling, and then, the singer-girl continued, "What are your plans for the day? There is the dance tonight, but right now I think they are playing pall mall in the garden."

"I'm sure they have already formed the teams. No one wants an interruption, or to have to make up the teams again." The giggler, her voice still muted. "Maybe I'll just go down to the library."

"Don't do that. It is such a nice day. We should enjoy it, even if we just watch. There are hours to go before the party, and I want to fill in the time." That was the singer again. "I have a beautiful gown my mother ordered special for this party. I cannot wait to wear it, so I need to do something to keep busy."

"I know who you want to notice you." Susan the spoilsport jumped in. "I saw him out there playing pall mall. You won't have any trouble finding him. With that red hair, he will stand out like a flame."

"Susan!" Giggly Girl seemed to have developed a spine, Grace thought with approval. "Anthony Throckbridge is a very nice man. He can't help that he has red hair. Besides, he has not a spot on his reputation, and I think Cyrilla is lucky that he has shown interest in her."

Was Cyrilla the songbird?

"One dance is not showing interest, it's just being polite." Susan again, still not giving up with her snide digs. "I was at that ball. Everyone commented on that hair."

Grace wished she dared open the door and slap the girl. Why were the other two even her friends? Although friendship was a strange thing. She thought of Ava, who never managed her own finances right, and had bilked Grace out of money with empty promises of repayment until she had been forced to cut off the relationship. Despite the relief of being away from the drama, Grace still thought of her, and missed her.

But Cyrilla had taken care of the situation. "He is a kind man. Not only that, but he also has quite a sizable estate of his own. Whoever wins him will be a fortunate woman. I want to go out and watch the game. Perhaps they have finished, and we can get on the next teams. Patricia, if you want to go find Lily, she might be out playing with the others. I'm sure she will be happy to put us on her team for the next game."

Patricia must be the giggly one. It was nice to have a name for each. More gown rustling, the sound becoming more dim and farther away.. Grace could picture Cyrilla walking off with dignity. She seemed to be mature for her age. Maybe she was older than her voice sounded.

"Susan, aren't you coming?" Cyrilla's voice came from a distance. Apparently Susan and her sharp tongue stayed behind.

"I don't want to play pall mall. And I don't want to stand around watching like a wallflower."

"If you are certain?" Cyrilla sounded worried, and Grace imagined her going through everything she had said to see if something might have hurt Susan.

Patricia didn't seem to be as concerned. The brightness was back in her voice as she called, "I will see you tonight."

More faint rustling, and the hall went quiet. A sniff broke the silence, followed by a sob, and then a second, and a third. A flurry of sounds accompanied the weeping, a door slammed shut, but not even that could block out the weeping.

Grace felt a tightness in her throat, a sudden urge to go out and give the imaginary Susan, if not a hug, at least a squeeze of the hand. Whatever had made her so sour, underneath that prickly exterior a young woman still had her feelings hurt.

Maybe Susan needed the two friends who seemed willing to put up with her.

Another door opened, then shut. Close by, but she could not tell whether the sound came from the right or the left. Shuffling steps drew near, followed by the sounds of a metal bucket landing hard on the floor right outside her room. The splashing of water as if the bucket had overflowed, then something wooden banged against the door and then landed with a clatter.

A knock came at the door. Grace jumped as she heard the mop bang against the door again, and the splatter of more water on the floor.

It was too late to hide. The bedroom door opened inward, and a young woman in a faded grey gown that might once have been purple, wearing an apron that had seen some use, lugged that noisy and obviously heavy bucket. A square wooden shape that must be a scrub brush bobbed on top of the water. A cloth dangled from her apron strings on one side, and a well-worn feather duster shoved in handle-first seemed in danger of falling out of the strings on the other.

This had to be the maid. Shouldn't she be wearing black, though? Or was that from a later time?

A glimpse outside the door pulled Grace from the maid's clothes. This wasn't her house, nor were there any medical workers in a hospital. In fact, the space beyond the open door didn't lead her back to the real world at all. Instead, dark wood floors matched the one in this room. On the bottom half of the wall, rich panelling in more of that wood. Did someone cut down a forest to build this place? Cream colored plaster filled the top.

Perhaps they had run out of trees by then.

"Oh!" The maid's surprised gasp drew Grace's attention back from the hall. She wondered which of their eyes were the widest, and who was the most surprised.

"'Scuse me, my lady. I din't mean to interrupt. I din't know someone 'us in this room . . ." The girl's voice trailed off.

The poor thing looked so tired, and too young for work this heavy. "It's okay. Do whatever it was you were going to do. Don't let me interrupt."

The girl remained where she stood, still holding that awful heavy bucket.

Grace couldn't stand watching her try to hold that bucket. "You can put that down, please. I feel tired just watching you. If you came in here to work, please go ahead."

"If you're sure?" The young maid hesitated, and gave Grace a strange look, but said nothing else.

Grace nodded. Jumpy young thing, wasn't she? But it would be rude to say that, even in a dream. "Pretend I'm not here." *I want to see more of this,* Grace thought, and wondered what part of her brain concocted the bucket and brush.

The maid gave her one more look, set the bucket on the floor, splashing a puddle over the edge. Even though it wasn't that warm in this place, sweat left a sheen on the maid's face, and dark circles ringed her eyes. She was young, probably only fifteen or sixteen, with clear skin, and slender arms. The white cap she wore had crept up, showing black hair pulled into tight braids wrapped in a circle around her head.

She scurried around the room with the duster, brushing over the walls, the dressing table, the posts of the bed, even the corners. With a glance at Grace, she cranked a window open, stuck the duster out, and gave it a vigorous shake. Most of the dust stayed outside; she quickly closed the window, and tucked the duster back into her apron string. That done, the maid moved to the fireplace, straightened the screen around the commode, and smoothed the bed covers.

Then she pulled out the brush, got on her knees, and started by the windows, scrubbing the brush across the floor. Grace ached to get down and help. It was agony to watch anyone work so hard and not be allowed to step in.

As Grace watched, she was struck by the girl's face, pert and young, a slender nose, fine cheekbones, and a dainty chin. Her cheeks hinted at dimples. A face that pretty should have been smiling, but was not. Under the grey sack she wore, Grace would bet the young maid had a body to match that youthful visage, and probably a heart that yearned for gowns to flatter it instead of this plain grey thing.

At last the torment was over.

The teenager got to her feet like an old woman, dropped the brush into the bucket with a sense of finality, and yawned, smothering it with her hand. A blush turned her cheeks red. "'Scuse me, my lady."

Grace ached for her. Cramps started in her own arms and legs. Sympathy pains? The odd sense that this was real returned. Would she have the snug binding around her chest, the tugging on her scalp, even the ephemeral cramping, while unconscious?

Maybe she *had* been hurt in the tornado, and the pain had crept through as a vague awareness.

"I'm sorry. That's such a big job for you. If I wasn't in this get-up, I would have offered to help," Grace said. The apology felt necessary.

"Oh, no!" The girl looked more shocked than she had upon seeing Grace. "You cain't do that! I never heard such a thing!"

"I'm from America. Everyone works in America." She paused a moment, thinking of the super wealthy, rumored not to work at all, but before she could qualify her statement, the maid interrupted.

"Well, you ain't in 'Merica now, and things are different here." The maid looked around the room, apparently checking to see if she had overlooked a chore, and asked, "Will ye be needin' anything?"

Answers. Explanations. Electricity. Oh, and my cell phone to call 9-1-1. "No. Thank you."

The girl picked up her heavy bucket, bobbed a curtsey, and slipped out of the room. The door to the hall gave a definite thud as it closed, sending vibrations up through Grace's feet, and cutting off the view of that hallway.

Grace looked at that door, and propped her hands on her hips, screwing up her courage. The maid had already seen her, and the sky hadn't fallen, the wind hadn't whisked her back, and the mirror was still exactly where she had placed it. Refusing to turn and stare at the dressing table to check, Grace kept her gaze on the large wooden barrier between herself and the world outside.

If that door represented the barrier between consciousness and unconsciousness, it was time to find out. Moreover, if she really had been spirited away into another era, by George, she wanted to see it.

Grace grasped the round, beautifully etched knob, and twisted it slowly, easing the door open to peek through.

3

No modern world waited, no shattered walls or jumbled mess. No pain from the feared injuries. Instead, the same scene she glimpsed when the maid came in was still there, a long hallway to her right, the plastered upper wall's creamy smoothness broken with large, dark-wood doors, almost like a hotel. About halfway down the hall, she saw a broad opening, and what looked like the top of a staircase. A beautiful heavily-carved wood staircase.

From where she stood, or rather, from where she peeked, Grace could not see it very well but it looked like twining leaves and vines decorated that banister. At a guess, the railing was nearly as thick as her arms. Did the carving follow all the way down?

She counted six doors before the landing, with hers the last one before the end of the hall. Some instinct, one she did not question, told her to stay away from that banister, and the wide opening beneath.

To her left, marking the near end of the hallway, the lone door beyond hers was narrow, nondescript, and painted black, unlike the rich wood ones that lined the corridor. If she had a guess, she'd call it the servants' entrance. Or exit, a quick flight from the well-dressed guests that would wander in and out of the elegant rooms.

One door per room, that made six rooms on this half of the floor, and if her count was right, six more doors on the opposite side of the landing. Twelve rooms on this floor alone. Twelve *large* rooms, if her own was any indication.

How big *was* this place? She couldn't think of any movies, any documentaries, that would give her mind this detail.

In those soft slipper-like shoes, ears tuned for the sound of anyone coming behind her, Grace eased down the short distance toward that black exit, took a deep breath and pushed it open, slipping through before she changed her mind.

A narrow staircase, plain, unadorned, a black iron railing—the only banister—curved downward just enough that she could not see the bottom. The stone steps showed wear in the center from decades, centuries probably, of feet. Light struggled through a series of grimy, many-paned, narrow outside windows as tall as herself, following the stairs downward into hazy greyness. As she passed the first window, she heard laughter and gave a start, nearly losing her balance on the stairs.

She flung a hand out to catch herself and the brick scraped her palm in sudden pain. The view out the window pulled her attention off the small injury, drawing her like metal filings to a magnet. The panes were small, the glass was dirty, bubbled and wavy, but tables and people filled a wide swath of green grass. Off to one side, a group of five or six men and women played an enthusiastic game of croquet.

The women wore long, high-waisted gowns as elegant as the one Grace had on, but with some kind of lacy under-blouse to hide the cleavage. The men wore strange suits with long coats with high lapels, and fancy ties—what were they called again? Oh, yes, cravats—around stand-up collars. Servants handed around plates of food to some of the group sitting on wooden chairs a few feet from the game.

And everybody wore a hat.

Odd, that the dream gave everyone but herself a hat. Even the little maid had a cap. As Grace continued down the dim, sloping stairs, though, that little incongruity became comforting. Dreams did that, throwing in things that made no sense when one woke.

But her palm ached where she scraped it. The sympathy cramps in her legs and arms were gone, unlikely if she was injured. Wasn't it?

At the bottom, the staircase ended in a small enclosure with two doors at right angles to each other. Sounds came from behind one door, along with delicious smells. The scents had unnerving realness. Did the kitchen hide behind that door? Her mouth watered and she turned that direction.

"Don't 'e go 'elpin' yerself to whatever ye think ye can sneak," a sharp female voice snapped, and Grace jumped back even though the voice carried the hollowness of distance, as if it drifted up a staircase.

"I ain't gonna eat nothin' I ain't entitled to," a young male voice retorted with the same hint of echo. Grace crept over to that door to hear better.

"Ye know we cain't eat until the quality is done." The woman again.

"They won't miss wot I et," the young man said, the voice taking on a whine.

"Ah, well, ye can take two, but no more, ye 'ear?"

"Iffen 'e can 'ave some, wot about me?" This sounded like a teenage girl.

"An' me?" That came from a child, ten years old, maybe eleven, not childish, not yet adolescent.

"Very well, then, one each. Any more'n 'at, an' I promise we'll all be in trouble."

Feet scurried in a faint scraping, no doubt racing for the promised treat.

She was not going through that door, for sure. It led to a passel of servants. One she could deal with, several at a time, no. Not until she knew where she was.

The other door, then. Grace eased the second one open a crack and found herself in a long, narrow dining room. The dark wood table—the same wood as the rest of the house—in the center and the majestic chairs that lined both sides defined the room's purpose. She had never seen a table like that. Ever. The legs' diameter was as wide as her body and carved down to the enormous claw feet at the bottom.

She crept further in and knelt down to peek at the legs of the chairs. They were not nearly as thick as the table's, but the carvings matched, as did the claw feet.

Who could afford such furniture?

She looked at the furnishings surrounding her, trying to find out where she might have seen anything like these to pull them out of her memory when she needed them. Nowhere in any of her auctions or flea markets, even the estate sales she prowled for pieces that would fit the designers' requests, had she seen decor like this.

The rest of the room matched the table in style and import. A fireplace on one wall, with a mantle of the same wood. Curtains of a grey velvet, the outer curtain pulled aside to show a sheer lace inner curtain. Someone intended this room to impress. The walls were painted a rich burgundy, lending another air of majesty. Between windows that she estimated were between seven and eight feet tall, and half that wide, hung paintings of stern-faced people from a time long gone.

A white chair rail ran around the room, and a sideboard that covered most of the inside wall matched the table. She wanted to go over and look at the sideboard, open the small doors and see what it held inside, but the sounds of the servants in the kitchen were still all too close. Someone could walk in at any minute.

Straight ahead, on the far wall, another door. She couldn't stay here and risk being caught, so Grace hurried over and pressed her ear to it.

A deep voice, this one so close she stumbled back, barked out, "Move that bucket out of the way! We have guests! You, mopping where you can be seen, leaving spots where people can slip and fall? Now take that away!"

Grace flattened herself against the wall by the door's hinges, hoping that if the sharp-voiced man walked in, she could hide behind it, and slip out before he realized she was there.

But the door didn't open, the man didn't walk in. Instead, heavy footsteps, his or the person he was talking to, faded away.

When would this dream end? Why was no one trying to wake her? Unless they were, and these voices were her mind putting the conversation of rescue workers and doctors into a setting she liked?

She'd gone through a couple of doors now. Would this next one be the one that led her back to reality? Grace pressed her ear to the door again, but no sounds came from the other side. Nothing to do but open it and find out.

Grace eased the door open and held her breath with every inch. Sounds whispered, but all at a distance. They probably belonged to the people outside.

She faced a large foyer, and the bottom part of the bannister she had seen from above. The staircase was, as she suspected, fully carved, and swept down from the floor above like a woman's gown, curving wide at the bottom. All the way down, the whole thing gave the appearance of a single piece of wood. Leaves and flowers flowed in an endless pattern, and if she wasn't mistaken, little birds hid in the design.

Once she tore her gaze away from that stunning staircase, Grace soaked in the echoing expanse. The floor was some kind of polished stone, and she noticed a lingering hint of darkness where the poor beleaguered servant had mopped and left the floor to dry on its own. To her right, tall dark double doors hinted at the outside.

Directly opposite, across the foyer, another set of double doors clearly led into a room, one door tightly shut, the other ajar. Sunlight seeped through the opening, luring, welcoming. It was also a warning that someone had just come out—or gone in. And a second warning that it looked out over the outside, and anyone out there could look in just as easily. And see her.

On her left, the foyer branched off into an angled hallway, where another door was barely visible. It looked shut. She couldn't stand here forever, dithering. Even though it was a longer dash, after a glance toward the huge doors leading outside, Grace picked up her skirts and ran across the floor as fast as her soft shoes would take her.

The first thing she discovered was that someone had the job of keeping the entry polished and took their job seriously. The second thing was that her shoes had no traction.

The third, much happier discovery once inside that door, was that no one else hid there. Even better, it was a library! Shelves and shelves of dark wood filled with hardbound books lined all four walls, the only breaks in the repetition being two tall windows with heavy outer curtains pulled aside, showing sheer forest green curtains beneath, enough to let light in yet still protect the furnishings.

She smelled leather, and wondered just how much money was tied up in this one room, with leather-bound tomes from floor to ceiling. Several wingback chairs and a chaise, all upholstered in a green velvet the same color as the curtains, sat around the room for comfortable reading.

Grace closed the door with care, and leaned against it, soaking in the silence and the sweet scent of books. They all looked like first editions, the kind she'd sometimes seen inside the locked cases at antique stores, not a paperback in sight.

Those books drew her. One could tell a lot about another by what they read. It didn't take long to discover that there were no Stephen Kings, no Agatha Christies, Tom Clancys or Rex Stouts, not even any James Pattersons or John Grishoms on those shelves. No Charles Dickens or Louisa May Alcotts, either, for that matter. Those works, she decided with another look around, would be right at home here. Especially in a first edition.

"Oh!" The word popped out. On one shelf, within easy reach, she saw a familiar name. A few volumes of the trusty Encyclopedia Britannica sat by themselves, as if out of place. Grace hurried over to the shelf and looked more closely at them. The volumes were not misfiled, part of a larger set separated from the rest. The whole set, she realized from the alphabetic breakdown on the spine, was only three volumes. As she pulled one volume down and flipped it open, Grace knew with a strange foreboding what she would find. Sure enough, the print was that nearly illegible old script where the "s" looked like "f," and played havoc with her comprehension.

Her Roman Numeral knowledge was rusty, but if she deciphered it properly, the copyright date was 1771, and the book was labeled—the one thing she could easily read—"Volume the First."

It looked original.

Tremors started in her hands, and the letters on the page blurred as the volume wobbled. She shoved it back onto the shelf and hung onto the wood for support while she absorbed everything.

A 1771 first edition of the Encyclopedia Britannica. Corsets, and soft-soled shoes. Servants both inside and out. Carriages and a gravel drive, and men whistling for horses, men wearing breeches and clogs.

She looked down at the gown she wore, blinking to bring it back into focus. Her teeth chattered, the sound audible in the silent room, but she was not cold. Not outside, at least. No, the chill came from deep inside, a building panic of disbelief. Grace wanted to cling to the thought of a tornado, injuries, and being unconscious, the hope she might open her eyes and see a paramedic, a doctor, the white walls of a hospital.

Instead, she still saw the peach-colored gown of rich silk, a tapestry rug beneath her feet, and those silly embroidered shoes that would hardly last a day of normal use.

The same mirror she had purchased in Minneapolis now fresh as the day it had been made, the skinned palm, the maid with the odd costume and the tired eyes, and the brush to scrub the floor bobbing in the battered bucket. The worn stone stairs and the bubbled glass windows.

She released her hold on the shelf and turned around, examining the room itself instead of the books. Tucked neatly between the shelves, a desk out of the same dark wood that filled the house fitted into the layout, a long, narrow desk with a leather inset on the top. A three-tier stairstep of shallow, rather narrow drawers sat on either side of that shiny surface like bookends, convenient for a quick reach. Two drawers underneath ran the desk's entire length.

Every drawer, those on the top and those beneath, had scrolled metal knobs. A chair of matching wood, complete with a leather-padded seat, sat pulled out as if someone had just stepped away.

Might the person be right back?

Grace stared at the door going back to the foyer, still tightly shut, spared a second to listen for sounds—hearing nothing too worrisome—and hurried over to that desk. She didn't believe in snooping through someone else's personal property, but this was an emergency.

She pulled open the small drawers on the desk's top, one by one. Each held oddly shaped letters, folded over and over. None were in envelopes. Even the paper was different from what she was used to. Instead of the typical 20 lb printer paper, or even the fancy water-marked kind she'd always admired but could never afford, these were thicker, cloth-like. Each of them either still had the wax seals she'd only read about or showed where the seals had been by the circles that left the paper thinner and torn.

One name appeared most often on the envelopes, Fairfax. The name from the girls in the hallway.

She put the letters back unread and moved to the next drawer. Handkerchiefs, neatly folded, with embroidered initials she guessed were GA, but couldn't be certain.

In the last of those upper drawers she checked, Grace found a neat row of feathers. Next to them, an elegant silver-colored bowl with a matching lid, closed now, hiding what it held. With one finger, Grace lifted the fancy carved lid, and found liquid ink.

Ink. She looked at those feathers again and picked one up. It had a neat tip, carved, not like the feathers she'd ever seen before. Everything made a bizarre kind of sense, the feathers, that little bowl of ink. These were real, old-fashioned quill pens.

Okay, that took care of the tiered top of the desk. Grace tugged at the upper of the two long ones underneath. Locked. "If only I knew how to pick a lock," she said to the air. But tempting as the idea was, that would have been one step too far.

She moved to the bottom one. Only long sheets of thick ivory paper like the ones in the letters, a few more neatly folded handkerchiefs, a strange knife, and several quills, normal ones not turned into pens yet.

Cooking food scents drifted into the room, faint on the air, a counterpoint to the fragrance of flowers from outside the window. Nothing in her education, nothing in her imagination, could make things this realistic. Until now this had been more of an adventure, not truly anything to alarm her. Just little nibbles of concern, but more fun.

Like a dream she might wake up from, one that needed to be savored while she had it.

A newspaper, bigger than a poster, peeked from under the paper pile, and Grace carefully slipped it out. It had the uneven thickness of having been read and refolded but not on the same creases. She carried it over to the better light from the windows and stared at the date on it. 1810.

"Oh. Dear. God." She sank down onto the nearest green velvet wingback chair with a puff of her skirts, looked around like a thief to make certain no one was peeking through the windows. As she glanced back at the newspaper, she saw a faint red smudge.

Blood. And rather fresh, at that. "Oh, no!" She turned over her hand to discover that the palm she had scraped was still raw and leaving small bits of blood, just enough to make a smear across paper. Or on the Encyclopedia Britannica? She might have left smudges on the shelves, too. The paper slipped out of her fingers and fluttered down to the floor with a whisper.

Grace hurried back to the desk, jerked open that long drawer and plucked out one handkerchief, then wrapped it as best she could around the bleeding scrapes, tucking in the ends, and hoped they stayed.

She was bleeding. Really and honestly bleeding from scraping her hand on a brick wall. She smelled food. Her hair wasn't matted and covered with dust from a tornado, but styled with ribbons and braids. A corset wrapped her middle.

"This can't be." She flopped down into the chaise. The distinctive sound of horsehair rustled beneath her.

Leather-bound books, a horsehair-stuffed chaise, and quill pens? Darkness formed around the edges of her eyes, and a whole hive of bees set up a ringing in her ears.

This was real. Really real. That whirling wind had not been a tornado, no one was rummaging through the remnants of her little house trying to find her broken body. She was not in Minneapolis anymore.

Grace bent double and pressed her head onto her knees. Gradually her blurred vision cleared, and the whine in her ears faded away, leaving only the quiet of the library. Distant laughter drifted through the air, coming from the far side of the house.

Something must have happened to the fabric of time that caused her to slip through and land here.

Wherever *here* was.

Grace lifted her head, and made herself sit upright. The room stayed still, her vision was clearing. She rose on shaky legs, walked over to a small gap in the sheer curtains, and looked out the window. It was beautiful out there, a path leading out into depths of greenery and splashes of color announcing where flowers grew. From somewhere nearby the scent of roses teased her nose.

She thought back to when this all started, at the flea market where she bought the mirror in which she had seen herself exactly as she appeared now, and the chairs—*oh my gosh!* Chills ran down her arms, the hairs rose on the back of her neck. The chairs! Those flea market chairs, and the designer who needed them done within a couple weeks.

She had to get back! Grace pressed her unbandaged hand to her chest, where her heart pounded as if trying to get out.

First she had to find out how she got here. And why.

Shouldn't there be a reason? Her gaze skittered around the room again, searching for a clue. Not that she would necessarily know one when she saw it, but nothing she had seen since landing here held any connection to her, other than knowing a bit about history.

The newspaper lay on the floor where she had dropped it, drawing her attention like a magnet. Maybe she could find a clue there.

Grace took the paper over to that wingback chair, away from the window chaise where someone walking past outside might see her, sat down with much shuffling of all that fabric, and started to read.

She was deep in the second page when the door opened. She froze, and huddled into the chair, drawing her feet up onto the seat so they didn't show from beneath, and held her breath, hoping whoever it was would get a book from the shelves and leave.

4

Garrett pushed open the library doors and slipped inside, embarrassed to have to seek refuge in his own house, all the more so since this party was his mother's idea with the whole-hearted backing of his sister.

"It's past time you wed," had been his mother's refrain for several years. Much as he loved her, that broad hint was easy to ignore.

He did just fine as an unmarried man. He was just thirty years old, far too young to consider marriage, and he said so on more than one occasion.

His father, once on his side, no longer agreed. "By the time I was your age, I had already fathered you," the earl growled on their last meeting. "The inheritance was ensured. You are my only son, you know how much depends on you."

"Certainly I am the only son, but that doesn't mean I have to rush into something as permanent as marriage yet," Garrett had argued back. "For heaven's sake, what if I grow to hate the poor empty-headed girl I wind up with? No, far better to take my time."

Which comment earned him a glare from both parents. "Garrett, I find your comment very insulting," his mother said.

"I am not talking about you," he had answered. "But even you, Mother, must agree that the current crop on the Marriage Mart leaves a great deal to be desired."

Arguing with an earl, even when the earl was one's own father, did not get one very far.

He no sooner arrived back in London when Madeline, pushy younger sister that she was, popped in for a visit, obviously aware of his parents' concern. "A country party is just the thing. You have that glorious estate. You should host an event, invite the most respectable women where you can see them outside the social whirl. Who knows? You might like one of them. You want to get out of London anyway."

"I just got back," he had reminded her.

"Well, I need out of town. Remember my delicate condition." He could still see her as she leaned back in her chair, smug with success. And no doubt hiding a letter from his mother in her reticule.

But she *was* with child, a visit out of town was a kindness for his youngest sister, and too many women of his acquaintance, wives of friends, were throwing out similar broad hints about him settling down. At least out of the City, there would be fewer to fight off.

The older they were the more desperate they were, and not above trying dirty tricks to get him alone. Appearance of compromise was as good as the real thing. He shuddered. A man did not actually have to get a woman into bed. Just being in the same room unchaperoned, and there you had it. Off to the vicar and a life in chains.

Hence his current predicament, hiding in his library in the middle of his own erstwhile simple house-party, momentarily safe from the small coterie of women he agreed to allow the visit.

He flopped down on the sofa (*chaise longue*, his mother would have corrected him) that his father insisted be a fixture in every library. A man might fall asleep reading in an ordinary chair, wake with a crick in the neck and be uncomfortable for a day or two until it resolved itself.

He agreed with his father on this score. A library always needed a sofa, especially one long enough to let someone of his height stretch out and relax.

At least until one of his sister's none-too-subtle bride choices came searching. He leaned back against the arm of the sofa and let out a low, heartfelt groan. If one couldn't groan in the privacy of one's own library, where could one groan?

At a muffled sneeze nearby, Garrett bolted upright. "Who is there?" He stood, hands on hips, thoroughly annoyed, even more so since the woman—and that was a thoroughly feminine sneeze—had been here first. Manners said he should leave, but manners could go hang. If she planned to waylay him in his house and in his own library while in such a thoroughly foul mood, he might be tempted to pitch her out the window. They were on ground level, it would not hurt her.

But that was out of the question. Not even the worst of tempers would justify throwing a woman out into the garden.

Sure enough, a woman's head peeked out from behind one of the tall wingback chairs, eyes wide with alarm as she stood up slowly. This guest was very pretty, with blonde hair that even in its careful arrangement showed a natural curl, and brown eyes, unusual with that color hair. She was taller than most of the women he knew, not overly tall, but just enough, and with the right amount of roundness to her.

Easy to kiss without bending double. He blinked, wondering where that thought came from.

"Hi," she said, her voice warm and mellow.

High? That was a strange word, since neither of them was off the floor at all. He glanced at the nearest sliding ladder and wondered if she wanted something on the upper shelves. "I beg your pardon?"

A rush of vivid pink swept up her cheeks. "I mean, hello. Excuse me. I was just trying to get some personal space. Everything is so . . . surprising, and I'm a tad out of place here."

He didn't recognize her accent, the vowels so short, her speech so brisk, and some of her phrases were strange, but he got the gist of the meaning. He hadn't seen her before. Until this moment, he believed he had met all his guests, especially the female variety. But this one looked startled, maybe even afraid, and he refused to allow any of his guests to be frightened by some unmannerly male. "Tad? Who is Tad? If he is making a nuisance of himself, just tell me and I will have him ushered off the property."

Her eyes got bigger, if that was possible. "Tad? I wasn't talking about any Tad—oh!" She stopped abruptly and rubbed a hand over her face. "I probably sound like a nut, but it will take me a while to get up to speed. Let's see, how should I have put it?" Her delicate brows furrowed, then her forehead cleared. "I'm so rattled my thoughts are jumbled. Let's start over." She walked around the chair and came toward him, her hand outstretched for a shake. "My name is Grace, and it's a pleasure to meet you."

No woman of his acquaintance would introduce herself by a first name only. That was for a woman of another sort entirely, but she hardly looked like one of those. Nor did women extend their hand to him, they curtseyed. He stared at her hand, then at her, but apparently someone had already made her uncomfortable.

Rather than make her feel worse, Garrett took her hand gently. "How do you do, Miss Grace . . .?" He paused, waiting for her to supply her surname.

"I'm fine." Under her breath, it sounded like she added, "I hope."

That was not the answer he expected. He tried again. "We have not been introduced. I apologize. As host, I thought I had met everyone here." He *should* have met everyone here. In fact, he was quite certain he had, Madeline would have seen to it. Where had this woman been that he missed the introduction?

"You have a lovely house." A hesitant smile accompanied her compliment.

However he overlooked her before, he would make up for it now.

"My name is Lord Fairfax. As I mentioned, I am your host." He raised her hand to his lips, but kept the kiss to the merest brush of his mouth, watching her as he did so.

Her eyes widened, her head jerked as if something poked her. "*Lord* Fairfax?" His name came out on a whisper. "You're a real lord?"

"Yes."

Red rushed up those smooth cheeks, and she stared at him as if he had two heads. He raised an eyebrow. Most women welcomed an introduction to him. He had never seen one startled by it. *Where was she from?* Everything about her shouted that she was as surprised to be here as he was to find her.

She dropped into a quick, unpracticed curtsey. "How very nice to meet you."

Despite the brief contact, he caught the faintest of fragrance, something light and clean. Wholesome. "Apparently I misunderstood about Tad. If no one by that name has been harassing you, I feel compelled to ask why you need to take refuge in my library. I assure you, it is my duty to make certain all my guests have a pleasant time, so tell me what I can do to ease your time here."

She bit her lip. He stared at her teeth on that soft rose plumpness. Remarkably clean white teeth. She muttered something that sounded like "tell me how I got here," but since her mouth had distracted him, he could not be certain. He dragged his attention back to her striking brown eyes, remarkable with that blonde hair. "I beg your pardon?"

"Nothing." She waved a hand to brush his question aside. "Really, it was nothing." Then she returned to lip-biting. Movement drew his eyes down to her hands, where her fingers twisted around each other.

Those nervous actions reminded him of their predicament. What was he thinking, being alone with a woman? Hadn't he just begrudged the presence of every woman in his house? "I will leave you to yourself then, unless there is something I can do for you. If you are lost in the house, I will send a servant to show you to your room."

Her eyes went bigger than ever, and this time there was no

mistaking the alarm there. "Oh, no, that's not at all necessary. I'm sure I can find it myself." After a brief pause, she asked, "Aren't your guests allowed to browse? If not, I will stop, but the house is fascinating. So—authentic."

She had a strange way with words. "Authentic?" He glanced around the room, although he already knew it well. If she meant it was an authentic example of an English gentleman's library, "Yes, I suppose it is."

Where was she from, and how did he miss seeing her these past few days?

The lovely woman blushed as if she feared she had said the wrong thing. "Well, now that I have your permission, I will get back to my browsing. Thank you for letting me look around your house."

"It is my pleasure." He bowed his head and gave in to the urge to tease. "That is why I am having this summer party, to let my friends from the city enjoy my *authentic* house." No matter how much he resented some of his guests, even the need for this party at all, this particular woman was not unwelcome. So far, at least. Perhaps she was a local woman here for the day, visiting a friend from London. "To whom do I owe the honor of your visit?"

"Fate, I think," she said, once more evading his question. Her hands clenched and unclenched in her gown.

Fate? Hardly a *whom*. "Come out into the garden with me," he offered, because one or the other of them had to get out of this room before someone discovered them alone and unchaperoned. "Perhaps the house will be more familiar from outside."

He walked to the windows that looked into the garden of which he spoke—windows large enough, nearly reaching the floor, that he used them as doors whenever he needed a quick escape—and pushed them open. The sun was warm, and the flowers' fragrances perfumed the air. "We can enjoy the flora as we stroll."

He held an arm out, inviting her to proceed him.

A rueful smile tugged at her mouth, and she lost the battle to hide it. "Oh, why not? No man where I come from has such gorgeous manners. I really can't let them go to waste."

He frowned, troubled again by the possibility that someone had not treated her well. Despite her denials, he wouldn't put it past several of his guests to take advantage of a woman who looked like her.

Miss Grace reached out and curled her fingers over his arm for support as she stepped around him and over the low sill. He looked down at that hand, surprised by the hint of tan there. None of the women he knew would dare go out without gloves or at least a parasol to protect their skin. Her tanned skin belonged on a maid, not a woman of quality, yet her clothes and hair were as fine and elegant as any of his other guests. Wherever she came from, she certainly was not of the lower classes.

Who was she? Garrett gently lifted her hand into the proper position around his elbow, smiled to take the sting out of his correction, and started down the path. The scent of flowers was particularly pungent today, the colors brighter, even the green grass had a new glow.

It had to be the sunshine. Clouds threatened for the previous days, but happily today the sun won.

Miss Grace smiled up at him and took a deep breath. "I'm sorry, I can hardly breathe in this getup. All these scents and I can hardly get enough air to enjoy them."

He blinked at her forthrightness. No woman ever referred so openly to the corset, despite how much everyone knew its drawbacks. He remembered hearing his sisters whine for weeks while they were getting used to them. She was like a lady who never had a governess to train her.

Society was filled with beautiful women who left him cold. Much as he hated to admit it, he was drawn to her, and not just because of her beauty. It was a combination of the shyness that came and went, her strange way of speaking, her lack of comfort with—or awareness of—the simple customs, her odd habit of talking under her breath.

Even the vocabulary he wasn't quite familiar with charmed him. He could make out her meaning, but the phraseology was new. She had held out her hand and introduced herself in the library, yet wasn't comfortable walking with him even in the garden's openness, a place beyond reproach, and did not know how to properly hold a man's arm. She talked far too openly about the corset's effects without using a single untoward word.

It was a welcome change to have a woman who didn't throw herself at him. He was long tired of jaded women who had seen it all and fell into the category of courtesans despite their entrée into the upper levels of the *ton*.

As he told his parents, he didn't care for the latest crop of girls on the Marriage Mart, girls barely out of the schoolroom. The older crop of unwed women had not one prospective wife. Where had this one been hiding?

"Do I know your family?"

Grace stopped walking, dragging him to a halt. She had expected some questions, but not this one. Her family? She took a breath against the stab of alarm and the tightness of her corset. "Oh, I'm sure you don't know them."

How could he? They weren't even born yet! For the first time since her mother died, she was relieved, because Mom would be frantic if she was out of touch too long. Her father—well, he wouldn't even notice, being so wrapped up with his new family.

The pain of her mother's loss seemed oddly distant, bringing a flash of anger at whatever sent her here. She was not supposed to forget her mother!

The man—what was his name again?—raised an eyebrow. "It might surprise you how many people I know."

"Not mine. I'm from far away." Far, *far* away. "It hardly matters, does it? I won't be here much longer." She didn't think so, at any rate.

Grace glanced up at him. Thick dark hair showing glints of red in the sun, piercing light gray eyes, and those shoulders! She'd always had a weakness for a man with broad shoulders. He had the arms to match, their firm muscles sliding under his coat sleeve, her fingers feeling every movement.

How did one address a lord? Mr. Fairfax? Lord Fairfax? Or did she shorten it to a simple *my lord*?

Grace stole another quick glance. She had read, when doing odd research on fabrics while restoring an antique chair, that men in this time padded their clothes to make their physique appear bigger. Fairfax didn't seem the type, and from what she felt under her hand where it rested in the crook of his elbow, that was no padding. He was definitely big enough to toss her off his property if her answers weren't satisfactory.

"Very well." His chest expanded in a sigh, the raspy texture of his coat brushing her hand, and she wondered if he was losing patience with her. "Where does your family come from?"

Ahhh. Finally, a question she could answer. Her grandmother had found a delighted audience in Grace. She grew up hearing stories about the huge family estate that some daughter way in the past had fled to marry an 'unsuitable' man, who was not unsuitable at all but merely had the misfortune to be born into a lower class.

A daughter who ran away with only a few jewels, none of which remained from what she knew, and an old box that her grandmother used for her own small collection of jewelry, with a name carved into the bottom. Cokewell. The two lovers went to America, where the man's skills with horses would be useful. Apparently it worked out as expected.

Other than that, she didn't know much about her English background. Maybe this man would recognize the family name. If he did, he might know where that original estate had been. Or rather, where it was now.

If it still stood, maybe she could go visit or at least look, even if from a distance. She decided to put Grammy's stories to the test. "My grandmother's family is from Norwich," she said, and watched his expression.

He merely nodded, the bland response an anticlimax. "Indeed? You're a long way from your grandparents, then."

"Where is this?" Grace waved her free hand to encompass his property.

"Not far from Northampton in Northamptonshire." His right eyebrow arched, and he gave her a suspicious look out of suddenly cool eyes. "You did not know where you were going? How did you get an invitation, then? And how did you even get here?" That eyebrow went down into an impressive frown.

Grace sighed. She was no good at lying, something her mother had appreciated, and Fairfax looked like he could spot a lie right away. "Honestly, I didn't know where I was going. I was just…taken here."

"Ah." He looked down at her, and his lips thinned. "I can guess what they planned. Still, logic says they would tell you the destination, even if the journey was already underway. Your presence leaves me with a quandary." He scratched his chin in thought. "You will not tell me who gave you the invitation?"

Grace shook her head. "I can't."

His brows came together, then smoothed out as he seemed to have made some decision. "I shall not press you. I respect loyalty. Your maid is sleeping in your room with you, so I shan't worry about—" He broke off.

Maid? She was supposed to have a maid? What would he do if he found out she did not have one? Still, she met his unwavering stare. Each held the other's gaze too long; his eyes warmed, and what began as an attempt to prove her honesty edged toward something more...intimate.

Grace floundered to change the subject. "This is a lovely garden." Even though she hadn't noticed more than the fragrance, and couldn't describe what they just walked through if asked.

Fairfax gave a single nod. "Yes, I like it. I have an excellent gardener working to ensure that it stays so." They walked on in silence as she tried to memorize the feel of the path under her feet, and the soft breeze on her face.

Under her hand, the muscles in his arm tightened. With a suddenness that surprised her, he stopped in the walk under a feathery tree, released her arm, and turned to face her. The mild expression was gone, and he looked every inch the lordly landowner, ready to hurl the upstart peasant off his property if he didn't like the answers he got. Grace made herself meet that gaze, trying to keep her expression as innocent as possible.

In a firm voice, he said, "I do not mind your protecting whoever invited you. However, you should understand right now that despite what you were likely told, I cannot, I *will* not, have unattached women wandering about trying to trick me into marriage, so do not think to capitalize on our time together in the library."

Grace gasped and jammed her fisted hands on her hips. "Marriage? Who said anything about marriage? I don't even know you! What makes you think I would want to *marry* you?" Until this moment, she had rather liked him.

His posture did not change. "If you insist, I excuse you of being part of the plot, but someone in your immediate circle appears to have set a trap for the both of us. I must put a stop to this prevarication. Just who is your family, and why did they think you would stand a chance with me?"

Just stick to the truth, she thought. "My last name is Harding. Grace Harding. My dad is Thomas Harding."

"Dad?"

"My father," she amended.

He had his hands on his hips now, too.

She sighed. "I'm American."

To her surprise, he relaxed, his face cleared. Maybe he wouldn't panic after all if he learned she came with no maid. "So that explains it," he murmured, his gaze roving over her. That relaxation didn't last long, however. "You truly are a long way from home. Why England? Our countries are not on the best of terms right now. There are whispers it might turn into a war, but you must know that."

"War? I'll have you know, our countries are too on the best of terms!"

"I know not who is telling you such things, but I assure you, matters are quite tense. You are fortunate you made it across the ocean safely."

Suddenly her history classes of years before became immediate and real. The War of 1812 hadn't happened yet! She supposed, with correspondence going by boat, letters and diplomats took months instead of hours or minutes to get back and forth. She knew the Battle of New Orleans, the final battle of that war, happened after they declared peace, so two years to get a war going made sense. "I think I see what you're talking about. My knowledge of histo—" she caught herself. "Of the feud between our countries is sketchy at best."

"You were about to say 'history,' were you not?" His gaze drifted to something far off. "One might think the *'feud'* "—he put a mocking tone to the word— "to which you refer would be a thing of the past, but it seems to have been a short-lived and uneasy peace."

A thing of the past? Short-lived? Did he mean 1776, the Revolutionary War? She didn't know what to say and wished her memory of history would wake up and guide her. "One would think so." Surely that was benign enough.

His gaze returned, and he frowned at her for a long, silent time. Or at least it seemed long. Grace tried not to fidget under that piercing stare. Only guilty people fidgeted, didn't they?

"If you can give me the name of your party, I will return you safely to them."

She stepped back and shook her head, panic fluttering in the pit of her stomach. "Oh, no, I wanted time alone. Please don't send me out in the middle of that crowd."

His brows went up in obvious surprise. "If you wish to be alone, I shall leave you to your own devices."

Before his warning about expecting any romantic encounters—if only he knew!—he had been pleasant company, and she felt a pang at being abandoned and unguided again. Grace saw what must be the front doors, big and dark and marked by stone steps. "I see we are at the entrance." *Coming up all too quickly, and with it the risk of being seen by more people, none of whom would know her.* "Thank you for bringing me through your garden."

Her host bowed. "I must thank you for putting up with my intrusive presence when you so obviously wished for privacy."

"Oh, stop it," Grace managed a laugh. "I was the one intruding, not you. You have been very nice."

"Nice," he said, stretching the word out. "Yes, that is my goal, to be nice." With a nod of his head, he turned around and walked back the way he came.

Drat! Grace thought as she watched his direction. If she guessed right, he was going back to the library.

So much for slipping back the way she had come. Now she had to go through the front doors and into that massive foyer with halls, rooms, and windows all over. The foyer was clear once; she highly doubted she would be that lucky again.

She tried to see through the windows against the glare of the sun but the light just bounced back a reflection of outside. Being here was full of risks for her.

If she ever got her hands on the genie that sent her here, Grace thought, she might gladly strangle him. Her handsome host could have pushed her harder for answers. Next time she saw him, he most likely would try again.

It was time to check on the mirror and try to go home.

Laughter sounded, close. Grace dashed up the stone porch steps before anyone else saw her. The door was heavy, but she braced herself and shoved it open. That huge curving staircase was directly ahead, but she had to hide immediately, because a backward glance showed the crowd of guests she'd heard around the corner was now in plain view through the wide front window.

She would be visible all the way up.

The servant's staircase was her best bet, and she only knew one route to it. Grace pushed open the door to the dining room, her heart in her throat, but it was empty a second time.

Grace had just reached the door to the servants' stairway and pulled it open, concealment within her grasp, when a tall, cadaverously thin man in a tuxedo-style suit fairly fell through from the other side.

5

"Watch where you are—" he started in a deep scolding tone, but gave her a sharp look, and stopped. "Excuse me, my lady," he said in a calm, puzzled tone, "may I help you?"

Caught off-guard, unable to come up with a single explanation, Grace put a finger to her lips, and slipped past him and through the door. Just as it closed, she glanced back and saw him staring after her, a frown creasing his forehead.

Once out of his sight, Grace's legs gave out, and she slumped down onto the stone staircase, her peach-colored skirts floating down around her. That man with the puzzled face must be the butler.

He would no doubt ask Lord Fairfax who she was. If the two men got together and compared what they knew—or didn't know—about her, what would they do? Once he found out no invitation had ever been extended to any Grace Harding, would she soon find herself out on the road, rejected and penniless?

Suppose someone else touched the mirror and got whisked back in place of her! Grace bounded to her feet, picked up her skirt, and continued up the stairs, desperation pushing her onward.

Scents of the picnic drifted through the windows along the stairway, and Grace's stomach gave an early warning. When was the last time she ate? She tried to retrace her day. Her *other* day, the one back in her own time, in her own home, doing her own job.

Breakfast. At the top of the stairs, she stopped to catch her breath. A hysterical laugh started to bubble up. Breakfast was her last meal, two hundred something years ago. The distance traveled both in time and space made her breath, which had just begun to ease, catch again.

Focus on what you can manage. She ran her tongue over her lips, and wondered if anyone had brought water up, even for washing. Right now, she'd settle for any kind of fresh water until she could sneak down to the kitchen and raid the—

Oh. There was no refrigerator in this time. And with what she heard from the girls earlier, there was a big party tonight. A party meant food, in every era. No doubt the kitchen would be packed with staff rushing back and forth, keeping the dishes filled. Or the buffet stocked. Or however they did it.

If she wanted food, she would have to go downstairs, join the party, and get some.

Grace pulled the door at the stairway's end open, scurried the few steps to her room, and slipped inside.

Garrett was crossing the foyer when the door to the dining room opened and Jones walked out. Despite the man's stoic expression, it was most obvious something disturbed him.

"Sir. I need a moment of your time."

"Yes? Is everything going well for the dinner tonight? Or is something else wrong?"

"The dinner is well under control. It is something else. I do not recognize one of your guests. I believe we have an interloper, although she is dressed well enough to pass. A young woman in an orange color gown, with blond hair? I am familiar with all the guests and their rooms, and I cannot connect any name with her. What is more," Jones leaned forward, unusually dramatic for him, "she took the servants' stairs instead of the main staircase."

"Taking those stairs alone is not enough to condemn her." Garrett refused to let himself smile at the memories that rose, the only boy among a family of girls, and the stratagems he used to hide from his sisters. "I know the very woman you mean. I have just had a conversation with her." Jones had been with his father before being passed down, he was certainly entitled to know everything about the woman. "She claims to be from America."

The worry remained in his butler's face. In fact, it deepened at the news. "There is something else about her, sir."

"Yes, Jones?"

"Did you notice something, well, *familiar* about her?"

"Familiar?" Tempted to say *no*, because she was American, who could he possibly know from America, Garrett hesitated. "I don't think so."

"Her coloring, sir. Brown eyes and that light hair?"

Would the man not just come out with it? Suddenly, a face popped into Garrett's mind. A dear friend of his parents, an elderly man with more money than he could count, curly hair fading into white but still showing a hint of its previous color, and eyes that made a striking contrast. "Cokewell?"

Now *that* made sense. He had not wanted to think it of her, but if his mother had her fingers in his prospective wife-choosing, what better family to pick than that of her husband's oldest friend? Any of his children, or more likely grandchildren based on the woman's age, would be his equal in Society in all but title.

Cokewell was a man of great dignity and enormous intelligence who changed the way his farming was done, and in the process made his family's fortune. The man's work had attracted the Prince Regent's attention, and his support.

Undoubtedly his mother was behind Miss Grace's presence. Mother was serious about marrying him off, wasn't she?

But if Miss Grace was connected to Cokewell, why didn't she just say so?

Jones dipped his head once, for him a vigorous nod. "The very name. I don't know what the relationship is, but I will be most shocked if there is not some connection." He straightened even more than usual.

A contradiction stabbed at him, piercing his certainty. "She said she is from America. How can there be a connection to the man?"

"I will endeavor to find out whatever I can about her, and her origins."

"Question her maid."

A frown creased Jones' usually impassive face. "I know of no maid. That is, I know which woman all the maids here belong to. If she has one, she must be keeping the woman in her room."

"Are you sure?" Garrett felt his own brows come together. "Surely even in America, a woman would travel with her maid."

Jones' face hinted at a smile. "I cannot speak for Americans."

"Check with the servants. Perhaps the maid is merely keeping herself out of your way. We are dealing with a possible uninvited guest, after all"

At the moment, the foyer was empty. A couple servants crossed the expanse, footmen carrying candles over toward the ballroom. Most of the guests were still outside, or dressing early for the dance and supper.

The party was only a few days old, and he was already tired of it. Without Madeline's presence, he would tell them all to pack up. Bride-hunting had to be the most annoying task ever laid on a man.

As long as Madeline was here, though, he could use her help. He did not know anyone more capable of sniffing out a mystery. And if she was in cahoots with his mother and the two of them had plotted this out together, he would know soon enough.

He would spring Miss Grace on his sister tonight at the ball. If Madeline was in on some *marry-off-Garrett* plot, her face would give her away.

Grace's gaze went straight to the dressing table, and the air left her lungs in a relieved rush.

The mirror was exactly where she left it. She hurried over and hesitated. How absurd, after all the nerves, all the pitfalls that surrounded her, to be afraid to pick it up now!

Holding her breath, she lifted the hand mirror, and waited for the windstorm.

Nothing.

Not a breeze, not a sparkle, not even that strange flash of static electricity from the first time she touched it. She looked back at the dressing-table mirror, and there she was, still in the peach gown, hair still in that fancy hairdo.

She shook the mirror. Still nothing. "Don't panic," Grace told her reflection. And then she laughed. "Of course! How silly of me!" She had been cleaning it back in her time. That must be the key.

But this place had no tissues, no paper towels.

Handkerchiefs? She looked around, and at the bottom of the armoire, so slender she had not even noticed before, were three small drawers. When she pulled the first one open, sure enough, a neat pile of lacy handkerchiefs sat there, clean and ready for use. Strange fabric for blowing one's nose, she thought. Give her a tissue any day for normal use, but she only needed to polish glass. She snatched one and scurried back to the little vanity mirror.

This time no amount of rubbing made the tornado come back. Not even a breeze.

Alarm slid down her arms, standing the little hairs upright, and making her scalp prickle. It was one thing to enjoy oneself and be reluctant to return so soon. It was quite another not to go back at all.

She sank down on the bed and looked at it. "Why did you send me here? And why won't you let me go back?"

There was no reply, just her own reflection staring back at her, face leached of color, brown eyes wide with worry. Her hands clenched around the sterling silver handle, its carvings digging into her palm.

How did she get it to turn back on?

She'd only been here a few hours. Maybe she was supposed to stay until the party was over, although what that would accomplish, she had no idea. Her stomach clenched, and a heaviness settled around her midsection. That *had* to be dismay.

Unless it was hunger. She still hadn't eaten.

First things first. Hide the mirror somewhere an unsuspecting maid would not find it. Whatever whimsical or malevolent genie sent her here might enjoy sending the wrong person back.

She turned around, scanning the room for hiding places. The only spot that might work was somewhere in the armoire. Everything else was too spare or too obvious.

Why couldn't she have landed in a house where people liked *stuff*?

Her eyes travelled up to the top of the large piece. An elegant design edged it, like crown molding in reverse. There must be a hollow behind that filigree, a place no one would think to dust because it would never be seen.

She hoped. Grace set the mirror down on the bed and dragged the dressing table chair over. When she climbed onto it, she was still too short to see over the top, but there was a space behind the molding. And yes, it was dusty. No one had looked up there for a very long time.

It took only seconds to slide the mirror behind the wooden carvings. There! It was as safe as she could make it.

Maybe the next time she pulled it out, it would be dusty enough that a good rubbing would wake it up.

After she put the chair back in place, Grace walked back to the armoire and opened it. Gowns, gowns and more gowns, hanging on hooks that lined the sides and back.

On impulse, she picked out one, green with lace around the neck and a cap-style sleeve, and held it up. It looked very much like it would fit.

If the peach gown had been gorgeous, this one was even better. The fabric shimmered with every movement, and the bodice richly decorated with real hand embroidered white and darker green lace flowers. The same design ran around the skirt, all the way around, lots and lots of tiny stitches. More of that embroidery ran along the edges of the short sleeves, and when she looked closely, she picked up a fine pleating that looked at first like a stripe.

The lace around the neck was far more intricate than it had looked at first glance, and lacked the crisp feel of the polyester and rayon machine-made lace she was familiar with. Who knew they had such beautiful fabric in this time?

Something about the shimmer caught her attention, and she lifted the skirt up to get a closer look. Was that real silver thread?

Grace swiveled and stared at the armoire filled with gowns. That was a lot of clothes for a short visit. Maybe there was a woman in this house, a wife or sister. She held the gown up to herself, stifling the guilt at touching someone else's clothes.

Strange, though, that this was the room into which she had been dropped. A room with an armoire full of those that looked exactly her size.

She returned to the armoire, hung the gown back onto its hook, and pushed the skirts of all the other gowns out of the way, somehow knowing there would be shoes to match each one.

There were indeed shoes, more of the flat, slipper-like ones she wore. Not a dressy pump or high heel in sight. Green for the color of the gown she just put away, complete with the silver shimmer, yellow shoes for the yellow gowns hanging over them, pinks for the pink, and so on down the closet.

She slipped on one of the shoes that matched that green gown. It fit. To perfection. As if it had been made for her. Chills ran down her arms, and she pulled it off and put it back, feeling like a thief.

The door opened without warning. She whipped around and found herself staring into the startled eyes of the pretty young maid from earlier. Blue. The girl's eyes were a deep blue, almost navy, not brown at all.

"Oh!" The girl's mouth dropped open. "Pardon me, miss. I thought ye might be out. I just—I was going to—"

If that had been herself, Grace thought, she would have come in here for a few minutes of peace away from watching eyes, a chance to sit and rest. But this was another time, and from what she saw so far, servants never got a moment free.

"Hello again. Don't let me disturb you." As she looked at the teenager, she realized the answer to one problem stared her in the face. "I missed the picnic outside. Is there anything left to eat? Or can I at least have some water to drink?"

"Water? Ye don't want to drink water. The nuncheon has been put away already. The servants are gettin' the supper ready for after the dance. But I can ask the cook for something for ye, and I can bring ye a cup of tea."

"Oh." She had been on the other end of a demanding customer, she didn't want to become one of them herself. "That would be very nice. Thank you." Grace looked at the girl. "I'm Grace Harding. What is your name?"

"Me name?" The maid looked surprised. Did no guests care enough about the poor workers to find out who they were even talking to? "Bella."

The pouch and the tin caught her eye. "Bella, can you tell me what some things are?"

"If I can."

Grace beckoned the maid to follow her as she took the few steps to the dressing table. The soap sat in the large bowl with the pitcher, and she had draped the silk cloth next to it. But the sponge was back in the pouch for safekeeping.

With a wave to the soap, Grace said, "Someone left these, I presume for whatever guest got this room. I know what soap and a washcloth are, but . . ." she opened the pouch and pulled out the little sponge. "What is the sponge for?"

"Why, yer teeth, of course!" Bella poured water into the beautiful china pitcher sitting in the lovely bowl. "Don't ye use a sponge for your teeth?"

Sponge? Teeth? "No. I've never seen anything like it before."

Bella looked up at her, and clapped a hand to smother her giggles. "What do ye use for cleaning teeth?"

"I use a toothbrush." The words came out before Grace gave a thought to whether she was breaking some time-travel rule. When was the toothbrush invented, and would Bella even know what she meant?

"Oh!" Bella's eyes went wide. "I've heard of such things, but I never saw one. Do they work?"

Grace had to fight an inappropriate laugh. "The ones I use do."

"I'd like one some day." Bella looked at the strange little sponge with envy. "I don't even get a sponge most of the time. I use sticks, and rinse with soda or salt. If I'm lucky, I sneak a comfit and chew it. They are delicious!"

Curiosity took over. "Can I have one? Is that allowed?"

"'Course. Yer a guest. Just ask an' some'un'll get ye whatever ye want." Bella nodded without hesitation. "I can have some'un get ye yer tea, or ye can go down. There's sweets sittin' out. Take whatever ye need."

Grace made up her mind. "I'll wait here."

"I'll let staff know." The girl grabbed the mop and bucket, bobbed a quick curtsey, and slipped out the door.

She couldn't hide here all day. Bella must not have been able to get away from her work, because a different maid had brought, not just a comfit, but buttered bread and a lovely china pot of warm tea and matching cup and saucer. The comfit had been very sweet, with a surprising fruit center.

A dessert to clean teeth? Goodness, what was she going to do if she didn't get home to the right century? Grace could feel the cavities brewing just thinking about it, and longed for her toothpaste and dental floss.

Not to mention that after all that tea, she now had to use the bathroom. Grace looked over at the screen hiding the chamber pot. A blush heated her face. She clapped her hand over her mouth as the nervous giggles bubbled up. Laugh or cry, she squirmed with the need to relieve herself. *If this is a nightmare, please wake up.*

But the scene didn't change, so Grace did what she had to do.

The sounds coming from below increased, laughter and the discordant notes of instruments tuning up. Apparently the party had moved inside. Sooner or later, she had to make an appearance. Both her host and the butler knew she was here, and so did two maids. It would be more suspicious to hide out.

Wouldn't it?

Besides, she'd soon starve to death. She would need all her strength and wits to figure out how to get home.

A sudden melodious chord came, and then the musicians started into what must be a dance, swirls and trills and a faint vibration through the floor. The piece wasn't in the least familiar, but it pulled her into the mood, light and sprightly.

One more glance at her wide eyes in the mirror, and Grace

squared her shoulders. "Time to make my appearance." Her stomach in a knot, she gathered her courage, grabbed the knob, and jerked the door open before she could change her mind.

It was a long walk to the top of the stairs.

Three men, all dressed in brightly colored cutaway coats embroidered with fanciful designs, skin-tight breeches buttoned under the knee, tight boots, and shirts flowing with ruffles, stood at the bottom of the stairs. She didn't think her soft shoes made any sound, but one of the men turned and looked up at her.

"I do not believe we have been introduced." The speaker nudged one of the men beside him, and the other two turned to stare.

She hadn't come from the future for nothing. Grace straightened her shoulders, and started down the stairs, her feet slow with dread, but her head held high. As she went, she met every man's gaze without flinching. *Do not show fear.*

She thought fast. *What would Elizabeth Bennet say?* "I heard the music and smelled the food."

Now that they faced her, she took note of their features, and tried to memorize them. Tall-ish, with different shades of dark hair and eyes in equally different colors, one blue, the second green, and the one on the far end with brown eyes. The pants were different colors, cream, burgundy and black, but all had the sheen of silk.

Three pairs of eyebrows rose. "It ain't ready yet. The guests will eat in an hour, p'rhaps more."

Grace felt her face fall. "An hour?"

The men looked at each other and back at her. "Yes. After the supper dance."

She shouldn't ask, women from this time would know what it was, but her mouth kept going. "Supper dance?"

Eyebrows that had gone back down popped up again, like surprised slashes across their foreheads. "You don't know wot a supper dance is?"

The excuse that came in so handy earlier with Fairfax came in just as handy now. It also had the benefit of being the truth. Fairfax accepted it. Hopefully everyone else would, too, if she said or did anything else awkward, which might be every few minutes. "I'm an American."

"Oh." The word came out in stereo.

Two of the men seemed satisfied with her answer, but one was not so easily convinced. "They ain't got supper dances in America?"

"Not where I live." *Live.* The word echoed in her head, and the image of the mirror, as unresponsive as if it were dead, appeared in her mind. Would she ever live there—or *then*—again?

"Oh." The third man sounded, if not convinced, at least pacified.

Do not brood about the mirror, Grace ordered herself. She gave the men a nod and walked down the last few steps and past them, making certain to keep her shoulders straight and her head up. With every step, she was certain she felt the stares of those three men still waiting by the staircase drill into her back. They might be following her although she heard no footsteps, but she didn't turn around to check.

The ballroom loomed in front of her, men and women moving in the intricate steps of a dance she had never seen, colors blending and contrasting as they wove in and out to the music.

Are you really going to walk right into the middle of a group of people you don't know, in a century to which you don't belong, people who can throw you out if you slip up, just to get some food?

Her stomach growled, the meager meal from earlier all but gone. The answer was yes.

As she neared the ballroom doors, those same doors she had avoided earlier, her daring flagged. Walking through those wide doors took every scrap of courage she had left. She sidled along the wall, dodging around a circular table with a large bouquet of fresh flowers, no doubt picked from the garden she walked through earlier.

As she eased further in, she noticed chairs by the windows, lovely antique chairs of elegantly carved wood but not as large as those in the dining room across the foyer. The smaller size hinted at being designed for a woman.

The dance circles moved in strange ever-changing steps. Grace kept one eye alert for dancers that might get too close as she headed for those chairs, and sank down to watch.

Perfume and body odors assaulted her, almost covering the scent of candle smoke from the two chandeliers glowing overhead. Necklaces sparkled in the flickering light. The room was light enough to see, but it could do with several bright LED lamps to beat back the shifting shadows.

Her gaze scanned the crowd. Moving people were hard to count, but she guessed there were several dozen in the room. The center where the dancing took place held three groups of—she did a quick count—four couples.

A few more guests lined the opposite wall and the far bank of windows, left out of the dances like herself. Either that, or they were staying away from the smells of sweating couples, she thought as another wave of body odor drifted past.

She thought of Colin Firth getting out of the bath in "Pride and Prejudice." Maybe that was cinematic license.

Grace turned her attention back to the dance.

Whatever these dances were, they bore no resemblance to what she enjoyed at home. She knew how to waltz—sort of—and bounced around to her favorite artists while she worked, but this was a lot of ornate steps, lots of back and forth and circling.

One group got off rhythm as a male dancer, tall with familiar thick dark hair, caught her eye. He missed his partner's hand as he passed the woman in the center of the circle. She, fortunately, was paying more attention and grabbed for that hand then, on light feet, added an extra skip as she swung around him, completing the move. They got into position just as the dancers joined hands and revolved the other way.

He did not turn his head back toward her, but the woman he partnered did. A quick look, bright and curious, as the music swelled to a stop.

The dark-haired man bowed to his equally dark-haired partner and led her off the floor—straight toward herself. Grace knew before they reached the edges of the room why he was coming.

Fairfax was coming to drag *her* into a dance. Which she did not know and had never even seen before today.

6

Grace watched as Fairfax approached, purpose in his face. Music started again, the circles reformed, but she only noticed from the corner of her eye.

Don't stare at him! Follow the dances, she ordered herself, but her eyes wouldn't obey. The couple drew closer, and his gaze trapped hers like a physical link.

When a man walked over to one woman with another woman at his side, it was never a good thing. She tried to smile, but her mouth felt frozen. Smile or no, she would not let them tower over her while she sat. Grace stood, and locked her knees. Fairfax bowed, the woman did a quick curtsey.

Grace copied it as best she could, drawing on the "princess" games she and her friends had played when they were kids. Everyone had seen curtsies on TV and in the movies.

It must have been acceptable because Fairfax drew the woman with him forward. "Miss Grace Harding, I would like to introduce my sister. Madeline, Lady Cavenaugh. I told her that you are from America, and she wanted to meet you. She has not met anyone from the colonies before."

Sister? Grace's attention snapped to the woman, her gaze suddenly picking up on the similarities. The same light green eyes, the same dark hair, the same unruly curls, although the sister's—Madeline, was it?—had been constrained in some kind of fancy style, curls pulled up, held by some kind of hairpin Grace could not see. A jeweled comb was tucked like a tiara into the brown swirls above her forehead.

"Hello! How do you do?"

"I do well," Madeline said with a smile. "So you truly are from America?"

Oh dear. Grace tried not to wince. She knew almost nothing about everyday life in colonial America.

"So is America as untamed and full of wild beasts as we hear?" Madeline's gaze was alert and interested, the color so like her brother that Grace blinked.

"There are certainly wild animals, but they stay away from the cities." For the most part, except for a rash of coyote sightings around Minneapolis and the occasional bear. Deer survived in parts of the city, but never where she lived. She had no idea whether deer or bear —or coyotes, for that matter—wandered through the streets of the Revolutionary cities. "It may be different for those in the country, but I live in town."

Madeline's smile dimmed a fraction. "Oh, well, I suppose it was too much to expect a tale of fighting off bears, or running from wolves." She raised an eyebrow. "I do have that right? There are wolves?"

Grace felt her lips curve. It was tempting to say, *Oh, yes, they brought the wolves back from the brink of extinction and are repopulating them.* "Yes, you're right about that. There definitely are wolves."

"Do they really look like dogs?" Madeline's face seemed more pale than a moment ago, but she continued the conversation. "That is what I heard."

Grace had only seen them in zoos, but in the days of television and movies everyone knew what they looked like. "Yes, they do. Big, shaggy dogs." She was certain of it now, Madeline had lost color. "Are you feeling well? You look pale. Do you need to sit down?"

"I suggested that very thing when the dance ended. She requires a few minutes' respite." Fairfax cupped his hand around his sister's arm, and seemed to hold her up. He moved her toward the chair Grace had just left, and seated her with solicitous care.

Madeline gave a single, weak laugh as she settled herself. "What he is trying not to say is that I am with child. Perhaps you would be willing to partner my brother?"

Grace bit back a groan. Instead of one host to outmaneuver, she now had two. "Thank you so much for the offer, but I don't know this dance. I would hate to embarrass any of us."

Madeline tilted her head to look up at her brother. "What do you think? The quadrille?"

His brows came down, and he looked over at Grace. Tightness pulled up her arms, and she knew if she looked down, her knuckles would be white from the tension of her clenched fingers.

"Why not? A quadrille would be just the thing." He turned and raised his hand to someone across the room.

"If you partner her, you'll be close enough you can give her the steps." A smile tilted Madeline's lips, and she shifted her gaze to Grace. "You have no idea how good it is to have the room stop spinning. I think I'm just going to close my eyes and enjoy the music."

She did just that, closing her eyes, and leaning her head against the wall.

Fairfax held out his hand. "I think we have been dismissed. If you would be so kind?"

Grace had seen a few Jane Austen movies, even read some of her books. Without a well-researched background and family connections, they would consider her unfit for the gathering. Not only that, they would hustle her out of the party, and the house. Yet he was going to dance with her? In front of all his guests?

What was this about?

His hand hadn't moved.

Grace glanced over at Madeline, but she was paying no attention. Or doing a good job pretending. There was an alertness about her posture, the tilt of her head, that made Grace think she missed little. Even though his mouth didn't curve, Fairfax seemed to smile. It showed in his relaxed stance, the ease in his expression.

"You are sure you can keep me from making a fool of myself?" Her hands untangled from their tight bundle, and one of them started to lift, even though she was certain her brain hadn't given any such command.

That was all the invitation the man needed. He tucked that hand into the crook of his elbow, his other hand coming over to hold it in place.

They stood like that, waiting for the dance to end. Grace looked down at that big, gloved hand on her own ungloved one. Was it there as protection? Or a manacle?

The circles reformed, changing slightly. She thought the partners had changed, but she hadn't paid close enough attention before.

Fairfax walked her into the crowded floor. Their dancing circle waited, everyone staring at her with open curiosity. If they only knew! Her teeth wanted to chatter, so she tightened her jaw.

Fairfax whispered into her ear, "This is my favorite dance. You will catch on quickly. I'll make certain another couple starts first, and I'll explain as they go. Then just follow what they do."

He stopped to whisper something to one of the men. As Grace followed her host into position, she analyzed their group. Four sets of couples, one at each point of a compass, square dance style. The music started, bright and sprightly, something that might have made toes tap even in her own time.

"Curtsey to the man next to you," Fairfax hissed and turned away to bow to the woman on his left. Grace followed his instructions, turned right and gave a quick curtsey to the total stranger at the nearest point of the compass, then turned back. Her heart pounded and her brain spun as she tried to follow what was going on.

Fairfax's voice came in her ear, the sudden brush of air making her jump. "See how they pass in the center, clapping the other's hand as they go? Remember, meet and clap and go across, I'll join you in the center as we form a line."

The couples at their sides (North and South, she named them) started the dance, their actions matching Fairfax"s description. As Grace watched the movements, and her feet bounced to the music, she thought with a whisper of panic, *I'm supposed to remember this?*

North and South joined into a row of quick bows and kicks, and then the couples separated back to their places. She tried to memorize the steps.

Fairfax whispered the coming routine, his breath once again sending chills down her skin. She had to fight the urge to rub the goosebumps off her ear. With that distraction, it was hard to keep track of the movements. The dancers threw in quick steps, skips and flutters, as if the music lifted them. Was she supposed to do the same? What wouldn't look like she was making it up on the spot?

It was their turn. Fairfax hissed just loud enough for her to hear over the music, "Forward, and clap as you pass."

By Grace's reckoning, that would put her across the circle from Fairfax, with only the sketchiest idea of what to do next. But the man across from her moved toward her with the music, and a strong hand on her back gave her a gentle push.

Her mind went blank for a moment, but she moved toward the center, and thank goodness, Fairfax's words came back. She met the man's raised hand, making a soft slapping sound before going across together.

Her new partner gave her an odd look, no doubt wondering if he should recognize her from somewhere. A giggle clogged her throat.

Somehow the steps of the dance were easier when she had Fairfax's guidance, a pull as he drew her toward him, pressure as he moved her away, helping her do the together-and-back steps as the line did some bouncy and skipping moves.

Grace felt her feet move. But it was more than that, she realized. The dance seemed to have been hiding deep inside her brain, and it came out, drawn by the music, the steps becoming more fluid, the movements making sense.

The song ended with a flourish. She glanced around, and saw other women curtseying on both sides, so mimicked them. The audience applauded and began moving out of the center of the room.

Fairfax caught her hand, tucked it in his elbow, and drew her off the floor with the other dancers. His brows drew together in a frown, although his mouth curved on one side. "How much help did you really need?"

"I needed every bit of help you gave me." Something made Grace slide her hand free and curtsey. "I am very grateful, and I thank you."

They reached Madeline. That same alertness Grace sensed before was in the woman's face as she looked between them.

"I must now leave you." Fairfax gave a brief dip, and said in a low voice, "I do not know how it is in America, but here, if unattached couples dance more than twice a night, it is presumed there is an understanding between them, and an engagement had better appear in the paper shortly thereafter. I am certain you would like that even less than I."

"Oh!" Grace clapped her hand over her mouth to stifle her gasp. An *engagement*? Here? Two hundred years from her own time? She could only hope she didn't look as horrified as she felt. Stupid time mirror! "No, I agree, I don't want to cause any talk."

"I did not mean to alarm you. I can see you have a lot to learn about my country." He looked down at his sister. "Well, Madeline, are you better?"

"No. I would prefer to sit out a few more dances." She looked up at Fairfax from her seat on the chair. "Amazing what one can see from the sidelines. Several of your guests are curious about Miss Grace.

People are watching her instead of their own steps. She is certain to have requests for dances."

A pit opened in Grace's stomach, and this time it wasn't from hunger. "No, really, I don't know these dances. I honestly prefer to sit out and watch."

Madeline's gaze darted up to her brother. "Garrett, you may leave so we can become better acquainted."

Aha! He had a first name, and it was Garrett. Grace tucked the knowledge away. She might never be able to use it, but at least she knew it.

Something from the floor caught Fairfax's eye, and his gaze shifted beyond Grace. "You have an admirer already."

She turned to follow his gaze, and her stomach tightened. Sure enough, a man was coming across the room, dodging between the other couples gathering in formation. Not much taller than herself, with brown hair long enough to curl over his ears, sideburns that went most of the way down his cheeks, and a high collar with an elaborate tie-thing whose name escaped her, he looked rather young, but had a smug, cocky air.

The young man reached them and looked at Fairfax first. A tint of red crept up his neck. "Might I request an introduction to your guest?"

A quiet snicker came from behind, but Fairfax kept a straight face. "Certainly." Turning to Grace, he gestured toward the man. "Miss Grace Harding, may I present my friend Mr. Wrigley. Wrigley, Miss Grace Harding."

Wrigley caught her hand and bowed over it. "Would you care to join me for a dance?"

That blush made it hard for her to turn him down flat. "Actually," she saw the red creep higher, and felt her willpower slip. "I'm from America, and we don't do the same dances as you have here. I'm afraid I would embarrass you, and myself. However I thank you very much for your kind offer."

"I don't mind."

Before she could say, *but I do*, the sets of lines forming around the room and the music caught her attention. An old memory from her childhood rose, sketchy with the years, but still there. "I know what this is!" she said with surprise. "It's the Virginia Reel." It probably wasn't the exact dance she had learned in elementary school, but close enough that she thought she might get the hang of it.

Fairfax's eyes lit. "Aha! I can see there will be no more excuses. Out on the floor with you."

"Off with you," Madeline chirped from behind her, a teasing echo of her brother.

Wrigley held out his arm like Fairfax had. He didn't have the panache that the older man had, at least not yet. Maybe in a few years he would be a force to reckon with, but right now, he was charmingly young. The high color on his cheeks had faded. Despite her cold fingers, the thumping of her heart and the fluttering in her stomach—which could just as easily be hunger—Grace didn't have the heart to embarrass him further.

She wished she dared glare at Fairfax and Madeline, but that was out of the question. Instead, she followed her new dancing partner over to the nearest double row.

She had to give him a chance to change his mind, she thought. "Mr. Wrigley, when I said I knew this dance, I meant I had done it only a couple times, and that was years ago. I might recognize it, but you will have to remind me of the steps. If you'd rather not go through that,"—her words came faster as they drew nearer to the double lines of waiting dancers—"you can take me back."

"It cannot have been that long. I'm sure you will remember. Just follow my lead." He sounded rather cocky. "I will give you cues if I think you need help." With a flourish, he put her at the end of the nearest line, and took his place across from her.

The music began, but the beat was in counterpoint to her own pounding heart, and hardly loud enough to hear over the thunder in her ears. If only it was Fairfax! He gave hints she could follow.

Wrigley danced lightly into the middle, but not toward her. Grace realized he was heading diagonal, to the far end of the line. And if he headed diagonal, would it alternate? And was she next?

The man at the end where Wrigley had gone moved toward her, the two men merely changing places. Hoping she was reading the dance right and the next steps were hers, Grace stepped out to meet him.

This was not the fun dance she had with Fairfax. Instead, she spent most of her time trying to recall what the next move was, with the man opposite becoming more and more irritated. There were one-handed circles around each other, in the center where everyone could see, then double-handed, then one time he didn't hold out his hands at all, just moved around her, and she tried to do what he was doing, always one step behind.

"You haven't danced this much, have you?" the man muttered at one pass.

If she'd had time, if it had been that kind of dance, she would have relished stepping on his foot.

Gradually, a pattern emerged from what she at first feared would be chaos. And with it, her heart lifted. Laughter bubbled up, and the moves came faster.

Now that she didn't have to concentrate so hard, something caught her attention. Wrigley smelled. A lot. Thank goodness they didn't spend much time in close proximity. Unfortunately, he wasn't the only one who could do with deodorant, and the air became ever more pungent.

Wrigley seemed to have found his confidence, and his curiosity. Each time they went under the arch of joined hands, he had another question ready. "Who is your family?" "When did you get here?" "How long will you be staying?"

One good thing about them not being together long, and the room so loud, there wasn't enough time to give detailed answers!

7

Garrett leaned down to Madeline and spoke under the music. "So. What do you say? Have I let someone unseemly remain in my house and mingle with my guests?"

She didn't answer right away, just watched Miss Grace dance, always half a beat behind. "I don't think so. Besides, she could not have gotten in without an invitation, although I don't recall sending one. Did she arrive with one of your guests?"

He frowned as he turned his attention to his guest. "No, not any of mine. If you didn't invite her, and I didn't either, then how did she get here?" He watched her struggle with the steps. "Despite her words, she does *not* know this dance."

"She never said she did. She said she knew something *like* it." Madeline smiled. "She is catching on, though, if slowly."

Jones's words nagged Garrett. "Does she look familiar to you?"

"No." His sister looked up at him, her eyebrows raised. "Am I supposed to recognize her?"

Garrett tried to follow his guest through the revolving, shifting line. Was Jones right? His butler was hardly a man given to fancies.

"Jones thought he saw a family resemblance. It's a name you should recognize."

Madeline stood. Garrett didn't think it would help much, there were too many people for her to get a good look without climbing on the chair. But his sister was quite observant; that was why he'd enlisted her help.

"Family resemblance? Does he think she's a relative of ours?"

"No, not our family. Look at her hair, and think of those dark eyes."

Just then, as if by fate, one of Grace's curls popped loose, and bounced in time to the music as she danced. "Oh!" Madeline's eyes widened, and she grabbed his arm, pulling him to look at her. "Did Jones say Cokewell? I know some of the granddaughters, and most have that same combination of light hair and those deep brown eyes."

Garrett's heart sank. "The very name. She claims to be an American, and from her speech and that informality, I would say that part at least is true. She came over to shake my hand, hardly the behavior of a well-bred Englishwoman, but perhaps fitting an American. Does being from America fit any of Cokewell's family? I don't know the story that well."

"I recall something about a daughter who ran off with a man the family did not approve. The couple might have left the country, but where they went I can't remember. I wish I could recall more." Her hands were still on his arm. He appreciated the strength in them. She looked at him, her face serious. "I will ask around and see if anyone brought her, but if she is here without a chaperone, American or not, she has already jeopardized her reputation. Cokewell is no one to taunt. You know how close he and Prinny are."

Garrett shifted to look at the dancers. Miss Grace's bright hair and bouncing curl made her stand out. That, and the half-beat-behind steps of her dancing. "The party has been going for several days already, and I have not seen her before today."

He turned back to Madeline. "Neither have you, obviously, nor Jones, and he knows everything going on. If no one brought her, the only other explanation is that someone in Cokewell's family sent her without an invitation. It is most presumptuous of them to assume she would be welcome. The family has plenty of wealth, they have no need of ours."

"Assuming they hoped to have her compromised and thus get a husband that way. That is what you are thinking, is it not?" Madeline's face and voice were sober.

"It is indeed." Garrett felt his gaze go back to his guest, and forced his attention back to his sister. "And why me? There are other men to pick on."

Madeline's eyes lit up. "I might be prejudiced because you are my brother, but if I were Cokewell and had to go through all of London to pick a man for my daughters—or granddaughters as might be the case here—I could think of no one better than you."

He didn't care who saw. Garrett put his arm around her shoulders and gave her a hug. "I love you, too."

Grace caught the scent of food, and her stomach churned, interrupting her concentration. How long would the dances go on before dinner was announced?

The music ended with a flourish. A titter of excitement, or perhaps relief, ran through the room. Everyone else must smell the food, too.

The dance circles broke up, and Grace let her partner lead her off the floor. No one came up to ask her for another dance. When the men all moved toward her host, she could tell this part of the night was over.

Madeline stood, and walked toward the double doors, where she joined her brother. Couples formed, men and women pairing off, likely husbands and wives, she thought. A line started to form.

Like a brightly colored parade, the men and women crossed the foyer. She glanced around. There were a few men behind her, none with partners, but no one offered her an arm. Grace turned back, walking with the measured pace of the women ahead, and hoped she wouldn't make any serious mistakes..

The dining room that had appeared so big when empty now looked stuffed as the party scurried for chairs. Even though the chandelier was lit, every candle blazing, and sconces she hadn't seen before glowing on the walls, just like the ballroom, the flickering lights didn't eat away all the shadows. The room could stand a few electrical fixtures and some bright bulbs.

A massive centerpiece of flowers and greenery sat in the middle of the table, blocking the greater part of the view of anyone on the opposite side. How convenient. No one could expect her to talk with anyone across from her. That only left her to worry about those on either side.

Fairfax sat at one end of the table, while his sister Madeline sat at the opposite end. One of the doors opened—she recognized it from her earlier scouting about the house as leading to where the kitchen had to be—and a uniformed servant came in, carrying a large tureen. Obviously a soup, and she looked down at the line of utensils beside her plate. She knew that one always started with the outer piece, but best to wait and watch everyone else.

When a bowl was placed in front of her, Grace recognized pieces of onion and carrot. The green bits of leaf she recognized as parsley, but what appeared to be meat floating about in the broth and greens baffled her. Oyster, maybe? Aiming for the meat-like bits, Grace scooped up a piece. The bite didn't taste like anything she'd ever had before, but it was utterly delicious. She took another bite, only to find out that that one had a different flavor. As did the next.

Aha! It was a combination of meats. She settled in to eat when someone down the table said in a loud voice, "Turtle soup? We are favored indeed. Your cook is to be praised."

Turtle? Grace stared down at the bowl in horror. Her stomach lurched. She was eating turtle soup? If only she dared stand up and rail at the group, tell them what their appetite had done to the turtle population by her day.

She couldn't finish it. She just couldn't. It didn't matter how delicious it was; it didn't matter that she was a good hundred and fifty years away from the ban on harvesting turtles. People in this era may not know better but *she* did, and while it was a small stand for the ecology and might not affect the devastation by her own day, it was her stand to make.

A voice came in her ear. "You don't like turtle soup?"

Grace looked up. The man was leaning far too close. His teeth had not been pretty before he ate. She focused on his green eyes instead, and the straight ash-blonde hair that draped too near his eyes and dusted his high collar.

She wanted to educate him about the fate of sea turtles, but she didn't know what effect that information would have. She'd already disrupted time by coming here. So she lied and hoped it wouldn't bother the chef. "No."

The waiters, or perhaps these were the footmen she always read about, came and removed the dishes. They were too well-trained to comment on her nearly full bowl. Another phalanx of servants brought in the next course.

Grace looked down at the plate in front of her. Fish. She wasn't a fan of fish, but she was hungry, she didn't know how long or even if Fairfax would let her stay, and it was important to get as much food as she could while she had the chance.

"The fish is superb, isn't it?" Her neighbor popped a bite in his mouth.

"It's fine." As good as fish ever got, she supposed, and took another bite herself.

"I hear you are an American. Would I know the place you're from?" He popped another bite in.

She would say this much for the man: he had a fabulous metabolism. He was eating like a horse, and he didn't have a spare ounce on himself. Grace wanted to pretend she hadn't heard the question, but doubted she would get away with it. "Probably not."

He swallowed the mouthful. "Try me."

Grace's eyes narrowed. He was certainly curious. "Minneapolis." Which did not exist in this day, she was positive.

He stared into the distance, thinking, and she watched his brows furrow with the effort. Finally he said, "You win. I admit, I have never heard of the place."

"It's not a big city." At least for her time. Big enough, but there were so many cities across the nation much bigger.

"What about your family? Do you have any connection to our noble families?"

"Not that I know of." Grace took another bite of fish and hoped he was done with his interrogation.

"Not to worry." He scooped up another bite, but this time instead of popping the food in his mouth, the fork stayed suspended when he started talking again. "Fairfax is not a snob. But you no doubt already know that, as I saw you speaking with both him and his sister. Have you known them long?"

Grace's bite got caught in her throat, and she started to cough. The offending piece came free, and she could swallow again.

"Forgive me. I should have offered you wine." Her neighbor grabbed her beautiful goblet, and picked up the carafe of wine. He filled the goblet half full, and handed it over.

Water would have been nice, but she didn't see a single pitcher on the table, and her throat needed something wet. She raised the goblet to her lips, and felt someone's gaze like a physical touch. It might have come from anywhere along the table, but Grace followed the direction of that tingle.

From his seat at the end of the table, her host stared at her, his expression blank. She didn't know what he thought, but she could hardly call *I'm fine* down the length of the table.

His gaze didn't waver. Grace looked at the glass of wine in her hand, hovering in front of her mouth, and back to him. His eyes were still on her, unblinking. She couldn't leave the delicate glass suspended all night, someone would notice, so she took a sip. He still watched as she swallowed. She was surprised she didn't choke a second time, but the wine went down smoothly. Heat went up her face at that steady gaze. Grace hoped the chandelier's pale light hid the blush.

"I asked how long you have known Fairfax." Her wine-giving male table neighbor was insistent.

That pulled her attention away from her host. "Not long."

He—whoever he was, she should get his name—gave a snort. "I saw you looking at Fairfax. I advise you not to put too much hope in that direction. Being from America, you have no way to know but every gal what's not married already has her eye on him. Even some married ones do, too. He is not likely to turn his attention to someone from your country when he can have his pick of women here."

If only he knew her sole goal was to get back home safely! Since he could ask questions, surely she could ask her own. "What is your name?"

The man blinked as if surprised, then cleared his throat. He flicked a quick glance toward the head of the table where Fairfax sat before turning back to her. "I suppose we can consider ourselves properly introduced. I am Durney."

Durney? Was that his first name, or his last? Maybe men and women weren't supposed to be on a first name basis. Even Jane Austen's Mr. Darcy was only known as 'Darcy' through most of the movie. "And I am Grace Harding."

"Is that Miss Grace? Or Miss Harding?"

"Well, either, I suppose." There had been a difference in *Pride and Prejudice*, but she couldn't recall which daughter was called what. She only remembered Lydia butting ahead of Jane in line going into the house after her marriage to Wickham, taking the first place as the only girl wed.

"What I mean is, are you the oldest daughter?"

She felt a sharp pang of loneliness, but shoved it aside with effort. "I am the *only* daughter." At least from her mother. If her father had produced any daughters, she hadn't heard about it.

"Very well. Then you are Miss Grace from America." The laziness that had marked him slipped, and she saw beneath it sharp intelligence. "You said Harding was your surname? I don't recognize it. But Fairfax clearly knows you." He forked up the last piece of fish, but watched her..

She was saved from having to respond by the arrival of the next course, carried in by a parade of those well-dressed footmen. Meat, with asparagus and peas, and a small collection of vegetables. She recognized the dandelion leaves in the mixture, and bit back a smile. Memories of staring up at the clouds watching for airplane contrails while nibbling on the weeds in the yard as a child drifted past, bringing a soft twinge of nostalgia.

She picked up her knife and cut the meat. It was so finely baked that it hardly needed cutting.

"You like lamb?" Durney asked. "I am a beef and venison man myself, but Fairfax has a chef to rival none."

Grace stared at the meat in dismay. "Lamb?" She knew people ate lamb, probably most of the world even in her day ate lamb, but all she could think of was soft, fluffy babies with little twitching tails following their mother about the pasture. She put her knife down and switched to the greens.

"My mistake." Durney gave her an odd look, and dug into his meal with gusto.

Grace picked at her food, and watched the rest of the table eat. For all the din of conversation, it was impressive how quickly the meal disappeared.

The footmen came back to collect the dishes, and then the oddest thing happened. Everything on the table was removed, not just the empty plates. The bouquets were removed, the wine goblets, every serving dish, even the neatly laid out tableware. The white tablecloth was removed, and she caught a glimpse of any number of stains, but was distracted by a second tablecloth that had been hiding beneath the first.

The centerpiece and goblets were replaced, and new silverware set out again. No sooner was the table freshly relaid when more servants came in with another course of food.

Thank goodness, was all she thought. What she'd eaten so far would not last long. The next course turned out to be chicken in a mushroom sauce. She couldn't eat mushrooms but once she scraped the sauce off, the rest of it was delicious.

Another dish followed the chicken, more meat and more vegetables, and after that a strange paste that had a decided meat flavor to it, and some fresh-baked bread. Grace smothered a yawn. *When will this dinner end? And how much can these people eat?*

More than they already had eaten, she discovered. Still more plates came in, small eggs in a sauce, then sardines. Whether it was so much food or the time or her body's reaction to all the changes, another yawn hit so fast she didn't get her mouth covered.

She was pleasantly full, and now she only wanted to sleep. Whatever everyone else did after the meal finished, she was going to bed. If she had a bed here that is.

Fairfax was in no hurry to toss her out. No one else disputed her being here, other than Durney's warning her off from plotting to marry the man.

The room upstairs must be hers. Why else would she be dropped there? No one had popped in and challenged her claim to it. She needed time to think and sleep. Maybe she'd wake up in her own bed in the 21st century, and this would only be a strange interlude in her life, taking on a dreamlike quality in the years to come.

She didn't know how to feel about that. It would be wonderful to have her own things around her, to know the rules of life, but as an adventure, this was exciting. Thrilling, even. Mixed with moments of terror, of course, but still an experience she was glad to have had.

But how to excuse herself? Grace looked up and down the table, waiting for some indication she could leave without causing a scene. No one wanted to move, not even when the servants came back through the door.

The table was cleared, again. cloth and all, and the polished wood of the table revealed. *We're done.* All her muscles relaxed in relief, but no one stood up. *What are they waiting for,* she wondered. The door through which the staff left opened again.

Servants bearing still more food came in. So this is why everyone stayed put. Grace smothered a groan.

A small bowl was set down, a fluffy lemon yellow dessert accented with a slice of strawberry. The scent of lemon, clean and crisp, tickled her nose. Her eyes opened wide, and the sleep that had been dragging at her eased. The creamy sauce looked so good that despite her stomach's protest she had to take one spoon.

it was as tangy as it looked. Not as sweet as the desserts she was used to, but the flavors were all fresh and sharp, each flavor, the mellowness of the cream, the bite of the lemon, even the sweetness of sugar, all came together in a zing of flavor.

She tried to do it justice, she really did, but not even the fear of possibly being thrown out once they discovered she was an imposter and having to survive on this lone meal could fit the whole dessert, small though it was, inside.

At last, at last, they really were done. She knew because people stood up and strolled toward the door. Music drifted from the ballroom, the small band tuning up again.

Obviously they were all going back for more dancing. Probably a good idea to work all that food they had just eaten off before going to bed, but she was tired and being on display again was too much. Grace followed the women out, but when they kept going across the broad foyer, she turned left, toward the stairs.

8

The hairstyle was still beautiful, despite one curl having fallen down and the others beginning to loosen, easing the tug on her scalp. She would never be able to duplicate it.

Maybe it wouldn't matter. Maybe today was more dream than reality. Grace stared at her reflection in the dressing table mirror, trying to burn the fanciful style into her memory for when this adventure came to an end, and reached up for the first pin holding it in place.

With mixed feelings of regret and relief, Grace pulled one fastener after another out as the curls and braids slid free, gathering a pile of strange pins in the process. She rubbed the sore spots along her scalp, and watched her normal self return in the mirror. Blonde hair down and loose, brown eyes nearly black with fatigue, face as clean of makeup as if she had already washed it off for sleep.

What would Fairfax think if he saw her in the cosmetics of her century, with her lashes darkened to hide the light tips, her lips glistening, and a hint of blush on her cheeks?

At the thought, her face colored, filling in the glow from the missing blusher.

But he wasn't here, and would never see her at her modern best.

The silver brush and comb set that matched the mirror, equally pristine and elegant, drew her. She bypassed the brush and picked up the comb. After the strangeness of the day, the familiar routine of combing out her hair was comforting.

That done, she realized she didn't know how to keep the curly mass out of the way for sleeping. Normally she just put it in a loose braid, and used hair elastic to keep it that way. but there was no elastic here. She made do with the braid, and tied it with a ribbon she found in the dressing-table drawer. "The odds of that thing staying in overnight," she muttered into the table's mirror, "are slim and none."

Now to take off the beautiful gown. She couldn't find any hooks and eyes, just a tie at the top. The style was delightfully forgiving. Once that tie was undone and the bodice slid over her shoulders so she could turn it around, she discovered there was a grouping of three ties holding the fancy belting under the bodice together. Simple enough, and she might be able to dress herself in the morning without help. The dress slid to the floor.

Now to get out of this corset. No wonder women of this era had maids! Grace squirmed and twisted until she found the tip of the string. "Aha!" Just a pull, she thought, and the bow should come untied. But the string was so short she could not get a grip on it.

More twisting, and finally she got hold. A good tug, and *aaah!*, she felt the bow begin to slide. More pulling, more bending and twisting to keep that string moving. Breathing got easier with each tug.

When the corset loosened enough to twist it around to the front, she continued to work the lacing through the hand-stitched holes, careful not to tear the fabric, and finally the garment was free enough to slide down her hips.

No more corsets until she got a maid! Maybe no more corsets at all, if she could get away with it. And she thought bras were bad!

She found nightclothes neatly folded inside one of the small drawers at the armoire's bottom, each one with a high lace neck, long ruffled sleeves, easily as long as the gowns in the armoire, and maybe with as much fabric. She would swelter if she had to sleep in them!

But the drawers seemed frighteningly short on other sleepwear options. Grace looked at the pile of clothes she had taken off, and focused on the short slip, pale white in the dimness. Too long for a top, but too short for a dress, it was perfect for summer sleepwear.

Ideas of straw mattresses, or stuffing of pine needles, was not enough to keep her from that bed. Whatever was inside, it was surprisingly comfortable, or else she was just too tired to care. The mattress smelled of the outside, a hint of the pine needles she had expected, along with the sweet scent of freshly cut hay. A thick featherbed lay on top. Even the pillows were filled with down and something that smelled like lavender.

She sank into the featherbed topping, curled onto her side, closed her eyes, and waited for sleep to come.

Unfortunately, her brain didn't cooperate. Her legs tingled with exhaustion, her eyes burned with the need to rest, but her mind whirled more than the dancers downstairs. The house still hummed with people and music, even in her room at the far end of the hallway.

After the current dance faded away and her brain still refused to turn off, Grace got out of the bed and walked over to the window. She worked it open, and leaned against the frame, wishing she could Just. Shut. Down.

The moon lit the surrounding ground, turning the gravel drive into a path of silver and gems, and the fence itself glowed as if painted with a luminous finish. Even the grass was dipped in silverplate. It was all an illusion, no more fanciful than the moonlit nights in Minnesota, but nothing could be mundane in this experience.

She rubbed her forehead again, and yawned so wide she heard the crackling in her ears. In her own time, back in Minneapolis, she had managed—usually—to go to sleep even with noisy neighbors, loud radios, and car traffic even in the middle of the night, but today could hardly be considered normal. The wonder would be if she managed sleep at all.

But she wanted to, so badly!

Another yawn stretched her jaw, and finally, *finally*, this one seemed to mean business. "Bedtime," she whispered into the air. Grace pulled the covers over her head to muffle the sounds that still drifted in through the window she had forgotten to shut and wafted melodically under the door, curled up and closed her eyes.

Garrett watched the dancers go around while he tried to stay inconspicuous. Madeline had taken herself up to bed, her coming child making her more tired than usual.

His uninvited guest had mysteriously disappeared. Perhaps she wasn't really staying here, and whoever brought her had taken her away. She was quite the most distracting woman he had met in a long time, but hearing Cokewell's name used in connection with her had been a jolt.

Her very presence here made no sense. Cokewell was not a man to use such a stratagem as leaving a woman unchaperoned—at least he presumed she was unchaperoned, neither he nor Jones had seen anyone around her to guard her good name—and thus tricking a man into a compromising situation to force a marriage. If Cokewell wanted his granddaughter to get married, he would simply approach the man of his choice and suggest a match, or give her a sufficient dowry to attract a husband.

But Madeline mentioned a family rift. Which might mean Cokewell had nothing to do with her presence. Or Cokewell might have had an indiscretion in his past and be unaware of her existence. That was always a delicate situation, because even if she herself was legitimate, if her parent had been born on the wrong side of the blanket, Grace would have no claim to the man and his fortune.

Perhaps she had no connection to the man whatsoever, despite the resemblance. Curly blonde hair and brown eyes were unusual but surely there were others in England. He would have to ask around—carefully, as he did not wish to damage her name—and see if anyone in the area recognized her.

She had been the subject of conversation and speculation at his side of the table at supper. Several asked him who she was. He had merely said, "She is the granddaughter of a friend of my father."

And then hoped he told the truth. Madeline had been at the far side of the long table, too far away to fill in any details. Good thing he had the reputation of a man who could keep his own counsel, as a great many questions had gone unanswered. With whom had she arrived? Where had she been during the Season in London?

He admitted to her being American, which only added to her stature. An American way out here in the countryside of England! Who would have thought!

Tomorrow he would have to find out whether that resemblance to a wealthy family was coincidence or who she truly was, and what she was doing here.

9

Sunlight leaked in, teasing Grace's eyelids. Morning always came too early. She snuggled a bit more under the blankets, and breathed the fresh-woods scent that seemed to fill the room. Just a few more minutes before she had to start her day. She wanted to look at the chair frames she bought yesterday and match fabrics—

Images flashed past, a graveled drive and carriages, a room full of dancing men and women in odd evening clothes, and a handsome man named Lord Fairfax.

Was it real? Or had it just been a dream?

She pushed herself upright, leaning on her hands, the blankets falling to her waist, the chill morning air raising goosebumps all over her skin, and opened her eyes. One look was all she needed. Armoire, commode behind a screen, tall windows with heavy curtains. With a groan, Grace flopped back on the down pillows, and pulled the covers over her head.

She was still locked in the past.

The morning was nearly silent, only a couple birds chirping outside the window for company. She wondered what time it was.

Hiding under the covers didn't change anything. Now that she was awake, she smelled the lavender of her pillow, and the pine from the mattress. A feather had worked its way through the ticking of the down mattress and poked her hip. She slid an arm free and worked the covers off her head, the sun still shining through that gap between the curtains.

"Get up," she ordered herself, and took another breath of the pine-lavender air before she forced herself upright the second time. Her hair had come most of the way out of the braid, and she discovered the leather tie—still tied, fat lot of good it had done—in the covers. She pushed the tumbled curls out of her face, and sat for a moment on the edge of the bed in the cool morning, letting her legs dangle, while her mind came to terms again with where and when she still was.

The quiet was oddly refreshing. No traffic outside her window, no honking of horns, no sirens announcing possible disaster. She rubbed her hands down her arms to bring warmth against the lingering chill, unusual for a Minnesota summer morning, but possibly normal for England?

She looked at the fireplace, small twigs sitting on the grate. Logs sat in a small basket on the floor. She didn't remember that from yesterday. Perhaps a maid brought them while she was at the party, and she had been too tired to notice when she got back.

Surely the room would warm up as the day went along.

Her teeth began to chatter, and goosebumps rose on her arms. How did one light a fire here? She jumped off the bed and scurried over to the small fireplace, shivering in the improvised nightgown.

A small metal box sat on top of the mantel, and Grace felt a leap of hope as she pried off the top. That flicker of excitement fizzled as she stared down at a couple odd bits of differently colored metals sitting on a crumpled bit of charred cloth.

Okay. So this must be the flint she had read about. She knew the basic premise, snap the two metals together and get a spark which presumably would ignite the cloth. But then what? Grab the burning cloth with her finger? Tip the box over onto the fireplace wood?

It felt like too much work. *Just hurry up and get dressed.* She turned and looked at the armoire.

Where the mirror hid on top.

Exercise was good for warming up. She scurried over and picked up the dressing table chair, her only ladder, carried it to the armoire, and climbed up, reached up and pulled out the mirror. Back on the bed under the covers for added warmth, yesterday's handkerchief in hand, she set to work rubbing again.

Nothing.

Tears prickled in her eyes, but Grace blinked them away. Whatever the reason she was dropped here, she would not make it back yet.

Her shuddering breath sounded loud in the quiet.

The quiet!

She froze, mirror in one hand, handkerchief in the other. Everybody else was still sleeping. Who knew what time they had all decided to call it a day and went to bed? The last she remembered, the party was still going strong.

If she wanted to browse outside, or slip back into the library and borrow a book or two, possibly get something to eat while she was at it, this was her chance. A hot cup of English tea would be welcome.

With the mirror safely hidden again, Grace splashed some very cold water into the washbowl and gave herself the best sponge bath she could manage, given the strange soap and the odd sponge to serve as a toothbrush and salt to fill in for toothpaste.

Maybe she could find an isolated pond and have a nice dip in place of a shower. The little bowl and pitcher just were not doing the job.

Why couldn't she have landed in a time when they at least had plumbing?

Now for which gown to wear. Grace looked at the selection in the armoire. The green one with the silver threads. Probably much too fancy for the daytime, but she had wanted to wear that since she first saw it.

It took some doing and she had to turn it around to tie the bow, twist it back to the front and work her arms through the sleeves, but leaving off the corset simplified things.

Next, her hair. Grace worked loose the last few plaits that still held together and brushed the tangles out, then looked at the curly mass in the mirror. She came in a fancy hairdo, but no way could she duplicate it. It was tempting to leave it loose, but she hadn't seen a single woman with hair down yesterday. *When in Rome*, she thought. With a shrug, she rebraided it, retied the leather string around the end, twisted it around her head until the tie felt hidden, and jabbed all of the pins from yesterday in as best she could.

It would either hold or not, but she was going out to explore. She took one last look in the dressing-table mirror, and poked her head around the door.

The hallway was empty. Further down in one of the other rooms, someone snored. Grace smiled and tiptoed down toward that elegant carved staircase, where the first rays of the day cast a glow up from underneath. She walked down it slowly, letting her fingers trace the birds and leaves carved into the banister.

At the bottom, she did another quick scan. Partially behind her to her left where the hallway split off at an angle, the library with just the suggestion of light beneath the door beckoned, the memory of the newspapers she had just begun to read in yesterday's brief visit luring her inside. She needed to know more about this era if she had the slightest chance of convincing anyone she belonged here.

Her deficiencies in her previous studies were becoming all too real now, but who would ever have guessed she would need historical trivia in such detail?

Small damp patches spotted the foyer floor, and warned of servants who might be up and about cleaning all evidence of last night's party. Now that her host knew of her existence, she shouldn't have to worry about them rushing off to tell the boss.

The library was dim when she shut the door behind herself. The glow she had seen was the rising sun seeping through the sheer green curtains. They opened by a hanging cord at the center, and she dragged it along the window, watching the room brighten.

Even if there had been a light switch, the sun made electricity unnecessary.

Newspapers. She examined the desk, the matching chair tucked into the kneehole as if some servant had come through to make things pristine. The letters of yesterday were gone, but the papers were left out, now neatly folded. She picked up the top paper, sat down on the chaise by the window to get the most light, and began to read.

She found that Napoleon Bonaparte had married an archduchess of Austria. Apparently Josephine was a thing of the past. She remembered that he had divorced her.

There were some articles on Russia and tensions because of French troops in Prussia. Where was Prussia again? Something about Poland and Russia, but she couldn't have drawn the borders if she had a gun to her head. Wasn't modern-day Germany in there somewhere? Russia's winters had defeated Bonaparte, but she had no idea when that happened in relation to this *now*.

Grace kept reading. There were reports of Marquis Somebody or other being robbed at gunpoint by highwaymen, but apparently other than the loss of some jewels, no one was seriously hurt. She didn't recognize the victim's name, didn't know how high in rank the title was.

The click of the door opening behind her jolted her out of her reverie. Her host, Lord Fairfax, stood there, arms folded, handsome face neatly shaved, thick dark hair combed, fully dressed in buff-colored pants, an embroidered vest, and a blue suit coat. He even had taken the time to put on a fancy cravat, tied in some fluffy bow.

The sun caught his cheekbones, painting them with a wash of

gold, and making his light eyes glint. Even across the room, his presence seemed to dwarf the space, and her heart started a quick patter.

Grace didn't know if that odd flutter came from being caught in his library without invitation, or if it came from his height, his pale eyes, and the fit of his clothes.

The men she dated had frequently amused her, usually bored her, sometimes worried her—one or two actually scared her and she feared for their future wives and girlfriends—but none had caused her heart to beat fast and her attention to fixate on him, her ears to turn toward the sound of his voice.

This was bad. Very bad. And here she was in a gown she had put on without assistance—and without a corset.

She looked from him to the newspapers and back, set them down on the chaise and rose to her feet. "I hope you don't mind my reading your paper, I rose early and . . .

"No, you are welcome to it. I have already found out all the news I need to know." He didn't move, just stood in front of the door leaning against the jamb.

She glanced at the window, trying to remember where the shadows had been when she first entered. "What time is it? How long have I been in here?"

He pulled a watch from his pocket and flipped it open. "I don't know what time you came down, but it is not yet eight o'clock."

Eight? In her time everyone would be up and about by now, business would be open, and the workday officially begun. From the lack of sounds in the house, that was not the case here. At least not among the upper class.

His gaze dropped to her mouth, and lingered for a moment before he looked back at her. Her lips tingled, and she licked them, but the tingle stayed.

He cleared his throat and moved his shoulders as if his coat didn't fit. For the first time since he walked in, she thought he seemed uncomfortable.

She hurried into speech. "Where I come from, we usually rise early and I wasn't sure what the arrangements were for breakfast and there was no one around to ask, so I stopped in here to read for a while."

His lips curved in a faint smile. "I can certainly show you where the food is. You need not hide out and wait." He stepped back from the doorway, and extended his arm in invitation. "Follow me, and I will take you." He looked past her and his gaze drifted down to something behind her. "Leave the papers where they are. The servants will take care of them."

No one picked up after her at home. If she wanted things tidied, she had to do the job herself, and it was hard to walk away from the unfolded newspaper. Her fingers itched to pick it up and put it back to the neatness she had found it in, but Fairfax waited.

They walked side by side along the same route as the group had taken last night, across the foyer, past that wonderful staircase, and into the dining room.

It looked much different today. Morning sun lightened the burgundy walls, and the grey velvet curtains were only partially open, as if the morning sun was too bright for the eyes this early in the day. The heavily carved sideboard with its still-closed doors now held serving plates of food, starting with simple rolls and a choice of jams including marmalade.

She hated marmalade. Her father loved the stuff, one more reason to despise it. Her gaze went past to the rest of the food, small plates of bacon, and beyond that, eggs. The room was empty except for her host and herself.

Plates were stacked at the near side, and the beverages were at the far end. Tea, she could tell that much from the classically shaped teapot sitting after the eggs. A second pot, silver, taller, high-spouted, with a wooden handle, sat next to the teapot.

From some hidden recess of her mind, Grace thought, *chocolate*.

She must have seen one in another of her flea-market trips, been told what it was, to be so certain.

Chocolate for breakfast. Her mouth started to water. She picked up a plate and started down the row of food. A roll with jam—but not marmalade—some bacon, eggs, and on to that lovely silver pot. Two sizes of cups sat between the two pots, one taller with a flaring rim and no handle, the other a typical elegant teacup.

She couldn't carry the plate and a cup with no handle, so she turned to the long table, set her laden plate down, and went back for the bigger cup and the chocolate pot.

Fairfax gave her a strange look, but let her pour out the—yes indeed—chocolate while he poured his own tea. "You like chocolate?"

She smiled at him. "Oh, yes. Very much. I like it best as candy."

"Candy?" His brows furrowed, but he followed her to the table and set down his plate and cup to pull out a chair. "Where are the footmen?" he muttered, then took his own seat.

When it came to the subject of chocolate, Grace was not easily distracted, and answered his question. "Yes, of course, candy. Bars with nuts, bars without nuts, stuffed with nougat or mint, I take chocolate however I can. The only kind I'm not fond of is with the cherries inside."

"America is certainly a land of wonder, then." Fairfax took a bite of his bacon, and chewed quietly, his eyes on hers as he ate.

Chocolate candy was a wonder? She must have done it again, letting slip something out of time. And he was waiting for her to keep talking.

There were plenty of other subjects that wouldn't get her in trouble. "I can see a little woods from my window. Might I take a walk there?"

He swallowed his latest mouthful, dabbed at his lips with the napkin, and shook his head. "Not alone, if you please. I trust most of my guests, but poachers have been found on my land. If you want to go for a walk, I will escort you." He lifted his cup of tea, and held it in front of his mouth as he added, "It is the least I can do for a guest."

Grace felt her lips curve up, for two reasons. She was going to get out of the house again and even see that lovely woods, and he still considered her a guest.

The trees were thicker than she had guessed, a helpful screen from curious eyes. A path of stones led through them, luring her along as she followed Fairfax. She paused several times to enjoy the scents, the sharpness of the spiny-leaved hedges, the freshness of clean ground, the sweetness of woodsy flowers, and from a distance, the heavier, darker whiffs of the barn and stables.

The air was so free of pollution and city smells that breathing was almost painful. It was like a blind person suddenly receiving sight, one fragrance after another came at her with such clarity, and in such profusion. Some scents she knew, others she did not, but this little woods had to have been laid out by a very skilled gardener with great thought to the pleasures of the seasons.

Grace stopped at the small clusters of flowers as she walked, and picked a blossom here and there. Not many, not enough to mar the display, just enough to press between the pages of a book and keep her memory fresh.

Assuming she could bring them back.

The trees led up a small rise, and at the top they suddenly ended, leaving the view unobstructed. The hill sloped down to a pond at the bottom, small enough that a bridge crossed from one side to the other. Water lilies floated on the surface, and reeds swayed in clumps around the edge. A bird skimmed just above the ripples, leaving its image for a fleeting moment on the water before it soared again into the sky.

On the far side of the pond, a pavilion only large enough for two delicate iron chairs and a matching table marked a perfect picnic spot.

Nothing sat on the table, but she could imagine it laid out for a couple, and pictured them taking a few minutes away from the children while the nannies and governesses took their turn.

She envied the woman who would have the right to sit here and enjoy this beautiful place.

10

Garrett glanced down at his guest, then his gaze caught. She looked . . . wistful, standing there in a soft green gown, her braided hair in a loose knot obviously not done by a skilled maid, a small cluster of flowers in her hand.

She was truly lovely, surrounded by the greenery and lit by the early morning sun. He could forget about the mystery that surrounded her, that she was American and here uninvited and unexplained. And perhaps the biggest worry of all, forget that her grandfather might be Robert Cokewell.

If simple hair and eye resemblance were to be believed.

At this moment, with the two of them alone, the sun rising and the greenery as her backdrop, he had the chance to find out more about her. Perhaps she would talk now that there was little chance of being interrupted. "It is a lovely morning, is it not?"

She looked up at him with those striking brown eyes, smiled and said, "It is." Waving her hand to encompass the scenery, she added, "How lucky you are to have your own park."

He accepted the praise with a quick bow of his head. "I agree. I am most fortunate." Movement in the distance caught his eye, and he leaned closer. In a low voice, he said, "Turn around slowly, and look to your right. There's a doe and two fawns. They're getting bigger now, but they will be with their mother for another year."

Instead of keeping his eye on the doe, he watched Miss Grace turn the direction he pointed. "My father didn't punish the poachers on our land, just chased them off, but so many of our deer were shot that it took us years to even begin to rebuild the herd. Now I have men regularly patrol to stop them."

Her dark eyes, so remarkable with that light hair, softened. "Animals are being destroyed at an alarming rate. We have that problem in America, and it's awful. The buffalo were nearly wiped out, and now we're losing"—she froze for an instant—"we're losing so much of the pristine landscape that was here before."

"Buffalo?" The word was new to him.

She bit her lip and hesitated, staring off into space before bringing her gaze back to him. That shadowed look flicked away almost at once. "It is a giant wild bull."

"Giant? Are you not safer with it gone, then?"

The shadows left her eyes, and the light of a crusader came back. "That's the problem. It's so short-sighted. The ecol—well, nature is all interconnected. When one species is wiped out, another depended on it for survival then dies. And whatever depended on *that* one dies off. It's like dominoes." She smiled, despite the seriousness of her subject. "That's why it's such a good idea that you save those deer. I feel bad for the villagers who used them for food, but there must be something else they can find. Maybe there are streams nearby for fish. Someday someone will find out how vital your rare deer are, and if there are none left, well, it'll be too late to fix it then."

He felt himself staring at her, but could not look away. "You are a rare woman, Miss Grace. I have not met another woman in London, however well-taught, who concerned herself with the interconnectedness of nature, as you call it. It is not something that interests women. Most women, at least."

She frowned, although it was more of a glare. "Perhaps you never asked. Women are interested in a lot of things, more than you would expect."

He *felt* his spine stiffen. "I have several sisters. I assure you, I am well aware of what interests women, and I have never heard them talk about such things. They are concerned with their families and houses, as they should be."

Miss Grace's eyes snapped fire. "Families are houses are all very well, but women are capable of more than that. Are your women allowed to attend college? Have careers? Own businesses? Because in America . . . they do."

What was behind that little pause? He let the remark about attending university pass. Surely she was exaggerating. "I am not sure what you mean by 'careers' for women, but women work in England. We have modistes, and bonnet makers, weavers and lace makers. In every village, I am certain you will find women providing valuable services. Not to mention the governesses and nurses. So we are not as backward as you think when valuing our women."

Her brows came down in a fierce scowl, and she opened her mouth, then seemed to think better of it because she shut it without saying anything. Her hands clenched into fists, and he stifled a smile. He could almost see the steam coming out her ears. She turned back to stare at the deer as if they were a welcome distraction from the building disagreement.

For such an opinionated woman, she seemed to give up too easily. A smile tugged at his mouth. "Nothing to add? No other criticisms?"

Miss Grace grimaced. "Nothing that won't get me into trouble, and I suspect I'm in enough trouble already."

"Trouble? Hardly. An exchange of opinions is always welcome conversation." He looked back at the deer. Something spooked them. Their heads came up almost in unison, and they fled back into the safety of the wood.

Now that the distraction was gone, he glanced down at her, to find her staring at him, a small furrow lingering between her brows. "Are all American women like you?" He cocked his head and waited for the answer.

In a startling change from a breath ago, she began laughing, harder than the question called for, but once she started Grace seemed unable or unwilling to stop. "Yes," she gasped out, "they are. Pretty much."

Fairfax took a step back. There must be some joke he was not supposed to understand. He did not enjoy having anyone use him for humor. "Perhaps America has something to teach us, then."

Her laughter finally trailed off, but her brown eyes still held the traces of her mirth. Her rosy lips were soft and full, the tension that so often pulled at her mouth eased. He had not seen anyone laugh like that in a while, and was glad he was the one to pull it out of her.

He thought of the young men back at the house. Whose idea was it to leave her here unchaperoned where she could so easily be compromised?

No carriage had arrived with anyone that looked like her. He knew because he had asked the staff, discreetly of course; that was the reason he had risen so early. No one had carried luggage in for her nor had a carriage arrived that was unaccounted for. And yet she had a new gown on today, not the right kind for a morning walk but she was an American. She was unfamiliar with England, and its customs.

Garrett realized he was staring at those brown eyes again. Madeline and Jones had seen the same resemblance to Cokewell, but they both might be reading too much into coincidence. Or the man might have by-blows, and she could easily be one. The mere resemblance to Cokewell's daughters did not make her presence unannounced at his house party acceptable.

He had been putting this off, but it was time to find out just who she was. "We are unlikely to be interrupted, and I need some answers. For both our sakes, neither of us is leaving this glade until I get them."

Her eyes widened, and he saw a shadow of fear fill them. "I've given you all the answers I can." But she did not hold his gaze, instead looked past him. The frown came back.

"Is that so?" He folded his arms and braced his legs. Madeline had often laughed at him when he did his "lord of the manor" pose. Hopefully, it worked better on Miss Grace than it did on his sister. "You told me about your father, but who was his father? What about your mother? Who was she?"

Even though he did not like what he was about to say, he had a responsibility to his family and his guests. "I promise you, if I am not satisfied with the answers, you will not be staying."

Grace met his gaze, and what she saw knocked any untoward emotions out of her mind. He was not joking. What would happen, where would she go, if he threw her out? She was nobody!

A name suddenly popped into her mind, one burned into the bottom of the jewelry chest she had inherited from her grandmother, a little carved chest with tattered red velvet lining still fastened to the wood under tacks that had once held it in place. Grammy always claimed it had come down in the family, but the name on the chest's bottom wasn't Harding. How Grammy knew it was a family heirloom, she had never said.

Grace often wondered if it had been stolen or sold, or pawned or purchased sometime in the late eighteen hundreds, or early nineteen hundreds. That would still make it an heirloom, just not from their family. But Grammy had always insisted . . .

It was all Grace had. "Cokewell."

He went still, his face losing all expression so quickly that Grace knew that name meant something. In a quiet voice, he asked, "Would that be Robert Cokewell?"

"I only know the one name, Cokewell. Nothing else."

His hands clenched, the knuckles going pale with the force of his grip.

Grace had the sneaking suspicion she had tumbled into something bigger than she could handle. If only Grammy had been more knowledgeable about the family history! "I don't know. No one ever talked about it."

No one ever talked about it? Someone that influential, a connection so desirable, and even in America no one ever said anything about it?

Unless she was a by-blow; then, yes, he could see the family not discussing it.

Cokewell. Jones and Madeline had good instincts. His butler would not dream of gloating about the accuracy of his suspicions, but Madeline had no such restraint, and she would taunt him about his ignorance at every opportunity.

His arms were tight. No wonder, as he realized his hands were clenched. Garrett forced himself to loosen his fists, lest he frighten her, and tried to remember the stories he had heard from his father about this family.

There had been something about a younger daughter . . . how long ago was that? Cokewell was not titled, but had so much influence he could have been. The rumor was that the Prince had tried several times to force a title on him, and each time Cokewell had managed to avoid it. It took quite a man to stand up to Prinny.

Madeline mentioned a daughter who ran off with someone unsuitable. He could not remember just how the affair was discovered, hardly remembered anything other than her brief summary, but Madeline did believe the couple married. Which made any children legitimate.

Much better a fate than being a by-blow.

Could the runaway daughter have a child the age of Grace?

His uninvited guest silently watched him, her face innocent. Worry etched a tightness around her eyes and mouth.

To have a daughter flee across the ocean, that was quite a family feud, Garrett thought, but then, few situations like this ended happily. Most of the time, the daughters—or on rare occasions, sons—lived estranged from their parents with no more than a few hundred miles separating them.

He knew a case himself where the daughter lived in the village her parents owned and neither had contact with the other.

America would be a logical refuge for a couple who wished to begin anew.

If Miss Harding's connection to Cokewell was real—and the more he looked at her the more he accepted *some* relation existed—then she had powerful connections. Cokewell's wife had been the youngest daughter of a baron with a lineage that went further back than Garrett's own. With their help, Grace's future would be assured, and she could make the finest match in England.

If that was what she was after.

What if the rift between the family was too severe, and they continued to cast Grace off as thoroughly as they had cut ties with her mother? What resources would she then have? "They sent you over with no one to provide support, no family to contact, no letter of introduction?"

"It would seem so." Her eyes grew larger. American or not, different cultures or not, he suspected she was beginning to understand the true state of her predicament.

"Tell me this. Did your family even think to send you with a maid?"

She shook her head. "I didn't need one there."

He knew how complex women's clothing was. The thought that she had no need of a maid stretched credibility. It was hardly something a man could ask, however. Garrett sighed. "No chaperone, not even a maid."

"No."

His neck felt stiff, his hands clenched. "Why *my* house?"

"This is where I was dropped." She took a quick breath and added, "Off. Dropped off."

"I will see that you get a maid before noon." He raised a finger of warning. "In the meantime, remember: stay with the women." A thought stopped him. "Do you know any of them?"

She gave him a wry smile. "Yes. Your sister. You forget, I met mostly men last night in the dancing."

Wrigley, the pup, might be safe—as long as she had no sense of smell—but Durney? "I will tell Madeline to introduce you to the women. In the meantime, the tale will be that you are a friend of hers, late to the party because of carriage trouble. She will be happy to back up the account."

He had a lot to do, and very little time. Garrett turned and left her there. She would be safe enough for now.

Grace watched him go. His stride was strong and confident, his stature straight and tall. Everything about him oozed self-assurance, a man who knew where he belonged. A man able to take on whatever was thrown at him.

Her situation, though, might be outside his abilities. Still, it was nice to have someone so willing to watch over her. It was awful being this clueless. At least she had being American to explain away her unavoidable blunders.

Get back to the women. Grace turned and left the pretty glade.

The air was still as soft, as pure, as when she first walked out here. The colors of the flowers seemed more vivid, but that might well be due to the sun climbing higher in the sky. At some point, she would love to do more exploring, but that was best done when she had a better idea of the property.

As she drew closer to the big house, she paused to look at the smaller buildings. Not that she ever expected to need the information, but they might make a good place to hide.

Should the need arise.

The biggest one was definitely a stable, she decided, when a whinny rolled out from inside. A group of men mingled outside the carriage house, polishing a sharp blue sporty little horse-drawn two-wheeled thing and exchanging raucous challenges about who would be fastest to the village and back.

She had to admit, the little vehicle had flash.

Men and their wheels! Grace smothered a smile as she crossed the drive and went up the steps toward the big outer doors. No matter what century, give them a vehicle and they couldn't wait to show it off.

Aggravating as it was to be told what to do, Fairfax ordered her to stay with the women, and her situation was precarious enough. Until there was a woman to stay with, her best option was waiting until the house came awake.

She had almost reached her room when one of the doorways suddenly opened, and a woman scurried through, nearly knocking Grace down. They both stood there, hands on hearts, trying to catch their breath in mutual surprise.

"Good morning." The other woman caught her breath first.

"Good morning," Grace echoed.

The woman had a lovely, sweet face, soft green eyes and straight rich dark hair pulled into a loose single braid that someone had wrapped into an intricate knot on her head and tucked under a fancy hairnet-style white bonnet. Her yellow cottony gown had pink flowers and stripes woven into it. Soft white lace edged the bodice, and some kind of filmy top underneath the pretty gown filled any signs of cleavage.

Grace touched her own chest, and wondered if she could get one of those tops to hide the swells of her own breasts.

Smothering a yawn, the woman said, "Is breakfast set out yet? I don't know what it is about being in the country." She smiled, an impish smile, as if they shared a joke. "I always wake before I am ready. I can see you do as well. What time is it?"

"I don't have a clock." Grace felt her own lips curve.

"Nor do I." Eyes that had been bleary a moment ago suddenly sharpened, but the woman's face remained pleasant and friendly. "I noticed you last night, but we were not properly introduced. I am Lily Stratham. My husband is Mr. Stratham. You danced with him last night."

Mr. Stratham? That was a bit formal for a wife to call her husband. Unless this was another of those cultural gaps and a wife could not say her husband's first name in public? Grace dragged her mind back to the conversation. "I don't know any of your dances. I was so busy trying to figure out what to do that I could have danced with a monkey and not noticed."

Lily laughed. "Danced with a monkey." Her laugh softened to a gentle smile. "If that was your first time dancing our English dances, you did well enough for yourself."

Grace noticed her new friend did not say she had done a good job. Just *well enough*. Which could mean anything from *you surprise me with how quickly you learn*, to *at least you didn't land on the floor*.

She gave a quick laugh. "You're being very tactful. Thank you." With a flutter of hope that she might have a new friend, she added, "My name is Grace Harding."

"Miss Grace. What a lovely name. It is a pleasure to meet you. I was on my way to get something for breakfast. Will you like to join me?"

"Thank you, but I've already eaten." As soon as the words were out of her mouth, Grace realized this was the perfect opportunity to gather as much information about this time as possible. Having an ally

—and a woman, and possible friend—would help tremendously. "I would love to join you. We can become better acquainted."

"Excellent!" Her new friend wasn't in much of a hurry to get down to eat. Instead of heading for the staircase, she asked another question. "Is this your first season? I don't believe I've seen you at any of the balls in London. You have the most delightful way of speaking."

"You wouldn't have seen me. Last night was my first party since arriving. And I'm from America."

Lily looked at her in surprise. "America! You don't sound like any of the other Americans I've met." No suspicion, just bright-eyed curiosity.

This could be a problem. "So you've met other Americans?"

The woman laughed, a bright sparkling tinkle. "Not many, I assure you, but some, like you, do come over despite the threats of war. I can sympathize with your country about impressment, I understand how loyal your people are after fighting so hard for your liberty, but I hate the thought of rushing off into another war so soon. War seems such a terrible way to settle difficulties, don't you think?"

One thing Grace did remember about the War of 1812 was impressment, British ships stealing American sailors off vessels at sea and forcing the men into brutal naval service, where whipping was common for even minor infractions. Thank goodness America won that war! Not the thing to say to an Englishwoman, though. She kept her reply vague. "Yes, it seems there must be a better way than bloodshed. Always."

Lily shuddered. "That is too dark a subject for such a bright day. Since you've already eaten, you can tell me all about what it is like to be an American. I always think of your country as a wild place, full of dangerous beasts, if you will forgive me. I am eager to be set straight."

Almost certainly Minnesota doesn't exist yet, Grace thought, and floundered for something to say that had a chance of being accurate. "There is wilderness, but we have cities and roads just like you do."

Lily still made no move to walk toward the staircase. "Tell me, how have you found England? I hope you are well-treated." She did not wait for an answer, but twisted to scan the empty hallway yet again, then leaned closer, as if afraid someone would overhear. "I must confess, I long to travel, but my husband is not fond of sailing. I envy you."

Grace said the only *thing that came to* mind. "I like traveling." Most travel, that is. Her mouth kept going. "This trip was quite a journey."

"I can imagine. All the way across the ocean! Did it take a long time?"

"No." A giggle threatened. "It was surprisingly fast."

"That is good to hear." Lily's eyes twinkled again. "Fairfax seems to be quite taken with you. You have made quite a conquest there." She sobered."I should warn you, you will soon discover you have a lot of competition. Every unwed woman here came specifically to set their cap on him. The other men are just to even the numbers, I vow."

She leaned close to Grace and spoke in a low tone. "Lord Fairfax hosts the most divine parties." She smiled, and even though Grace knew the woman wanted juicy gossip to spread, she couldn't help but like her. "My husband says we won't go back for another week, although I do miss my babies."

"You have children?"

"Yes. Three. It is my first time leaving them for so long, but we received this invitation and I just had to get away. The nurse is very well trained, so they are in good hands." She took a deep breath, and rested her hand on her chest as if to calm her heart. "I hope you will forgive my boldness. I know it is frightfully presumptuous of me, but one of the first things you must learn as long as you are in England is that women are judged—perhaps too much—by their clothes. No doubt in America it is different, but here, even in a country party, proprieties must be observed."

Grace felt her hand move to cover her cleavage. Her face heated, and she knew from long experience that her face just turned red. "I suspect I'm wearing the wrong gown for walking around. This is a ballgown, isn't it?"

Lily caught her hand and gave it a quick squeeze before releasing it. "I did not mean to embarrass you. Please do not think that. I wish only to be helpful. Yes, your gown is more appropriate for the evening. No, the important thing is that you forgot your fichu," Lily said, and plucked at the delicate top under her gown, filling everything in up to her neck. "Don't they wear them in America?"

"Not where I'm from." Honesty was always nice, but it was going to be hard to keep track of which truths she had shared. "I don't know what clothes I have here."

"I always oversee the packing. Perhaps your maid packed it for you. Shall we go check? If not, you can borrow one of mine. And might I suggest that you change from a ball gown to a day dress? You don't want anyone to consider you overdressed for breakfast." Lily looked so eager to help that Grace could only smile. She might well learn the terms for all her clothes, and how to wear them. "Let's see what you have before we go down." Lily gestured toward Grace's door.

"Yes, let's." She stepped across the hall to her own room with Lily.

11

Garrett strode across the drive and up the stairs to the front doors. First things first, he had to alert Madeline. Then Jones.

Maybe Jones first.

The door swung open before he reached it, to his disappointment. He rather looked forward to flinging its heavy weight open, anything to drain the tension that burned through his veins, and set his muscles jumping. One of the footmen stood there. "Where is Jones?" The question came out too harsh, and Garrett forced himself to take a breath.

"He is dealing with the servants in the kitchen at the moment, my lord."

"Get him, please. Tell him to meet me in my office. And send my sister's maid to find her. Don't wake Lady Cavenaugh if she is sleeping, but if she is up, please ask her to join me."

The office door clicked shut behind him, closing him in the masculine setting. He walked over and threw back the dark green curtains to let in the morning light. The small fireplace on the right wall was dead on this summer day, but the ashes beneath the freshly laid logs reminded him that it could get cold in the evening.

He felt a bit chilled now. An American in his house when tensions were so high between their nations, and the complication of her possible connection to Cokewell.

Garrett sat down at the large, ornate desk where he did all the business involved in managing his property. His boots made a nice sound on the wooden floor, but the rich green and gold rug muffled the rest of his steps. He let out the groan he had been holding in.

An unchaperoned American with connections to his father's closest friend—not to mention a man with the Prince's ear. He glanced over at the cabinet on the wall opposite the fireplace, and thought of the decanters and glasses he had locked away inside for the duration of the party. No. Right now he needed his wits about him.

There had been not a single hint of her presence until she showed up in his library yesterday. Every guest was accounted for except her. She hadn't ridden in any carriage, or with any guest, according to his most-observant butler.

The tap at the door pulled him away from his thoughts. He straightened. "Enter."

Jones stepped in, and pulled the heavy door shut behind him. It hardly made a sound under his careful touch. "You sent for me, my lord?"

"Yes, Jones. You were right about the woman. I asked her for a family name, and she did indeed say Cokewell." He frowned. "She seems to know little to nothing about the man. Her own grandfather. Doesn't that strike you as odd?"

Jones's shoulders lifted in the hint of a shrug, then settled back in his usual stance. "Perhaps not, sir. If the rift was big enough in the family, I would rather be surprised if she *had* heard of the man."

"America is not on the moon, Jones, and Cokewell is not unknown. Surely she would have been told *something*. Her parents could hardly keep such a connection a secret."

Jones shook his head. "You did say she knows the name. She might have been forbidden to speak of him if her parents were worried that he might reject her as they had been."

"If that is the case, why send her over here at all? And now that she is here, I must presume on that connection. I have no choice. She was left in my home without a chaperone. Whoever brought her over from America did not see fit to stay and ensure her welcome."

Jones gave no sign of being surprised. "I had not noticed one myself. I have accounted for all the servants."

The drumming of fingers intruded, and Garrett looked down at his desk. The sound came from him. He stilled his hands. "It gets worse. We need to find her a maid. Americans! Not only has she no chaperone, she does not have a maid."

One quick, satisfied nod from his butler. "I suspected as much. I did not notice an extra one of those, either."

"Find her a lady's made right away. The sooner she gets one, the greater the chance of saving both our reputations."

"Yes, sir. Do you have any preference which type of woman? Older, younger?"

For the first time since entering the house, Garrett felt a smile tug at his mouth. "I believe our unwelcome guest would much prefer someone closer to her own age, but an older woman would lend more respectability to our situation. Plus, a woman with more experience would likely know how to keep her mouth shut. We don't have time to send out for one, so we will have to make do with the staff here. See who you can find among the staff."

"I will see if I have someone who will suit. I might not have a mature woman available, however. Most of our maids are young, in order to be strong enough to do the hardest chores."

Garrett shrugged. "Do the best you can. The most important thing is discretion."

"Of course, my lord." Jones gave a quick bow, and walked out the door, pulling it as quietly behind him as ever.

He had done as much as he could for now. Garrett stared down at the paper in front of him. Madeline had still not made an appearance, although it had hardly been enough time for her to put herself together. Female input would be helpful right now.

How did one ask such a well-known man if he had a missing granddaughter? And what if he did not? Blonde hair and brown eyes, while unusual, were not unheard of.

If word got out about an unaccompanied female in his house, and his guests learned they had shared the house with such a woman, he might start the rumors he was hoping to prevent. His father would be horrified, and it would not do his own reputation any good. The ripples would reach as far as his sisters, even if they had not been here. Just the fact that their brother had sunk so low would be enough to stain the whole family.

He looked back down at the blank paper on his desk and scowled. Cokewell had to be notified, the letter had to be written. He dipped the quill into the inkwell, and tapped off the excess.

Dear Sir: I hope this letter finds you well. My father sends his greetings.

He did not need to ask his father first. If his father knew he had written Cokewell and *not* sent well-wishes, he would be most disappointed.

Garrett looked at the measly sentences, sighed, and got into the heart of his message.

I have a young guest here at my house party who claims a relationship with you, although she has made no move to presume on the connection. She is an American, with the surname of Harding, and is unwed. There are several things that convince me there might be some merit in her assertions. She is blonde, of average height, and has curly hair, but with brown eyes. I would put her age at twenty or a bit more.

I do not know if any of these facts are familiar to you, but I beg your assistance in determining her true identity.

Sincerely,

Garrett Atherton, Earl of Fairfax

There. It was done. A quick roll of the blotter to dry the excess ink, and he sealed it and set it on the edge of his desk with his other correspondence. His mail would go out with unusual dispatch today.

He turned around and pulled the cord for Jones. The man was there so fast Garrett wondered if he'd been waiting outside. "See to it that this letter gets mailed today."

"Yes, my lord. I will see it done." Jones took the folded paper.

"And Jones? Is my sister up yet?"

"I believe so. Her maid was just in the kitchen for her tea." Under that rigid exterior, he could tell Jones was surprised that he would even have to ask.

"She gave no indication when Lady Cavenaugh would be down?"

"No, sir."

"Send a maid with the request that Lady Cavenaugh join me when she is ready. I will await her here."

Jones nodded, and stepped outside, shutting the door behind him.

His day's work, the record of rent payments and the latest on the crop report, were finished when the tap came on the door. "Come," he called, and Madeline entered with a whisper of her day gown, some flowered thing in a pale blue. Under her white cap, her hair was lightly put up, a sign she did not give her maid much time to style it.

She looked a touch green this morning. "Are you well?"

Madeline sank into the nearest chair, and slumped, not her usual posture at all. A hand drifted toward her belly. "This coming babe is making me positively ill in the mornings."

"You did not need to make the journey from London at all, if this is going to be a trial for you." He rose and came around the desk, to sit in the other chair. "I know Mother put you up to coming. You should have told her to come herself if she was so anxious to see me wed."

She smiled, a pale version of her normal cheerfulness. "But how much fun would it be having your mother watch over you as all the debutantes on her list vied for your attention?"

Garrett winced. "True, but I hate to see you so under the weather."

She patted his hand. "It does not last long. The rest of the day, I feel perfectly fine." Then she leaned back in the chair, looking for all the world like a monarch waiting to be entertained. "So why did you send for me?"

"Our uninvited guest? Miss Grace?" Madeline nodded. "You and Jones were right. She does claim some relationship with Cokewell. But there is a mystery there, because though she knows the name, she insists she knows nothing more. What do you think of something like that? Is the tale too absurd to be real? To know the name yet not know of the man?"

A frown furrowed Madeline's brow. "She *is* American. Perhaps the man's fame has not reached across the ocean." The frown deepened. "It is strange that she came here, to you. Why not go directly to his house?"

"You did say there was some family rift. Should I write Mother? No doubt she knows of the situation."

Madeline straightened. "No! Do not spread the tale any further. If you are going to write, go directly to Cokewell. If the rift is as I remember hearing, he would not appreciate it going beyond the two of you." She caught herself. "Well, the three of you. We must presume Miss Grace knows at least something. Her discretion speaks well of her."

Garrett smiled. "I have already written Cokewell what I know of her, and given her description. Jones is sending my missive. Now we wait." He leaned back, mimicking her posture of a moment ago. "Are you up to playing a role?"

Her brows lifted this time, a switch from the frown. "Role?"

"A minor stratagem. I need you to play her friend. If anyone asks, you invited her."

A light came on in her eyes, offsetting the lingering green of her skin. "What a wonderful idea! We can say she was late. Perhaps her carriage broke down on the way. People saw us talking at the dance last night. It should not be hard to convince everyone that we are at least acquaintances."

"The very thing." He rubbed his jaw. "The American issue is difficult, but not insurmountable."

Her brows came back together, and she stared off into space. "That is true. How would we have met?"

"Perhaps we can convince her to say we met in London." She did not sound confident.

He shook his head. "Too much chance of her making a mistake. I am certain she has never been there. At a guess, her ship came in on the west side of England, and she was on her way to London when she was left here."

Garrett felt his hands curl into fists, and forced them to relax. "I wish I could break through her loyalty to escorts. She will not tell me their names, but that might work in our favor. If she will not tell me, she will not expose them to anyone else."

The room was quiet for a moment, only the ticking of his mantel clock and the soft sound of their breaths, before Madeline said, slow and hesitant, "Unless you see an objection, a broken carriage is believable. She might welcome our plot. It would release her from this need to protect those who left her here."

He leaned forward, elbows on his thighs. "There is that remarkable resemblance to Cokewell. If we noticed it, others will also."

"But if he denies her . . ."

Garrett stood. "We will deal with that when and if it happens. No one will blame us for presuming she belonged to him." He looked down at her. "I do love you. Thank you for your support in this." He held out his hand to help her rise.

She smiled up at him as she put her hand in his. "I will find her, and explain the plan." He eased her to her feet, and she brushed down her skirt, wiping away the creases. "Cokewell might surprise us and claim her."

"So Miss Grace is here until the party is over. She is an interesting woman." Madeline's eyes twinkled up at him. "I have seen you with her several times, more than any of the other debutantes. She is not so young and green as they, which is one of your complaints. I found her company pleasant last night."

She slipped her hand through his elbow. "I think I can eat now. Take me to the dining room?"

As he reached for the doorknob, his sister giggled. "What a match it would be if our family and Cokewell's were united in marriage."

He glared at her. "Don't get ideas in your head. I will play the gracious host, but that is all. The party will end in a week or so, I will go back to London, and you can write Mother that you did your best."

12

Lily examined the bulging armoire, the rainbow of colors. "Such a wealth of gowns!" She pushed them around, catching any that fell off the hooks, checking them over, and then rejecting one after another, until one of them caught her eye. "Here, this is what you want." Grace caught a flash of pink as Lily flung it onto the bed. "Let's get you unlaced."

Grace obligingly turned her back and felt the gown begin to slide off her shoulders. A gasp came from behind.

"You don't have stays on!" When she looked back over her shoulder, Lily's brows were puckered in a frown. "I know some women *choose* to go without, it is more respectable to wear one. You are new to England, but this is your first lesson. Always wear stays. No matter how forgiving the gown."

"Stays?" Grace glanced down at the short slip she wore, the sum total of her underclothes. "Do you mean the corset?" After the struggle to get out of it last night, she was going to be stuffed back in?

It seemed so, because Lily spotted it where Grace had tossed it. "Oh, Grace, no woman likes them, but you cannot walk about without being properly dressed." She walked behind Grace. "Raise your arms and let me get this on you."

Grace sighed, more of a groan, but she muffled it enough to make it sound like a cough, and complied. She felt a faint tugging and the corset—or stays, she guessed she would have to get used to calling them that—lifted higher against the slip-like undergarment as Lily pulled the strings. Oh, for a simple bra that only went around her breasts, Grace thought, as the stays tightened against her ribs and waist, and she felt her posture straighten as the boning forced her into stiffness. Lily grunted from behind and the tugging stopped. Grace had to smile at the odd noise.

The other woman came around the front and gave a nod. "There. Much better. Now for the fichu and gown, and you will be ready for the day."

With surprising efficiency, Lily had her in the lace fichu cleavage-cover and the pink dress, all the fasteners fastened. It was exactly the kind of gown she had always wanted to own but never had a place to wear, a floor-length diaphanous weave of muslin in a spring pink color over a slender petticoat of the same color, decorated with embroidered yellow flowers—no doubt all done by hand—layers of filmy fabric floating around her legs. Not as much fun as the beautiful gown she had taken off, but lighter and flowy. She twisted from side to side, enjoying the drift of the fabric.

Lily smiled. "It is very fine fabric. Very expensive." Then she became brisk again. "You should have something on your head, too. Let me see what you brought." She pulled open one of the drawers at the bottom of the armoire. "Ah, yes, exactly the thing."

Out came a ruffled thing, a little cap covered in embroidery with a silk ribbon that must tighten it. "How do I keep this on? Is there a front and a back? Or doesn't it matter?"

Lily's brows rose. "You don't wear caps in America?"

"Sometimes, but only to protect the head against sun, and nothing this fancy." She thought about the baseball cap, and a giggle threatened in her throat, imagining wearing this fancy ruffly thing at a ball game, or even working in the garden.

"Here, let me show you. Sit down and I'll get it fixed, and then we can go to breakfast." Lily waved toward the little dressing table chair, and there was nothing to do but sit.

Lily clucked her disapproval. "I think your hair is coming down. Let me get my maid. Stay here."

Grace grinned. "Aye, aye, captain."

With a strange look and uncertain smile, Lily slipped out the door. Grace touched her hair. Sure enough, pins were coming loose all over. No doubt some lay scattered around the path in the woods, and on the stairs.

A moment later, Lily reappeared with a young woman in simple clothes and a tentative smile. "Here's my maid, Jane. We will have your hair all fixed in no time."

Jane turned her around, and set to work. Every remaining pin came out, forming a pile on the dressing table, the leather strip came off from her braid, and nimble fingers unbraided the whole thing. Watching in the mirror, Grace was enthralled at the magic of the young woman's skill. New braids took shape, wrapping around her sides and up her crown, going around and around until only the curly ends remained, a soft hair crown.

"You should have brought your scissors to trim her front," Lily scolded her maid as she watched from the side. "Her hair is so curly it would make a perfect frame for her face. Don't you agree?"

"No!" Grace blurted out the word even though the conversation hadn't included her. She didn't care for bangs. With her curls they became frizzy fluff, and she had no intention of going back with them.

"No?" Lily's brows went up. "They are all the rage."

How to explain? "They might be the rage here, but not where I'm from."

"Oh, very well, but they would look so nice." Lily handed Jane the cap, and it fitted neatly over the curly braided bun the maid had created. "There! Now we are ready to go down."

The maid waited for them to leave, silent as a statue, and slipped out behind them.

They walked together into the dining room, and Grace stopped short. Fairfax and his sister—what *was* her name again?—sat side by side at the near end of the long table, a cup of milk and a plate with bread and jam in front of her, and a cup of steaming tea in front of him. Both looked up at their entrance. Color rushed up the sister's face, and his expression went blank.

Almost as if they had been caught talking about her, Grace thought, and was sure she was right.

"Oh, Madeline! How lovely to see you." Lily's greeting was so effusive they might not have seen each other in months rather than the night before.

"Lily, Miss Grace. Please, join us." Madeline waved to the chairs directly opposite.

Grace turned to Lily. "Go ahead and get your food. I'll just sit." She remembered the chocolate, and looked down the line of food. Sure enough, the fancy silver chocolate pot still sat there. "After I get some chocolate."

She might be overdoing it, but without her fix of modern sweets, this was as good as she was going to get.

When she sat down, Fairfax looked at the cup, and then up at her. A faint smile quirked one side of his mouth. "I am pleased you like my chef's chocolate."

Without thinking, she made a teasing face, wrinkling her nose at him. "I like chocolate no matter how I get it."

"I know." He raised his cup to cover his mouth. And to hide the smile she was certain lurked there.

Madeline gave him a quick look. "You do? And how did you learn that?"

"Miss Grace and I were both up early this morning. The food had been laid out, so we joined each other for breakfast. She has already taken a walk outside." He glanced at his sister. "She is not one for sleeping late."

Lily looked between Fairfax and herself. Grace could see the wheels turning in her brain. "The fresh country air does the same for me. I was just telling Miss Grace that very thing."

Fairfax bowed his head in acknowledgement. "So it does. I find myself rising earlier than usual here, as well." He looked down at his sister. "Would you like to take Miss Grace out for a tour of my garden?"

Madeline smiled brightly. Too brightly? "The very thing for a perfect start to the day."

He turned his gaze on Lily. "Mrs. Stratham, your husband expressed an interest in my horseflesh. Would you mind telling him that I have time this morning, if he still wishes to see them?"

Lily gave Grace a quick, apologetic glance. "Certainly, my lord. I will do that as soon as we are done eating."

"Thank you." He went back to slipping his tea, and watching Grace.

Something was going on. The chocolate tasted more bitter than it had a moment ago.

Conversation was desultory. "Lovely dance last night," Lily said. "Your musicians were quite good."

"Thank you. I hired them from London. Even musicians need a break from the dirty air." He took another sip of tea.

Sooner or later, the cup would be empty, Grace thought. He was only using it as a screen for his expressions. Yes, something was definitely going on.

"I admire your cook." Madeline this time. "The bread is delicious. What kind of jam is this?"

He gave his sister another strange look. "Elderberry."

"Oh. Of course it is. Your chef must add a little something to it to enhance the flavor."

"I would hardly know." He actually set the teacup down this time, and rose. "I am off to the stables." A bow to Lily. "Mrs. Stratham, if you would give your husband my message, I would be delighted to see him."

Madeline gave a teasing wiggle of the fingers, and unless Grace missed her guess, a wink. "Good. Now that he is gone, we women can enjoy a good gossip."

The chocolate in Grace's stomach seemed to turn into lead. A good gossip, after all the meaningful looks and the made-up excuse to send Lily off on an absurd errand so she couldn't join them in the garden.

What did he suspect? And now Madeline was in his misgivings, too. A pity, because she really liked his sister. Lying to him was hard enough, lying to her would be more difficult. She had slipped up, mentioning buffalo, women and careers, and who knew what else?

"Let's go to the garden." A footman appeared from nowhere and pulled out her chair. "The garden is beautiful."

Grace felt a footman behind her, the faint vibration as he set his hands on the chair's back, and started to rise. The chair slipped away and she found herself following Madeline and Lily out of the room.

"I had best give Lord Fairfax's message to my husband right away, before he makes other plans." Lily turned toward the stairs.

"We will see you later." Madeline continued down the hallway that passed the library.

Grace had not gone further than that door, and her curiosity overrode her nerves. There was nothing much to see, just a short hallway barely longer than the library itself with a heavy paneled door at the end. Daylight streamed through a fan-shaped transom window above the door, both welcoming and warning in a golden glow.

Madeline opened the door, and motioned Grace to follow. "This is the best place for us to talk. We can hear anyone coming."

She didn't want anyone to hear what they said? Grace's spine stiffened. The looks, the ploy to get Lily out of the way, and now, a conversation Madeline didn't want overheard. She looked at the red roses climbing up trellises that she had not seen on her other trip through the garden, trellises that formed a beautiful wall of blooms around them. Yes, this location was chosen on purpose. "What are we going to talk about?"

Madeline walked a few steps further, and looked back. "Yes, this is a good place." She stopped and turned to Grace. "We need to invent a story on how you got here." She raised a hand. "My brother tells me you are protecting your escorts. I will not force you to betray them, but questions will be asked."

"What kind of questions?" Grace's fingers tingled, as if her nerves were so alarmed they pressed against her skin.

"How did we meet? You are an American. How could I meet an American? Particularly since you are connected to Cokewell. The resemblance is striking."

Despite her unease, that tidbit stopped her. "It is?"

A smile tipped Madeline's mouth. "Yes. Your blonde hair and brown eyes? That is a Cokewell trait. All of his daughters have the same things. Not all of the grandchildren inherited them, but enough did. We can pick them out in a crowd."

"Oh." Maybe there was some connection to England, then, and Grammy's stories were true. She needed to know more. "What is he like? Cokewell?"

Madeline's eyes went wide. "You truly do not know him? Garrett said you did not, but"—she looked around—"Good, there is no one around to hear." She reached out and touched Grace's arm, a fleeting gesture of appeal. "If you are hiding a family secret, you can tell me. I promise I will keep your confidence."

They might want another answer, but she only had one to give.

"Honestly, I know absolutely nothing beyond that one name. My"—she caught herself before she said *grandmother*, which in this time would be the wife of the man in question, not the one she had known as a child—"mother has a box, and the name is on the bottom. She told me it was a family heirloom. I know nothing else." She could add the tale of the groom and the daughter, but the mere mention of a groom, a lesser class, mingling with the blue blood of the wealth surrounding her, held her back.

"Oh dear." Madeline bit her lip. "That might be a problem."

"Why?" She did *not* need any more problems.

"My brother has written Cokewell. We should hear back in a couple days." Her head tilted, sympathy warmed her pale green eyes. "We do not know what his reaction will be to finding he has an . . . American granddaughter?" She made the relationship a question, as if uncertain whether Grace might be a product of a more recent liaison and be a daughter instead.

Grace said nothing, she couldn't speak, her breath felt trapped in her throat. *He had written the man?* What was he thinking? More precisely, what had *she* been thinking? She never should have used that name on the jewelry box!

"Well." Madeline became brisk. "You are here. We must make the best of the situation. For now, you and I must concoct a way we might have met, and stick to the story."

"Ah." Concoct a lie, then. Would lying make the time genies angry? And would that make it more or less likely for her to stay?

She had to leave this in Madeline's capable hands, because she didn't even know how to describe what might have—should have—brought her here. She had never even been in a carriage, nor ridden a horse, the only two possible ways they would believe.

"You have never been to London?"

A vacation trip to modern-day London on an airplane, and a double-decker bus ride around the city probably didn't count. "No."

Madeline shook her head. "Then we cannot say I met you there.

We discussed claiming you were late to the party because of problems with your carriage. A broken wheel would work. But you would have been on your way somewhere, a perfectly logical explanation."

That sounded simple enough. "Do I need to memorize the name of this mythical inn?"

"Let us say we met at The Red Rose. It is a lovely place just beyond Northampton, right on the route to London for your Season. We will say the carriage wheel suffered too much damage and could not be repaired, hence this side trip to my brother's country house." Her eyes had begun to sparkle as she wove her tale, and now she looked almost like an eager child awaiting praise.

The story sounded plausible, and simple enough to portray since she wasn't an actor. The simpler the better. "I can do that." For a heartbeat, she had the urge to hug Madeline. Both she and her brother were taking a risk, Grace knew that much from the books and movies.

Risk or not, there might be a bit of self-preservation mixed in. She would go with generosity; she was in no position to alienate her hosts.

"Very well." Madeline gave a big sigh. "That is settled. You and I met at The Red Rose, and I offered to let you stay here while your carriage is being repaired."

The simplest plans always had a glitch, and this was Grace's biggest worry. Best to get it out in the open now. "What will we do when the party is over? I have no place to go."

That last was the wrong thing to say. "The people who brought you here, surely they will come find you. They know where you are."

Did they? Grace supposed whatever was behind this jaunt through time must have kept track of her, but since she didn't know what activated the mirror or when it would turn back on, she had best plan on a stay of some time. "They seem to have abandoned me."

Madeline gasped, her hand over her mouth. "Surely not! You should not say that about them. I am sure they left you here with the best of intentions."

It was Grace's turn to sigh. "I wish I could believe that, but I fear I don't trust them." Or *it*, whatever *it* was. "At all."

Madeline straightened her shoulders, and her chin came up, as if ready to take on whoever dared to challenge her. "We will simply wait for Cokewell to respond. I am certain he will happily take you back with him."

Grace didn't want to ask, she knew she should let it go, but this was too serious. "What will happen if he doesn't? Accept me, I mean."

Madeline sobered. "We will deal with that if and when it happens. Perhaps we will hire Bow Street Runners, and find your escorts. In the meantime, we must stick to our story. Now, we have another issue. You do not have a maid, do you?"

Grace shook her head again. "They aren't necessary where I come from."

"They are here. We must find you a maid. I will make certain one is sent to your room shortly."

A maid to help her dress. After this morning's dressing fiasco, Grace was not going to turn one down.

13

"We are supposed to be walking the garden, so let us do so." Madeline slid a hand through Grace's arm and began dragging her through the trellises. "My brother has a wonderful gardener. My grandmother had these planted, and he treasures the responsibility of keeping the house and the gardens exactly as she left them."

Grace looked around, paying attention to the plants this time. She recognized the purple bellflower because she grew them herself. Little pink flowers bloomed next to the pebbled path, and hollyhocks grew against the brick wall. Here and there, tall blue spiky flowers filled in gaps that needed color.

Beneath her feet, some crunchy surface made up the path. She looked down. Was that shells? Or just small pebbles? Grace peered at it.

Shells. Definitely shells.

She smelled lavender, but couldn't see it. Somewhere the purple flowers must be in bloom.

The path curved around the house, and the library windows came into view. She had complimented Lord Fairfax on it, but had been too nervous to actually look. This time Grace paid attention. Peony bushes grew here and there, little islands of green. Grace knew the blooming season was over but she had seen them too often to mistake the leaves. Each peony island was surrounded by yellow and pink primroses.

And there were the lavender plants she had smelled, their small blossoms putting out a scent almost too pungent for the size of the flowers.

She and Madeline continued around to the front of the house. "Is there anything you want to see? I can ask for a carriage and driver to take us around if you would like to explore the countryside. We can go to Northampton and shop, if you wish. It would be a full day's journey. You would enjoy that, would you not?"

Grace stopped and turned to Madeline. "But I have no money. It's no fun if you can't at least buy something. I've never been much for window-shopping."

Madeline's head tilted, and a slight frown furrowed her brows. "But we are not shopping for windows. If any in your room are broken, just tell my brother, and he will have them fixed."

She had done it again. "No, where I'm from it just means all you can do is look through the windows, but you don't buy."

Madeline smiled. "I see. You Americans have the most interesting way of saying things." She walked toward the path outside the hedge.

Grace felt her lips curve as she recognized the route to the pretty little lake where the deer walked and the pavilion waited. As they crossed the rutted drive, a familiar voice called her name. "Miss Grace, Grace!" When she turned around, sure enough it was Lily, a beautifully attired young woman on either arm, one in pink, one in a pale green.

The duet of 'hello's' gave the identity of the two girls away. Grace might not have seen them, but she had been trapped in the room that first day, and had plenty of time to listen. At a guess, the giggling girl, the one in pink, was—what was the giggler's name again? Oh, yes, Patricia.

It only took one glance to see the resemblance between Patricia and Lily. The same hazel eyes, with the same shape, same angle, same dark lashes that wouldn't need mascara in her time, even the same tilted nose. On top of it all, they were the same height. Only the shade of Lily's dark hair was different, a slightly darker brown than her sister's.

She remembered Patricia saying her sister advised her not to marry an older man, they were too set in their ways and only wanted heirs. Grace couldn't imagine Lily unhappy with her husband, or giving out that advice. There must be more girls in the family.

The last of the three was the girl in green, with a sulky mouth, and a hint of frown lines already showing between her eyebrows. Her light brown hair was pretty, curls showing even in the pinned-up hairstyle. With a little life in them, her brown eyes would be equally appealing, but they were flat. This unhappy person had to be Susan, the complainer. She was skinny as a rail, and taller than any of them. Nearly six feet, Grace guessed. In the future, she'd do well as a basketball player if she was at all athletic.

If these were Patricia and Susan, that meant Cyrilla of the lovely voice would likely be found on the arm of a young man with red hair.

"Hello, Miss Grace," Lily said cheerfully. "Come meet my sister, Miss Patricia Griffiths. And her friend, Miss Susan Williams."

She had guessed right. "Hello, Patricia," Grace said. She caught herself. "Miss Patricia. Miss Williams."

"You have them confused. Patricia is Miss Griffiths, Susan is Miss Susan. But we are friends, so their given names are fine." Lily corrected Grace gently, and finished the introduction. "Girls, this is Miss Grace Harding, visiting from America." She bubbled on. "So you two have been in the garden? I was thinking it is the perfect place to start the day."

Madeline smiled at the trio. "I had just planned to take Miss Grace out to the lake. Perhaps you would like to join us?"

"Yes, indeed." Lily—or was she supposed to be called by her formal name of Mrs. Stratham when in a group? Grace wished the rules were more clear—spoke for the others. "We would love to see the lake."

They all turned toward the pebbled path.

"Lily, I am glad you made me put on my half-boots." Patricia looked down at her feet. "My shoes would have been ruined."

"You were going to wear your half-boots anyway." Susan was still as sour as she had been outside the bedroom. "You wanted to see where Cyrilla and her young man were going."

"Well, someone should chaperone them!"

Madeline frowned. "Are they being watched? We should send someone out to find them. I don't want any scandal connected with my brother's party."

Grace tried not to wince. A potential scandal already hung over their head in her own self, and that letter Fairfax had sent off to Cokewell.

"She had her maid along. I am sure nothing untoward will happen."

To change the subject—and because the discussion with Fairfax this morning came back with the familiar setting—Grace asked, "What do women do in their spare time here?"

"Do? Women?" Lily's eyes went wide. "I am sure it is much like what you do in America. I write letters mostly. Before the children came I loved to read gothic novels, but have less time for that now. I do make time to embroider, and paint, and I play the pianoforte. I meet with my housekeeper and the cook, and help plan meals. If there is any extra time, I sit in on their nanny or their tutor, and watch. And of course visit with friends for tea and the latest gossip." She said the last with a mischievous smile. "What do you do to fill your time?"

What would she think if Grace told her the truth, that she tore down tattered upholstery, replaced creaky joints on furniture, refinished wood, purchased fabric, and rebuilt the things again? What started as worn ended up fresh, ready for another few decades of use. It was a one woman business, but it was hers and she was very good at it, if she said so herself. She didn't make much profit but she had no debt, an independent twenty-first century woman.

But how to tell Lily that?

She took a breath, and said in a matter-of-fact tone, "I repair furniture."

Patricia must have overheard, because she turned away from her friend. "Oh? Like embroidery? I embroider pillows. There are several in my mother's parlor. She says I'm quite good. I've filled in several holes on the chairs with my embroidery."

So much for changing the lives of these women yet. Pillows were a step up from samplers, though. "I'd love to see your work."

"Do you embroider?"

"No." She had an electronic sewing machine that made fancy stitches, but she could hardly take credit for that.

"So if you don't embroider, what kind of sewing do you do?"

Grace nearly choked on a crumb in her throat. *Keep it simple.* "I can sew on buttons, and stitch up hems. I can fix holes in seams and sew on lace. I have made whole gowns." And slacks and blouses, even coats. With manufactured patterns, but she couldn't say that. Even the amount of hand sewing she had done might come in handy in case she got thrown off the property.

"My goodness." Both Lily and Madeline stared at her. She didn't know which had spoken until Madeline said in a slightly appalled tone, "Were you a modiste?"

She might not know much about this time period, but she certainly knew what a modiste was. Looking between the two women, Grace couldn't tell if that would be a good thing or not. Perhaps that would put her in the wrong class. "No. It's just, in America women are taught lots of skills. We have to be independent, and know how to do things on our own."

"Don't you live in the city?" Susan was finally intrigued by something.

"Yes, I do, but I still learned to do things for myself. For most people being self-sufficient is a necessity." They had no idea just how big and sprawled out her country was. A trip to the city must have been a risky thing. Even in the Minneapolis of her day, she had seen raccoons running in the alleys, often smelled skunks, and heard about bigger wild game venturing into the suburbs. "America is a huge country. And wild."

"Are you not afraid to live there?" Patricia's eyes were big with either admiration or alarm, Grace couldn't tell which.

"No." She thought about the locks on her doors, and the alarm system she had been convinced to install. "Sometimes. But more from people than from animals."

"We send our criminals to Australia." Madeline sounded oddly callous, hardly fitting with her sweet exterior. "That is on the other side of the earth, far enough to keep them from returning. Perhaps your country should do that. Let Australia be a land of criminals."

Grace bit her cheek to stop her smile. What would they think if they found out that someday the country they dumped their human refuse into would become a sophisticated, wealthy, glittering land?

They stepped out of the trees onto the rise that looked over the pond. The pavilion on the opposite side was not empty this time. A platinum blonde woman, near-white hair tumbling down her back as if someone had run fingers through it and dislodged whatever style it once had, and a red-haired man stood there, arms around each other, lost in a passionate kiss.

Grace could almost feel the steam from where she stood.

Four gasps came almost simultaneously. "Cyrilla!" Susan's voice shrieked the loudest. The couple jerked apart.

Cyrilla. So this was the songbird, the woman with the lovely voice from outside her room. At least now they knew where she had been.

Priscilla turned to Madeline, wringing her hands in dismay. "How do we get over there? We must decide what to do! He was kissing her! They have to get married now!"

Grace saw the blush on the girl's face even across the pond. And her smile. The man at her side stepped in front of her and looked up at them without a hint of remorse on his face, even though his blush was visible all the way across the pond. The bane of red hair, she thought as she watched the tableau.

The man stood tall, and held out his arm as if to keep his companion out of sight.

"Mr. Throckbridge!" Madeline's voice was sharp as a knife, and shrill enough to pierce the distance between the two groups. "How could you abuse my brother's hospitality this way? She is an innocent!"

Lily moaned. "Miss Cyrilla. What am I to tell your mother and father? I promised I would take the best of care with you."

Miss Cyrilla's hand closed on his arm. Her companion patted it, never taking his attention from the group on the hill above them. "You have nothing to worry about." His voice came calm and strong. "Miss Cyrilla has just agreed to become my wife. I will be leaving shortly. I must go to London and meet with her parents. We have settlements to discuss." He turned and looked at Cyrilla, his back toward them but she could guess the expression from the young woman's face, glowing with happiness, a soft smile curving her lips.

Grace looked at the joy there, and felt a pang of relief. It must be relief. It could hardly be jealousy. Cyrilla looked so delighted, so joyful.

She could only hope that bliss never faded under the stress of daily life. Perhaps girls grew up faster in this time, more capable of dealing with reality. In her day, teenage marriage had a lousy success—or failure—rate. Here, if memory served, divorce was not an option.

And from the look and sound of things, these two were going to wind up wed, and soon.

14

Throckbridge led Miss Cyrilla across the little wooden span, holding her outstretched hand as if a knight from centuries ago. Grace heard an envious sigh from one of the group. If she had to guess, the sound came from Madeline. He gallantly kissed Cyrilla's gloved hand, never taking his eyes from hers as he bent over it, then bowed to the women en masse before he turned and strode away.

This time the sigh came from Cyrilla. She stared at the path where he was no longer visible, and folded her hands over her heart, her face alight with her smile. "Is he not the most wonderful man?"

Lily sighed a very different sigh. "I must confess, he has comported himself well." She turned to her charge. "Cyrilla, you should not have let him kiss you."

The young woman looked unrepentant. "I could not help myself. My heart was so full, I had to express it." She met the accusing stares around her. The smile faded from her face.

Lily's straight posture—no doubt a result of years of wearing these awful corsets—drooped. "As long as that is as far as it went, I suppose I can excuse it. But I am glad he will not be around to tempt you into further excesses." She put one arm around Cyrilla's shoulder. "But I will be glad when I can let your parents take over."

Cyrilla's delicate pale skin got even whiter. Grace would have thought that impossible a moment ago. "You will not tell them about the kiss? I want nothing to stop this wedding. They simply *must* let me marry him!"

Grace wondered just how far that kiss had gone. She could tell Madeline and Lily wondered the same thing, but with two other teenage charges who were supposed to have pure minds, they dared not ask.

"I am certain your parents will give their consent." Lily's voice was like iron. She sounded like the mother she was.

Grace suspected her new friend would tell Cyrilla's parents everything, and the wedding would go off without a hitch.

"We should go back to the house." Madeline turned and started down the path Mr. Throckbridge had walked a moment ago.

Grace looked back on the ridge. No doubt it had lost its appeal for the others, the scene of some violation of the mores of this time, but she would love to come back.

It was still a peaceful place to her.

They cleared the woods and stepped out into the curving drive just as Mr. Throckbridge walked up the steps to the big front door. She didn't know if they made a sound, or if the chemistry between the two lovebirds was strong enough to alert him when Cyrilla was near, but he turned and froze in place.

Grace felt the jolt like a pulse in the air as their gazes locked. A flush rose up his pale red-haired complexion. A quick glance at Cyrilla showed the same flush on her face as well.

Throckbridge raised a hand and stepped inside.

They strolled across the drive at a brisk pace, considering their leader was a pregnant woman. Madeline stopped at the foot of the steps, and looked back at them. "Do feel free to continue your stroll. There is no need to come in. The day is young. If you wish, Miss Grace, you can show them around the garden."

In other words, Grace thought as she nodded agreement, Madeline didn't want her brother's reaction to this egregious breach of his hospitality to be overheard.

She turned to the other four. "The gardens are lovely. Would you like to see them?"

"Of course." Lily spoke too quickly, but the three girls echoed her. Cyrilla glanced back at the main door, a wistful look on her face, before turning to follow them.

"There is the most beautiful patch of lavender. You can smell it from the other side of the garden. And the roses are on trellises, which makes a nice privacy wall." Privacy might have been the wrong thing to say in front of Cyrilla, but her man was leaving today. She highly doubted she gave the girl any ideas. They already knew where to find privacy.

Her charges turned along the side of the house toward the garden path. Grace risked a glance behind, but the door had already closed.

At least this time, the conversation between Madeline and Fairfax would not be about her.

"Where is my brother?" Madeline untied her bonnet and peeled off her gloves, handing them to the footman. "Have these taken to my room."

"He went out to the stable with Mr. Stratham."

So that had not been just a stratagem. "I will take my bonnet and gloves back." He handed them over, and Madeline put them on again, tying her bonnet with sharp jerks.

He opened the door without waiting for her to ask.

The stables. She rested a hand on her stomach and hoped it would handle the smells without rebelling. She would have a groom drag Garrett out of there. Mr. Stratham needed to hear the news as well; they might as well come out together.

The groom barely inside the stable agreed to get the men, so Madeline moved away from the door—and the smell of horse—and waited.

Garrett appeared first, coming out of the dimness with long strides. "Are you well? Should I send someone for your husband? I believe he is with the men riding to the village." He caught her arms. "Do you need to sit down? You should have sent a footman."

She could have, Madeline thought, but had needed to walk. "I have some news I did not wish to spread around." She turned to Mr. Stratham. "You need to hear this as well." Looking from one to the other, the words tumbled out. "Miss Cyrilla was caught kissing Mr. Throckbridge out by the pavilion."

A moment of grim silence fell. "That cad!" Mr. Stratham's voice was almost a shout. "I am responsible for her. He has abused my trust!" He turned to Garrett. "I must call the man out!"

"That will not be necessary," Madeline spoke quickly before the two pushed past her to find Throckbridge and do some stupid manly thing like actually plan a duel. "He had just proposed when we came upon them, and is packing right now to go back to London to discuss arrangements with her parents. He would hardly admit proposing, and in front of several witnesses, if he did not intend to follow through."

The tension level lowered somewhat, although Mr. Stratham's hands were still fists, and the muscles of her brother's neck and jaw were tight.

"Country parties are known for scandal, but I would rather this happened in someone else's house." Garrett's eyes glittered with lingering anger. "How far do you think they have taken this?"

They simply must let me marry him! Cyrilla's desperate cry held more than just the urgency of young love, Madeline feared, but she would not turn a suspicion into salacious gossip and possibly ruin the poor child's reputation. "They were both still fully clothed." She would not mention the tumbled hair. Hairpins fell out on occasion, but she would be a fool to think Cyrilla's completely undone hair happened because every pin slipped free of its own accord.

Yet she did not believe their affections had gone beyond passionate kissing.

This time.

Madeline shoved down the looming question of what might have happened before today.

Mr. Stratham stepped around her. "I must go talk to my wife. She is undoubtedly distraught over this. We both gave our word to the Parkers." He faced Garrett again. "Forgive me for abandoning the party so early, but I believe our best course is to take Cyrilla back to London and her parents."

Garrett bowed his head in gracious acknowledgement. "Think nothing of it. There are plenty of people here. I fear your absence will hardly make a ripple."

Madeline had to bite her lip to keep from smiling. Nothing would make Garrett happier than to be able to send everyone home.

"I will go back with you," he continued, and turned to her. "This is hardly the place for you. Let me walk you to the house."

"Thank you." She slid her hand through her brother's arm. The men kept their pace slow for her, but she sensed the lingering tension in Mr Stratham, walking on her other side. Madeline turned to him. "I am sure all will be well. Throckbridge is an admirable man. If he says he is going to London to make the wedding arrangements, I am certain he is doing exactly that." She had a feeling she would be saying that for the next several days. The news could not be kept secret long.

No doubt Cyrilla was bursting to share her good fortune already.

"The man had better do as he promised." Stratham's voice was tense, his words sounded like they scraped out between a clenched jaw. "If he thinks he can despoil a maiden and skip out on his responsibilities, run off to some property outside of London and hide until the furor settles down, he has another think coming. I will be hot on his trail all the way."

Was Lily already packing? Madeline felt her pace pick up, and did not think the men had changed their speed.

Much as she did not think Throckbridge the kind of man to abandon an innocent, it did not hurt to follow him to London.

Grace didn't believe Lily heard a single word she said. Her new friend seemed to be on the verge of tears, and she kept giving Cyrilla worried glances.

Was a kiss that big a deal here? Grace had seen more graphic scenes on the bus, and in the malls.

They made it around to the door through which Madeline had led her outside. Thank goodness for the girls, because they happily told the American in their midst all about the English flowers she did not recognize. Lily's silence went, if not unnoticed, as least unremarked.

They went back through the same side door Madeline used. The house was much more quiet than she expected. As they neared the library and the foyer, a soft hum of voices drifted from the ballroom. Or parlor, its real purpose when not needed for dancing.

The conversation barely paused when they entered. Teacups sat around on two small tables. A game of cards was going on.

The party had seemed bigger. People must be out walking, or in the village.

"I have such news!" Cyrilla's lovely voice drowned the soft conversation.

Next to her, Grace heard Lily moan, "Oh, Cyrilla." She interrupted whatever Cyrilla was going to say. At a guess, the girl was dying to tell everyone about her engagement, and Lily didn't want it out.

Perhaps they didn't trust the young man much. He seemed sincere to Grace, but Lily talked over Cyrilla, speaking quickly. "We will be leaving for London."

Grace gasped, her head whipping to stare at Lily. Leave? She caught the shocked *why?* before it slipped out. No wonder Lily had been so quiet in the garden. She had been planning their escape.

Grace kept her mouth shut, and her confusion to herself. Cyrilla was young, yes, but Lily wasn't all that old and she already had several children. They married young in this time.

"Oh, dear. Say it is not so." That comment came from one of the women at the card table.

"Yes. Something has come up, and we must go back." The sadness of the garden had hardened into a firm resolve.

Another woman spoke up. "But the party is barely started. Surely you need not leave so soon."

"Come, girls. We must go up and begin packing for the journey." Lily gave each of the three a stern look. Susan and Patricia curtseyed to the group in front of them, then turned to leave without a peep. Lily grabbed Cyrilla's arm and tugged.

"But I want—" Her pretty chin lifted, and she didn't move. In fact, Grace could almost see her planting her feet.

Lily only tugged harder. "Cyrilla, we must *go*."

Grace looked at the group of total strangers staring at them, and back to Lily. Patricia and Susan were almost at the door. What was she supposed to do? Did Lily want her to stay with these women? With all the tension swirling around her, the last thing she wanted to do was fend off the inevitable questions.

"Miss Grace?" Lily's voice still had that edge. "Would you be willing to join us?"

Gladly, Grace thought. Aloud, she said, "Certainly. Anything I can do to help." She curtseyed to the room of curious women and followed Lily. Maybe she would learn just what the issue was.

They were barely out of the parlor when Cyrilla jerked her arm out of Lily's grasp. "Why won't you let me tell them? You are acting like it is the worst thing! He is a good man, and I was so happy!"

"Keep your voice down," Lily hissed. In a quiet tone, she went on, words tumbling out as she hurried them across the foyer. "It has not appeared in the papers yet. Nothing is official until then. You cannot presume to speak for him until he has made it official."

She fairly pushed Cyrilla up the stairs. "He *said* he was going to London, but he certainly left in a hurry. We can only hope he does what he promised, but if word gets out that you were seen kissing him and we get to London ahead of him, we must assume he was merely toying with your affections."

Aha! So that was the problem. No one trusted the man. Maybe it was nothing personal against him, and men did that all the time here. Maybe he had a reputation that Cyrilla was only too willing to overlook in the starry eyes of young love.

"He would never do such a thing to me!" Cyrilla's voice raised. Maybe not loud enough to reach the parlor, but if the women in there were listening hard, they might have heard enough.

The big outside door opened behind them, and Grace looked back. Lord Fairfax entered, followed by Madeline and another man. The unknown man saw them on the staircase, and his gait picked up.

"My dear." His voice carried, and Lily stopped, whirling around so fast on the step that Grace feared she would lose her balance.

Thank goodness the steps were wide.

"My dear! I am so relieved you are here!" She turned back to the girls, Patricia and Susan now on the landing, Cyrilla next to her on the same step. "Go up to your rooms and begin packing."

As she passed Grace, she hissed, "Go with them, see that they pack."

Grace just nodded and followed the girls, feeling like an uncertain goatherd trying to herd fractious goats.

Cyrilla seemed to feel she had a potential ally as they headed down the hallway. "He loves me. He does!"

This was one argument she did not want to jump into. "He has the most wonderful red hair."

"I think so, too, but most people find it not at all the thing." Cyrilla stopped. For a second Grace feared she might have a struggle on her hands, but she realized they stood in front of a door. "My room." That stubborn little chin raised again. "I suppose you were told to make certain I packed."

Grace grinned. "You suppose right." She knew how to employ guile. She had learned a bit from her father before he abandoned them. "Just think. The sooner you get to London, the sooner you will be able to see him again. After all, he's on his way there, too, and the party isn't supposed to end for . . . a few days yet." That was vague enough.

Cyrilla pushed the door open. Grace walked into a room much like hers, but with a smaller armoire and the windows faced out over the garden instead of the drive.

"Do you have a suit—trunk?" She didn't know how old *suitcase* was, but she knew the word *trunk* was old.

"It is on the other side of the bed." Cyrilla walked over to the armoire and pulled open the doors, then stood looking helpless.

Grace found herself looking at a selection of gowns much like her own. Did these people bring every stitch they owned when they went on a trip? "Put them on the bed, and we will get them packed." Then she remembered the conversation about a maid. "Can you send for your maid? It might take the three of us to get them packed safely."

Now to check on the other two.

And wonder what it would be like without the comfort of Lily's vivacious personality around to guide her after they left.

Lily was gone. Grace waved at the carriage as it pulled away, and turned to find Madeline at her side.

"I have a maid for you." Madeline slipped her hand through Grace's arm and led her back toward the house. "You will meet her later. She is very efficient, and very good with hair."

An efficient maid. Was that better than a friendly one? "What is wrong with my hair?"

Madeline pressed her fingers to her mouth. "I am sorry. I did not mean to imply . . . It's just that your hair is so curly, I assumed you would prefer someone skilled."

Grace managed not to touch her hair. Lily's maid had worked so hard on it. It didn't seem to like these old-style hairdos. "You are right. I am grateful."

She was, too. She had not looked forward to going through dressing and undressing by herself again, and this was fast.

A maid. Giggles threatened. What would her friends think if they found out? The giggles died. Her friends would never know. Even if she went back, she could never ever tell them.

The thought of a maid drifted through her head as she wandered the garden with Madeline. It came back later when she slipped into the library to read and research while the woman napped, and jumped back into prominence when Madeline reappeared near sunset.

Grace's stomach rumbled, but she knew it would be hours before supper.

"There you are! I have been looking all over for you. It is time to dress for the dance, and you haven't met your maid yet." Madeline tugged the newspaper out of Grace's hands. "Put that down, and go upstairs with me. We need to dress, and I am eager to see what you brought from America."

Grace rose, and followed Madeline up the stairs.

"Your maid is waiting." Madeline stopped outside Grace's room and smiled. "She is skilled with both hair and clothes, and will know exactly what to do. I believe she has already selected your gown for this evening."

Grace pushed her door open, and stepped inside, Madeline right behind her. A candle was already lit, and in its small puddle of light, a woman possibly in her forties rose from the chair by the windows. She wore the mobcap and white apron over a dark flowered gown that marked a servant. Medium brown hair peeked out from under that white cap, and green eyes bright with intelligence met Grace's gaze without any hesitation.

"Hello," Grace said, and blew out a sigh, part relief at finally having a maid to help her get dressed, part sadness that she was not young Bella. "I don't know if anyone told you, but I am from America and don't know how things go here, so I will need your help." She added, "Did they tell you that?"

"Yes, my lady," the woman said.

This was not the friendly, chatty maid Bella would have been, but Madeline said she knew what the job entailed, where Bella's training had likely not gone beyond the finer points of cleaning. "What is your name?"

"Martha, miss." Martha walked around behind Grace. "Ah'll just get you out of this gown and inta your ballgown."

"I will leave you in Martha's capable hands, and see you downstairs." Looking smug, Madeline stepped outside and pulled the door shut behind herself.

"I know exactly what ta do with your curls. You will look the very thing." Martha turned Grace around, and began unlacing her gown.

Strange as it was to be undressed by a total stranger, it was nice to know the clothes would go on right.

15

SHE WAS ACTUALLY DANCING. ON HER OWN, WITHOUT NEEDING whispered commands. Amazing what a few days of practice—or learning by desperation—could do.

Her current partner was a nice man she had seen about the place. Some names were familiar now, but mostly the women. Grace had learned that a generic *my lord* or *my lady* covered a lot of gaffes when the names didn't come.

No one asked how she belonged. She mentioned the lack of curiosity to Madeline, who merely replied, "I did tell you the resemblance to Cokewell's family is striking."

If Mr. Cokewell had received the letter and responded, neither Madeline nor Lord Fairfax mentioned it.

The dance came to an end, and her partner bowed, then walked her off the floor. "It was a pleasure, Miss Grace."

Which told her nothing at all. Every single man she had danced with said the exact same thing.

Dancing wasn't the only thing she learned in this new world, she thought as she curtseyed to the man before he left to find his next partner. The last few days had been full of new experiences, and normal things made different just because of the setting. And the clothes.

She had walked about the property with the women in her long, rustling gowns, admired the gardens from under a bonnet and parasol, and ridden into town in a small open-top carriage. Madeline told her it was a curricle. Grace found it frightening, and missed the security of seatbelts, steel doors, and a solid roof overhead.

Her skirt kept blowing out the side and fluttering near the wheel, and gave terrors of it getting caught and pulling her out to be run over. The thing rocked and jostled over the uneven ground. She found herself constantly grabbing for something firm for fear she would be bounced out. *So many ways to die on wheels.* She pressed herself against the seat back and braced her feet.

"Have you never ridden in a curricle before?" Madeline had asked the first time they rode to the village.

"Only in ones with roofs. And doors." She grabbed at the edge of the seat again as they hit another bump.

The village's main street was neat and tidy, a tribute, she supposed, to Lord Fairfax's care. If poor houses and ragged children hid off the side streets, she didn't get a chance to wander.

Madeline offered to loan her money—"as Cokewell will surely be good for it when he responds"—but Grace needed nothing. The time tunnel seemed to have anticipated her every wish, as long as she was happy staying.

The mirror had not changed. She checked it several times, and each time it was still clear, if becoming more dusty.

The party intruded on her thoughts as she walked over to the refreshments table and helped herself to a small glass of lemonade. Dancing was thirsty work, and there was always something to drink set out along the wall.

Another figure appeared at her side as she put the empty glass down. Grace looked up, ready to make an excuse and sit out the next one. The visitor was a welcome one, though, Fairfax himself.

"Miss Grace, might I request the pleasure of this dance?"

"Of course." She rested her hand on his arm and followed him onto the floor.

They lined up across from each other, and the steps came easy again. There was little chance to talk until they had to promenade down the length of the line.

"I received a letter from Cokewell today." No inflection in his voice, just a statement of fact.

And then they had to separate. The next time they came together, she asked, her heart in her throat and all the fun gone out of the dance, "What did he say?"

She had to wait again for them to cycle back for the answer.

"He will be arriving tomorrow."

"Tomorrow?" The shriek came out loud enough to drown out the music, and Grace felt the color rise in her cheeks.

The steps took them apart before he had a chance to shush her, assuming he meant to.

After that, the night was a blur. She danced with the men who asked her, wishing each time that he was Fairfax so she could try to pry out the rest of the letter's contents.

Somehow, despite being host, Lord Fairfax managed to make himself scarce. He did not appear at the buffet supper, either. Her dancing partner got her a small selection of food, but Grace could hardly make herself eat.

Supper done, everyone moved back across the foyer to the ballroom. Grace knew if she went upstairs, she would not sleep. Might as well fill the hours with mindless partying, and wear out her nerves with dancing's exercise.

"Grace?" Madeline eased up to her. "If you do not remove that storm cloud from your face, no one will ask you to dance."

"I don't mind. I don't know if I can concentrate on the steps." She fixed her gaze on her companion, and an idea slipped into her brain. "Did your brother tell you that Cokewell responded? And will be here tomorrow?"

Madeline gave a start. "He replied? Garrett said nothing to me." She caught Grace's hands and squeezed. "Grace, that is wonderful news!" A quiet laugh bubbled out. "I told you Cokewell would claim you. Did I not?"

"Your brother told me the man was coming. Nothing else. Nothing at all. And he certain didn't say that Cokewell claimed me." Grace wrapped her arms around her middle, her cold fingers seeping through the muslin of her gown. "I said Cokewell didn't know me. He will come and deny me, and then what will I do?"

"Never." Madeline clasped Grace's forearms, and squeezed. "He would not make the journey only to deny you. If he is coming all this way, it is because he knows something your family might not have told you." She tugged on the arms she held. "Smile, now. I am certain the visit will bring only the best of news."

She linked her arm through Grace's, and started walking around the room's perimeter. "If we just stand there, they will either feel sorry for us because we are not dancing, or they will try to get close and overhear, then spread what they imagined and get it all wrong. If we walk, they will assume we merely wish to converse."

As they reached the far side of the room, next to the windows, Grace glanced outside. The light from the chandeliers made the windows more like mirrors, the dancers' reflections moving against the glass, but she was certain she saw Fairfax standing across the curving drive, under a tree next to the path to the pavilion.

She turned to Madeline. "Is it too late to walk out to the rise and look at the lake?"

"Keep walking," Madeline ordered. "And yes, it is too late." She patted Grace's arm. "I promise you, everything will be fine."

Grace's legs felt like lead, and her heart beat a painful thud in her chest. Thank goodness for Madeline and her poise. Was this her last night in Lord Fairfax's house? Last night of being an almost-friend with Madeline? Wearing these fabulous gowns, having a maid to help her dress, eating sumptuous food prepared by a French chef?

Something had driven Fairfax outside, away from the brightness and music of his own house, to hide in the darkness.

Grace looked over at Madeline, smiling at the dancers who caught her eye. Asking her to find the letter was disrespectful. Rude.

Tempting.

Madeline would never do it, anyway.

She wanted to turn and look out the window again, see if he still stood there, staring into the night. That would not do, so she tried not to cling too hard to Madeline and forced her legs to keep moving.

Madeline found a chair, finally, and begged off from more walking. "The dance will be over soon. Someone will come to take you out." She patted Grace's hand before sitting down. "You must stop this worrying. If Cokewell was not at least curious, he would not have replied, let alone taken the trip."

The music swelled to a stop, Dancers eased off the floor in pairs, and the couples changed. Durney stopped in front of her and bowed. "Would you join me for the next dance?"

Much to her surprise, her feet remembered what to do. She tried to peer out the window every time the turn took her that direction, but she was too far away, and only saw their reflections in the glass.

With the next turn, she saw Fairfax back in the room, dancing with someone else. He did not come and ask her for a second turn on the floor. Grace accepted yet another dance and tried harder to pretend all was well.

It was late; the quiet was most welcome. Garrett leaned against the tree, and took a deep breath of the clean air. One more day of this party done. Just a few more days of this, and he could send everyone back to London. He was tired of being host, pretending interest in girls barely out of childhood.

And then there was Grace, dropped into his party out of nowhere.

He had not lied when he said Cokewell was coming, but he could not tell her the rest of the letter. That privilege belonged to the man himself. It was too private, too painful, for an outsider to share.

"I cannot tell you the joy I felt when I received your letter. I had heard nothing about my daughter since she ran away with that groom. A grown granddaughter! All those lost years.

"Regrets, my young friend, are bitter. Learn from an old man, and save yourself this pain."

Did the man long for a warm reunion? A granddaughter who would rush into his arms, bringing greetings from a penitent daughter?

He was in for a wretched awakening, if so. A granddaughter who did not know more than his surname, and had not come with any greetings.

At least none she was willing to share.

Garrett looked up at her window. A faint light glowed behind the heavy curtains. Her window was open to the night breeze.

What was she thinking? He remembered the shock on her face, could still hear her appalled shriek, *tomorrow!*

Perhaps tomorrow some of the mystery around his guest would be solved.

The curtain moved, and he held his breath. Then there she was, a slender figure in a shocking short white camisole, leaning against the window. Her head bowed like a bent flower stem, pressing against the glass. She sighed, so hard he could see her shoulders rise before sagging as if all the weight of the world sat on them, and then she brushed at one cheek.

A tear?

There seemed to be more than enough regret to go around.

Something tugged at the middle of his chest, and he rubbed there, but it was deeper than the skin.

Garrett pushed away from the tree and walked back to the house.

16

Just after the midday meal, the sky went more overcast than sunny, but Grace decided she was willing to take the chance of getting wet. She needed the privacy of the garden, and huddled on the bench she stumbled upon behind one of the peony bushes, letting the air with its faint chill wash over her. The greenery provided no concealment, but with her back to the house, hopefully any passer-by would realize she was not in the mood to talk.

More guests than usual stayed for the luncheon. Some of the men decided to eat here instead of riding to the village pub, no doubt after looking at the sky, but there had been little mixing. They seemed at loose ends, as if they knew what to say to women on the dance floor or out walking, but talking over a cold repast in the middle of the day was foreign territory.

Grace was certain Fairfax had kept his counsel about Cokewell because it never came up; no one asked questions she could not answer. Instead the women talked fashion and modistes, and gossiped unmercifully about those who had not been invited, who was having an affair, whose husband hadn't paid the modiste's bill yet, who found out one of her necklaces was paste.

The men talked horses. No doubt at the pub they would have ventured into other subjects, but the presence of women muzzled them.

A day ago, she would have enjoyed soaking up all the colors, the sounds, the voices, the scents, flowers and bread, tea and fresh berries, but her secrets had grown so large that they threatened to explode out of her.

Being here stopped feeling like a dream a couple days ago, but there were moments when the reality crashed down and she would lose her breath beneath the panic of her situation.

Did anyone notice? Did her eyes get as wide as they felt, her heart beat hard enough to move her gown, her skin go as pale as the faint ringing in her ears hinted? Thank goodness for the gloves she wore most of the time when around others, because her clammy hands would have been a giveaway, had they missed any of the other signs.

Cokewell said he would be here today. On the strength of a name carved in the bottom of a jewelry chest. It felt like a cosmic joke—at her expense. How long before she found herself tossed out as a fraud?

Maybe he would have a minor carriage disaster like the mythical one Madeline had invented for her. Nothing serious, nothing where he could get hurt, just something to stop his arrival. Maybe she would disappear today, be back home before he came.

Grace rose. She shouldn't have let herself get this far from the mirror. She had checked it last night, climbing up after Martha went up to her own room. Getting the woman out so she could pull the mirror down had been a challenge. Martha took her responsibility seriously and never left before Grace was safely tucked under the covers.

Did the woman wait outside the door to make sure she was sleeping? Grace had held her breath and listened, until at last she heard the scuff of her maid's solid shoes.

Did Martha ever long to wear the fancy things she dressed Grace in? She wasn't at all the kind one asked, so Grace figured that was a mystery that would never be answered.

The mirror looked pristine. Even the dust was fresh and new, a faint layer as if apologizing for being there at all.

And now that thing had gotten her into the predicament of her life.

She hadn't reached the side door when the rattling of a carriage, its wheels crunching on the crushed rock outside the large doors, caught her attention. Voices came, "Welcome, sir!" Another voice, "Ah'll be takin' yer 'orses to the stable, sir." And then Fairfax's voice, a distinctive rumble but no words.

Grace turned and hurried along the path, to peek around the corner of the house. A large carriage with a stand for footmen on the back and drawn by four horses waited in front of the step. A footman in different livery than she saw around here lowered the steps, and held open the door. As Grace watched, an old gentleman climbed out of the carriage.

She caught her breath on a gasp. She *knew* that man—or at least that face. She had seen it in a miniature painting on a pendant in her grandmother's old jewelry box. She had forgotten that necklace until now. As a child, she played with it, wore it around the house, even to school a couple times. No one thought anything of it, and when she grew older, she just assumed it was a rather nice bit of costume jewelry.

Obviously it was not, and now she wished she *could* return, if only to grab that pendant and bring it back here.

And here the owner of that face was, in the flesh. She might never be able to convince him of her identity, her time, but whether or not he believed it, she knew now that some relationship existed.

Maybe he really was her several-times-great grandfather after all.

And maybe, her practical side reminded her, the jewelry box had no connection to them other than being purchased some time in the past and appropriated. Family legends had a way of doing that.

No point in hiding. Someone would come for her at any moment. Grace pressed a hand to her fluttering stomach, took a deep breath—which did nothing to calm her racing heart—and walked around that concealing corner.

A drop from the threatening skies fell on her arm, and another, then more. She looked up at the clouds, just as lightning arced across the sky.

She started to run.

Just what she needed, to arrive at the door soaking wet, but the cluster at the carriage headed for the door as fast as they could. No one paid attention to her; their goal was to get this distinguished guest inside.

Grace huddled with the footmen, glad for their height to take some of the wetness, and slipped inside without being noticed.

As the door shut behind the dripping group, she kept to the side of the double doors and watched.

The butler came hurrying up, a maid behind him with an armful of towels, and began handing them around. Grace found herself looking at Bella.

"Well, hello there!"

Bella curtseyed, and handed over the next towel. "'Ere you go, miss."

Not a flicker of recognition in her eyes. Grace realized that with so many guests, Bella wasn't likely to remember anyone specific. They were all just faces and demands.

Poor girl.

But the silence in the foyer jolted her from her thoughts. Grace looked over the towel on her face.

Fairfax and his guest, the man from the pendant–Cokewell–stared at her.

Fairfax spoke first. "I did not realize you were outside." He turned to Cokewell. "Allow me to introduce you."

The old man stared at her, skin pale, brown eyes wide under

bushy white brows. His greying hair was still thick and curly, like her own would be if she cut it short, and showed hints of its original blond. He grabbed Fairfax's arm, and held on. "That is her." He might have meant it as a question, but it came out as a statement. "This is my granddaughter."

"Yes."

Without waiting for his host to lead him, Cokewell straightened, the color came back into his face, and he strode over to stop in front of her. His gaze was both warm and piercing as it ran over her face.

"Hmph. I could see better without that bonnet, but what I do see of your hair tells me you have the family color and curls. You certainly have my eyes." Despite the gruffness of his tone, his hold was gentle as he picked up her hand where it hung by her side. "Give that towel to the maid, and let us go somewhere both warm and private."

He looked over his shoulder at Fairfax. "Can you think of a place that fits?"

Fairfax dipped his head. "You may use my office." He gestured toward the door behind the stairs.

"Follow me?" Cokewell extended his arm. Grace did as he asked, handing the damp towel to Bella, slipped her hand into his elbow, and made herself follow him.

She sensed eyes on her back as they crossed the foyer together. Her brain felt like a hamster in its wheel, spinning and spinning and getting nowhere.

What was she going to tell him? He looked like nobody's fool, and she wasn't good at lying.

The door clicked shut. Cokewell ushered her to one of two matching chairs in front of a massive desk, and took the other himself. Grace didn't know where to look, but got the impression of dark wood and deep green. Dark wood wainscoting, dark wood desk and chairs, dark wood shelves. Deep green walls, deep green curtain, deep green and gold rug beneath her feet.

A man's room. This much darkness in decorating would drive her nuts, she thought, but men seemed to like the heavy colors.

Cokewell cleared his throat, a gruff rumble. "Fairfax has told me a most surprising story. Why don't you tell me your side? You are from America, I understand?"

Grace nodded.

He cleared his throat again. "So tell me, missy, why did you not come directly to me? Does my daughter still hate me so much? And is she still alive? What about the man she left with? I hope you are legitimate. It will be more difficult if you are not, but I think we can find a way to work around it."

Grace took a bracing breath, then raised her eyes to gaze again at this man, this person straight out of her past. His face, so familiar from the old pendant yet so oddly unfamiliar, like an animation come to life, was startling in color. His eyes were as brown as her own, with full, nicely arched grey eyebrows. Up close, they, too, held the faintest memory of his original ash-blond hair color. His face was ruddy and sun-worn, his hands a slightly darker shade of tan.

Her mouth took on a life of its own, leaving her brain oddly disconnected. "You're my ancestor. I've seen your portrait in a miniature pendant. "

"Ancestor?" His brows went up almost to his hairline. "I know I'm an old man, but I'm not *that* old."

Her brain began to work, of a fashion, but her heart read him and made the decision. She wrapped both arms around her waist to hold back the urge to reach out and touch him. "I have a story to tell you. You're not going to believe it, but I swear to you, every word is the truth. My name is Grace Harding, and just like you were told, I was born in America."

She took a deep breath. Well, as deep as she could with tight lungs and a snug corset. "Just not the America you are familiar with. I would keep the accepted story going, except you are going to ask me about family I don't know, and have never heard of. Never even knew they existed."

Grace clenched her hands in her skirt, wishing she did not have to say this, knowing there was no choice. She had hidden this from everyone, but if she was going to be accepted by this kind old man, going to become part of his family, he had to know the truth. "What I am about to tell you is something I would not have believed myself, had it not happened to me. I thought it was something out of science fiction, or fantasy."

She struggled for another deep breath, wishing the oxygen could bring with it a way to convince him. "I was born not quite two hundred years in the future. I am living in a past I only knew of from books and movies."

17

He drew back and those expressive eyebrows came down in a frown that would have frightened her if she hadn't been going strictly on instinct. "What is this you're talking about?"

"I don't know how it happened," she said in a rush. "I was at a flea market—at an outside store that sells all kinds of things. And I bought a mirror, an old silver mirror that was all tarnished and foggy, but there was just something about it that drew me and I had to own it."

He was still frowning, but he hadn't shouted for Fairfax. Grace took that as a good sign. "I haven't told Lord Fairfax this. He doesn't know when I'm really from. I didn't tell anyone, in fact, not until you, but I couldn't"—tears threatened—"I couldn't *not* tell you. I don't know if I can convince"—and then she remembered the quill pen and the pile of paper. "Yes, I *do* know how to show you." She jumped up, then turned around and held her hands up, as if that could hold him in place. "Stay there for just a minute."

Grace dashed out of the office and across the foyer to the library, ignoring the startled glances of the people who hadn't left for their rooms yet.

"Miss Grace?" Fairfax was the only one to speak. "Is all well?" He took several steps toward her.

She didn't slow, just called over her shoulder, "Everything is just fine."

The inkwell was where she had last seen it. She scooped it up, pulled a quill and some paper out of the drawer, and dashed back across the foyer.

Fairfax still stood where he had stopped. He looked at what she held, and his brows went up.

Maybe she should have asked permission.

But her many-times-great grandfather was waiting. She hurried back in, flopping down in the big chair behind the desk where she had the whole top to draw.

The quill wasn't very cooperative, but after a few tries she got it to work, and under her skilled fingers, long used to sketching ideas for customers, a computer monitor appeared, and a car, a plane, and an old-style telephone, since she quickly rejected modern cellphones as far too bland to reveal anything. She slid each piece of paper across as soon as she finished filling it.

Grace reached across the desk and tapped the fluffy tip of the quill feather against the sketch of a telephone. "We have a way to communicate quickly now. This one is called a telephone."

She looked up at him. A hint of interest flickered in his eyes, partially obscured by the lingering suspicion. She went on, "I don't know *how* they work, I only know *that* they work. We have motors now, that push and pull our carriages. And we learned to send ships up in the air . . ." she faltered, trying to think of something believable to liken it. "Something like kites only bigger." She looked down at the sketch of the airplane, now held gingerly in his strong hands. "Much, much bigger."

He looked down at her pictures again, sliding each aside after looking at it and moving to the next. "You are not making this up?" He raised his gaze to her under his eyebrows, as if he couldn't tear his eyes from the papers in his hands.

Grace smiled, feeling hope. "No. There's even more, so much more, but I don't know how to make you believe it." How could she tell of men walking on the moon? Or the orbiting space station? The Hubble Space Telescope? Even cameras? So many things she could not —should not—even try to explain.

Cokewell stared at the drawings, angling the paper to get the best light. Grace's lungs felt tight, air struggled to get inside, and her heart beat slow thumps in her ears as she tried to read the man across from her. This was the biggest gamble she had ever taken, much bigger than leaving a regular job and starting her own business. That was just money. This was her *life*.

Finally he put the pages down. "You have my eyes," he said as if surprised, then tapped the papers on his lap. "These drawings are unlike anything I have ever seen. I might think you were making up tales, but I cannot explain these pictures. We are inventing new things all the time. Dredging canals to haul food to market? Who would ever have thought we could make rivers bigger by our own sweat and blood? I once believed only God could make a river, yet I have seen man do that."

One large finger traced the telephone sketch. Grace wondered if he even realized he was doing it. His gaze measured her, as if trying to see through her skin into her mind. "A river is not time, although they both flow in one direction. Or so we always thought. Your story stretches acceptance, but then you know that. And yet you told it to me, knowing that I might not—probably would not—believe it. I see the very eyes in your face that I see in my own mirror every morning when I check my toilette. I see my curls in your hair, even the color I once had. And I see in your face some resemblance to my wife, and a greater likeness to our daughter."

He cleared his throat. His eyes cooled. "I do have one question I must ask before I can accept this. If you did not know of me, if this tale is true, how did you know my name? You don't have the Cokewell surname, but you hardly would as my daughter—if she married her groom—would have taken his name. So why did you choose me for your tale?"

"I inherited a box. An old, old box with your name carved on the bottom." A smile trembled on her lips. "Only I didn't know whose name it was. Fairfax caught me off guard when he asked for a name. Because the box was so old and I had been told from childhood it was from the family, I used it. I had no idea the name—*your* name—was so famous."

He went very still. "Describe this box."

"It has a curved lid, of dark wood, with carvings all over the top. Three flowers that are supposed to be roses. The sides are done in some kind of swirl. It looks hand-carved."

That was a stupid thing to say. In this day, probably everything was carved by hand. He still listened, though, so she continued. "There had been a lining at one time, kind of a reddish, but there are just bits left around the tacks. And on the bottom someone had carved your name. Cokewell. My mother told me the family lore, that it was stolen in the early 1800s by a daughter who wanted to elope with a groom, but the family disapproved. So she took her own jewelry and the box it was in, and smuggled it away with them. Or so the story goes."

"Can you describe the jewelry, my dear?" His eyes were moist, which was better than sceptical.

She hated to shake her head, but if she was going to be honest with this kind old man, she had to be honest about everything. "I think only one piece survived. A pendant with your portrait, hanging from a necklace."

His eyes went wide. "A miniature portrait? Of me?"

Grace nodded. Hope bubbled higher. "Yes. That's what convinced me that there might be a link between us. I didn't know it was you, hadn't believed anyone who said I had a connection with *anyone* here until I saw you. I played with the necklace and pendant as a child.

Nothing else of any jewelry survived. I think it all must have been sold along the way. You see, over the centuries, there have been a couple serious economic downturns. One of them was called The Great Depression, and it was horrific. People lost their jobs, I don't know what would have ended it, but a terrible, ugly war broke out, and of course, there is nothing like a war to pull an economy up by its bootstraps."

He scowled. "What on earth do you mean? War is terrible for any country."

Grace caught her breath. She was about to release even more information, political information, technological information, to a man who might have the power, the connections, the grasp of economy, to use what she told him to alter history.

She didn't see any way out, though. "Nowadays—well, in *my* days—wars mean bullets and bombs and guns and planes and giant ships called destroyers and aircraft carriers, and those companies employ thousands of people. When wars break out, all of a sudden there are lots of jobs."

He sank back in the chair. Some of the color seemed to fade from his face, as if what she was saying had finally become real. "You are not making any of this up?"

Grace shook her head. "No. I wish I was, but I'm not. War is an almost constant part of my world."

The room went very still. Cokewell looked back down at the pictures she had sketched. A drop of water fell on one of the ink lines, blurring it.

A tear. He was crying.

"What is wrong?" She reached out to touch him, but the desk was too wide.

"I did not expect bad . . . I wanted . . . hoped to mend the breach with my daughter." His voice got rougher with every word, and choked on the last one.

He pulled a handkerchief out of his vest and mopped his eyes, then blew his nose.

A bird started chirping outside the window. Cokewell gave a start. "Forgive me, my dear. An old man's regrets." The sigh that came out was so filled with pain that Grace hurt just listening.

There didn't seem to be anything to say that would help, but she could give him a glimpse of some of his descendants. "I can't tell you about your daughter, but you have family in America. I have several cousins. My mom had a sister, my aunt. I'm an only child"—not counting the several half siblings she barely knew from the father who abandoned her, but he was no relation to Cokewell, he didn't count—"so your line goes on."

He made a sound that might have been a laugh. "More girls. I only had daughters, myself."

"My aunt had sons. They live on the other side of the country, I never see them, but we know who we are." Mostly through Facebook and Instagram, she thought, but that was not something she could explain. "They don't have your name, but they have your genes."

"Genes?" He gave a sharp bark of a laugh. "You use such strange words. You must be telling the truth."

"Genes haven't been discovered yet. Here, in your time." She felt a smile quirk her mouth. "I don't remember when they were discovered, but genes are in every cell of our bodies, and they hold all the information that makes us who we are. They make eyes blue or brown, hair blonde or brown, decide how tall you will be, even how long your fingers are. DNA has even been found in plants." Her smile slipped into a grin. "I can even tell you what the real scientific name for it is. Deoxyribonucleic acid. I don't know all the ins and outs, but every kid in America in my time is taught at least something about it."

"Such amazing things you know!" He was still pale, his eyes still rimmed with red. "They are so strange that if you did not resemble my family so much, I would find them impossible to believe." He lifted the papers. "These odd pictures you drew . . . I see wheels on the things you say run without horses, so I know that at least has a basis in something familiar." He shook his head, not in denial it seemed, just in amazement. "But going back in time? You will forgive me if I find that far too strange to accept easily."

"I can show you the mirror I bought, but it only looks like a mirror. There is nothing about it that gives away its true purpose." She didn't even know what that purpose was yet.

"I would like to see it, if I may." He shuffled her sketches together, and straightened the edges. "May I keep these?"

Grace nodded.

"Good." He folded them, and slipped them inside his waistcoat, then rose with more ease than she would have expected from an old man.

She stood up herself, and headed for the door. "I'm one floor up."

They left the library and as they moved toward the massive staircase, heads turned again all around the foyer. There weren't as many people as it seemed but everyone there, from Jones to Bella with her cloths mopping water off the floor to Durney, looked from her to Cokewell and back again.

Fairfax was nowhere to be seen.

The foyer went quiet, as if no one wanted to gossip in front of such a respected man.

The silence followed them most of the way up the staircase. They had not reached the second floor when the whispers started. Grace looked over to see his reaction.

His mouth was in a firm line. "I think everyone has noticed the same resemblance as I did when I first saw you, but I would rather they speak to my face than behind my back."

"I'm not used to being talked about at all. I'm just a normal person, and I've never done anything worth gossiping about." He still had not given her a definite sign of acceptance, but she felt hopeful.

"And yet here you are. Tales of your sudden appearance will spread about London."

London. Her presence might now change events as far away, as influential in history, as London.

He looked at her from the corner of his eye. Grace caught that glance, and the calculation there. What was he planning? To drag her to London and present her there, draw even more notoriety to her presence?

They had reached her room. Grace pushed open the door. "Here we are. Come on in, give me a moment to get the mirror out of its hiding place."

He stayed where he was. "You hid it?" He sounded more amused than curious. Since he wasn't certain about travel via mirror, she could hardly blame him.

"I don't want someone to accidentally be whisked through time." She turned back when he didn't follow her in.

He shook his grey head. "A man does not enter the bedroom of a woman. Leave the door open, and bring the mirror out to me."

"Okay." Grace pulled over the dressing table chair, and climbed up. The mirror was still there, not that it wouldn't be. Holding it tight— the last thing she needed was to drop it—she clambered back down and over to the door. She peeked out to see if anyone else was there, but other than Cokewell, the hallway was empty.

"Might I see it?" Cokewell already had his hand out.

The oddest burst of panic made her hesitate. What if it woke up now? His hand still waited, so she took a deep breath, braced herself for disaster, and held it out.

Cokewell took it casually, as if it held no terrors, and turned it over to check the back, examined the handle, looked at his reflection. "This? Very pretty thing, but it looks normal to me."

"It does, doesn't it?" Her shoulders were still tense, her fingers tingled with the need to snatch it away. How obnoxious that it didn't have anything special about it, no sparks, no static, no ripples across the glass.

Such an innocent-looking thing to be filled with such danger.

18

"You don't recognize it?" So much for any hope that the mirror was connected with him. Not that it would have been, of course, but for her to be dropped here and find ancestors, it wouldn't stretch imagination that the mirror had returned home, too.

At least it hadn't whisked Cokewell away. Yet.

Cokewell handed it back. "No, my dear. It doesn't look at all familiar. You would be better off to ask my wife."

His wife was still alive?

He must have seen the question in her eyes. "Yes, my wife is alive."

"Why didn't she—" Grace caught herself before she finished the sentence.

"Come with me?" He smiled sadly. "I was afraid to shatter her hopes. I wanted you to be my granddaughter, but I was not going to expose her to a broken heart again."

Broken heart. She had just done that to him, broken his heart, or at least cracked it. A man didn't cry in front of a stranger unless he really hurt, and he had done that very thing.

So what now? Her place here depended on him. He had been very kind, but what was he *thinking*?

She had taken the biggest risk of her life—of both her lives, now and then—trusting him. Grace looked down at the mirror. "Let me put this back." They both needed a moment to think.

He still waited when she met him at the door. Her fingers twisted together, her hands fairly trying to tie themselves in knots. She didn't realize she was doing it until a trail of cold sweat trickled down her spine. With jerky breaths, she blurted, "I know the chance I took telling you my tale. I promise you every word is true. I'm not here to take advantage of you or your family. I don't know what you want to do with me. I am well aware that the situation I am in is dire. I have nowhere to go, I know no one in this time period, I have no connections, no money. I am at the mercy of you or Lord Fairfax."

"Be calm." He reached out and caught her hands. "If you faint I don't think I have the strength to pick you up from the floor." His brown eyes were soft and kind, fine lines crinkled the corners, and a hint of a smile quirked his mouth.

Looking at the gentleness there, her heartbeat slowed. Hope reared its fragile head.

Cokewell smiled a real smile. "You really are so very much like my daughter in many ways. I do not understand any of this, but you say you don't know how it happened, either. Your words, your pictures"—he patted the place in his waistcoat where he had hidden the sketches—"all have the ring of truth. I know your tale is fanciful, but I believe you, my child. You are correct when you say you risked much by telling me such wonders."

He took a deep breath, as if surprised at what he had said. "You appear sane to me. I can see you are a woman of courage and good character. It took both to try to make things right with me despite the chance I would reject you. I cannot say I accept everything you told me, but if even some of it is true, I am pleased with my future relations."

Her heart slowed to almost normal, and her breath smoothed, not completely but enough. Hope grew bigger, and she couldn't take her eyes from him. In a whisper, the strongest voice she had just then, she asked, "What are you saying?"

The old brown eyes began to twinkle. "I am going to claim you as my granddaughter."

Grace went limp with relief. She didn't realize she'd been holding her breath until she exhaled. She reached out a hand in entreaty and Cokewell took it. Raising it to his lips, he gave a very formal kiss.

"We are agreed then? You are my granddaughter?"

Grace clung to his hand "Oh, yes! Thank you! Thank you so much!"

He patted it. "I recognize the miniature portrait you speak of. I also know the box you described, only it is currently lined in red velvet. You have described the very box, you have the appearance of family."

A sigh, with a hint of the sadness she heard earlier. "If I cannot ever have the pleasure of seeing my daughter again and mending the rift between us, I will claim whatever family I can have, and be glad of it." His hand tightened on hers, and she knew he did not realize he was leaning on her for that moment.

Tears tightened her throat at the pain in his voice. And then something occurred to her, something that she hoped would not exacerbate the pain, but lessen it. "What was your daughter's name? If I am to pass as her child, shouldn't I know it?"

His eyebrows rose as if the idea had not occurred to him before either. He let go of her hand easily, as if the weakness of a moment before had never been. "Isabelle. My daughter's name was Isabelle."

Grace gave a start. "My grandmother's name was Isabelle. Do you think it possible that she was named after her own grandmother? Or great-grandmother, however far back that was?"

His face brightened even as his eyes filled with tears. He had to clear his throat before he could speak. "Likely. How lovely that someone remembered her name."

More worries popped up to taint the moment. "Do you remember the name of the man she ran away with? We have to come up with a family for them, and make sure the tale is reasonable."

"You are right. Someone may think to ask." He frowned. "Unfortunately, I cannot remember the fellow's name. He was just a groom, I'm not sure I ever knew it."

"My real father's name is Thomas. Thomas Harding. Will that work?"

"Well enough. No one will look for any servants from that time to check on the tale."

"Are you sure? What if they married here before they went to America? Won't there be records?"

"We shall have to hope not, so your tale will stand." His face firmed. "Now that you have someone to watch over you, I will take on the duties your father would have—*should* have—done. You will come and stay with my wife and I, and we will bring you to London for a season, find you a good husband the way it should be done."

Her heart clenched. "Oh, no, don't do that. Please."

His brows came down in an impressive frown. "And why not, my dear? That is the way it is done here, and here is where you find yourself."

"But, sir—"

"Grandfather," Cokewell corrected in a stern voice. His eyes went firm, the brown becoming darker, if that was possible. "You must remember that from now on."

Grace found her lungs had grown tight again. "Grandfather. After all I told you, you know I can't marry in this time. What if the mirror sends me back?"

"It won't. I am certain of it." His gaze held hers. "You were sent to me, however it worked, and you are meant to be here." He leaned over and gave her a light kiss to her forehead. He adjusted his waistcoat. "You may stay for the rest of the day, it is too late to begin the journey, but have your maid begin packing. Tomorrow we will go and introduce you to your grandmother. I must tell Fairfax."

He turned to walk away, but looked back after a couple steps. "Call your maid, and begin. We will leave early. It is two days' drive."

Garrett waited in the open doorway of his office. It had been quiet upstairs, no accusations, no weeping. He wished he had sent a footman, even a maid, up to peek, see what was happening, but that would be an abuse of his authority.

Cokewell would be down and inform him of the decision regarding Miss Grace. He was certain of that. After all, she had been under his roof now for several days. He had a right—no, a *need*—to know who he had been sheltering.

The sound of footsteps came from the staircase. A man's. He would bet a goodly sum that the footsteps belonged to Cokewell, and straightened his shoulders.

Sure enough, the man himself came around the swooping banister. He did not immediately notice Garrett, the curve of the stairs and the location of his office behind them prevented it, but Cokewell had been here frequently when his father lived in this place, and knew where the office was.

Just as he had done a moment ago, Cokewell's stance stiffened, as if he were a general about to launch a campaign, and he turned. Those dark eyes under that light hair pierced the distance between them, and he started over with a determined stride that belied his age. "Fairfax. Might I have a word?"

"By all means. I have been expecting you." Garrett stepped back from the opening and walked around to the chair behind the desk, heard the man enter, the door shut. He did not sit until Cokewell had taken his own seat. Grace's grandfather looked relaxed, a good sign.

Cokewell met his gaze, his eyes calm, even happy. "I am in your debt for taking such care of my granddaughter."

So they had all been right. "It was my pleasure. My sister has enjoyed playing hostess to her."

"Give her my thanks, will you, but I am taking her home with me. It was a pleasure to see you again, but I must get her to my home and my wife." His eyes sharpened, and Garrett stiffened in his chair. "Whatever tale you told to protect Grace's reputation, you will stick to it. Is that clear?"

Was that all? "I assure you, Cokewell, I have no desire to besmirch anyone's reputation, least of all my own. Miss Grace had carriage trouble, a broken wheel, and my sister met her at The Red Rose on her way here. It would not do to leave her there, even though it is a reputable inn, so she was taken to our party to await your arrival."

Cokewell nodded, and his eyes mellowed. "A most wise decision." He winked. "I will of course cover the cost of the carriage repairs."

Garrett smothered his own smile. "Exactly as I expected, sir."

The two men rose almost as one. Cokewell extended his hand, and Garrett took it gratefully. The man did not release it right away, though, and his brows came down, his eyes glinted a warning. "I will see you in London in a few weeks' time."

"Yes, sir." And he would be expected to pay a call on the Cokewells when he got there. The command came through loud and clear.

19

The horse hooves clattered on the road, and the carriage rocked, but it was nothing like riding in an open gig, Grace thought. Amazing the difference two full doors and a roof made. She hadn't felt the need to grab something and hold on.

She watched the sun ripple over the fields turning golden, and fanned herself to ease the heat. Martha sat silent and still, but Grace knew she was ever attentive to any need. A handkerchief? Her maid managed to pull one out of her satchel, a virtual duffle bag of supplies.

Some of the surprises were food, and Grace had found herself grateful for a snack more than once. Dried berries, nuts, cheese wrapped in oilcloth, they all came out of that satchel. Martha even insisted they stop at several wells, and had seen that Grace drink.

Which of course necessitated other stops.

She watched her grandfather sleep on the other side of the carriage. Grandfather many times removed, but still a real live relative. The more time she spent around him, the more convinced she was that the connection existed.

Funny how things held true down the generations. She saw her grandmother's smile in the curve of his mouth, heard hints of

Grammy in his chuckles. Even the lift of one brow when he teased her was the same. The brow might be thicker, but the arch was an exact match.

She patted the reticule at her side, where the mirror hid. She could have packed it in one of the trunks—Lord Fairfax had sent his servants into the attic to find some she could use—but she dared not risk it breaking, and had ridden just enough in carriages to know it was a real possibility unless she kept it close at hand.

Martha would have thought them insane if she overheard them together this morning. Grandfather had taken her into Fairfax's office early, and shut the door.

"We must settle what to tell my wife." He seated them in the two side-by-side chairs, and patted her hand as he spoke. "She is no fool."

"What do we say about your daughter?" Grace had asked.

"We will have to tell her Isabella is dead." His flat voice had told the sadness that still haunted him. "She would have written us long ago if she wished to do so. Since she has not, we must assume she cannot."

Grace didn't know that the woman really was dead in this time, and shuddered that someday his Isabelle would make the treacherous journey back to England to settle things with her parents.

Or even send a letter, a much more likely happening and just as frightening for her position here. But they needed some way to explain Grace's presence and their daughter's simultaneous absence, so Grace agreed.

"You are gift enough to ease my wife's heart," he had stated several times, and she almost believed him.

The carriage hit another rut and gave the worst lurch yet. Grandfather gave a half-snort, opened his eyes, looked blearily around, but finding the carriage still upright closed them again and promptly fell back to sleep.

You could get used to anything if you live with it long enough, Grace thought, and shifted on the seat, hard underneath her bottom.

She would be surprised if she wasn't bruised when they got to the hotel and stopped for the night.

They would be in Northampton tomorrow afternoon sometime. She would have another grandmother. The thought would have been lovely if not for all the secrets.

And lies.

Like those she had been forced to tell Fairfax. Had he spent a moment's thought about her since she left? Or was she one less guest to entertain?

Would she see him when she got to London? Grandfather insisted her unknown grandmother would introduce her to Society once they got there.

Which did not mean she would even see Fairfax, or that they would be at the same parties.

She might have seen him for the last time, and those trunks he had given her might be the last things she had to remind her of him.

Grace looked out the window again, anything to distract her from her thoughts, and got the same shock she felt every time something was so English, so . . . *historical*. From behind a spreading tree, a man in knee breeches, clogs, and a loose vest carried a bucket of water toward a house, no doubt from a nearby well. A child scampered beside him, a boy in what looked like a one-piece coverall except that it buttoned at the ankles.

The house was little more than a shack, crudely made with a thatched roof and smoke puffing out a leaning chimney. The door stood open to the warm sun. A woman was inside, standing by a fire stirring a pot.

In a long dress, on this hot summer day. Grace didn't know how the poor woman did it. She herself was melting, perspiration trickling down her back and sides, dampening her neck, and she wasn't anywhere near a fire. The carriage moved slowly enough that she watched the man walk all the way to the house, and in.

Minnesota was green in the summer, but there was something

different in the green of England. Or perhaps it was the clear air, no hint of smog or exhaust.

Instead, she breathed in the dust kicked up by the horses. The alternative was to close the windows, but she had tried that and the carriage turned into a sauna, so she used a handkerchief to block the worst of the dust and was grateful for the slight breeze.

Air conditioning was a long, long time in the future. She tried to put it out of her mind, and focused on the story they concocted to ease her grandmother's sadness. She had to borrow her aunt's boys ruthlessly as part of this mythical family she and Grandfather concocted.

The day dragged on, the carriage lurching and bumping, dust settling in a fine layer over the seats and her gown. Even the handkerchief showed a faint brown tinge. They stopped at an inn for lunch, climbed back into the carriage and were off again, jouncing over the road. More of Britain, green trees, hedges along some of the roads, rock walls in others, and everywhere trees and fields, small houses, cows and sheep.

Sunset finally came. "Watch for inns," Grandfather instructed. They drove by several before he said, "Ah, yes. This is the one." They pulled into a bustling yard with another carriage, well-worn and disgorging three women and one man, poorly dressed and looking worn and tired.

"The stage." Grandfather sighed, dismay in his tone. "As long as they stay in their rooms, all will be well. It is too late to find another inn. I will have the footmen keep closer watch on the carriage."

Scorn for the poor seemed to exist across time, Grace thought, and remembered the homeless in Minneapolis, sitting on the sidewalks or standing by roads and intersections, holding signs begging for money and being all but invisible.

These people at least had the funds for the trip. She thought of the couple with the little boy, and their meager house. How would they travel, if they ever wanted to?

The rich scent of cooking meat greeted them as they walked in, and Grace's mouth immediately began to water.

The main room was large, filled with long wooden tables and a sizable fireplace to the right, currently cold. Benches lined the sides of the tables, marred with scuffs, probably from boots scraping across as the men seated themselves.

Grandfather walked up to the tall scarred counter, and tapped sharply on the wood. A greying woman in a long apron, mobcap on her head, strands of hair slipping from underneath, came from around the wall that must lead to the kitchen.

"Two rooms," he said, and set a gold coin down in front of her. Her eyes flicked to it and back up to his face, one brow going up briefly, but her smile was merely professional. She had obviously seen coins that large before.

"Yes, sir. We will clear out after the last guest." She waved at someone behind her, and turned back to them. "You must be all kinds of hungry. The stew is about done, but I have fresh bread ready."

"That will do."

"I will go and see that all is done properly." Martha picked up her satchel and, with a stern glance at the proprietress, held out her hand for the key and headed up the stairs.

"Doesn't she want to join us?"

Grandfather gave her a strange look. "She is quite capable of seeing to her own needs." He took Grace's arm and steered her to the one table that had a real chair, seating her on the bench next to it. He took the chair for himself. "These old bones cannot take those benches."

After settling himself, he cleared his throat, and fixed his dark gaze on her. "My dear, you must learn how to handle the servants. Be stronger with them. Martha has you totally cowed. Remember, you are her mistress."

She started to protest, not sure what she was going to say, just not wanting to relegate her rigid maid to a nonentity, but he stabbed a finger toward her. "You must remember your position. I know you think of yourself as one of them because you were in trade, but you must never discuss business. I am willing to overlook much just to have you here, but I forbid you to tell anyone you were a shopkeeper." He leaned forward. "I need your promise, Grace, and you will give it."

Another piece of her other life slipped out of her grasp with the demand. She took a deep breath. "Very well. I promise."

Supper was a truly delicious stew of meat and some kind of grain, more grain than meat, and a fruity wine, as well as the ubiquitous tea.

The meal done, they went upstairs to their rooms. Grandfather's key opened the room across the hall from her, and Grace felt suddenly uncertain. The lock on the door was not a deadbolt, just a skeleton key lock, hardly any protection at all.

But she *was* tired, and needed sleep, and Martha would share her room.

"Let me get you out of those dusty clothes." Martha had a way of making everything so matter-of-fact, so Grace turned around and let her maid undress her, leaving just the chemise, as the rest of her clothes still sat in trunks on the carriage. Someone must have been assigned to stay up all night to guard them, but that meant wearing clothes a second day. She had never done that in her own time, not even with daily showers and deodorant. Grace cringed at the thought of wearing the same clothes tomorrow.

But there was nothing else to do, so she folded the gown and corset, and draped them over the back of the room's only chair.

Once she was under the covers, Martha undressed and gingerly climbed into the far side of the bed. There was no other place for her, and Grace had wondered where her maid planned on sleeping.

Somehow, just knowing there was another person closer than across the hall made it easy to fall asleep.

20

THE DAY WAS A REPEAT OF YESTERDAY. VILLAGES, FARMS, HORSE-drawn carriages at inns along the way. Snacks came from Martha's satchel, bread and cheese tasting so fresh she must have replenished her supply from the inn's kitchen.

A quick spurt of rain helped both to cool the air and settle the dust. They stopped for a meal at an inn, and were back on the road again.

Grace realized she was more relaxed today, the rocking of the carriage on the rough road less noticeable. Grandfather took his midday nap, something she suspected was his normal daily routine. He wasn't a young man, and the thought hurt. Perhaps that was why the time tunnel had taken her here, that at least in this time she could ease the loss of his daughter.

The worry about how long she would be permitted to stay dogged her. Grace shoved it aside with determination, and looked outside the window at the lush green of England again.

When Grandfather awoke, he looked around, and blinked. "Why, we are almost there."

Ignoring Martha's presence, he reached across the carriage, not so great a reach, and took Grace's hands. "Your grandmother will be thrilled. I did not write her, as we would arrive at almost the same time as the mail."

Grace stared into her grandfather's eyes, wishing Martha anywhere else so she could beg him for reassurance, and go over their story again. *What if I make a mistake*, she wanted to ask, but of course she could say nothing of the sort.

He must have read her fears, because he pressed her hands together like a prayer, and held them firm. "All will be well. I will stay at your side, but Lavinia will be so happy." He let go and leaned back. "We will leave for London before the Season begins. There will be balls and *soirees*, and nights at the opera. We must hire you dancing tutors and your grandmother will want you to get the best modiste."

"But I already have enough clothes." Grandfather had seen the trunks loaded onto the carriage; he knew what she had.

He shook his head. "I know your grandmother. She will want you to have more than enough." The carriage slowed, and a long drive came into view.

The horses turned onto a smooth road of fine white rock. An impressive house came into view. Not as big as Fairfax's, but big enough to have four towers, one on each corner. The red brick front contrasted with a white carved-stone panel that rose straight up from the massive arched double door, almost like an arrow pointing to the entrance. Windows on either side showed three stories, and even the curving towers had windows just as big as those across the front. She couldn't tell how deep the house went, but what she saw was enough to startle her.

Silly, because she knew the man to be wealthy. He was friends with Fairfax's family, after all, and they would hardly mingle with someone lesser.

The carriage rocked to a stop in front of the door. Two steps, not a staircase but still wide and deep, ran the length of the front door, which swung open as they climbed down. A butler, obvious from the uniform and stiff posture, stood aside, and a white-haired woman rushed out, to stop at the foot of the two steps, her hands folded over her heart, her gaze flicking from Cokewell to Grace and back. Her face was sweet, with smile lines on the outside of her eyes and creases in her wrinkled face showing years of smiles there, too. Her hair hid behind her mobcap, but bits curled out from under.

"What did you find out? Who was it? You silly man, to take off like that and tell me nothing. I have been frantic with worry." She looked at Grace. "And who is . . ." Her voice trailed off, and her green eyes went wide. "This cannot be . . ."

"Yes, my dear, this is our granddaughter. Isabelle's daughter, come to meet us."

Her mouth opened and shut, then her eyes filled with tears. "But where is Isabelle?"

Grandfather pulled his wife into his arms. "I am sorry, my dear. Isabelle is dead. But she sent her daughter with her last breaths."

Grace watched helplessly as Cokewell's wife—now her Grandmother—sobbed in her husband's arms, then pulled away and rubbed at her soft, wrinkled face as if trying to hide the evidence of tears. She held out her hands with the lacy half-gloves, and Grace took them gently.

"My dear, forgive my shocking display of emotion." That green gaze swept over Grace's face. "You have your grandfather's eyes."

Grace smiled, and let go of her new grandmother's hands. "And his hair." She pulled off her bonnet. "See?"

"Oh, my yes. How lovely." Her eyes went moist again. "Come in, come in. We must talk. You must tell me everything." She linked her arm through Grace's, holding on tight.

Bonnet in one hand, the other trapped by Grandmother's arm, Grace looked over her shoulder at Grandfather. *What do I do now,* she tried to ask with her eyes, but he merely beamed, smiled, and followed them in.

Grace was ushered into a magnificent room done in beautiful

white wallpaper striped in blue. Large paintings hung on each wall, a pastoral scene here, a sea view there. Some smaller paintings held portraits, and she wondered if they were more of her ancestors. She would have to look closer later.

Matching chairs sat around a low round table where a small silver tray held a floral teapot and teacup. An elegantly carved cabinet with doors filled one side of the room. Grace wondered what it held.

A white fireplace broke up the longest wall. Grace could not tell what kind of stone, but possibly marble, or limestone. Open curtains showed the drive and the grass beyond. Sunlight poured through the wide window, making the room even brighter, and more welcoming.

On one of the chairs, a bit of partially embroidered fabric sat as if it had been dropped when the stitcher saw the carriage arrive. This was the first time Grace had seen a real family home, albeit a wealthy family's home, and it was oddly welcoming.

"Sit, sit," Grandmother led her to one of the chairs around the table. "There is a little tea left, but we need fresh." She bustled over to a silken cord hanging on the wall, and gave a tug.

Grace suddenly realized this woman was as nervous about the meeting as she was.

With much clasping of hands, Grandmother came back and picked up her embroidery, setting it in a basket. With a deep sigh, she said, "Now. There is so much to catch up on."

It was Grace's turn to take a breath. She folded her hands in her lap to keep them still. "Well, my parents were married." Now for the cousins. "I have two brothers, and they both have the curly hair, but it is dark. I am the only blonde."

"Yes." Grandmother's voice went a bit flat. "Probably from their father. I recall he was a dark Irishman. Isabelle thought him so dashing." Her delicate eyebrows came together in a frown. "I know he is your father, but I still resent that he took my daughter away."

Time for a bit of her own kind of embroidery, words instead of needles. Her own parents' marriage would hardly work, so she borrowed her real grandmother and grandfather's. "But they were happy. Most of the time, at least."

"So there are three of you children."

"Yes."

"And do you live on a farm, or in the city?"

There was a limit to how many lies she could keep straight. "I—we—live in the city."

"And how old are your brothers?"

"Seventeen and fifteen."

"Younger than you, then." Grandmother's hands were still clenched. Grace bet if she could see the knuckles below those open fingertips, they would be white with tension.

She had to relax this poor woman. "Yes, I am the oldest. There is a bit of a gap between us." She reached across, and touched her grandmother's arm. "I loved my mother. She was wonderful with me, and had the patience of a saint. I was not an easy child to raise. Always wanting to do more, to *be* more."

"Then it is a good thing you were born in America. I think it is probably easier for women there."

Grace laughed. If only she knew! "Yes, I have discovered that already."

Sobering, Grace looked at her many-times-great grandmother, and then over to Grandfather, where he stood by the fireplace, leaning on the mantle. He had forced the promise not to talk about being in business, but did that apply to the grandmother, too?

She took a deep breath. "I promised Grandfather I would not discuss this with anyone, but I think you need to know. I have my own business in America. You call it being in trade." She met Grandmother's gaze straight on. "I'm good at it, too."

The woman turned to her husband, a touch of alarm on her face. "Did you know this?"

"Grace." He sounded disappointed. "Is this as long as you can keep a promise?"

"She is my *grandmother*." Grace lifted her chin. "She needed to know."

He scowled, then his brows lifted and a faint smile tilted one side of his mouth. "You see, my dear? She is much her mother's daughter, and has a will of her own." He gave a single, firm shake of his grey head. "I wish you had not told her, but now it is in the open." His gaze firmed. "But it goes no further. Is that understood?"

"Yes." She could agree to that.

Grandmother pursed her lips, and a tiny frown creased the wrinkles on her forehead. "If we are to bring you out . . ." She turned to her husband. "That is what you planned, is it not? She is to find a husband in England? She was sent here to find one?"

"I can only assume that is what her mother intended."

"Then we will do so." The tears were back. A sob tore out of her throat. "How I wish you could have been her!" Grandmother pushed herself to her feet, and hurried out of the room, one hand over her eyes as if no one could see her weeping.

Grace and Grandfather stared after her.

Grace stood herself. "Is it my fault? Is it because I told her I am in business for myself?" Guilt pricked her with sharp thorns.

"No." Grandfather pushed himself away from the fireplace, and came over, to put his arm around Grace's shoulders. "It is more than that. Isabelle hated being forced to paint and play the pianoforte, hated having to learn to dance. And she especially hated having her brothers go to Eton and Cambridge while she had to stay at home."

With one more squeeze, he turned her to face himself, hands on shoulders as if to guarantee her attention. "Lavinia loved our daughter, more than words can say. We had given up hope of a daughter, but Isabelle was so independent!" He chuckled, a wet sound that showed he was not so far from tears himself. "The Good Lord only knows how we managed. We should have expected her to do something outrageous, but we never ever thought she would rather run away than conform."

"And now she gets me, who is just like Isabelle was."

"You see why I do not believe you will go away? We have lost one daughter; we cannot survive another loss like that." He stepped away, and headed toward the door. "I must take care of my wife. Make yourself at home. The tea should be here any moment."

Grace had just reached the nearest small portrait when someone cleared their throat behind her. "Miss? Someone rang for tea?"

She spun around to see a maid older than herself in the required mobcap and apron holding a larger tray than the one on the table, with a teapot and two cups, plus some small cakes. *You must remember your position.* "Oh. Yes. If you could put it on the table? And take away the other one, if you would. Thank you."

The maid set down the tray, and picked up the other one. *Maid!* Grace suddenly realized that she had been so absorbed in herself and her grandmother that she forgot about Martha. "Can you tell me where my maid is?"

"Certainly." This maid stood straight and looked Grace in the eye. A woman who knew her worth and didn't care if she worked for a living. "She is in the kitchen eating. We are getting your room set up. Once it is ready, she said she would go up and inspect." That last word came out tinged with scorn, as if it took a lot of nerve for anyone to think their efforts might not be enough.

Grace smiled. "Yes, that sounds like Martha. Thank you."

The maid nodded, and walked out without another word. Grace was alone again.

Might as well eat, she thought, and sat down to help herself. The tea was delicious, with a delicate flavor she couldn't place but enjoyed. The cakes were just as good, with fruity sauce over the top instead of frosting.

She was on her second piece when Grandfather came back in.

"Is your—is Grandmother okay?"

He nodded. "It will take her some time to accept that her daughter is gone. You do bring back memories, but once she begins to prepare you for the Season, she will find happiness again. She will want to take you to every modiste she trusts, and get you fitted from the skin out."

"But I have clothes!" That might become her mantra, she thought.

"Not enough. We will hire a dancing instructor. I know you draw, but do you paint? Speak another language?" His eyes narrowed as he looked at her. She could see him measuring her against the young woman of this day.

"No to both. I don't paint, and my only language is English."

"We will have to hire a music teacher. You must at least know a bit of the finer arts. And language. You cannot learn much in the short time before the Season begins in earnest, but if you can understand even a few French words, it will help." He sat down on one of the other chairs, and helped himself to one of the cakes.

Modiste, and now dancing, playing an instrument, and a new language. She scooted forward on her chair. "Do I really have to learn to play an instrument? And I do know some of the dances."

He shook his head. "Not enough, and they must become second nature. And yes, you must learn at least some of the womanly arts."

"So when did she want to take me to London?"

He smiled. "We are nearing the end of August, we should leave within a week. September will be here before you know it."

A tingle of excitement ran along her skin. *London.*

21

Garrett waved to the last of his guests. An entire week passed since Grace and her grandfather left, seven days of pretending he was enjoying himself shooting with the men, dancing with the few women who remained after the Strathams took their brood of girls, eating the best his chef had to offer.

Seven long days of utter boredom. The summer party had been bad enough before Grace arrived. After she left, it had become interminable.

And he knew what he had to do. In fact, Jones was packing right now.

He was going to pay a visit to Cokewell's estate, and see if Grace was as intriguing there as she had been here. Was it just that she was different from the young woman that she caught his attention?

Or was she interesting enough to bring him back to London for the Season?

The last carriage disappeared behind the stand of trees, and he turned to vault up the stairs. When Garrett reached his room, Jones had the large trunk filled, and was packing away his best boots in the smaller one.

"The carriage is being readied, sir." Jones carefully placed the next pair of boots in, and laid a cloth over them. "One more pair, and you should be set. Would you like your greatcoat as well? You will be closer to the ocean in Norwich."

Garrett gave it but a moment's thought. "No, that will not be necessary. Just inform me when the trunks are loaded." He got to the door before turning back. "And do have the chef pack food for the journey."

"Yes, my lord."

Garrett went back down to his office. He had some accounts to review before he left. There had been little time to check the rents during the party, and make certain the repairs that some of the tenants requested were done.

Then he could focus all his attention on Grace, and see what she was like among her family.

A carriage rattled up to the porch, and Grace looked up from her embroidery, the one 'womanly' skill she had taken to easily.

She nearly dropped her needle when she recognized the emblem on the door.

Fairfax? Or Madeline? The carriage door was opened, the man himself stepped out, and looked around.

What brought him here?

He caught her gaze through the window, and a slow smile curved his mouth as he dipped his head in a courtly bow.

Heat warmed her face. If that expression was what she thought it was, he had traveled all this way to see her. Not her grandfather, but *her*.

She set the needle, put the little square of fabric on the small table, and turned to the parlor door. The knocker echoed through the house, and a footman appeared. She heard Fairfax's deep rumble, and then he was right outside the doorway, handing his gloves and hat to the footman.

"Tell Cokewell I will wait in the parlor."

Grace found herself on her feet. Fairfax just looked at her without entering, his gaze going over her face and body, then lifting to meet her eyes. That smile from outside came back. He walked over with the slow measured steps of a pacing tiger.

Goosebumps rose on her arms. She was actually grateful for the long sleeves of her day gown. He picked up her hand—ungloved in deference to the embroidery needle—and raised it to his lips, warm and surprisingly soft. His eyes never left hers.

Did he give her hand a gentle squeeze as he let it go?

He straightened, still holding her gaze. "I am most grateful to find you here. I feared your grandparents might have spirited you to London already, and I would have to go all the way there to find out how you were faring."

Grace thought of all the classes she was taking. "Grandmother is determined to make me into a proper catch, so has tutors coming for all manner of things. I am learning how to dance every dance you can think of, and to paint. *And* I'm struggling with French." She gestured to the fabric she had set down. "The only skill she approves of so far is my embroidery, but I already knew how to sew before I came."

"A proper catch, huh?" He frowned, and she wondered what prompted that. "So they are determined to marry you off, and keep you from returning to America?"

"Exactly." She suddenly remembered her manners. "Won't you sit down? I'll ring for tea." She went over and pulled the cord. When she turned back, he was still standing.

Right. She had to sit down first. Sure enough, as soon as she seated herself, he sat as well. Grace glanced at her embroidery. Was she supposed to pick it up, prove her skills? Or was she supposed to focus on him?

If she tried to stitch now, she would prick herself for sure.

A maid appeared in the doorway. "You rang?"

"Yes. Tea and cakes, please." Grace turned back to Fairfax. "So the party is over now?"

He grinned. "Yes, thank goodness. I left right after the last carriage was out of sight."

She folded her hands to keep from patting his arm in sympathy. "So why did you have the party if you didn't like it?"

One brow went up. "Madeline did not tell you? My parents insisted I try harder to find a wife, just as your grandparents are trying to find you a husband."

And of all the places he could have gone, he was here.

The maid arrived with the tea and cakes, setting it down on that low table. "Thank you," Grace told her, and picked up the teapot. "I'll take it from here."

Grandmother had drilled her on the proper way of pouring tea, so Grace went through the entire routine. Sugar? Cream? He refused both.

She handed over his cup, and he set it down without even tasting it.

"Is something wrong?" She examined her own cup, but it looked fine to her.

"I did not come here to drink tea. I wanted to make certain I had not committed a grave error in sending you off with your grandfather." He seemed to be closer than a moment ago. "You must tell me truthfully. Is all well with you here?"

A bubble of warmth filled her chest. "Yes. Yes, you did the right thing. All is perfectly fine. I am coming to love both my grandparents, and I would never have known them without your help." She set down her own cup and, proper or not, reached out and touched his arm. "I owe you a great debt."

Grandfather appeared in the doorway.

"Fairfax! Welcome." His face was bland, but Grace knew he had seen that quick touch. And put two and two together and got five.

But then, she was doing the same thing.

"What a pleasure to see you. I owe you thanks for what you did for my family. How long are you planning on staying? Surely you did not travel all this distance just to leave again?"

Fairfax rose and extended his hand to Grandfather. The once-common gesture surprised Grace. She hadn't seen a simple handshake since arriving here, so the rules on who one did and didn't shake with were blurry. But Grandfather took it without hesitation.

"No, I have taken a room in town. It is early to go back to London, but there was nothing to keep me at my country house longer."

"You are more than welcome to visit us as often as you wish while you are here. And you are right. There is some time before the Season begins in earnest." Grandfather's eyes began to twinkle and Grace braced herself. "As long as you are in the area, I believe my granddaughter would love a different dancing partner for her lessons."

Grace felt her eyes go wide. What was he *doing*?

But Grandfather went on, "She is growing bored with only having the instructor and myself on whom to practice."

Fairfax smiled. "I would be happy to assist."

Neither of them looked at her.

Grandfather glanced down at the tray on the table, then over at Grace. "If you are not hungry, would you like to stretch your legs? I do not have the garden here that you have, but it is a lovely walk along the road, and the path goes into the trees. We have a pond hidden behind the house, if you would like to see it."

"I would be happy to take Miss Grace for a stroll." Fairfax turned to her. "If she is willing?"

Grace rose. "I would love a walk."

The footman brought the hat and gloves back. Amazing how masculine a man could look doing something as simple as pulling on gloves, she thought, and tried not to stare.

She and Fairfax were ushered out the door by her smiling grandmother, who had appeared out of nowhere with Grace's own bonnet and gloves. "You must take care with your complexion, my dear."

They walked down the white rock drive in silence for the first few minutes. Just the usual *nice day* and *are you warm enough?*

How did one apologize for a grandfather's unsubtle throwing them together? In her own time, she would have blurted out an embarrassed apology. Here elders were treated with more respect. Grace framed several attempts in her mind, but none felt right.

Besides, she would love to dance with Fairfax again, even if only in practice.

Once they were on the road and walking through the dappled sunshine between the trees, Fairfax was the first to really speak.

"Are you looking forward to your trip to London?"

From what she could see of his face around the edge of her bonnet, his jaw was tight. The possibility that he didn't like her going to find a husband gave her a happy tingle. "Oh, yes! I'm not so happy about the thought of being paraded like a prize horse to the highest bidder, though."

He jerked, she could feel it through her hand where it curled around his elbow. "Is that how you see yourself? As a horse being sold?"

"Yes." Now this was something she could opine about. And he, since he seemed once to enjoy her American ideals, probably expected it from her. "I suspect most young women feel the same. It's different for you men here. You have all the choices and options women here don't. For us, it's marriage with the hope of security, or spinsterhood with poverty, and that is considered a fate worse than death."

She stopped, and he had to as well. "Some day we women will force you men to see us as equals. We're just as smart, if not smarter, than you men."

That faint smile returned as he looked down at her. "I know women are clever. They seem to outwit us at every turn."

"I'm not talking about cleverness." Grace pulled her hand out of the crook of his arm, whirled to face him, braced her feet, and slammed her fists on her hips. "Clever implies sneaky and underhanded. I'm talking about women learning science and business and mathematics. Women teaching in the colleges you won't even let us attend right now."

He raised a hand in surrender. "I have sisters. I know they are capable of learning." He caught her hand and tucked it back into his elbow, turning her back to the road. "I cannot change the world for them, much as I would like to try."

That was an improvement on the usual male attitude, she thought.

"Now," he patted her hand. "Shall we find this pond your grandfather spoke of?" He looked at the scattered trees, and the fields dotted with the buds of early autumn flowers. "I don't see a path. Do you know how to get there from here?"

Grace had to laugh. "No. I only know the path from the house."

He chuckled. "So Cokewell wanted us to take a longer walk, did he?"

She nodded, and felt the blush start.

His grey eyes twinkled down at her. "Shall we keep going and see if the path reveals itself? We would not want to disappoint your grandfather if he sees us coming back so soon."

Sure enough, not five minutes' gentle stroll later, the fence along the front of the house turned sharply right, and a path done in the same white stone as the drive appeared. Fairfax looked at her with one raised brow, and they turned down it. Birds called overhead, and from behind them on the road, the sound of a large carriage rattled by.

They continued the stroll. Birds twittered and fluttered in the trees that shaded their route, not so close as to crowd the path but close enough to keep the sun out of their eyes. A small rabbit darted across the path in front of them, and a little reddish squirrel played hide and seek around the trunk of a tree as they passed.

"This is beautiful." She sighed in delight. "I wonder why my grandparents haven't taken me this route before."

"They are not young anymore," Fairfax said gently, as if afraid to remind her that there wasn't endless time with this new family. "I am sure they would rather take you on paths they can traverse easily."

Grace sobered. "I think you're probably right."

"No doubt they hope to see more grandchildren before they get too old." His voice was flat, almost emotionless.

"I had not thought of that." A sudden surge of anger at the time tunnel that whisked her here and might as quickly whisk her back surged along her nerves, tingling down to her fingertips, making her feet heavy. She stumbled, and Fairfax's free arm suddenly came around her waist, holding her until her legs steadied.

"I am sorry if I startled you." He released her slowly.

She wished she could lean against him for another moment, but that was not allowed in this time, and he would never tolerate it.

Or would he?

"You will be careful which men you permit to court you, will you not? I know not what kind of men you are accustomed to in America, but there are cads aplenty in the ton. If you do not know which men to avoid, you might find yourself caught in an untenable situation." He felt stiff beside her as they began walking again, his arm tight beneath her hand, his voice as flat as the path beneath their feet. His footsteps were louder on the ground, as if he was stomping.

He didn't look like he was stomping. It must be her imagination. What had he asked again? Oh, yes, men and courtship. "I'm sure my grandparents will watch the men who visit me with eagle eyes."

He stopped dead, and turned her to him, one finger lifting her chin until she had no choice but to meet his crystal gaze. It was not a hardship to look at those eyes, filled with what looked like worry. "Cokewells have been away from London society for some time. Their knowledge of the men to avoid is years out of date. You cannot rely on them alone."

He didn't say what she hoped to hear, however. No *I'll have to stay close and keep them away from you.* No *check with me before you let anyone date you*—although the proper word here would be *court.*

Fairfax suddenly chuckled, and she looked up quickly at the sudden change. "Perhaps it will not be the problem I fear. You are a strong-willed woman with definite opinions. Many men will be intimidated by that."

She had to laugh herself. "I don't want that kind of man." The next thought slipped in, bringing a stab of longing. *You don't seem intimidated.*

He looked down, and their eyes met. "I did not think you would."

The pond suddenly came into view, the angle different and new. Not surprisingly, Grandfather and Grandmother sat on the bench built at the same time the pond was laid out.

"Your chaperones are hard at work, I see." Fairfax turned her toward the curve in the path.

As soon as they got close enough that the parties could speak without shouting, Grandfather said, "You had little trouble finding the turn?"

"No. It was quite obvious."

Grandmother looked between the two of them. "A lovely day for a walk, is it not? And such delightful company."

Fairfax gave a full, gracious bow. "The company was indeed charming."

Grace wondered if that was simply his perfect manners. Regardless, it gave her a tingle of happiness.

Beware, she told herself. *Nothing has changed.*

Fairfax released her hand, gave her a polite bow, then did the same to her grandparents. "I thank you for your hospitality, but I must be off now. I have some things to do in town. I am glad to see that you are all doing well together."

Perhaps it was her grandparents less-than-subtle hints, or perhaps he had satisfied his sense of responsibility.

Grandfather made no attempt to hide his disappointment. "My

offer still stands. If you have time, Grace's dancing instructor comes in the early afternoon. It would be an honor if you stood in as a new partner." He looked at Grace. "Is that not right, my dear?"

"Of course." And she didn't say it just to avoid embarrassing her grandfather. Fairfax had seen her at her dancing worst. It would be rather fun to show how much she had improved.

Fairfax did not come back that day. The dancing instruction came and went as usual. Grace had to admit to herself that she didn't really expect him to appear, but it still stung.

Nor did he come the second day. While she didn't expect him to show up twice in one day, was it some breach of etiquette to drop in two days in a row?

"He might have returned to London." Grandfather brought the subject up at dinner. He nodded at her bowl of untouched mushroom soup. "Have your soup. Do not let his absence disturb you. You will see him when we get to Town ourselves."

"I can't eat mushrooms." Grace had explained that before, but the chef never seemed to remember. The soup was a convenient change of subject. She did not want to brood over how disappointed she was.

"He is quite a catch." Grandmother ignored the mushroom soup topic and picked up the previous conversation. "But there will be plenty of other men to choose from."

The third day since Fairfax's unexpected visit began as a repeat of the days before. French and painting and music lessons, with no obvious signs of great improvement on any of them.

And no Fairfax. Halsey, her dark-haired, jovial and surprisingly fit middle-aged dancing tutor, came after the midday snack with his piano player, a young man with curly blonde hair and bright blue eyes, and an intensely serious manner. The two men were such a contrast that they hardly seemed to be father and son, but they were.

The sun streamed in the second floor music room window, and the room warmed as Halsey walked her through the steps of the cotillion.

It seemed unfair that she had to dance just as the house was getting warm. Wouldn't it be better to dance early in the day, so she wouldn't be all hot and sweaty?

They were in the middle of practicing the steps for the cotillion—difficult to do when there were only two people and the places for the phantom dancers were marked with books on the floor—when a footman stopped in the doorway, and cleared his throat.

"Lord Fairfax for Miss Grace."

It was a good thing they had stopped dancing when the footman interrupted or she would have tripped over her own feet.

"Show him in!" She heard the exclamation mark in her voice, and caught herself, adding with more calm, "Please."

Then there he was, in the doorway, resplendent in fawn pantaloons, a blue coat, and a stunning embroidered vest that cleverly included both colors in a rich tapestry.

He looked, she thought with a renewed flutter of hope, like a man trying to make a good impression. Was he courting her? Or just showing respect to a friend of his family?

As he had done the first day, he handed his hat and gloves to the footman, and stopped in the doorway.

"Am I late?" His eyes twinkled, clear and unmistakable even from where she stood.

She knew she was smiling all over her face. "Not at all." She waved him in without thinking. "Come in, come in."

He strolled in, each step measured and graceful, a man comfortable in his body. And what a body it was!

He stopped in front of her, and took her gloved hand with his naked one in a dance hold. Businesslike, not as man to woman. Grace felt the difference like a physical pain, and wished she dared turn her hand . . . just that much.

But she didn't.

He turned to Halsey, standing by the piano. "Did I hear the music of the cotillion?"

Halsey smiled. "You did indeed. I am teaching her the Strasburg version today."

"Ah, one of my favorites. Will you object if I serve as Miss Grace's partner?" He must have pulled her closer, or it was just the warmth of the room, because she felt heat wafting off him. Heat, and the most delicious smell.

Halsey rubbed his hands together. "This will work well. I will play the next man in the circle, and we will alternate."

"My thoughts exactly."

Halsey's son didn't wait for a cue, but began the sprightly music, and Fairfax bowed to her. Halsey was there when it came time to join for the first circle around the books.

Somehow the skips and turns came naturally, even if they had to pretend there was a full circle. The various exchanges, swapping arms behind and turning, made more sense when there was an actual change of partner.

There wasn't a lot of physical closeness in the dance, but Grace would have known each time Fairfax took her hands even if she kept her eyes closed. There was a strength in his gentle hold, a naturalness in the way their fingers linked. A reluctance as their hands released.

Of course, she might have been imagining it, too.

"You are becoming a good dancer," he said in her ear as she went under his arms for the turn.

She felt the blush go up her face, and didn't know if it was from the words themselves, or from the whisper of his breath against her skin.

Then they reached the part of the dance where the arms crossed in front and her arm rested on his forearm, light and brief but long enough to feel. A muscle flexed under all the clothes, and his fingers tightened on hers.

And she was glad that he had surrendered his gloves when he came. She wore hers, it was *de rigueur* and he must know that, but he had come in with his hands bare.

There were so many rules to follow! But right now the music was bright, and his hand came back to hers, and they were dancing.

22

Six weeks later

Grace stood against the wall in her grandfather's London house, pulled at the string around her wrist with silk-gloved fingers, and hoped no one in the crowded ballroom could tell how annoying the thing was. A fan and a pencil dangled from the yellow satin cord that matched her gown's color perfectly, swaying with every movement, ready for more men to come and claim a dance with her. There were already a few names scrawled on the spines, men who had requested an introduction and a dance. She only hoped she recognized them when they showed up.

There was only one man she wanted to dance with, and he hadn't even arrived yet.

She wasn't sure she would spot him when he did come, not through this mass of people. She scanned the crowd, colors shifting as everyone searched out friends with the eagerness of one who hadn't been seen in weeks instead of days. A few of the women's faces were familiar after the past weeks in London, and some she even put a name to. Grandmother had dragged her to a few *soirees*, plus Grace learned a modiste's shop was a fabulous place to meet other women.

Word had spread she was the granddaughter of the Cokewells, and every door seemed to be opened to her.

Across the room, through the sea of pinks and blues and lilacs and greens, punctuated by the blacks and navys and burgundys of the men's evening suits, she thought she caught a glimpse of Lily, but it was hard to tell at this distance.

It still boggled her mind that her grandfather owned a house big enough for a ballroom the size of a gymnasium, and could even afford to finish the entire room in a soft shimmering ivory-colored wallpaper.

Even in her own time, with wallpaper available everywhere, it got costly.

Every candle glowed in the chandelier overhead, and all the sconces on the walls were lit as well. Obviously, her Grammy's tales of coming from long-ago wealth were true.

"Are you looking for someone in particular?" A deep voice, tinged with humor, sounded in her ear over the din.

Grace whirled around, to find herself staring at a richly embroidered scarlet and gold waistcoat under black evening attire. Her gaze went up past the intricate white cravat, knowing who she would see, but even so, her heart gave a thump as she met Fairfax's grey eyes, glinting with humor. "Oh! You startled me." She felt color rush up her cheeks.

"It has been many weeks. Your grandfather told me he brought you here the end of September."

"Yes. They have been easing me into the London whirl." She wasn't sure 'ease' was the right word, although Grandmother called it that. Instead, there had been weeks of paying calls on women her grandmother's age between visits to the modiste, weeks of sipping tea with strangers speaking English with a strange lilt, of eating cakes—some kitchen staffs were better at baking than others—and trying to make up believable stories about her imaginary life in America.

Not a word about business. Grace sometimes felt her breath catch when she realized how old the furniture she sat on was, and what it would be worth in her day. Assuming the chair or divan or bench she sat on survived until then.

Chandeliers dripped real wax from the ceilings, and candle smoke drifted across every room.

She pretended to write letters across the ocean, and gave them to Grandfather. She presumed he burned them when Grandmother wasn't looking.

Or did he keep them?

"So do you like London?"

"I know I only see the pretty parts, but it's . . ." Amazing? Architecturally stunning? Endlessly fascinating? She settled for, "Like a world apart."

His head tilted as he weighed her words. His grey eyes were fixed on hers, and her mind went back to that single day when they practiced dancing together in her grandparents' music room in the sunlight. "I am certain, although you have your own cities in your America."

It took a breath to pull her mind back to their conversation. "Yes, but it's a young and wild country."

He chuckled. "Ours must have been the same at one time, but it is hard for an Englishman to admit."

She smiled back at him. "I'm sure it is."

He pointed toward her wrist. "Do you have any dances open, or am I too late?" The faint weight on her wrist lightened as he pulled up the fan and pencil.

He bent to read the names there. His lips pursed at one point, and a frown furrowed his brow, but he said nothing, just looked up at her. "I see you still have the supper dance open."

Grace had to grin. He was the only man she dared confide this to. "I might have implied that my grandfather was taking me in to supper."

He scrawled his name there, and let the fan and pencil swing back down. "Might have? Or did?"

"Did."

"Well, I have now saved you from lying by implication." He leaned a bit closer than Grace knew was appropriate. "I would like to take you on a ride tomorrow in Hyde Park. I have already cleared it with your grandparents. I think you will enjoy it."

"Carriage? Or something more open?"

"Oh, my curricle, of course. I want you to see the scenery."

Her smile wavered. "I'm still not comfortable riding in a curricle. I hope I don't embarrass you by hanging onto the sides for dear life."

He frowned. "Madeline said nothing of the kind. No doubt she thought it a secret." Then he gave his head a quick shake, as if pulling away from his thoughts, and smiled. "I promise I will drive slowly."

She took a deep breath. A ride with Fairfax in Hyde Park, pretending to be comfortable in a small and open vehicle rocking with every shift of the horses, her skirt wafting too close to the wheels, and with everyone staring at her. "Okay."

"I assume that is a yes?"

There was no need to think more about it. After all, a trip through London with the one man who ever made her heart flutter? "Yes."

"I will be there to pick you up at four in the afternoon, then." He bowed, and walked away.

A ride in Hyde Park. Grandmother must have been over the moon with excitement when he asked. She had been disappointed when Fairfax never returned to the country house after the dancing lesson. Old women had the prerogative of saying so in the privacy of their house, doing it loudly and often, while young women had to suffer in silence.

Grace looked at the fan again. She could not read the name just before his, but Fairfax must be a pro at this; he would remember which dance was his. Her only job was to listen politely, and concentrate on her newly learned dancing skills.

From one side of the room, a burst of music cut through the roar of conversation. Couples began to form patterns on the floor, and a man she barely recognized stopped in front of Grace. "My dance."

Grace took a bracing breath, put her hand in his, and followed him into one of the groups. Music swirled once again, a melody Grace recognized from her lessons, and the party began in earnest.

Grace curtseyed to her latest partner as he bowed, then left her with her grandparents. She peeked yet again at Fairfax's name on her fan. He was her next partner.

And then they would go in to supper together.

Grandmother was thrilled. "It is quite an honor, you know. He does not usually stay this late. You must have caught his eye. A visit to our country house, the supper dance at your first ball? The signs are very good."

Grace fidgeted with the cord of her fan, and tried to hide the happy tingle those words gave her. It would not do to get her hopes up. "I know he feels a sense of responsibility for me. That's why he came to visit your house."

"That is a very good start to a marriage," Grandmother said in a firm voice. "You would hardly want a husband who felt no sense of responsibility. If a man will not care for his wife, he will not care for his children, or his land."

Grace shook her head. "I don't know if I agree. Men can be devoted to their ca—horses, or their land, and their wife and children rank far down on the list. As long as they're fed and the house is clean, they're perfectly happy to go back to their hobbies." She had seen that over and over again. In fact, she had a friend who divorced her husband because he was married to his sports, and would rather watch his games than talk to his wife.

A tall shape appeared at her side. "I could not help but overhear you discussing the flaws of men. You have a jaundiced view. A man can enjoy his horses without forgetting his wife." He bowed and extended his hand. "I believe this is our dance. We can continue our discussion on the dance floor."

Grandmother dipped her head. "I am certain my granddaughter is in good hands. Enjoy the dance."

The lively music of a country dance started. Grace had grown to love the dance, but it didn't allow much time for conversation. The partners spent most of their time across from each other.

Fairfax strolled slowly to the forming lines. She could feel his gaze on her. How much had he overheard? Hopefully not Grandmother's comment about his potential as her husband!

"So you think men cannot love horses and women at the same time?" Humor lightened his voice.

She automatically glanced up. His grey eyes sparkled with the same amusement. "I didn't say all men. Just that I know some who were great at the courting business but lousy husbands."

He sobered. "I know those men myself. I assure you, not all men are that way."

The music started in earnest, the dance began. Grace's heart lifted with the notes. The steps brought the two of them together, and apart, and each time they drew near, even if only to circle, she saw . . . something in his eyes. A warmth? Humor?

Around them, couples exchanged words when they circled or promenaded down the line, but he stayed quiet. Just the faint smile that tilted the corners of his mouth. She wanted to pry, wanted to think of something to ask, but her mind had gone blank. There was only the music, the movements, and that smile in his eyes.

G arrett circled Grace again, and moved around the woman next to her in the steps of the dance, then came back, his eyes returning to her again and again. She enjoyed the dance, he could see it in her sparkling eyes and smiling mouth, and a new warmth filled his chest.

Almost unwillingly, his mind slid back to that day weeks ago when he had dropped in during her dance lesson. Even as he did it, he knew the visit gave her—and her grandparents—hope, but he could not stay away.

More than concern for her welfare had driven him there. He knew it then, knew it more now. He did not need to take her in to supper. The supper dance did give rise to a certain amount of justified speculation, but tonight he did not care.

He'd had other choices, other dances to sign his name. Not many, but other men might have chosen the supper dance and the chance for conversation over the meal. He had seen the few empty spaces, but some whim made him take that dance for himself.

In truth, he rather suspected she was meant to go in with her grandfather. After all, this *was* her ball, her first introduction to the *ton*, and Cokewell *was* her grandfather.

But Garrett had missed her these past weeks. He stayed away on purpose, even after word reached him through Madeline that Cokewells were seen about London with their beautiful American granddaughter.

He saved that note. It sat, at the moment, in a locked drawer in his desk.

He wanted to pay another call on them. Madeline had even shown up at his doorstep after he had been in Town for a week. She flopped into the chair across from his desk and glared at him. "*When* are you going to call on Grace?" Not even the honorific *Miss* Grace. Just Grace, as if she took for granted that any formality was unnecessary.

He had merely raised an eyebrow. "Hello, my dear sister. Nice of you to send word you were coming. And how are you today? Feeling well? The babe not causing any more problems?"

Her glare had gone from disgruntled to disgusted. "I am fine. The babe is fine. *You*, however, are not. A perfectly good choice for a wife that I *know* will not bore you, and will bear you hearty, strong children, and you have not even paid her a call!"

In that moment he had seen, not his sister sitting across from him rounded with child, but Grace. He had blinked, and it was Madeline again, but the thought left him shaken for the rest of the day.

Now, circling a slender Miss Grace in her pale yellow satin gown, it was hard to imagine her with a swollen belly.

But the vision had not left him.

His power of light conversation, however, had. He could not take his eyes off her. Her dancing skills were vastly improved, and she now held her own with any of the other women here, but her enthusiasm, her unfettered enjoyment of the dance, set her apart.

She might not have come to England of her own accord, but this was a woman who knew how to make the best of things, to throw herself into wherever she found herself.

The music ended. Either the musicians were as hungry as the rest and cut it short, or his thoughts so consumed him that the dance had flown past.

He bowed and held out his arm to Grace—*Miss* Grace—glad that etiquette for a ball was so second-nature that it required little thought.

"Shall we go in to supper?" He felt his face smile. They came so easily around her.

"Of course." She leaned close, and said *sotto voce*, "I happen to know what is being served. I slipped down to the kitchen earlier, and asked."

He leaned down and mimicked her, "And would I be considered rude if I asked?"

"Not at all." She pulled back enough to look into his eyes, her own sparkling. "After giving you such a broad hint, I would be disappointed if you didn't." But she just moved beside him without answering as the line crept toward the dining room.

He laughed, and did not care who noticed. "Very well, minx. What is being served?"

She grinned at him. "We are having a fish soup, followed by some kind of fish called a turbot." Her brows came down in a mock frown. "I have no idea what it is. Never heard of it before, but Grandmother assured me I have eaten it. If I did, I didn't know what it was."

The line moved closer to the dining room, and he eased her forward. "Just fish? That sounds a rather boring meal."

"Oh, sorry, I got distracted for a minute there." She lifted her free hand and pretended to count on her fingers, raising one for each item. "Ham in a wine sauce, hens in a mushroom sauce." Her eyes went big. "Oh! I forgot to tell you. I can't eat mushrooms. I'm allergic."

"Another American word?" He raised an eyebrow.

Grace blinked, and her face clouded. "I suppose it is. It's used all the time where I come from. It means they make me sick."

"Well, then, I shall make certain you do not get any of the mushroom sauce."

"Thank you." She looked down at her hand again. "Where was I?"

The line moved forward again, and the dining room doors came into view. "Ham, mushrooms and hens."

"Oh, right. Then chicken fricassee and partridge in aspic, a cheese brioche, and a bunch of desserts."

"Sounds delicious." They passed through the doors. Grace was seated on the long side of the table closest to her grandfather, who of course took its head, and Fairfax had the chair at her right.

All the sermons he had heard about the right hand being a sign of favor rushed through his head. He looked down the table at all the other young men, most of whom probably wished they were in his seat, and was suddenly glad he had the favored place.

He waited until the soup had been served before speaking. "Now that you have been in England for a while, tell me. What do you think of my country?"

She set her spoon down. "It is fascinating. So very different from what I am used to." Her eyes were sober as she looked up at him.

He nodded. "I am certain your grandparents are very careful where they take you. I commend them for that. Just like parts of London are dangerous, parts of the countryside are as well. They would certainly know better than to let you put yourself in danger, in the city or out of it."

She straightened, he felt an argument brewing, then she sighed and sank back again, turning her attention back to her soup with studied indifference. "I suppose."

A vein began to pulse at his temple, and his fingers clenched on his spoon. "Tell me you are not so foolish as to wish to wander the dangerous parts of London."

Her brows snapped together and she turned back to him. Anger snapped in her eyes. "I am not a fool, and I don't appreciate being called one."

"My apologies, Miss Grace. I spoke from fear."

"Of what?"

Goodness, she was a bold one! "Not *of* anything. Fear for you, and your safety. Fear that your lack of knowledge of London's environs might make you take chances and get injured. Or worse."

Her frown faded, her expression softened. "Thank you for being concerned, but you don't need to worry. My grandparents watch over me so carefully I sometimes feel trapped. I'm not used to being so . . . smothered." She met his gaze with a firm look of her own. "In my own ti—country, I learned to use good judgment. I do have some common sense, you know."

He caught a frown on Cokewell's face out of the corner of his eye. It was time to change the subject. "So what is your country like? What differences do you notice?"

Her eyes went wide, and he was certain he saw alarm there.

Keeping his voice soft, as he did for a frightened horse, he asked, "Did I say the wrong thing?"

"Not at all." Her hand touched his arm briefly before she caught herself and pulled it back, whipping her head toward her grandfather for a quick look before turning back. "It's just that . . . I keep expecting to go back."

"Have the people who brought you here tried to contact you?"

"No." She stared at her spoon, and drew it through her cooling soup without making any attempt to eat.

"Then they no doubt believe they have done their duty. I am certain you have nothing to fear." He wished he could touch her as she had touched him. Instead, he contented himself with a smile. "So let us talk about what you wish to see on our drive tomorrow."

Garrett leaned against the back squab of the carriage, the driver shut the door. He felt it sway as the man climbed up to his seat. A lurch, and the carriage clattered down the cobbled street.

Grace might as well have been in the carriage with him, she was so present in his mind.

Independent little miss.

He did not seriously think she would try to wander around London, but the restrictions of Society pressed hard on her. America must truly be a land of freedom for her to chafe so.

Would a trip through Hyde Park be enough? Or would she rather see more of the city? Her grandparents no doubt drove her about the park to show her off, possibly endless times.

Perhaps he could find another respectable park to satisfy her sense of adventure.

23

Sunshine poured through the sheer green curtains over the windows. Grace sat in her grandparents' parlor watching the clock and waiting for their butler to announce Fairfax's presence. At least, she assumed he would come inside. Perhaps with horses, a man had to wait with the carriage to keep them from doing stupid horse things.

A marble mantel clock ticked loudly in the silence. The warm rays through the windows provided all the illumination the room needed, brightening the papered walls of interlaced green leaves and bright red birds, and making the stone fireplace glow.

Grace's gaze flicked from one piece of furniture to the next. If she was home, she would still be nervous for a first date, but she could watch television or listen to the radio.

That clock made the only sound. The furniture and wallpaper, delicate candlesticks instead of electric reading lamps, a settee that was harder than it looked—however wonderful and old—weren't enough distraction for today.

On one side of the room, her grandfather hid behind his newspaper. Closer by, in the direct light of the window, her grandmother was reading also, probably one of the gothic novels she loved. Grace wished she could read now, but she was supposed to be ready for Fairfax's arrival, concentrating on him, not herself.

Pacing helped, but she had done that already and been told to sit several times. Grace folded her fingers in her lap, and resisted the urge to tap them together. At her side, on the small table next to her chair, a pink bonnet waited next to a pair of gloves, both a perfect match for her gown.

She had never been a hat person, but even she had to admit some of the bonnets Grandmother had ordered for her were cute. Small brimmed ones with a snood-style back that covered the hair, straw ones with ribbons that wrapped the crown or dangled down her back. And hatpins. Real, jeweled hatpins that could literally take an eye out if she wasn't careful where she pointed it.

Today's hat was a pretty little poke bonnet, a shallow crown with a graduated brim and feathers that curved over the seam. It tied with a satin ribbon, and she was positive it would come untied at some point during the ride.

A carriage rattled along the street, making her start, but it continued past without stopping.

"Grace, my dear." Grandmother looked up from her book. She sighed, the sound audible in the still room. The resounding quiet had grown familiar, even comforting, after these weeks. "You must learn to relax."

"What?" Relax? She was sitting down. If she had been pacing the room, she could see that it would annoy her grandmother.

"Your leg is jiggling."

Grace looked down at her gown. Sure enough, her right leg was making the skirt flutter.

"Take a deep breath. He will be here when he gets here, and not a moment before." Grandmother smiled and looked back down at her book.

Deep breath was stretching it. The ever-present corset insisted on pinching her lungs. She doubted she would ever get used to it.

Another carriage clattered down the street, but this one stopped. Grace took another breath. Did she stand? Stay seated? Put on her bonnet? Yes, she decided, anything to be busy, and settled the pretty thing on her head with hands that insisted on trembling ever so slightly.

The air in the room changed, a current of movement that hadn't been there a moment ago. Grandfather peered over his paper and looked past her, at the door. "Yes, Davies?"

Grace turned around in her chair, her fingers still holding the loops of the bow.

"Lord Fairfax." Davies stepped aside, pulling the door fully open as he backed, and Fairfax walked in, carrying a top hat with his gloves draped over the edge. He handed the hat and contents to the butler, who took them and backed out, pulling the door shut as he left.

Grace felt her lungs catch, her heart race as he crossed the room, and bowed to her grandparents. "Cokewell. Madam."

And then he took the few steps over to Grace. Another bow that even Grace recognized was done with elegance, and he extended his hand. She let go of the bow, set her hand in his, and forced herself not to giggle with nerves as he pressed his lips to the back and straightened.

"Are you ready for a ride?" His eyes twinkled. He must have noticed her impending laugh.

"Yes."

From her left, Grandmother cleared her throat with well-trained dignity. "Your gloves, my dear."

"Oh. Yes." Grace reached for them, and tugged them on, feeling all thumbs as Fairfax watched. "Thank you, Grandmother."

"It is a lovely day for a ride. I could not have ordered a better one." He tucked her properly gloved hand in his elbow and turned to her grandparents to bid farewell.

When they stepped out onto the porch and she saw what waited on the street, she blinked. "It has doors!"

He chuckled, the sound as warm as the sunlight, opened the carriage door, and somehow eased her inside without the carriage rocking too much. "I wanted you to relax, so I brought my landaulette. We'll leave the top down. It is a pity to waste the sunshine. We hardly get enough days like this."

Imagine you're riding in a convertible, she thought as he walked around the back and climbed in, settling next to her. She looked at the gap between her skirt and his leg, those corded muscles stretching the fabric, and wondered if that much space was required between an unattached man and woman.

Of course, even in her time she wouldn't let a man crowd her on the first date. Even so, the space separating them seemed a bit *too* wide.

The driver flicked a switch over the backs of the horses, and the carriage moved out with only a slight jerk. The street was empty of other vehicles, but it merged with a larger, wider one in short order.

The traffic on this new street was so thick with carriages and horses, and pedestrians dodging between them to get to the other side, that they barely moved for a while.

A familiar face caught Grace's eye, walking down the sidewalk, and looking in the window of a tearoom. "Is that Lily? I mean, Mrs. Stratham? And does she have her children with her?"

Fairfax followed her pointing finger. "I think it might be."

Grace raised her hand to wave, but he caught her arm in a lightning fast grasp, and set her hand back down on her lap. "Not here, not now. Even though most of the horses are well trained, we don't want to spook any of them with sudden movement. I will get you her address, and you and Mrs Cokewell can pay a call on her."

The carriage rattled on, and Grace was pleased to notice that she actually recognized some of the landmarks. The cabinet maker whose store she ached to browse, the haberdasher—for men only, a studio with portraits of people who were undoubtedly well-known to others, a perfumer that Grandmother had taken her into for her own custom scent.

She wondered if Fairfax noticed her perfume. That wasn't something she would ask even in her own day, so she just wondered, and watched the fancy carriages roll past.

Horses did their business on the street, the scent overwhelming her nose until they passed. Children hurried out with shovels to clean the mess and receive a few coins for their efforts. Further along, an old man in ragged clothes was stuck with the nasty job, and her heart twisted.

Normally she rode in her grandfather's carriage, enclosed within the solid walls and with only narrow windows. This was the first time she had had a good look, and not everything was pretty.

Despite the constant interruptions, despite knowing she was on show, despite the smell of horses and the crush of traffic, the charm of the place and the day seeped into her. Without thinking, she said, "This is much better than television."

"Better than what?"

She gave a start, but answered calmly. "It's just an American . . . pastime." Goodness, she was almost getting good at dodging her *faux pas*, although now that she thought of it, they were becoming further apart.

At her side, Fairfax nodded, seemingly satisfied.

The little vehicle rolled onto a street she hadn't seen before, and Grace sat up to take notice. Here, buildings sat close together as if a giant hand had taken either side of the street and pushed. Ham and beef shops sent the heavy aroma of cooking meat into the air, and Grace's mouth watered. A tea room was filled with customers needing a delicate drink before they headed out to spend more money. A coffee shop surprised her. Didn't the English drink tea? But the coffee shop seemed just as popular.

There was such a sense of familiarity as she watched the shoppers move in and out of stores that except for the clothes it might have been any strip mall or shopping street in her day.

A modiste's shop spread rich fabrics out in the window to shimmer in the sun. Women drifted in, and some of them brought their men in with them. An apothecary window had a large painted sign that offered medicines, herbals that had almost been lost to time until the back-to-nature movement of the 1960s revived it.

She turned carefully in her jouncing seat to watch the apothecary shop go by, and clung to that sight like a drowning woman. Medicine of a sort, just in case . . . well, just in case. She shoved the thought away, and turned back to the front.

She did not recognize the next street, nor the one after that. A big building loomed along one side, with pillars in the center oddly reminiscent of Buckingham Palace. Just beyond it, she saw a swath of green, the grass and trees she had been missing, but they kept going.

Another park opened in front of them, a wide space of green with a cool and formal touch. It looked oddly out of place, a touch of a sculptured French garden here in the middle of London. A long narrow pool, hardly a lake, more like a canal, sat along one side of the garden.

The driver pulled up the carriage, and Fairfax dismounted, coming around to open her door. "I thought I would introduce you to the pelicans of St. James Park. They have been residents here for about a hundred and fifty years."

"Pelicans!"

"So you know what they are?"

"Of course." They started down the long walk following all the other groups, strolling out in the open air. At the far end of the pool, a cluster of trees cast some shade over the path. Sure enough, a couple pelicans bobbed on the smooth surface of the water.

As they walked along the edge, Grace found her gaze drifting across that canal over to the buildings lining the opposite side of the street. She wondered if this was what Central Park looked like in New York. She remembered having seen a picture of the Park's boundary, buildings on one side of the street, the vast swath of green on the other. On a much smaller scale that was what she saw here, a long manicured area of trees and plants edged by this long, narrow lake, and a city surrounding them.

He seemed to notice her abstraction, because Fairfax patted her hand where it rested on his arm. "At one time there were cages hanging in the trees lining the far edge of the Park, housing falcons and other birds. They have been gone for some time, but the name seems to have stuck. It's still called Birdcage Walk."

A sudden shout broke the calm. Around them, the elegantly dressed people began to retrace their steps, nearly running.

"Time to leave, I think. My apologies for such a short visit and please forgive my familiarity, but you did want to see the other side of London." He wrapped an arm around her waist and walked back the way they came, moving fast and nearly lifting her off her feet. "Although this excitement is not the reason I took you here."

The line of carriages drew closer. Several were already pulling away.

"Most of the time, this is a pleasant park. In you go." He tossed her into the landaulette, still waiting where they had left it, ran around the back, and vaulted in himself, calling to the driver, "Move us out of here!" The half-door shut with a firm click.

In less than a minute, they had blended into the crush of carriages leaving the park. Grace openly clutched the door this time, and swiveled to look behind them. All she saw were more carriages, and hurrying people. "What was that about?"

He didn't turn his head as the driver guided them down the street. The sunshine seemed to have dimmed, but perhaps it was just hidden behind the buildings. "The park has a habit of attracting some unsavory characters. I had hoped we could enjoy the day without any of that."

"I think unsavory characters are just part of the problem of cities. We have the same thing in America."

"No doubt."

She felt the carriage slow, felt the tension drain from Fairfax as they moved into an area that looked newly familiar.

He shifted, his arm bumping hers. "Are you hungry? Can I tempt you to eat something?"

Eat? Until he asked, Grace hadn't even noticed the passage of time. She turned her attention to her stomach, and discovered that yes, she was indeed hungry. Breakfast was long gone. "I'd love something." She smiled at him, and he smiled back, a warm smile that started in his crystal gray eyes, genuine and spine-tingling. "Where do you recommend?"

"Take us to the nearest tea room," Fairfax called over the sound of the busy street. They pulled out of the traffic, and parked the carriage to the side. Grace had to bite her lip to keep from smiling. Parallel parking with horse and carriage.

The eatery was a simple shop that advertised muffins and butter as well as a choice of teas with names Grace had never heard before. When they stepped inside, the sweet fragrance of fresh-baked goods blended with the spicy tang of the tea.

Little tables filled the inside, with couples or groups of women seated there, taking sips from fancy cups, and tiny bites of muffins. Heat drifted from delicate cups with matching saucers.

A tall counter hinted at a raised platform on the other side. She could see a small kitchen behind a curtain, trapping the heat of the small furnace. One large teakettle puffed before the view was lost, but Grace had no doubt other kettles were heating because of all the pretty pots that sat in plain view.

Fairfax motioned for a waitress, and ushered her to a table. The tea came quickly, along with a scone and clotted cheese. He watched her over his cup. "Would you like to attend the opera?"

"The opera?" She wondered if he was supposed to ask her grandparents first, but shoved the thought aside. She was a grown woman, and he had asked her on a date. She was going to accept. And no doubt Grandfather would be delighted either way. "I'd love to go to the opera."

"I have invited your grandparents as well. I thought they might enjoy the night."

Some of the glow faded. If this was still a date, it would be the strangest one she had ever been on. "When?"

"Tonight."

24

Martha lowered the green silk gown over Grace's head. As the candlelight reflected a glow through the sheer fabric, a sudden memory surfaced, green curtains, a matching suite with chairs and a sofa. *She was supposed to have an upholstery job done and delivered to the designer today.*

As her maid tugged the skirt into place, pulled the small sleeves up over her shoulders, and turned Grace around so she could begin the lacing, her thoughts were still trapped in that lost world. Where was time on the other side? Were police crawling around her place, searching for clues, putting up flyers on corners, begging for information?

Had the designer given up and gone to someone else to complete the order? And all her business cards, sitting around at the fabric and decorating stores, her page on the internet, her ads running in the local papers. Were potential clients calling, was her phone's message box full? Did people, friends, family think she was dead?

Maybe this was a time bubble, time away from time, and when she went back, she would arrive at the same place and time she left.

If time was still moving in her real world, no doubt the police had contacted her father at his new family, her father who hadn't called her in years, who probably wouldn't even admit to siring her.

She shoved that other world aside fiercely. There was nothing she could do about it, and she would not let herself brood and ruin the evening. Tonight she had an opera to attend with Fairfax.

He was in this time, and so was she. That was good enough for now.

No one told her which opera by the time they pulled up before the majestic theater. Her grandparents clearly enjoyed the surprise. They exchanged smiles across the carriage, where she sat next to her grandmother.

"Your first opera," Grandfather said as he exited the carriage and turned back to help Grandmother down. "You have nothing like this where you are from. Our operas are renowned."

When Grace saw the announcements sitting outside the door, she caught her breath. Mozart! She couldn't see the opera's name, but it didn't matter. Mozart was her favorite composer, good company on days when the work got tedious.

The theatre was packed from the boxes that lined the walls, going up tier by tier, down to the floor where masses teemed. Funny, Grace thought as she settled in the chair in Fairfax's box. In her day it was the opposite; the wealthy got the floor and the poor ones the balcony, at least at the rock concerts she occasionally attended. She wondered when it changed, and some imp inside her turned her toward him. "Wouldn't you rather sit closer to the stage than way up here where you can hardly see?"

Grandmother gasped. "Grace! That is not the place for our class! You must not say such things. Someone might overhear."

Fairfax looked at her with disbelieving eyes. "Mrs. Cokewell is right. Sit on the floor? You can't even see the whole stage from there. No, I'd much rather sit up here."

"Hope for a good performance, my dear." Grandfather picked up her hand, and patted it. "The crowds below always bring something in to throw if they don't like something. They are harsh critics. That is hardly the impression I want you to get of our famed operas."

The orchestra began tuning their instruments, odd snatches of familiar bits, and the audience settled down, if having the sound go down a couple decibels was quiet.

Music, real music, after days of no radio, no stereo, not even a television commercial jingle. She sighed in delight. And then, with a grand flourish, it began. The music swirled and swelled around her. Grace leaned forward, arm resting on the box's edge, and watched the actors glide across the stage with melodies rolling out, the notes soaring up through the building as if flying directly to her. Familiar songs in an unfamiliar setting, but Grace let the past and the present blur.

She had missed this, Grace realized, missed having music for the taking. She shoved the ache aside, and soaked up the notes, the richness of the various instruments filling the air with their harmonies.

The crowd below them talked and laughed and shifted about, almost as if nothing was happening on stage. The people in the surrounding boxes weren't much better. Grace ignored them, wanting only the music, holding on to something she knew.

When the last crescendo faded away, she sighed, and turned to her host. "Thank you, Lord Fairfax. That was absolutely wonderful."

He looked down at her, and smiled. "I am glad it met with your approval."

"Oh, it did." A huge yawn cracked her jaw, and she covered her mouth quickly. "I'm sorry, I had no idea I was so tired."

He reached a hand to pull her to her feet, his gaze shadowed by the uneven lighting behind him. "You have had a busy day. Perhaps I should have planned this for another night."

"Oh, no! I'm so glad I came." Another yawn caught her at the end.

It was so late when they made their way out of the box that Grace wobbled on her feet. Fairfax pressed his free hand against hers where it curled around his arm. Some of his strength seeped into her. They walked with the crowd, bumping against each other on occasion as he kept her from being jostled.

Their carriage arrived. Grace was grateful for the roof, two full seats facing each other, and doors that closed them in tight. Grandmother got in first. Fairfax waved Grandfather in next.

Her grandfather sat next to his wife, not on the opposite seat where it would be men on one side, women on the other, protecting the supposedly innocent female—herself—from unnecessary male contact. Grace was suddenly wide awake. She knew that simple choice—leaving the only open space for Fairfax to sit right next to her—was replete with meaning. Without a word, Grandfather had given his blessing.

Fairfax helped Grace onto the small carriage step, all steady arm and a strong lift and she was inside.

She looked at him, still outside the carriage. His face gave nothing away. He merely vaulted in and sat down beside her.

25

Garrett stood on the balcony of his father's London ballroom and watched the dancers move across the floor. He picked out Grace immediately by her curly fair hair. Even in the fancy style her maid had put it in, that color and those curls were distinctive.

She was in a pale green gown, matching ribbons woven through her chignon. He had no doubt that if he got close, he would find emeralds in her ears.

Cokewell and his wife were more than generous with their lovely new granddaughter.

A whole week had passed since that night at the opera, when the man arranged for him to sit next to Grace all the way home.

It had not been a short drive. The streets were busy even that late at night, and he had been tormented by both her lithe shape and the tantalizing fragrance that drifted from her.

He thought he smelled it a hundred times over the past seven days. Each time he had turned to look for her, but she had never been around.

Once he was certain it drifted past him in White's. Impossible, since that was a male-only establishment.

When a man found himself so entranced by a woman that her fragrance was such a part of him he smelled it over the odor of pipe and cigar, it was time to do something about it.

She was almost certainly wearing that same perfume tonight. His hands clenched on the railing.

"Son?"

Garrett's head whipped around, and he found himself looking into the concerned grey eyes of his father. They were so alike he knew he was looking at himself in forty years. "Hello, Father. This is quite a ball. It has been a long time since you held such a party."

"Your sister's suggestion. She thought it would be good for you, help you find a bride since the summer party was not successful. There are more women to choose from here." Albert Atherton, Marquis of Huntley, rested a hand on his son's shoulder, a familiar gesture, but this time it didn't have the same calming effect as usual. "Something troubling you, Garrett? Your face is a veritable thundercloud. Is something happening down on the floor that I should know about?"

Garrett looked down at the swirling colors on the floor below, but only the pale green gown caught his eye. "How did you know it was time to propose to Mother?"

He could feel his father's startled jerk even though they were not touching. "You have chosen a bride?"

All the weeks of delay, of avoidance, hiding in his club after coming to town, turning down invitations to balls and parties, had not worked. Madeline had been right. *A perfectly good choice for a wife*, she had said.

He pulled his gaze away from that graceful swirl of green, and turned to his father. His shoulders eased, as if they had been tense for a long time. "Yes, Father, I think I have."

"Think?" His father raised an eyebrow. "Or know?" His face went sober. "You should be sure. Marriage is for life. You must give it thought before you make an offer. I waited the better part of the Season before I offered for your mother."

"But were you not worried that someone else might offer first?"

A faint smile tugged one side of his father's mouth. "What do you think forced my hand? I saw an entry in the betting book, her initials with another man's and the speculation that they would be wed within the month, and drove straight to her father's house." He chuckled, barely audible over the music and voices. "She was not best pleased that I had cut it so close."

Then this dignified man went stern. "If you have your eye on a woman, do not cut it as close as I did. I must have aged a decade on that ride."

Garrett shifted and looked back down on the crowd below. Grace was laughing at something her partner said. That laugh worried him. The *ton* was filled with men who would court her just because she was Cokewell's granddaughter. They would not see, or care, that she was too intelligent for her own good, and adventurous.

Would another man be wise enough, crafty enough, to curb her worst instincts without crushing her spirit?

He did not want her to change. He liked her as she was, and did not need her connections. He had enough of them on his own.

Father turned, too, and now braced himself on the balcony railing, leaning on his forearms, an oddly relaxed posture for him. "Ah. She is here, then? Dancing with another man? Jealousy is not a good reason to marry, son, so do not let that guide you. Even married people are required to dance with others. You want to marry a woman you can trust. Jealousy will eat you alive. You will never have a day's peace."

"I do trust her." It was true, Garrett realized as soon as he said the words. She had a rare sense of honor that made her see even servants as real people, likely due to her American upbringing. She had not taken advantage of her kinship with Cokewell, had needed someone to step in to bridge her resistance. This was a woman who would never violate her own code.

But that left her vulnerable to those who did not share her values. She needed someone who could stand up for her, fight back against those who might use her connections, her American-ness, to exploit her. War talk with her country had not subsided, but rather increased. If it happened, she might be in danger. "It's all the other men I don't trust. They don't understand her."

Father straightened from the railing and laughed out loud. A few heads beneath them looked up. "The man does not exist who understands women."

"It is Cokewell's granddaughter."

His father's mouth dropped open, then closed with a snap, and his eyes went wide. "Oh. I see." A breath passed, and a smile curved his mouth again. "The young woman from the summer party?"

Garrett groaned. "Madeline has been talking again."

That fatherly hand came down on his shoulder again. This time it brought the support he wanted. "Do not blame your sister. She is concerned about you, and wants you to be happy, as happy as she is. But yes, I have heard about the young woman, and not just from Madeline. I was not aware that she was here tonight, but your mother and sister handled the invitations. Of course the Cokewells would be invited."

Then Father's gaze sharpened. "You are right to worry about other men. I can count a dozen right now who would pursue her simply because of who her grandparents are. Whoever marries her has an immediate link to Prinny himself."

"I know that. It is one of the things I fear for her."

"If you believe she is the woman for you, do not waste time. Cokewell wants her well-married so she will stay in England, and he is not up on the rakes and cads this season. Now I am going to find my wife for the next dance." Father's hand squeezed Garrett's shoulder again. "Go down there and find her, get yourself a dance before her card is filled. And make an appointment with Cokewell before the night is over."

Garrett bowed to Grace as she came off the floor with her current partner. He waited until the man walked off to speak. "Miss Grace. Do you have a dance to spare for me this evening?"

She pulled up her card—not a fan this time, but a real dance card—and looked at it. "I have one dance left, but it's late and I don't know if my grandparents want to stay that long. That's why I haven't let anyone pick it."

I can take you home, he thought, but he could never say that. "May I?" He reached for her card, and she held up her wrist, waiting while he scrawled his name. "Where is your grandfather? I looked for him, but did not see him from the balcony."

She glanced around. Silly, that she would imagine she could spot Cokewell with her shorter height if he had not seen the man from the balcony's vantage point. "I think he went into the card room. Either that or he and Grandmother strolled into the garden."

Garrett hardly thought that people their age would dare venture into the garden at night. That was reserved for the bright light of day, when there was no danger of bumping into couples doing something they should not. "I will try the card room, then." He bowed again. "I hope to dance with you later."

Grace's next partner arrived, so Garrett dipped his head to the man in a cursory bow and strode off toward the card room. He doubted Cokewell would be playing, but the man liked to watch.

Sure enough, he was there, leaning against the wall and looking at the cards of the closest player. No one made a fuss; they all knew he would keep his counsel and never cheated, never gave a hint to the other players.

"Cokewell, sir. Might I have a moment of your time?"

At his nod, Garrett led the way out. "We can go into the hallway. It should be empty enough for us to talk. This won't take long."

Sure enough, the hall was bare of people. Garrett walked a little further than absolutely necessary to make certain their voices would not carry to anyone who might step out at the wrong time.

"This should be far enough." He turned to face Cokewell, surprised that his hands inside his gloves were sweaty. He wished he could rub them on his breeches like he had done as a child. But he was a man now, and men did not show nerves. "I would like to make an appointment to discuss something with you. Might I come over tomorrow?"

From the look in Cokewell's eyes, he knew exactly what Garrett would discuss, but was not about to make it easy. "What is this matter?"

"I wish to discuss settlements for your granddaughter."

Cokewell's head gave a single bob. "Tomorrow at two. I will be waiting."

Then he turned around and walked back to the card room, but Garrett was certain he saw a lightness in the man's step.

26

"I hoped you would come up to scratch. There have been men hovering around my granddaughter that I feared might make an offer I would be forced to consider. I am glad you came first." Cokewell sat behind his imposing desk, hands flat on the shiny polished surface. His office was as stately as Garrett's own.

Had he not been used to such a formidable room, Garrett might have been intimidated. The man knew how to impress. Heavy mahogany furniture, genuine silver multi-branched candlesticks that made the room bright and surely showed any sweat on nervous brows, dark blue velvet curtains, the scent of real leather in the books on the shelves, and the thickness of the rug beneath his feet.

It wasn't the surroundings that made Garrett's mouth dry. He looked at Cokewell, and his throat went tight. He was actually going to do this. He was going to wed Grace—and he hoped the settlements he spent most of the night working out would be proof of his esteem for both the man and his granddaughter.

Cokewell tilted his head toward the papers Garrett had given him. "This is all well and good, but it does not get to the real reason you are here. So tell me. Why do you want to marry Grace?"

Why? Garrett wondered whether any sound would come out if he tried to speak. He could talk settlements with ease, but did Cokewell want *feelings?*

The discussion with his father yesterday slid into his mind. He would tell Cokewell the same things he told his father. The words came when he needed them then.

His father wasn't the one who decided to allow or deny.

He cleared his throat, relieved when the words were audible, even firm. "She is not used to our customs, and needs someone who can allow her to be herself. She sometimes uses words that might frustrate anyone who wants a typical English wife. She is not that, and likely never will be."

Cokewell blinked. Garrett wondered if that was good or bad, but since he could speak, he had to get them all out.

"She is also American, and I have heard the whispers of war. What if someone tries to exploit her? She needs someone who has nothing to gain from her nation. She is also from a rough country, and seems without fear. She wants to see everything of London, and probably England, the good and the bad. What if she weds a man who wants to control her? She needs a husband who can let her explore, but curb only her worst impulses."

"And you are that man."

Was that a question? Garrett decided it needed an answer. "Yes. I believe I am."

The room was quiet. Cokewell looked at him, then down at his hands, still resting on the desk. When he lifted his gaze again, his eyes were shadowed. "There are things about my granddaughter that she might never feel she can share. If I promise she is of good character, are you willing to overlook that she holds secrets?"

"If you are referring to the possibility that she might be illegitimate, I think your acceptance of her has put that to rest."

"America is a land of workers. That is all I can tell you, but can you overlook a wife who is . . . the daughter of a tradesman?"

That pause felt strange, but perhaps Cokewell or his wife had struggled with the life their daughter lived after her elopement. Had she gone into trade with her husband? Grace often seemed to be bored, the sign of someone who had always been busy before.

Did it matter to himself, though? He saw Grace learning to dance, remembered her curiosity about everything, that concern about the effect man had on the earth, her strange new ideas. Did it matter that she might have been in trade? The answer came quickly. "It matters not to me. No doubt someone will wonder, and ask what her parents did. Your daughter's history is known, that she ran away with a groom. Almost certainly someone will take issue with it, but I am certain I can handle whatever complaints come. If they have any complaints on her background, I have an issue with *them*."

Cokewell gave a single nod. "You have my permission to wed her." Then his gaze sharpened, his brown eyes fierce on Garrett. "She is no young girl right out of the schoolroom. As you have said, Grace has a mind of her own. I might agree to your suit, but you must convince her on your own. If she says no, then the answer is no. I will not force her."

"Neither will I." Garrett's mouth relaxed enough to smile. "But I will do my very best to convince her."

If Cokewell's gaze had been fierce a moment ago, it became downright deadly now. "I will not stand for her being compromised."

Garrett stiffened. "You mistake my meaning. I would *never* do that to her."

Cokewell relaxed. "I did not think you would, but I had to make sure. I will send for her. You can take her into the garden and plead your case, but it is in sight of the windows. Know that someone will be watching at all times."

He reached behind him and pulled the cord. A moment later, the butler appeared. Apparently no one answered the office summons but him.

"Ah. Davies. Can you send my granddaughter to me?"

Davies' somber face flickered, but he gave a single bob of the head. "Certainly, sir."

The door shut. "She will be here soon."

"Of course." Garrett resisted the urge to drum his fingers on his knee, just sat and listened to the clock tick.

After several minutes, a tap came on the door, and it popped open. Grace stepped in, leaving the door open. Cokewell and Garrett both rose.

"Grandfather? Davies said you were looking for me." She seemed to notice Garrett for the first time. "Oh! I'm so sorry. I didn't realize you had company."

Garrett managed not to give a start of surprise. Unless he was mistaken, several clumps of dust were sticking to the curls on the top of her head, caught in the fancy style her maid gave her this morning, and where she could not see to brush them away. The nearest sleeve had a tint of grey at the underside, and it wasn't a shadow. He suspected if he could see the opposite sleeve, it would match. Her hands were ungloved, not even the kind without fingers that his mother wore when embroidering, and still slightly damp. She had washed them, but hadn't changed her gown.

He bit his lip to hide the smile. When he and Cokewell talked about her coming from a family of people in trade, he had not pictured her scrubbing. Or sweeping. Or whatever she did to get dust in her hair.

What *had* she been doing? Clearly her American independence kept her from heading to her maid before coming down to visit her grandfather.

He would have to look her over carefully before they went out anywhere.

Garrett imagined brushing those little clumps away, touching that curly hair for the first time, and his heart picked up, his throat grew tight again.

"My dear." Cokewell held out his arms, and she walked into them as if they had been hugging each other all their lives. He set Grace away, leaving his hands on her shoulders. "Lord Fairfax would like to see our garden. Why don't you take him on a tour?"

"Certainly. The late flowers are still blooming, but they won't last long." She started for the door, and smiled at Garrett as she passed. "Follow me."

Behind him, he thought he heard Cokewell choke back a laugh, but the smile still lingered in his voice. "Yes, Fairfax, follow her."

With a glance over his shoulder and an exchange of smiles, Garrett let Grace lead him out of the office and down the hallway.

If she says no, then the answer is no. I will not force her.

He himself would never force a woman, as he had told Cokewell, but he was not above some subtle convincing.

Grace walked down the hallway toward the back door that led to the garden. It wasn't a large garden, they were in the city after all, but it was pretty even this time of year. As she had said, the summer flowers were done, but the autumn flowers were still in bloom.

This English fall was hardly the fall she knew in Minnesota. In her own time, the first frost would be past by now. In an odd way it felt more like spring, cool days, and only slightly brisk at night without even the threat of oncoming winter. She could go out in a light shawl and be perfectly fine.

Of course, all her latest gowns had long sleeves.

She wondered as they passed a footman if she should tell him to have her maid bring a shawl, but they were unlikely to be outside long. There just wasn't that much to see. If Grandfather allowed her this brief time, she didn't want an interruption, not even for a shawl.

Besides, she too seldom saw Fairfax, and she missed him. Last night's dance was the first time she had seen him in a week. The first time since they shared the seat in the carriage.

She worried Grandfather's blatant hint scared Fairfax off, even though he hardly seemed the kind of man to turn tail and hide. No, he would come right out and tell Grandfather to mind his own business.

He had danced with her last night, and here he was. He didn't even protest when almost shoved out of the house with her. See the garden, indeed!

Grace glanced over at Fairfax, walking so calmly beside her. He didn't seem irritated. In fact, he looked rather smug.

This couldn't be his own idea, could it?

Don't be silly, Grace, she scolded herself. *If he was interested in you, he would have visited.* Paid a call. Whatever they termed it in this time.

At least dropped in on one of the balls they went to throughout the week.

As they neared the large doors at the back of the house, doors to the stone steps that went down into the garden, another thought struck her. Perhaps he had been trying to find a way to tell her not to get her hopes up.

Working out how to warn her off without insulting her grandparents might well have taken a week.

"You were right. This is a very well-planned garden." Fairfax held out his elbow, and Grace took it. She was used to this now. Why men thought a woman couldn't make it down steps without a man to help them was both irritating and sweet.

Another emotion climbed into the mix. Dread. If he meant to tell her not to expect more from him, she would prefer he just got it over with.

But it wasn't done like that in this time. Everything, even a brush-off, had to be done with ceremony. Courtesy.

Her heart seemed to slide down in her chest, weighted by the sense of impending pain. A rejection, however kindly done, was still a rejection.

And then the rational part of her brain reminded her, *you are only here temporarily.*

They reached the bottom of the short tier of steps. Fairfax walked calmly along the crushed rock path, past the sculpted hedge designed to look like a bench, the large clay pots that held the golden autumn flowers, the wrought-iron bench where one actually could sit after the hedge's bushy illusion. Keeping the same measured pace, like a man with all the time in the world, he headed toward the tree that had been formed into a sculpture of trunk and branches, and the climbing rosebush that covered the archway.

The season for roses was long over.

Fairfax walked with confidence, but he always did. That didn't mean he had been here before. Did it?

She had to ask. "You seem to know your way through the garden. This isn't your first time here, is it?"

He looked down at her, not missing a step. "There is a path. One can hardly get lost. Besides, my parents are good friends with your grandparents, you know that. Yes, I have been in the house, but it has been years since I saw this garden. I seem to recall there was a small gazebo of some kind. Is it still there?"

"Yes. It's just beyond the rose arch." Her heart picked up as they reached the climbing rosebush. Grace knew the gazebo well, a delicate tracery of whitewashed wood with curving open doors and windows. It was not meant for shelter, but for romance. In the summer, pink roses climbed over it and scented the air, and the sun peeked through the wooden lace walls.

He specifically asked to see it. Did he just want to visit old memories? Or was there a deeper purpose?

Her heart kicked up another notch.

"Ah yes. There it is." Fairfax gave a satisfied nod. "It will do."

Grace couldn't bring herself to speak, just let him take the lead. If she said what she was thinking, she might embarrass herself. Faint nausea twisted her stomach as building excitement and desperate dread fought. Worse, if he said what she longed to hear, she knew what she had to say. And it hurt. It hurt so much!

Why couldn't the mirror have given her a time limit? Told her she was here for six months, a year! If she knew, only *knew*, how long she was staying in this world, and if that was forever, she could give the answer she longed to.

Because now she was quite sure what he intended to say.

Ducking his head slightly, he stepped through the arched doorway onto the white limestone floor. His free hand lifted hers where it rested on his arm, and he brought it to his lips.

His eyes met hers, and something burned in them, sending her heart into overdrive. "I am glad you did not wear gloves. I like the taste of your skin."

Then he faced her fully, and took both her hands in his. The leather of his gloves almost felt like flesh; they were even warm. She knew what was coming, and her heart pounded so hard it battered her insides.

In his deep, warm voice, his eyes fixed on hers, he said, "I have received your grandfather's approval, but it all depends on you. Miss Grace, will you do me the honor of becoming my wife?"

Grace's throat burned even as her heart soared. *Tell me what to do*, her heart screamed at the mirror, but no answer came. How could she marry him never knowing how long they would have together? *Stall.* In a voice she didn't recognize as her own, she asked, "Shouldn't we get to know each other better first?"

His brows drew together. "Is that how it is done in America? Isn't it better to learn about each other after we are married? We will see each other every day. Courtship is by its very nature artificial."

"But we hardly know each other!" Her voice was only a little stronger.

"I know plenty, and I must wed soon. I am the only son. My family line depends on me finding a wife."

I must wed soon. If he had slapped her with a fish, it might have been less insulting. "So why me?"

He drew back, still holding her hands. "I should think it obvious. I have been watching for someone I could see myself marrying. Until you, I found no one."

So I'm the best of a bad lot? But Grace kept her mouth shut. The mirror had not turned on. Had not shown the first signs of tarnish, nothing to indicate that it really was the force that brought her here.

Maybe she was supposed to stay.

But how could she say *yes*? Grace looked down at their joined hands, her ungloved ones that had been working in secret in Grandfather's attic, Fairfax's so much larger ones concealed in expensive leather.

Hidden from her view, like his heart.

She remembered her grandmother's words once when talking about her own courtship. "He had the hardest time telling me he loved me." And Grammy had giggled like a girl.

The hardest time telling me he loved me.

Was this Fairfax's problem too? Was he trying to tell her he loved her?

And if she said yes, would her trip here be final? Was that what the mirror was waiting for? Her to choose?

"Are you waiting for me to present my case?" He jiggled her hands. "I know all I need to about you to see that you are everything I have been waiting for. I could never marry a virtual child, and that is what I have had to choose from." He paused as if to deliver momentous news. "Until you." He jiggled her hands again. "Will you put me out of my suspense and give me the answer I seek?"

What do I do? The words shrieked in her brain, pounded in her heart, beating faster as the silence stretched. *What do I do?*

She didn't know how long she could keep from crying. How could she do this to him? If she were to disappear as quickly as she came, what would that do to him?

But what if she could never go back? It felt like that lately, like she was here to stay and it was a one-way trip.

He brought one of her hands to his lips again, his mouth warm and dry. "I will wait as long as it takes. If you wish reassurance, if you long to go back and visit your family, I would never prevent you. I should like to meet them myself."

Grace cleared her throat, the sound too rough for the setting, and screwed up her courage. "I have told you I don't know how long I can stay. Consider how unfair it would be to marry, and have me suddenly be forced to leave."

His face softened, his eyes stayed warm. "I assure you, I can prevent that. No one can take you anywhere against your will once you are my wife."

Grace couldn't hold his gaze. The weight of her secret squeezed her middle until she could hardly breathe. What if she was stuck here after refusing him? Forced to stand by and see him wed someone else?

And that thought finally loosened her heart. *Say yes*, it said, then more insistently, *say yes*.

Maybe that was the mirror's reassurance?

Breathing around a heart that suddenly filled the space in her chest, she said, "Yes."

Garrett—yes, she would think of him now as Garrett, not Fairfax —gave her hands a convulsive squeeze, released them, and one finger touched her chin, lifting it up until her eyes met his. "Thank you."

Then his head dipped, his crystalline eyes glittering, and his mouth met hers. Soft at first, a quick peck, a touching of mouths, a sudden exchange of breaths, then a groan seemed to come from his throat, and his lips came back, the kiss grew deeper. She felt her mouth open of its own accord, and Garrett absorbed her.

27

Two long months later

"Fairfax is already at the altar," Lily told Grace in an excited voice as she peeked around the door of the small room where they waited. "It looks like every invitation sent was accepted." She shut the door again, cutting off the bright morning light that seeped through the narrow gap.

Madeline smiled from the chair where she was sitting. "I have to go out and take my seat. Everyone will be shocked that a woman so great with child is out in public, but I simply could not miss seeing Garrett getting married." She pushed herself to her feet.

Thank goodness for the high waists of this day, Grace thought. A pregnancy could be hidden for a while in the current styles, and Madeline had done so. But she was right. There was no hiding the bump now. Or the pregnant-woman waddle.

The last two months had been a whirlwind. Everyone wanted to meet the woman who captured Lord Fairfax's heart, and Grandmother had taken her on a tour of all the high-ranking women of London. Grace learned which families had the best chefs, which had children that wanted to peek around corners, and which had sons that didn't care if a woman was engaged to be married; they would flirt with anyone in a skirt.

Grace could tell her hostesses she captured Garrett's mind more than his heart, but she didn't want to think about that herself. He was handsome, not the most important thing but a definite plus. His smile made her heart sing. If she did not do the same for him, he would never admit it. And wasn't it better *not* to know?

He was kind, attentive, and very tolerant of her odd Americanisms.

In fact, he hadn't even fainted when she confessed that the dust in her hair—which she hadn't even realized was there, and how embarrassing to think he was looking down at attic debris while he proposed—came from scrounging through some of Grandfather's discarded chairs.

She promised Grandfather to keep her occupation secret, so no matter how much Grace longed to tell Garrett everything, she kept back that she had been more than looking. She was working again. She had sent the footmen out for the necessary tools. To be sure, she did it all in secret, her only cohorts the servants.

Stuffing a chair with fresh straw purchased and smuggled in from the nearest inn had been a new experience for her. And for the footmen. The maids were also in on the conspiracy, and worked frantically to sweep up the dried bits that fell out of the wrapped bundles going up to the attic.

But she had done the best she could, and the chair turned out rather well.

Right now it sat again in Grandmother's parlor, where it belonged.

Although Grandmother told no one how it came to be back. "You must keep this quiet, Grace. It will humiliate Lord Fairfax if word gets out. You will be a lady soon, and ladies do not go into trade."

Grace took a deep breath, and looked down at her wedding gown. It was not the white gown she had always imagined, but it was breathtakingly beautiful, a soft green undergown with a pale cream overlayer, so filmy it almost wasn't there, and covered with embroidered flowers in the palest hues. The elbow-length sleeves were slightly poufed, with a thick band of lace at the bottom that matched the trim all around the gown's train.

If anyone had ever told her she would be in love with a green wedding gown, she would have replied that they were crazy, but this gown was the most stunning thing she had ever owned.

The bonnet made to match was equally gorgeous, the green ribbon that tied under her chin an exact match to the undergown. Matching embroidered flowers had been sewn around the brim, and more decorated her gloves.

Grace stared at herself in the mirror, unable to believe this was her. She was still here in the England of the past, and she was getting married.

Lily came over and gave her a hug. "You are indeed a fortunate woman. I might be married, but I can see that he is the best catch of the Season. And he is fond of you, which is more than many wives can say." She picked up the bonnet. "Let's get this on without ruining your hair. This is not something you can do without looking, and I need to fulfill my duties as your friend."

Grace sat in the chair Madeline had just abandoned, and held her breath as Lily eased it down. "There! I did not feel a single hairpin catch, so everything should be as it is supposed to be." She stepped back and smiled. "You are a beautiful bride. Fairfax will be impressed at his good fortune."

A tap came on the door, and Lily dashed back to peek outside. "Oh! Mr. Cokewell! Is it time?"

His voice rumbled into the room. "Yes. You should go take your place. I am ready to walk her up."

Grace suddenly wondered whether her legs would straighten, or hold her up if they did. But Grandfather was waiting, and Lily turned around. "I will leave you with him. I must go sit down." She smiled, and vanished out the door.

Grandfather stepped inside and pulled the door shut. His eyes filled, but he blinked the moisture away, and cleared his throat. "You look beautiful, my dear. Your grandmother will cry when she sees you. Your . . . Garrett will be most proud." He held out his arm. Then he must have seen something in her face because his brows came down in a worried frown. "Are you well? You are not having second thoughts, are you? You have picked a fine man, and will be most happy."

It was too late to change her mind. Not that she wanted to. She had checked the mirror this morning, and it was as clear as the day she arrived. If she was here to stay, what was better than to marry the man she wanted?

Grace took a breath, discovered her legs did remember how to work when she got to her feet, and slid her hand into place.

One nice thing about a wedding so early in the day. It cut down the number of hours leading to the wedding to have the last-minute jitters build. She had endured enough of them last night, so getting the wedding over with would be a relief.

Even though she saw the church earlier, it seemed to have grown, but that had to be all the eyes watching her walk up the long aisle. It was just family and close friends clustered on the front rows, but they were all staring at her and the aisle was so long.

Her knees felt wobbly, and her hand shook so hard on her grandfather's arm that he looked down at her in surprise. His other hand came up and squeezed her fingers gently. After the first few rows, Grace decided to keep her eyes focused ahead. Garrett stood straight, and so very tall, a symphony in black and white, black coat and breeches, white shirt and stiff cravat.

He watched her with a fierce and unhidden intensity in his gaze.

And then she was there. Cokewell took her hand off his arm and looped it around her almost-husband's. The two men exchanged a glance.

I will enjoy this, I will pay attention, I will memorize everything, she told herself, and prayed she would be allowed to keep the memories . . . no matter what.

"Dearly beloved," the minister—his exact title slipped her mind—began the ceremony, "we are gathered here in the sight of God, and in the face of this congregation, to join together this Man and this Woman in holy Matrimony."

Behind her, only the sound of people breathing filled in the background.

He went on, in ponderous tones, to list the sanctified reasons for marriage. Children, of course, in this time before birth control, and to prevent fornication, and companionship.

Oh, how she wanted this marriage to be one of companionship! Most of all, more than anything, dare she pray for love?

Then came the ominous words, "Therefore, if any man can show any just cause, why they may not lawfully be joined together, let him now speak, or else hereafter hold his peace."

If she was not meant to go through with this, the mirror had better wake up now. She felt her heart thud, her lungs seize, while she waited to disappear.

Nothing happened. Not a tremor in the air, not a whisper of wind, not even the flicker of a candle.

Grace took the first clear breath in months.

It was time for the vows. Garrett came first, and she heard the words *love, comfort, honor* and *keep.* And especially the ones about *forsaking all others.* In a strong voice that she knew carried all the way to the empty back of the church, he said, "I will."

Her vows came, and the first words were "obey him and serve him." *They were really serious about that, both 'obey' and 'serve' in the same sentence,* she thought. The rest of the vow was familiar; *love, honor* and *keep,* and of course, *forsaking all others.*

She suspected that last bit would be much easier for her than for him.

But they weren't done. Grandfather answered to the question of who gave this woman. In her own time, she highly doubted her wedding would have that part.

Almost as one, they turned to face each other. Garrett took her right hand, and held it with a gentleness that captured every morsel of her attention. His gaze did not waver, those gray eyes remained calm. "I, Garrett Thomas Atherton, take thee, Grace Renee Harding, to be my wedded wife, to have and to hold, from this day forward . . ."

Then it was her turn, and the words came out so smoothly it was as if she had memorized them from another past. "I, Grace Renee Harding, take thee, Garrett Thomas Atherton, to be my wedded husband . . ." His eyes were warm as he listened, and his hand held hers, still without a tremble.

The book was extended, a single ring sitting neatly on the open pages, yellow gold, not wide but thick, the curving height proclaiming that it would be heavy on her finger. Grace glanced back up at Garrett. For the first time since the wedding began, he smiled.

The old ceremony sank into her as it linked them, she and this man from another time. Inexorably the ceremony continued, involving kneeling, and a prayer.

At last, the words came, "I pronounce that they be Man and Wife together."

The minister turned and walked away. Garrett tucked her hand back in his elbow and followed.

Where was the kiss? She had to follow, he held her hand against his arm, she had to move with him, but weren't they supposed to kiss?

"We have to sign the register," he whispered in her ear as they passed into a small room.

It was done, her signature next to his on a page beneath many others, a stack of paper turning yellow with age even now, a permanent record that she was here.

They walked back into the church proper, then down the aisle, Grace still clinging to Garrett's arm, her legs stronger than they had been on the way up. Faces smiled at her, and she made herself smile back, but it felt forced.

Didn't he want to kiss her? Or wasn't it allowed?

He lifted her into his open landaulette, his hands warm on her waist, and climbed in beside her. The driver clucked to the horses, and the carriage rolled off.

The sun baked down on their heads and cast his face into strange angles as they clopped down the street, between buildings that threw their own shadows in large blocks onto the cobblestones.

As they rounded a corner in the shade of a tall three-story building, he faded into milky grayness.

She gasped and grabbed for him, but the carriage moved back into the sunshine and he was still there, solid and smiling.

"Still not used to the carriage, I see." He chuckled. "That is fine with me. It means you will hold on to me more. I shall have to take you on many carriage rides."

He wanted her to be herself. He didn't mind her outspokenness. Very well. Grace turned to face him. "The minister never told you to kiss me."

His brows went up, and those pale grey eyes twinkled. "Is that some American custom, to kiss in a church?" He clucked his tongue. "For shame. You Americans must shock God."

Grace scowled. "It is a lovely custom, like sealing the marriage. It's another promise, and what better place to do it than in front of God?"

He shifted on the seat. "There will be plenty of time for that later." When he cleared his throat, it sounded tight. "I hope you are pleased with the ring. It has been in my family for generations."

Grace thought she knew what his little movement meant, and smiled. She glanced down at the ring, glad now to go along with the change of subject, and smoothed her hand over the glistening gold. "It is beautiful."

"Not as beautiful as you." The words were so softly spoken she wondered if she heard them right.

Grace turned her head quickly, and stared at him. It was the most personal thing he had said since he proposed. "Thank you."

In a soft voice that could not carry even as far as the driver, he said, "I very much approve of your gown. You looked a vision." Then his voice became normal. "You aren't afraid of getting it stained during the wedding breakfast?"

She looked over at him, his outline sharp against the backdrop of buildings, no haze, no blurring. It must have been a trick of the light. "I don't intend to eat anything that might stain."

He laughed. "You are going to go hungry if you keep to that."

She smiled, pleased at how easily it came. "Then I will have to be hungry. I'd rather have the gown on and eat little than to put on something else and fill my stomach.

He shook his head, his eyes still twinkling. "You continue to surprise me, wife."

Wife. She was now a *wife*. In 1810.

28

THE SUN STRETCHED LOW, THE SKY WAS FADING INTO DUSK. SERVANTS slipped like shadows around the house, closing the curtains, lighting candles, tending fires in the rooms they would use.

The guests were all gone. The wedding 'breakfast' had lasted into the early afternoon, bacon and egg, ham for those who preferred it, and freshly baked rolls that the poor kitchen staff had been up early baking. Tea and chocolate, and wedding cake. No, not the tiered cake she expected, but a dense, heavy loaf of fruitcake so filled with fruits and nuts she could hardly see the dough that held it together.

That cake could have served as a whole breakfast.

Grace sat in the smaller of the two matching chairs in the parlor, and watched Garrett stretch out his legs and stare at the fire. He still wore his wedding clothes, even as she did, only his added a somber darkness to the room. A glass of brandy sat on the small table at his side, the scent teasing her nose.

"It was a lovely wedding," she said. Even she could hear it came out wistful. Would he kiss her now? How long did she have to wait?

"We can still pack for a wedding trip, take a tour of Italy, if you would like. I won't hold it against you if you change your mind."

Garrett gazed at her from beneath lowered lids. When they discussed the wedding plans, he asked if she wanted a wedding trip, and Grace had said no.

She might be changing time enough just by being here in England. No need to traipse across Europe.

Did he want to travel? Grace tried to hold his gaze. "We don't have to stay in London if you don't want to. It's just—well, you already know the city. It's all so new yet to me. But it's your wedding as much as mine."

"Not just a wedding. A marriage." His eyes didn't flicker, were still steady and calm. "Have a glass of wine, my dear. It will relax you." With surprising grace, he poured one for her from an elegant bottle sitting on the same table, and handed it over.

"Thank you." Grace had to look down to hide her smile. Maybe a new bride from 1810 wouldn't know what he was doing, but a woman of her time knew exactly what was going on. She'd heard Ogden Nash's little ditty about liquor being quicker. Garrett wanted to relax her.

She might have been a modern woman, but she could use his cure. Grace took a sip of his truly excellent wine, then another, longer sip.

"Take it slowly, my dear. That is not tea." A smile colored his voice, deeper than its normal tone. He lifted his own glass to his mouth.

The nerves that had percolated under her skin all day seemed to lift. The wine was doing its thing.

The fire crackled and warmth finally reached them. Grace held out a hand to soak it up, feeling it prickle on her cool fingertips. Garrett set his glass down and leaned back. Grace blushed at the look in his eyes, all hot masculine anticipation.

"Are you tired?" His voice was as smooth as the brandy in the snifter he held. "It is early, but why don't you ring for your maid, and have her get you ready for bed?"

The wine left in her glass had little ripples across the surface.

Grace set it down. She didn't need false courage tonight. "I am sure she is already up there." The mirror had given her this; she was going to take it, every moment. She stood.

"I will be up soon."

At the heat in his words, Grace went still, her legs weighted in concrete. She turned and met his gaze.

Garrett's eyes were hot, and Grace felt her clothes tighten as her body began to respond to the seduction in his steady stare. He stood slowly, like a prowling panther, and stepped over.

Her breath caught.

He was going to kiss her, the kiss she had longed for all day. She couldn't move, not even if an earthquake shook the room.

Garrett stopped in front of her. His breathing cut the air, deep and quick, and his eyes captured her gaze, holding it as strong as a chain. His hands came up and framed her face, his touch soft and warm.

Then he lowered his head. She felt the warmth of his breath before his lips touched hers and lingered, learning the shape of her mouth as she learned his. Her heart hammered in her chest, stealing her own breath.

Unless that was him.

Their mouths grew fierce and demanding, eager, his tasting of brandy and hunger, and she matched his every move. His hands crept into her hair, and she heard the pins tumble to the floor, felt the intricate braids and twists come loose and tumble around her shoulders.

He pulled back. "I love your curls. At last I get to see them." But he didn't look, just came back for another taste, another drink, dipping into her mouth, stroking, teasing, until they had to break apart to breathe.

Grace gasped for air through constricted lungs, and raised her hands, slid them up those arms still protected by his layers of clothes, across his shoulders, and then down his front. His vest buttons stopped the slide of her fingers, and she slowly slid each one from its hole. The richly embroidered vest separated, and his shirt tempted her next. Garrett caught her hands as she reached for those buttons.

"Not here. I want complete privacy. I intend to take a very long time."

Grace watched his mouth move, and wanted to taste his lips again. Two kisses. They were married and she had only tasted two kisses from this man who was her husband.

He pulled her up and swung her into his arms. "Then we are agreed."

"Yes," Grace whispered as she clutched his shoulders, and watched his mouth again.

She stroked her fingers gently up and down Garrett's back, loving the smooth stretch of his skin. Muscles roped his back and thickened his arms, made his legs lean and taut. Riding horses must be wonderful exercise, she thought dreamily, and gave a single watery chuckle.

Whatever capricious fate or mirror brought her here could snatch her away again. That worry dogged her, but today it seemed particularly close and threatening, and now she knew, finally, what she would lose.

A lump clogged her throat, like a giant sob hung suspended, and she tried to swallow it down, but the first tear slid free. She wrapped her arms around Garrett in sudden ferocity, holding him to her as though her meager strength could keep them like this forever. His hand came up and stroked her hair as though he, too, was spent, but he could not know the terror that hung over them, the dread she carried every day.

The sob bubbled past her throat, the sound shocking and out of place. Garrett struggled onto his arms again and looked down at her. "What is wrong?" Guilt darkened his face. "I didn't hurt you, did I?"

"No," she sobbed, now that the dam had broken. "No, not at all. I just wasn't—expecting—*this*." This closeness, this belonging, this surfeit of pleasure he had poured over her.

This sudden and shocking fear.

His face lightened again, and he leaned down and kissed her, gently, reverently. "It was not casual for me, either." Then, when she couldn't stop, he separated their bodies, and rolled to his side, pulled her into his arms and let her cry.

29

Garrett was already at the table when Grace entered the dining room for breakfast, a plate of mail at his side, a letter in his hand. He looked up and smiled. "Good morning, wife. Did you sleep well?"

She felt the blush heat her face. His smile grew as she sat down in the chair nearest him. "It took a while to fall asleep, but yes, I slept well."

He laughed. "It was a very pleasant way to wait for sleep, do you not think so?"

Her face got hotter, but she had to laugh herself. "Very pleasant, yes."

His laugh faded to a smile, and his eyes glittered with the memory of last night. "I am glad to hear you say so. Do you feel like a drive, or would you prefer to stay home?"

The poker-faced footman set a plate down in front of each, fresh toast, fried ham, and an egg. No doubt the servants had held the food for her arrival. It was a sweet thing to do.

Grace smiled at Garrett. "Thank you for waiting."

"I dared not hold off much longer. The food would have gone

cold, so thank you for coming when you did." He picked up his fork. "It would have been a lonely meal."

Grace suspected he didn't mind eating alone. He had certainly tried hard enough to warn her off when they first met, but it was a lovely thing—a very husbandly thing—to say.

He nodded to the footmen, and they left, closing the door behind themselves.

"Well, my dear, back to the subject. What would you like to do today?" He lifted his teacup to his mouth, then said over the rim before sipping, "We could stay home. I can think of many things we can do to fill the time." His lids lowered, but she saw the glint in them.

She wouldn't mind, but if they went up to bed, they wouldn't get out for hours. Much as the idea appealed, she wanted to see the London her grandparents wouldn't show her. She started with an easy request. "Can we go to Buckingham Palace? I would love to see it."

"Palace? It is a grand place, but hardly a palace. You went past it once before. Had I known you wished to look at it, I would have pointed it out." He smiled. "But if you wish, we can certainly drive that way again, and satisfy your curiosity. In fact, we can stop at St. James Park again, and perhaps this time stay longer." He gestured toward her plate with his cup. "Eat. You will need your strength for later."

The glitter was back in his eyes.

She gave a shiver of delight, and turned to her food. Eating with his gaze returning to her over and over again was distracting, that steady look as tangible as a touch. She pretended not to notice, finally made it through most of her breakfast, set the plate aside, and smiled at her husband.

"Shall we go?"

He smiled back, and waved toward the pile of mail beside his plate. "Let me finish this first. Why don't you get acquainted with my house? It will be your home now. Decide what you want to keep. Whatever you do not like, we can bring up to the attic." His brows went up as if an idea had just occurred to him. "In fact, you can start there. You might find things you want to use."

She hadn't paid attention to the decor. Yesterday there had been the family, his side and hers, new 'aunts' and 'uncles,' to meet, make conversation with, try to impress. Today, there was just him, sitting at the table, absorbing all her attention.

She looked around the room for the first time. For an exclusively male domain, it was surprisingly bright. The bottom half of the wall was a soft Wedgewood blue, the wide chair rail and the wall above were white, giving the room a softness. The curtains over the long, wide windows filling one wall were the very same blue as the walls.

Garrett set down one letter, glanced up at her, smiled absently, and picked up the next. "You need not wait for me. Feel free to wander the house."

"I don't mind staying. It's a beautiful room." She wished she could get up and turn chairs over to check for a maker's mark. She pulled on her training, her experience, to make educated guesses. That dark wood inlaid sideboard, long, with scalloped openwork legs on each corner had to be a Chippendale. The chair on which she sat, straight legs and a lyre back, was probably an Adam chair, as was the armchair on which Garrett sat. Which meant the table was probably an Adam as well.

Her question just slipped out. "Is this table set an Adam?"

The letter lowered. His eyes appeared, his brows puckered in confusion. "Pardon?"

It was too late to put the words back into her mouth. "I was just wondering about the maker. Your furniture is beautiful." Words kept coming, the story she was hiding pushing out mindless chatter. "I've always been interested in furniture. I studied the history of the different styles and epochs when learning about reconstruction techniques. Each era has its own identifying marks, you know. Colors go in and out of favor just like designs do."

His eyes had gone wide as she prattled on, but now they narrowed as he looked at her. "Reconstruction techniques." Garrett repeated the words as if he had never heard them before. He folded the paper and set it by his plate. "Grace, what are you talking about?"

She took a breath, and let it out slowly, hoping to calm the sudden thunder of her heart. Hiding so much from him had been tearing her apart, but now that she had the chance to open at least part of her stash of secrets, there was so much riding on his reaction!

Under the table, she crossed her fingers. A foolish gesture, but it gave her hand something to do. "I'm an upholsterer. I recover furniture, fix loose connections, refinish the wood. Make them look like new."

The image of the chairs she purchased the day she was whisked here had almost faded from her mind. She couldn't even remember what they looked like. Maybe he would let her work on something from the attic, assuming anything there needed repairs. She would go crazy if she didn't have anything to do but embroider, shop, and attend parties.

"I see." His gaze was still on her, but no expression showed on his face. "I have a wife with unusual accomplishments."

Unusual accomplishments. Was that good?

Cokewell's words the day he gave Garrett permission to propose came back. *America is a land of workers. Can you overlook the daughter of a tradesman?*

How much did the man know? That she was not just a tradesman's daughter, but a tradeswoman herself? He looked at her eager, anxious face, her eyes wide with unease. His own words came back, but with a new sting. *If they have any complaints on her background, then I have an issue with them.*

But when he said that, he hadn't thought that his *wife* had been in trade. Her expression became worried, and that furrow between her eyes and the shadow in those dark orbs stung like a prick from his letter opener. He did not want her to feel that way.

He would think about this later. Right now he had to make her feel better. "Your grandfather warned me that Americans were workers. I should have expected that my wife would be among them."

That little furrow eased, but did not disappear. "Perhaps I should have told you more."

Would it have mattered if he had known more about her? He didn't want to think he was that shallow. He respected his valet, and trusted his butler and his man of affairs. They all worked. It did not affect his view of them.

But they were *men*.

Garrett pushed this new knowledge away, to be considered later. After he had time to absorb it, maybe even talk to Cokewell, see how much of this he knew.

Get the man's promise not to breathe a word.

He had offered her a trip through London, and he would keep his word. Better, he would make it a delight. He did not want to run into anyone from yesterday's wedding, and have them see a frown. Gossip that his marriage was already in trouble after a single day would hurt his wife. And likely bring Cokewell pounding on his door. "Aside from a drive past Buckingham House, what else do you want to do today? It is your honeymoon as much as mine."

Grace smiled, and the furrow disappeared. "I want to see the other parts of the city. I've spent the last weeks getting fitted for my gowns, or picking out bonnets and gloves and shoes. I want to see something outside the shopping districts. Take me to the parks, and Westminster Abbey, and the Tower of London, the Tower Bridge, and the Thames. Does it smell as bad as I've heard?"

He laughed out loud, glad for the diversion from his thoughts. "I have married a woman who would rather smell the Thames than go shopping. I certainly can take you about the city if that is what you really want. Perhaps not all in one day, but that will give you something to look forward to." He pushed the plate with all the letters he had not finished aside, and rose. "Are you sure you do not want to stop somewhere and buy something pretty?"

"I'm an American. We believe in work."

One eyebrow went up. "Seeing the sights is hardly work, you know."

Grace narrowed her eyes, but they twinkled, and one corner of her mouth turned up. "I'll be learning. All kinds of stuff. Who knows what I might find that will be useful in my new life?"

Garrett nodded. "Very well. This will be an interesting day." For both of us, he thought, but kept the words inside. "I will have the curricle hitched up, and we shall go for a ride."

He shoved back his chair, and stood, then bent over the table, and gave her a close look, his gaze analyzing her face. "*Not* to the docks, in case you were going to mention them. I will draw some lines in your exploring. Put on your bonnet and bring a parasol, and we will go on this ride you want so much."

The route began to look vaguely familiar. Garrett was as skilled a driver as any she had ever ridden with, which made the curricle slightly less terrifying. She saw the apothecary shop she had told herself to remember, and a modiste's shop. After a couple turns, a green park appeared, running along the left side of the little carriage. And there, up ahead, was the formal park they had tried to explore before being chased away by the disturbance.

Instead of going into the park, though, Garrett turned the curricle right and ran alongside it.

"Look to your right." He pulled the horse up. "Buckingham House."

She did recognize it from the previous visit to the park across the street, but the resemblance to the Palace of her day was still vague.

The fence running around the property blocked some of her view, but those columns along the front of the house—now those looked familiar. She looked at the design on the top of the gate, and that, too, rang a bell.

"Does it live up to your expectations?" He leaned forward, she felt the small vehicle shift at the movement, but her head was turned away.

This was the first time she'd been disappointed in this new world. "Somehow it looks less impressive up close."

He frowned. "It is a big enough house, I assure you. I have been inside, and it is most impressive. Perhaps some day I can get you an invitation, and you can see for yourself."

She forced a smile, and turned back to him. "I'd like that very much."

The brow that always went up when he was skeptical rose. "Somehow that lacks a bit of sincerity." He flicked the reins, and maneuvered the horses and curricle around, squeezing through the carriages around them.

Once they were facing back the way they came, he eased over to the side and pulled the carriage up. "Shall we go for a walk again? Perhaps this time we will not be interrupted, and you can see the pelicans."

Grace smiled again, a real one this time. "I'd love that."

Garrett flipped a coin to the driver of a larger carriage in front of them as they passed. "Keep an eye on mine, too, will you?"

"Gladly, me lord." The coin disappeared into a pocket.

She looped her hand around his extended elbow, and he rested his free hand on top of it. Even through both of their gloves, his warmth crept through. She knew now what the rest of him felt like, and shivered in delight.

"Are you cold? I had thought to walk in the shade of the trees, but we can go over to the canal, and walk in the sunshine."

"The canal, please." She looked up at him, glad her bonnet had a short brim so she could see his eyes. "Will I see the pelicans again?"

He chuckled, the vibration running along his arm and into her hand. "I will do my very best."

So they took the other path, and strolled along, Garrett pointing to the mansions on the other side of the trees, nearly hidden from where they walked. "If you look closely, there is St. James Palace, for which the park was named. If we were to walk to the end of the park, you could see the Horse Guards, but I think we will save that for another day."

Grace nodded. "If I see the pelicans, that will be adventure enough."

For the first few minutes, they had the path to themselves, but people began to meet them, coming back from the far end.

One well-dressed man stopped for more than the obligatory nod of greeting. "Fairfax. Good to see you. You missed the Changing of the Guard." Then the man noticed Grace, or—more likely, she thought—that this was a new and different woman than he had seen before. "Oh, I say! Is this your new wife? I saw the notice in the papers."

Garrett looked down at her, and smiled, but it felt formal this time. Not the smile he gave when they were alone. "May I present my wife, Lady Fairfax. My dear, an old friend, Mr. Knight."

"Lady Fairfax." He bowed, crisp and practiced. "Madam. It is a pleasure." Then he turned back to Garrett. "A small wedding, then? I did not receive an invitation."

Garrett laughed. "To a wedding? You? Are you not the same man who said weddings are catching and you never attend?"

Knight winced. "You know what they say about words coming back to haunt you. Turns out, my older brother's wife has still not produced the required heir. It appears that duty might now fall to me. I must thus join the Season's whirl and find my own bride."

Garrett clapped a hand on his friend's shoulder. "You might find the institution to your liking."

Which was a rather nice thing to hear, Grace thought.

"I can see it suits you. I have not had your success as yet. You might wish me luck. I certainly seem to need it."

"It is not luck, my man, but knowing what you are seeing when you find it."

"I wish it was that easy." The man bowed again, and walked off.

Grace frowned at the man's back. "Poor woman."

A start ran along the arm she held. "What do you mean? You don't know the man!"

"Oh, I'm sorry, I didn't mean his future wife. I meant his brother's wife. It's desperately hard to want children, and not be able to have them."

Garrett relaxed beside her. "Yes. That is indeed a hard thing." He stopped, and turned her to face him, leaving his hands on her shoulders. His crystal-grey eyes were warm, not with passion but with sincerity. "I want you to know if you are unable to bear children, I will never blame you. God either gives children or he does not. It is pointless to blame either party."

She curled her hands over his arms as they still held her. "Thank you. That is a very enlightened view."

He smiled, and they began walking again, side by side, not touching but linked nonetheless.

An odd sound, like a coughing bark, pierced the air.

"Ah. The pelicans." Garrett took her hand again. "Come, my dear. Let us see the pride of St. James Park."

"I thought we would attend the opera tonight." The horse clomped down the street on the way home.

It had been a delightful day. The pelicans floated majestically on the water of the pond, Birdcage Walk was less than impressive, as all the bird cages were gone but the trees were still there, and Garrett stopped at a chocolate shop on the way home and bought her a chocolate drink.

She had seen very little of the rest of London. Perhaps that would come later. Or possibly he hoped to dissuade her by keeping her to new areas of 'his' part of the city and hoping she wouldn't notice.

But today she would not complain. "I would love another night at the opera." Without chaperones this time, she hoped.

"Excellent. Why don't you have a rest when we get home? It will be a late night."

They rode home in comfortable silence.

Garrett gazed at the blonde head on his shoulder as the carriage rumbled home in the small hours of the morning, and wondered who he had married.

It had been a strange night, watching a new side of his wife.

Grace had hummed along with the music without missing a note, yet watched and listened to the plot twists of Almaviva, Figaro and Susannah like someone who had no idea what to expect next. When Cherubino jumped out the window, she gasped. How could she be so familiar with the music and yet not know the story?

He had heard portions of the opera played at musicales, but her familiarity was deeper than that. Her fluid hands had given her away. She unconsciously gestured with the conductor, expected the swells of the music, even seemed to know which instruments would come in next as her hands beneath the edge of their box mimicked the playing of a violin, the crescendo of the drums, and the fingering of the flute.

Somehow she—who could hardly play the harpsichord, knew nothing of any other instruments and he was quite certain could not read music with any fluency at all—had heard the entire opera yet never seen it performed.

Her hand crept up his chest and caught a button, curled around it, and held on for a moment before slipping back down and landing squarely in his lap.

He picked it up with care, and wrapped his fingers around her small ones, wishing he could take off the lace gloves and feel her skin.

What a mystery he had married, lucky man that he was. He recalled their first meeting, how she walked right up to him and reached out to shake his hand, something no other woman of his acquaintance would even consider. She claimed to do work he had only seen done by a tradesman, and knew the score of an entire opera without ever having seen it.

What strange women America bred.

30

"So how are you and my brother getting along?" Madeline leaned forward as best she could around her belly, and tried to grab the teapot left on the table between them. "It used to be so easy to reach. Now I lose my breath just bending over."

Grace had to laugh. "Here. Let me do that." She picked up the teapot, and poured herself a cup. "You will forget all about the inconveniences after the baby comes. Or so I'm told."

"I hope you and all your advisors are right." Madeline held out her cup. "Will you pour?"

Grace hesitated, wondering how much caffeine was in it, and if it was enough to hurt the baby. Madeline's brow rose, a match for her brother's so-frequent expression as she waited.

The woman had been drinking tea from the beginning of her pregnancy. It was a bit late to stop her now. Grace gave a mental sigh and poured.

After a long sip, Madeline sighed. "I needed that." She looked at the table, back at her cup, shrugged, and rested the bottom against her protruding belly. "Do not think I forgot my question. My husband tells me Garrett is not visiting the club as often as before. He also says

Garrett has never been away from White's so long." She took another sip of the tea and set it back down on the bulge. "Forgive my curiosity, but he is my brother, and I want him happy."

She clapped her free hand over her mouth, and her eyes widened. "That was most tactless of me. I want *you* happy, as well. But I know him better, and it warms my heart that you have made him that way."

Grace felt the heat rise in her face. Garrett had certainly been sticking close to home—and to their bed. Madeline chuckled a racy chuckle she never expected to hear from her married and matronly sister-in-law, so obviously the blush was as bright as she suspected. "We have been driving about the city. I told him I wanted to see more than the shopping areas, so we've been exploring."

"There is plenty to see in London." Madeline gave an approving nod. "Where have you been?"

Grace winced before she could catch herself. "Garrett has taken me to every major landmark in London. I've been to Vauxhall Gardens several times, we have driven past the Houses of Parliament, I have seen Somerset House, and walked around any number of the gardens in the City."

All very nice, but she had wanted to find an upholstery shop, go to the docks and see where all the ships came from, wander through a fabric store, find a carpenter's factory, if such a thing existed here. Learn how things were done before everything became so mechanized.

Be around people like her old self, working people, ordinary people.

It seemed that her previous life was slipping away, more each day. This new life of luxury was too appealing; servants to pick up after her, meals that arrived fully cooked, a house that looked like it cleaned itself —if one didn't look at the maids who worked hard to keep it that way. She had gone down to the kitchen at first just to talk to everyday people, but learned quickly that her presence made them uncomfortable.

"Is something wrong, Grace?" Madeline's voice broke through her reverie, soft and concerned.

"No, everything's fine." Which was only half a lie. "The house is beautiful, the servants are most helpful, and Garrett is very . . . attentive."

The room was quiet for a moment. "If all is fine, why do you look so wistful?" Tension ran through Madeline, palpable on the air. "You are not sorry you married Garrett, are you?"

"No!" That didn't take any thought at all. No, she wasn't the least bit sorry. In fact, some days she hoped he was the very reason the mirror had sent her here.

So why had he never once told her of his feelings? It was as if he did the logical thing, and having married her to keep her and her Americanness safe from whoever he feared might threaten her, Garrett figured his job was done.

How could she bring up love when he showed no sign of wanting to hear the word? He certainly never said it. Pretty compliments, but those were easy. And often meaningless.

Poor fool she, who believed every one and ached for more.

"We women take a chance when we marry, don't we?" She didn't realize the words had come out until she heard the ache in them. And to Garrett's sister, of all people!

Madeline nodded. "I know you are not talking of cruelties. Garrett would never abuse a woman."

"No, of course not! I was just wishing . . ." her voice trailed off.

"Ah yes." Madeline smiled, or at least her mouth curved up, even though her eyes were sober. "It is best to keep your wishes to what is attainable, and not wish for too much. It is a good thing we women are the more clever. I would never say the like to my husband, but men are so easy to manage." She sobered. "I know I am the youngest of both of us, but I have been wed the longer. It appears you want some advice. Am I wrong?"

Grace shook her head. "No. I was never married before. This is not as easy as I hoped it would be."

"Ah yes, we all come to that conclusion. Well, here is my advice. It is a wise woman who does not expect more from her husband than he is able to give. We must look beyond their words, if you take my meaning."

"Beyond their words?"

"Sadly, yes. For most women, marriage is a transaction. Only the rarest few marry for love." She smiled a secret smile. Grace already knew Madeline was one of those lucky women.

She also suspected most of the women in this society were not as happy.

Madeline blinked and came back from her thoughts, picking up where she left off. "Fortunate women find a husband who treats them well and gives them children. And who does not quibble at the odd request for an increase in the allowance. But if you long for words of love, my dear new sister, you may be disappointed." Madeline folded her hands around the cup resting on her bulge, and cocked her head, looking at Grace with wise eyes. "That is what you desire, is it not? Words of love and devotion from my brother?"

Grace's throat tightened. She only nodded. If she tried to speak just then, nothing would come out.

Madeline's face was soft again. "I know he thinks much of you. It is early days yet. You are just coming to know each other. Softer emotions and words will come later. Many men never find them easy to say. For them, actions speak volumes, maybe more than words. Then there are the men who cannot love, for whom wives are for getting heirs, nothing more. But that, I am positive, is not Garrett. For right now, enjoy the coming to know him."

Grace nodded in pretend agreement, and sipped at her cooling tea. Was it better this way . . . just in case?

31

Grace stood beside Garrett as they eased their way toward the wide doors. The ball was clearly in full swing. Music crept over the clamor of conversation coming from inside, almost drowned by the equally enthusiastic conversations around them.

Perfume drifted through the open doors. They took another step closer, stopped by the crush of people in front of them. Garrett had given her a striking pearl and diamond necklace and matching earrings, both of which felt heavy on her, and the cream-colored gown she wore was a veritable column of lace that fell in swishing folds around her, the most elegant thing she had ever seen.

People didn't seem to be in a terrible rush, or maybe everyone came expecting to wait. Garrett gently caught her hand on his arm and squeezed. She looked up at him.

"Are you all right? Let me know if you feel faint. Women do at these things."

Grace nodded. "I'm fine. Really I am." Besides, she wouldn't dare faint and risk possibly tearing this beautiful gown. She ran a gloved hand over it just to touch the intricate pattern again.

At last they were ushered through the doors and the room spread out before them, high arching ceiling and chandeliers blazing away overhead as if to set the roof on fire, the candles flickering in the currents of air caused by the crowds beneath. In one corner, a small orchestra played valiantly on, Grace caught glimpses of them through the sea of bodies. Garrett gave her hand a reassuring pat. The night had begun. Another ball, another night on display.

And display it was, with the shine of ice-blue, gold and rose-pink satin, the shimmer of forest-green or sage silk, more lace, white for the youngest women, ruffles on the hems, dropped bodices showing enough bosom to satisfy the randiest male, and diamonds, pearls, sapphires and rubies around necks, on wrists and hanging from ears, even woven through intricately braided hair, gems flashing fire under the perfect illumination of so many candles.

No security guards stood around to watch over the riches like the award shows, the only place in her old world where such a surfeit of gems ever appeared. These were worn as comfortably as if no threat could exist.

In this rarified world, that might well be the case.

"Lord Fairfax!" A deep voice spoke nearby, and Garrett turned.

"Good evening, sir. Pleasant night, isn't it?"

The man, elderly and packed into a suit that looked like it might lose some buttons any minute, chuckled. "At least the weather is dry, if one has to wait to get inside. Hear tell Prinny himself is considering attending. Any confirmation yet?"

Garrett shook his head. "No, Sir."

"And who might this lovely lady be?" The man was so good-natured and there was such a total lack of innuendo that Grace smiled at him.

"My wife, Sir."

"Your wife?" The man looked surprised, but just for a moment. "Well, it was about time, wasn't it? Usually rumors run rampant when a man of your stature begins to cast his eye on a lady, but I've been out of Town. Just got back in two days ago. This is my first ball. Presume your father is relieved, eh?"

"So he says." Garrett smiled at the man, too, and turned to her. "My dear, may I present Lord Welles? My lord, my wife, Lady Fairfax, granddaughter of Cokewell."

"Cokewell, is it? I should have guessed. My lady." Lord Welles bowed over her hand. "It is indeed a pleasure. Perhaps I will see you at your grandfather's one of these days."

"I look forward to it." She smiled again, and hoped it would happen.

"I must find my wife. I promised her I would claim the supper dance." The cheerful old man leaned forward and said in what would have been a low tone if the noise had permitted it, "When you reach our age, the supper dance is another way of saying we sit together, catch up on gossip and wait to go in to eat." He chuckled, patted Garrett on the arm, and walked off.

Garrett watched him go, and held out a hand. "That is quite a good idea. Let me have your card and put my name there. I will reserve my choices before anyone else can." He scrawled his name on her card, kissed the hand to which her dance card was tied, winked, and walked off.

"Grace! Grace!" A familiar and welcome voice called her name. She swiveled from side to side, trying to pinpoint the source.

A delicate hand clamped on her free arm. "I finally found you!" Lily gasped as if she'd been running. Maybe squeezing through a crowd like this was as good as the real thing. "You look wonderful!" She was a picture of elegance in pale green satin with lace sleeves of the exact color. Emeralds were woven through her dark hair, and a heavy string of matching gems hung around her neck. A matching design dangled from her ears.

The music stopped. Applause scattered through the room, and people shifted again.

Lily pulled her out of the crush. The air immediately felt fresher.

She leaned close to talk, pitching her voice low, her eyes alight with interest. "How are you? I have not seen you in an age! Are you as happy as you look? How is marriage treating you?"

"It's fine. He's fine." The warmth of a blush crept up her cheeks, and Grace hoped the lighting was uneven enough that her friend didn't notice.

Lily linked arms and started around the outer edges of the crowd. "Maybe if we keep walking, men will find us, and our dance cards will fill up in no time at all." Her face suddenly changed, the merriment morphing into respect as she curtseyed, and tugged Grace down with her.

Grace knew a cue when she saw one, and managed what she hoped was a very respectful curtsy. A tall, heavy-set man with dark hair, wearing too-tight clothes and a leer stood there, looking at her with a lascivious eye. He spoke to Lily instead, but Grace knew his attention was on herself. "Good evening, Mrs. Stratham. Might I trouble you for an introduction?"

Lily nodded. "Of course, Your Royal Highness." *Your Royal Highness?* Grace's ears began to buzz, but she heard herself be introduced. "This is Lady Fairfax, Lord Fairfax's new wife."

The man looked Grace up and down, then nodded once. "So it is true. I thought I heard whispers of the like around the room, but I discounted them. One must ignore half of what one hears at events like this and distrust the other half."

He laughed, and Lily laughed along with him. Grace managed a weak smile as she tried to keep her legs locked in place. Was this the Prince Regent who gave the name to this era? And did he have the slightest suspicion what his reputation in history would be?

He turned back to Grace, took her hand, and pressed a kiss to the back. Looking at her from under the heavy swath of hair, he murmured, "Enjoy yourself this evening, my dear. I shall look forward to . . . seeing you. Soon, I hope." That leering smile again, and he strode off with a bit of a waddle.

Grace frowned at his back before she realized what she was doing. "The nerve of him! He was flirting with me."

Lily gasped. "Grace! One does not say such a thing about the Prince Regent!"

"Maybe not." Grace tried to smooth out her face. The frown kept pulling her brows down. "But I bet they *think* it."

A young man came over, younger than herself, Grace was positive, with medium brown hair, medium brown eyes, a medium build and medium height, and bowed to Lily. "Mrs. Stratham, might I trouble you for an introduction to your friend?"

He looked innocuous, a relief after the prince. Grace felt a smile start.

Lily went through the introductions again, only this time the young man bowed to Grace. "If your card is not full, might I have this dance?"

Lily gave her a poke, and Grace nodded. She held out her wrist, and he scrawled something, then extended his elbow. With one glance back at Lily, Grace slipped her hand into place, and they walked off toward the line of people forming for the next dance.

The music started, and Grace gave her new partner a curtsey. The music was vaguely familiar.

"I didn't know Lord Fairfax was married," the man said as they came together before turning away again, which saved Grace a reply. He repeated himself when they came back together with the next moves. "Where did he find you?"

She had heard any number of similar questions since the wedding, and hardly blinked. "We met at his house in the country." They turned away for the next step of the dance.

"Indeed?" He picked up the conversation a minute later when they swirled back.

Grace blessed the fact that she could step away and let him meet the next girl in the line. Throughout the dance, she wished it was Garrett across from her, Garrett taking her hand as the partners crossed in the middle, Garrett coming around the end of the line to meet up with her and promenade down the center.

Even though she knew people expected him to partner another woman, she didn't have to like it, and was glad she didn't see him on the floor in any of the other groups.

She moved around the line, forward and back and down the line and around in the now-familiar dance. Her mind was so absorbed with thoughts of her husband that when her eyes caught him watching her from a doorway, Grace almost missed her step.

Garrett stood there, leaning against the jamb. A faint smile lifted his mouth, so slight she wondered if he even realized he was smiling.

But she saw it, and her feet felt lighter as she moved through the dance. Every time she turned that direction, he stood there, not dancing with another woman, just watching her and almost smiling.

Garrett held Grace carefully in his arms as he moved through the steps of the supper dance, and struggled with the urge to bend down and kiss her each time she glanced up at him, put his claim on her in front of all the other men.

He had abandoned her to herself for nearly an hour. The whole time he was off in the card room with the other men, losing money for the first time because of his distraction and being ribbed mercilessly for it, he battled the urge to come back to the ballroom and monitor the men who took her out onto the floor. Even newly married as the two of them were, it just wasn't done that a husband monopolize his wife the entire evening. He had never questioned it before tonight, but now he thought it a ridiculous rule.

So he tightened his grip just a little, kept his steps measured and smooth, and wished himself home. At least he was at her side now, and he intended to stay nearby the rest of the night.

Grace suddenly raised her head. Her entire face lit up, her brown eyes, such a startling contrast with the blonde hair, sparkling with utter delight. "This is nice."

Nice. She used that word often. If he were a man given to flowery words and phrases, he would have chosen something stronger. It was *delightful. Captivating.* He might even say *thrilling*, except he had something else in mind that fit the word better. "How long do you want to stay?" he whispered in her ear, smelling the faint lemon that drifted out of her upswept hair.

"My feet are tired, but I'm not ready to go home yet." She smiled at him, and once again he reminded himself that a man did not kiss a woman, not even his wife, in the middle of the dance floor.

The band ended with a flourish, and he pulled Grace to a stop. The room applauded, and he took advantage of the distraction to enjoy her as she clapped with the others. A smile curved her mouth, and the exercise had put a glow on her face. Unless that color was not from the dancing. He didn't want it to be his imagination, but she looked as glad to be with him as he was with her.

"I'm having such a wonderful time." Grace started walking off the floor without him, but she looked over at him as she spoke, apparently assuming he would keep pace with her independent stride.

He caught her hand, drew it properly through his arm as etiquette required, and began the slow promenade off the dance floor. They hadn't gone more than five steps when someone stepped in their path. It was Montfort, the worst womanizer in the ton, handsome, blonde, and tall.

He didn't like the man, had earned Montfort's undying hatred. A few years ago reports swirled around the ton that he abused his female servants. When gossip reached Garrett that Montfort was paying court to Madeline, he went immediately to his father and told everything he knew.

He knew Father never revealed where he heard the reports when he refused the man's suit for his daughter, but whatever else he was,

Montfort wasn't stupid. It hadn't taken long for him to accost Garrett at White's. "You'll pay for this," he had snarled.

That was the first time Garrett's initials appeared in the betting book, along with a nasty hint about cheating at cards. It had been an ugly period. Thankfully Madeline found her current husband shortly afterward, but Garrett kept a wary eye on Montfort from then on.

How the man managed not to get himself run out of the country Garrett never found out, but following the direction of his gaze, he had found a new way to torment, and a far-too vulnerable target. Grace was too new to England to know about such men. His teeth gritted.

"May I have the next dance?" Montfort bowed low and reached out for Grace's hand without waiting for an answer. Not that Montfort could have done much in a crowded ballroom, but—

"No thanks," his wife said before Garrett could open his mouth. There was a new, hard tone in her voice he had not heard before. He glanced down and noticed the curve of her jaw had grown tight. Did someone already warn her about Montfort, or did she sense his evil? With the same firm edge, she added, "My feet are tired."

"One more dance cannot hurt. You will be back in your beloved's arms before you know it." Montfort didn't even try to hide his mockery. His hand remained extended, as if that would induce her to take it.

"Thank you, but no." Garrett bit back a smile as his wife stood her ground. She was not a woman to intimidate.

"I'm sure Fairfax won't mind." Montfort took one step closer.

"You didn't ask him to dance, you asked me, and I said no." Her voice was even colder.

It was time to step in. "My wife has made her feelings known, Montfort. Find another woman to tease."

"It's just a dance," Montfort said. "What is the matter? Don't you trust your rustic American wife to be faithful?"

Garrett ignored the taunt.

Grace, however, didn't. "That's a disgusting thing to say! Why would I dance with you after that?"

"My dear, let it go." They had taken but three steps when Grace jerked to a halt. Her hand slipped away from his arm. He whirled around, to see Montfort holding her wrist in a tight grip, so tight the glove around her slender wrist was puckered. "You little—you think a nobody like you can—"

Before Garrett could grab at the man's arm and peel him away, Grace did something so quickly he didn't see what it was, a sudden move, a sharp flip of her arm upward that snapped her wrist out of his hand, and she was free.

Montfort stood, gaping, looking at his quarry as she backed against Garrett.

Now that Grace was safe, Garrett pulled her close. "Stay away from my wife, Montfort, or we will meet at dawn."

He could feel the fury coursing through Grace, a faint tremble against his hands as they rested on her shoulders. In a voice colder than a moment ago, she hissed, "No one touches me like that. No one says *anything* to me like that. From now on, you stay away from me, do you understand?"

Dull red crept up Montfort's face. He didn't seem to know what to do.

"Do you?" Grace hissed the words at him, and Montfort gave a slight incline of his head before melting back into the crowd behind him.

"Good riddance." She snarled the words at the man, who was now out of sight.

Garrett cradled the wrist Montfort had grabbed. "Will it bruise, do you think? Did he hurt you?" The man's gall appalled him. Grace's quick escape amazed him. Where had she learned to do that thing? "I am sorry you had to be subjected to that. I did not think he would attempt to make a scene in a place so public."

Who was this woman he married?

He glanced around, but the music had started, the groups were already formed, and only a couple faces looked his way. The whole thing was brief enough, disguised by the movement of couples and the shifting of the groups, that it had gone almost undetected.

"I think it is time for us to take our leave."

Grace looked up at her husband. His voice was mild, but his eyes were determined—and wary, and she finally realized what she had done.

There had to be a better way to handle things, but the creep triggered an old instinct. Working alone as she often did, she had invested in a couple self-defense classes, but until today had never used them.

It was a shock to have done it at all. One minute she had been a capable businesswoman, the next she was thrust into a world where men had taken her life out of her control, and that smarmy man triggered the very reaction she once practiced until it was second nature. There were things about being from the twenty-first century that she could not—would not—give up. She would not become a mouse and disappear into her husband's shadow.

Would not let a man paw her. And would not dance with someone who gave her the creeps. She had read about the gift of fear, that women needed to listen to their instincts, and so she had.

Her husband did not speak until they were in the carriage. He sat across from her on the opposite seat. She could not see his eyes. "How did you get free of Montfort's hold?"

The wariness in Garrett's voice was like a stab in her heart. "It was something I learned. He scared me. I'm sorry if I embarrassed you."

"You didn't embarrass me. You amazed me." He eased himself across the carriage, his movements smooth despite the bouncing and rattling along the road, and sat down at her side. He picked up her hand, the one Montfort wrenched, and slid his fingers with a feather touch across the area that was finally sore as the skin came out of its numbness. He asked again, "What was that thing you did?"

"It's just a quick move designed to help anyone get free if someone tries to abduct you. You want to break the grip in the gap between the thumb and fingers. That's where the strength is the weakest."

"Mmmm."

She wasn't sure if he was listening. His fingers kept that gentle soothing motion. Grace kept talking. They would be home soon. "Where I'm from, a woman is in danger a lot, and I decided to learn some self-defense. It was that or spend my life on edge and I didn't choose to live like that."

He let go of her wrist, and eased her head onto his shoulder. His other arm came around her. She felt the flicker of his breath across her hair as he spoke. "What kind of country is America that women have to go to such extreme measures? Don't your men protect you?"

He eased her away from his shoulder enough to tilt her face up. His gaze was on hers even in the dimness, she knew it even though she only saw the shimmer of those eyes. His warm voice sent tingles along her skin. "Grace, you are in my country now. You can trust me to take care of you. I am amazed by what you did, but taking care of you, keeping you safe, is my job. I have known Montfort for a very long time, and I know exactly what kind of man he is. There is no way I would have let you dance with him. My name carries with it a measure of protection, my wealth gives me status beyond most, and I am strong enough to take on Montfort."

"I know," she said. "Garrett, I had to make a point with that guy. I'm an outsider. I heard what he said, how he taunted you with me. I wanted to be the one to put him in his place. He was insulting *me*, not you."

"In insulting you, he insulted me."

She sighed. "Garrett, when he insulted me, he insulted *me*. It's *my* integrity, *my* honor. I am responsible for myself."

He shook his head, and his hair whispered against his collar. "You are not in America now. You are in England, and here, a husband takes care of his wife's honor."

Before she could argue, the carriage rocked to a stop. Garrett exited first, then turned to reach a hand to her.

Grace leaned forward and rested her hand on his cheek, wishing she didn't have a glove on and could feel him, skin to skin. "You don't realize how difficult this has been, coming to a strange place, with no friends, no family—that I knew of," she added as he prepared to speak. "I know you don't understand my customs. I want you to know that I appreciate you turning all alpha male on me."

In the glow of the windows behind him, she saw his brows raise. "I don't know what that means, but if you appreciate it, I will assume it is good." He lifted her hand away from his face and kissed the palm, leaving a spot of warmth that seemed to set up an echo in her heart. "I *will* protect you. It is my responsibility to see that you are safe." The words rang with intensity, a solemn promise, as binding as the vows they had exchanged weeks ago.

She felt the smile start down in her heart where the warmth of his lips settled, and work its way up, bringing a new awakening, an absolute certainty, as it came. "I love you."

Garrett's eyes went wide, his face paled in the moonlight. He said nothing, but captured her face between his hands, leaned in, and pressed his lips to hers, then slid her off the seat, into his arms, and held her suspended as he worshipped her mouth.

And he didn't even seem to care that the coachman was standing behind him, smiling.

32

Oddly enough, they suffered no repercussions from the event with Montfort. In fact, they got more invitations than ever. Grace's life took on a pattern, balls or musicales in the evenings, the occasional night at the opera, afternoon teas, *soirees*, and the sweet nights when she and Garrett didn't feel like going anywhere, and sat at home in the parlor to read before going up to bed, and the blissful fever they found there.

She also discovered a totally unexpected fondness for the gothic novels her grandmother loved. Having time to read was an unexpected pleasure. She missed her work, but found new purpose in learning how to run the household. The housekeeper showed her around, where all the household furnishings were kept, which were the good plates, and which for ordinary use. She watched them take inventory of all the silver, candlesticks so heavy they were hard to hold, equally heavy serving dishes that got hot enough to scorch the footmen's gloves.

She scavenged through the attic, and found old furniture that cried out for her skill. A skill she could not use here. The one fly in her gilded ointment. Garrett did not want a wife in trade.

Some things a modern woman could not give up, and cleanliness was one of them. Grace refused to stink. She didn't like to impose on the servants, but on this she simply had to hold her ground. A bath at least every other day. No excuses. She had even carried the water up herself one day. The servants were appalled when they caught her, but she made her point. The bathtub now sat in the dressing room attached to her bedroom.

On a scale of importance, she wasn't sure which rated higher, running water or electricity.

Her hair began to curl wildly as fall crept toward winter and the rains came almost daily. No efforts of the maid, hairpins, or rag-tied curls could tame it. She looked like a perm gone mad, and if not for Martha's skilled fingers, Grace would have been tempted to cut it short, something she never would have considered before.

Her previous life took on a dreamlike quality, as if this was her real time and what came before merely fantasy. And then something would happen, a sound, a smell, and memories jolted back. The future her, that *other time*, would tug at her heart, and she would miss so many things. The feel of driving a car, the taste of pizza, television, music as accessible as turning on the radio.

And then it would pass, buried beneath the pleasures of this new life and she could forget until the next time it happened. Her marriage was still new, less than two months old, and she wondered if the time would come when that future world would fade completely.

The mirror was hidden in the very back of a drawer, in a compartment designed not to be found by snoopy servants, far enough back that she could—almost—forget about it.

Another day in this life she had fallen into, and the cold early winter sun shone through the dining room window. The flatware sparkled with polishing, the breakfast eggs steamed on her plate, and the toast was still warm enough to melt the butter.

A footman came in and set the correspondence down beside her breakfast plate. Grace glanced at the silver palaver that held the day's mail, saw a date scrawled on the top one, and her heart gave a lurch.

Could she really have been married six weeks? She had been in this time for nearly four months. Autumn was waning, leaving behind the fallen leaves, colder nights, and number of rooms in which they kept the fireplaces burning.

Homesickness washed over her in a wave.

Garrett was saying something, but her mind couldn't focus on his words. She looked up at him; she saw his mouth work, saw a frown begin on his forehead, where a dark curl fell in an upside-down question mark, but she couldn't pull her mind back to the present. *This* present.

What was happening in her real time? Her cellphone's mailbox must be full, likely with increasingly irate questions. Customers would have pounded on her shop door, wondering why she hadn't called to tell them the furniture was done. Had her landlord unlocked her shop to allow them to pick up their furniture, unfinished though it was?

What about her bills? Had the postman noticed and reported her missing? Surely someone called the police by now. It had been summer when she was whisked away. Now winter was beginning. The decorator who gave her so much business would have moved on to another upholsterer. Did any of them still wonder where she was? Had her absence made the news?

News. Instant coverage from around the world, and all of it current, much of it happening live. While she didn't miss the violence of her own time, she did miss its immediacy, and its distraction. No movies in the living room or Star Trek reruns or HGTV, not even local weather. Here one knew it was going to rain by watching the clouds and paying attention to the colors of the sunrises and sunsets. Knew the news, albeit weeks old, from the paper.

Something dark, filled with dread, sent an awful shiver down her spine and weakened her knees. Grace was glad she was sitting down. Had she been standing, her legs would have given way.

As frightening as it was, she needed to check on the mirror.

"My dear? Did you hear what I said?"

She struggled to concentrate on his words. His mouth, that wonderful, masculine mouth, was moving, and it took all her energy to sit there and listen.

"I said we are going to the opera tonight. Did you forget?"

"We are?" And then she remembered he said something about it yesterday. Or was it the day before? "I didn't realize it was tonight."

He smiled. "Yes. It is tonight. I hope you have something to wear. There is not enough time to order a new gown."

Grace wrinkled her nose at him. "I have more than enough gowns. I'm sure I can find something to wear."

His gaze sharpened. "Perhaps you should sleep this afternoon. You are looking a bit pale." He frowned. "If you are not feeling the thing, we can always go another night."

She shook her head. "No. Tonight is fine. I just . . . lost track of what day it was." *What year it was, what century.* "Getting out will be good for me."

Yes, she needed to anchor herself again, see London as it was, as *she* was.

"Eat your breakfast. I have some letters for you here. Perhaps you can fill in the time with them, then take a nap. I will be back in plenty of time to get ready before we leave tonight." He shoved some of the pile in front of him over to her. "Here they are. Something to fill the hours."

Did she act like she needed to occupy herself? Had he noticed something she thought hidden? Grandfather forbade her from going back into trade, but Garrett had never said she couldn't. He never said she could either, only that she had *unusual accomplishments.*

But she had never asked.

Maybe he would let her do it again, even only for their own furniture. The thought lifted her heart. Perhaps that was all she needed. If she was busy, surely these moments of longing for that future time would ease.

Grace looked over the letters as she ate her breakfast, but the urgency didn't ease, and the food felt like lead in her stomach. Finally she thought she had eaten enough to satisfy her husband.

He shoved his chair back and rose, came over to lift her chin and kiss her on the lips, soft and lingering. "Take care of yourself, my dear. Get some rest so you can enjoy tonight."

She waited until she heard the door shut behind him before slipping out of the dining room and breaking into a run. Holding up her skirt was second nature now as she dashed up the stairs and into her room, to stop before her dressing table and catch her breath.

She looked at the drawer where the mirror hid. Her hand didn't want to move toward the drawer pull, but finally she yanked it open all the way. The mirror was exactly where it was supposed to be.

In the bright sunlight streaming through the window, Grace tilted it this way and back, looking for anything that might warn of time slipping away from her.

It seemed perfect. No cloudy marks, no pitting in the mirroring in the back. Not until she tilted it one last time, and there it was, the smallest bit of a blur.

Or was it?

She moved the mirror again. No, it was gone. Had it really been there, or had it been an illusion of the sunlight and her own fears?

She sat and looked at the mirror until the ticking of the clock reminded her that she was supposed to rest.

33

Wind whirled past the opera doors, and pellets of ice bounced off the glass edged with frost. The storm had surprised everyone when the intermission let them out of the sheltered confines of the big auditorium. "I wonder why the weatherman didn't predict this," she said without thinking. "I wore the wrong shoes for snow."

"Weatherman? Predict? Predicting the weather is outside man's ability," Garrett said in an authoritative tone beside her, and she felt his gaze.

"I mean, if anyone could understand the weather, he would surely be called a weatherman. Just think what money he could make." Her laughter was nervous, and a bit shrill.

Grace felt a flutter in her chest, and recognized panic. After supper she suggested they call Grandfather and ask if they were coming down for the rest of the Season. Garrett had looked at her with a baffled expression on his face. "That is quite a shout. How would you manage that?"

These lapses were happening all too often. And now, as they drew nearer to the big doors and the snow swirled outside, she had done it again. And in public, where anyone might overhear.

They reached the door. Garrett moved her to the side. "Stay here and let me go out and check where the carriage is in this crush. I don't want you to risk a fall."

She leaned against the wall where he left her, right by the big windows, and watched the carriages go past. The bright lights from the lamps inside reflected against the windows, making the carriages only dim shapes that came and passed. Even the rattle of the wheels and the clump of the horses' hooves were muted.

A taxi pulled up, its light just above the windshield glowing through the falling snow.

Grace jolted into shocked rigidity and stared at the taxi, right where a carriage and four had been only a second ago. "Oh, dear God," she whispered, fighting off the trembles.

"It is quite a storm," a woman behind her said, apparently eavesdropping.

But Grace didn't respond. She wiped a circle of the window clear and pressed her face close, cupping her hands to block out the light behind her, and searched for that incongruous image.

The taxi was gone. The line of large carriages in front of the theatre moved slowly ahead, and women in rich gowns and long pelisses or capes hurried outside to climb into the boxes. Horses shook the snow off their backs, setting the traces to jingling again.

Her grip on this world was slipping.

Garrett brushed through the doors and wedged his way over to her. Grace grabbed his hand as he drew near and held on tight.

She got a sharp look as Garrett squeezed her hand and let go. "Does this storm frighten you?"

"Yes," she said, too shaken to lie or hedge.

"Well, I'm here now. Our driver is an old hand at this kind of weather. We will be fine. Let's go out, the carriage is right outside the stairs." The crowd seemed to part before them. It must be his imposing presence. She felt a bubble of hysteria at the thought. "They're getting slippery, so hold on to me."

She would, O how she would!

When they reached the carriage, a sudden gust of wind caught the edges of her cape and whipped it apart just as Garrett clasped her to his side, closing the folds back together and holding the warmth in. He lifted her through the carriage opening as the driver squinted into the blowing snow and braced the door against it.

A horn sounded, blaring its raucous sound clearly even through the shouting people and the jangling reins and the howling wind. Behind her, Garrett jerked, and Grace flopped into the seat with even less agility than usual.

"What was that?" He whirled around. He had heard it, too. Was he coming through the time tunnel with her?

And then Garrett strode off, his boots kicking up puffs of snow ahead of him, and grabbed a small ragged boy with worn shoes and bare legs sticking out beneath a coat clearly rescued from a dustbin. The boy held a broken trumpet.

Grace felt limp as she saw the instrument. The *blaatt* had come from that.

Garrett jerked the trumpet away from him and headed back toward their carriage. The little boy with his thin, chapped face looked so hungry. For a moment Grace thought he might cry as he watched what was probably his only toy be carried away. She slid back out of the carriage and met her husband. Garrett glared at her. Without breaking her own stride, more a slithering slide, she snatched the horn out of Garrett's hand and kept going. The child's face had gone from sadness to the dawning of anger. How little the aristocracy knew about the struggles of the poor.

Grace held out the horn as she got closer and watched his eyes get big and wary. He even took a step back. "It's okay," she said, and held it out even further. "I won't let the big man hurt you. I'll give it back under one condition."

He reached out and snatched it so quickly Grace almost let go. As he tugged, she said, "He was just afraid you would spook the horses.

You can have it back if you promise not to blow it until the carriages are all gone."

"Ain't makin' no promises," he whined. "Gimme it back."

"Promise first." Footsteps were coming up behind her. She didn't have to glance back to guess whose.

The little boy saw him. "Promise," he yelped, and this time Grace couldn't hold on. But the boy ran off into the snow clutching his precious toy, so she supposed the horses were safe.

"Don't do that again." Garrett took her arm so gently it belied his sharp words, and helped her slide back to the carriage. He boosted her inside and the carriage sagged as he climbed in after her. "If I had not taken that from him, the horses would have spooked, just as you said. Would you rather have a sad child, or someone killed? It may have seemed cruel, but I thought of the potential dead and injured."

The air was so cold her breath fogged. They hadn't taken a carriage blanket, there hadn't seemed a need when they headed out, so Garrett tucked her close by his side and wrapped his arms around her. She pulled them tight, clinging to their strength, and tried to find warmth.

"Did you see his clothes?" If she was this cold inside a carriage, how brutal must it be on such a tiny, skinny body? "I'm afraid he'll be frozen solid by morning. I wish we could take him home with us."

She felt Garrett move, and his finger tilted her face up. They hadn't lit the carriage lights, so all she saw was a lighter oval against a background of black.

"I'm afraid we'll hear of a runaway horse trampling someone in a few days, and we'll find out a sudden noise frightened the animal. That could have been our horses, and you could have been the person killed. Grace, when I do something I have a reason."

"He was little and hungry and cold, and that's probably the only toy he has. Maybe the only one he's ever had. He might be a budding Louis Armstrong or Wynton Marsalis."

That stillness was back. "Who are they?"

She'd done it again. How close was she to going back? The minute they got home, no matter how afraid she was, she needed to check that mirror. She tightened her grip on Garrett's arm. If only she could hold on tight enough! "They're American musicians."

He seemed satisfied with that, thank goodness. "I'm sorry about the little boy, Grace, but you cannot change the world."

Couldn't you? "You might be surprised."

They rode home in silence. It was just too cold in the carriage to talk. He hurried her into the house, and handed their snowy outer clothes to the footman. "Hang these where they will dry."

"Yes, m'lord. Glad to see ya back. It's blowing a bit out there."

That was a long speech for a servant.

"Yes, it is, Jim." Garrett hurried her upstairs. "We need to get you into bed. You get ready. I will be in and help warm you up."

The words promised more than a cuddle.

After he had seen her safely into her room and shut the door with a quick kiss as a promise, Grace took a deep breath, sat at her desk, and pulled out the drawer. She knew, even before she picked up the mirror. She could tell just from the silver handle, suddenly dark with tarnish. She took it out, and turned it over.

Her hands shook as she tilted it toward the candle.

Gray banded the outer rim of the glass, almost as wide as two fingers. Her hands were still cold and it slipped free and into her lap. She caught it just before it slid onto the floor. Somehow she knew, almost as if it had spoken, that if it broke, she would disappear, perhaps for all time.

She heard Garrett dismiss his valet, his voice as clear as if he stood on the other side of the connecting door, and maybe he did.

Grace shoved the mirror back into its hiding place. A giant celestial clock was ticking and she didn't know what the outcome would be.

Garrett tapped on the door and it swung open. "You have not changed."

"My maid is asleep. I thought I would let her be."

"Can I play maid for you, and get this off? Beautiful as it is, you look better out of it." He came over and held out both hands.

She took them in a desperate hold and stood up, knocking her dressing table stool over. "Oh, yes, Garrett, I would love that!" She let go of his hands and flung herself against him.

Garrett's arms went around her, and he chuckled. "I see we will have a wonderful time keeping each other warm this evening." His mouth came down and captured hers.

34

The sun glowed through the curtains, dancing against Grace's closed eyes. Her head rested against Garrett's shoulder, and his fingers were stroking through her hair.

She was still here. The taxi's image slithered back into her mind, a chill wrapped around her heart, and she shivered.

"Cold, my dear? Did I wake you?" He didn't sound in the least sorry.

"Hmmm." Grace rubbed his chest. It was about as much movement as her drowsy body wanted to make, just to be here and know Garrett was still with her.

He smiled down as he rolled over to face her. "I have a surprise for you. Your grandfather wrote that he was planning to come this week for a visit."

"Grandfather? And you kept it a secret? Even after I asked to contact him?" Grace shifted to face him. "When do you think he'll be here?"

"Today." Garrett's teeth flashed white. "And you never said to contact him, you said to yell."

"It's the same thing!" Grace grabbed her pillow and pretended to hit him with it. Garrett snatched it away and threw off the covers. Cold air rushed in, and Grace grabbed them and hauled them over her, then burrowed down again.

She watched him walk to the fireplace, his muscles moving under the smooth skin. His shoulders were broad and his arms roped and tight with strength. "How can you get out of bed with no robe on? We need to turn up the fur—" she caught herself. *Not again!* "—fire." Her gaze wandered to the dressing table, and the secret within gave a chill the covers could not warm.

She had to show Grandfather the proof when he arrived. Together they would think of something. Maybe if she got it far enough away, its influence wouldn't reach her. It needed to be further away than the distance last night, from this house to the opera, but his village was halfway across England. Surely that was far enough.

Assuming he went back soon.

"Is Grandmother coming?"

"He did not say. You will find out soon enough." Garrett came back and bent over her, pinning her underneath the mound of covers. His mouth smoothed over hers, his lips teased and nibbled, and then he straightened and patted her leg. "Up you get. You want to be ready for him when he arrives. The kitchen staff is alerted to another guest or two for dinner. I had extra provisions delivered, so all they have to do is cook."

"All?" She cocked an eyebrow. "Do you have any idea how much work goes into cooking?"

He propped his hands on his hips. Grace saw the goosebumps down his legs. The man wasn't as impervious to the chill as he pretended. "And you do?"

She lifted her chin, but it lost some effect lying down. "Yes, sir, I do."

"Americans." He shook his head in mock disgust, and pretended to stalk off to his room, but spoiled it when he turned at the door. "I'll hold breakfast until you get down." He paused. "I enjoy your company to start my day. I haven't said it, and I should have."

That wasn't the only thing he hadn't said, she thought as the door closed behind him.

There might not be time to hear the words she ached for.

The mail sat at his plate when Grace came down. She leaned over, pretending to read, and Garrett slapped his hand onto the pile.

"No begging to go to anything that your grandfather doesn't want to attend. He and I will go over the invitations and then you can see which ones we have chosen."

"Chauvinist," she teased him, and turned her attention to the porridge.

He didn't smile, just sat there and looked at her as if she were an interesting specimen, the latest letter forgotten in his hand. "Grace." He spoke quietly, and Grace set down the spoon. Her heart gave an ominous thump. He sighed. "Do you miss America? Your home?"

Grace met his gaze, and couldn't read what she saw there, if it was sadness or just curiosity. "Why do you ask?"

"Because you get a faraway look in your eyes from time to time." He set the letter in his hand down. "Grace, there is the possibility of war between our two countries. I will happily go with you should you want to visit your country again, but it is not safe right now. I want to wait and monitor the situation. It might be nothing, but the tension is growing, and ships are being attacked."

"Oh, yes," Grace said, as she looked at his worried eyes. "I know about that. The War of—" she caught herself. 1812. A nasty, foolish, wasteful war.

"You read too many newspapers. Such things are for politicians. And it may not even happen."

But it would. It did. Only she couldn't tell him that. "Will you go fight?" Was that why the mirror was taking her away? So she wouldn't have to live through his death? But what difference would that make? If she went back, he would be dead anyway, by nearly 200 years. And her heart would die, too. She would grieve him forever.

Garrett's eyes sharpened as he looked at her. "Don't worry. There may not even be a war." He reached over and wrapped his large hand gently around hers. "We will wait and watch. We might be worrying for nothing." He let go and went back to his mail. "I will not attempt a trip back to your country until I know we can arrive safely."

"I don't want to go back," she said, and it was true. She looked around the room, illuminated by chandeliers and branched candlesticks on the sideboard. A footman came in to remove the plates at a nod from Garrett.

Grace cleared her throat, trying to speak lightly. "There are a lot of things I miss, not the least of which is my business, I suspect all my customers have gone somewhere else. I had more freedom there, but I have much to hold me here."

She took a breath to steady her voice, and managed a smile. "I didn't have a house like this, certainly not clothes like these. I didn't know how to dance and there was not so much time to read guilt-free. There was always something more important to do." She wrinkled her nose at him, and he smiled ruefully back.

She wasn't sure how he would react, but a fierce need had her turn her hand around so she was clutching his. "Most important of all, I didn't have you." Tears roughened her voice.

"You are not sorry you married me, then?" His eyes were fixed steadily on hers, and they held a tension, a stillness that had taken over his whole body, even his hand as she held it. His tone might be calm, but he wanted the answer very badly.

Grace rose from her seat, went around the edge of the table to sit on his lap, curled up and wrapped her arms around his neck. She pressed her lips to his, felt his heart give a sudden, faster beat against her. "I love you," she whispered against his mouth, and his lips joined hers fiercely.

But he never said the words back, and Grace felt the omission like a stab in the heart.

Grandfather arrived shortly after noon, when they were dressed again. They had rushed back upstairs after breakfast, coming together in a surge of need, as if Grace's fear had spread to her husband.

Garrett's man of affairs had shown up, but the poor man had to wait for nearly an hour. No one dared knock on the door, or else they just enjoyed the idea of their lord and his lady rolling about the bed in broad daylight.

When her grandfather was announced, the two of them were neatly dressed, the rooms were in order, and the man of affairs had gone off.

Grace suspected her grandfather knew exactly what they had been doing most of the morning. "My darling child," he boomed with his arms outstretched as if to embrace the entire room. "You are positively blooming. And how has your husband been treating you? Like a treasure?" He swept her into his big hug. "Your grandmother sends her love. She is resting, The journey was hard on her."

"I need to show you something before you leave," Grace whispered, and then drew back, and said with a smile at Garrett, "Yes, he is very good to me. Now, come in and tell us all about your journey here. The weather was awful." And haunting, with images of the past —or would it be the future? "How is Grandmother? Will she feel better tonight? Can she come for dinner?"

"Your grandmother is fine, just tired. Whether she can come this evening, I cannot say. There is always tomorrow, though, after she has rested."

He patted her hand. "Now, as for the weather, the sky was clear when we left. I didn't run into any problems until closer to Town. It was more the cold and ice that wore her out." He turned to Garrett. "I have read of a promising investment opportunity, but news is always old by the time I get it. May we discuss the matter? Perhaps you know more and can help me decide."

"If it is the one I suspect, I will warn you away." Garrett extended his arm toward the door. "Shall we discuss the reports in my office?"

"I thank you." Grandfather turned back and gave Grace another hug. "Man talk, you understand, nothing that would interest you. Read a book, embroider, whatever you like. We will be back soon, and we can catch up on the past weeks."

The men strode out. Grace wanted to seethe at the patronizing tone, but investments didn't interest her at all. Grandfather was right about that.

A book it was.

Several minutes later, she abruptly set the book aside. It was useless. She couldn't focus. The mirror haunted her thoughts, as if preparing her to go back. How else could she explain the taxi, as undeniable as the winter sun that streamed through the window?

Where did Garrett fit into this? Would he be allowed to come back with her? He had responsibilities here, a world into which he fit. In her world he would have to begin all over again, schooling, technology, transportation, science, money.

Did she want to watch him flounder as he tried to find his place in her modern world? Even if he adapted as quickly as his nimble brain could, he still wouldn't have the position and property that he had here.

Far better for her to be the fish out of water. A mother gone, a father who truly didn't think of her for months, maybe never without prodding, although she doubted her stepmother would extend herself that far. Who would miss her? Friends, of course, but their lives would go on. Skilled as she had been, her customers had probably already replaced her.

Unless this time had been a bubble, and the mirror would return her to the very spot and time she had left.

It was time to take action, whether the right one or not she didn't know, but she was going to stack the deck in her favor. She would give Grandfather the mirror, make him take it away. He didn't have to believe her. He just had to get that thing out of the house. His townhouse was several streets away, not far enough, but perhaps he would leave again soon. Not that she wanted him gone, but he had to take the thing out of London and back to his country house.

Wherever that mirror was, she would make it work to get her.

Grace slipped upstairs to her room and sat at her writing table. She took out a quill, sharpened it with the tiny knife kept for that purpose—funny how such onetime unthinkable things as sharpening a quill feather to write were becoming so natural to her—set out an inkwell and paper, and began to write. She had to leave a record, something for Garrett to hold on to. It took a moment to figure how to begin.

At the beginning, they always said.

"My dear husband, I have a story to tell you, and you may not believe it, but I promise you it is the truth. I want you to know, so you don't wonder where I am if I suddenly disappear.

"I was born in America, but not when you think. I was born nearly 200 years after this time. You are going to say that is impossible. I thought so, too, until it happened to me. I told you I was an upholsterer. That is true. I own—owned my own business and worked with other women whose job was decorating houses. I bought antique chairs and furniture and refinished them to match the new decor. I was at an outdoor sale one brutally hot day . . ."

The words poured out, the story coming faster than the old quill and ink could handle it. Oh, for a ballpoint pen!

"Know that if I am gone, I am not gone of my own will. If I can

find a way to come back, I will, because life without you is a poor thing indeed. With all my love, Grace."

Where would Garrett look, if she disappeared? The letter had to be visible, easy to find for a man who would be wild with fear and grief.

Did she matter that much to him? Or would his emotions be more muted, his recovery faster?

Grace cleared out the drawer in her dressing table where the mirror had been. Her writing papers lay on the bottom. The mirror came out, and the brush and comb.

With trembling hands, Grace set the note on top of those papers, then put the mirror on top so it could come out quickly when she handed it over to Grandfather. Nothing else would go there.

She felt wrung out with the reliving when she was done. After splashing cold water on her face, she straightened her clothes and went back downstairs.

35

It wasn't that easy. She got down to the parlor after finishing the letter, and both men were gone.

"They went to the club," one of the footmen told her. "They hope to learn more about the investment. Lord Fairfax said he would be back before dinner."

"With Grandfather?" The whole staff would be working on the meal all day.

"I could not say."

She suddenly remembered Garrett was supposed to take her for a final fitting on a new gown. No doubt Grandfather's arrival and the challenge of this mysterious investment had knocked the appointment right out of his head.

Oh, well. He didn't come with her very often. This wouldn't be the first time she went alone. And this gown had to be finished and delivered, one less hanging thread if she got whisked away. "I need to go to the modiste's for one more fitting. Can you get the carriage ready? I will need a footman."

"Certainly, my lady."

"Send someone up for me when the carriage is ready." She turned and walked back up the stairs to her room, trying to pretend all was well, then stood in front of the dressing table, her stomach heavy with dread.

There was nothing else to do. She would never forgive herself if it took Grandfather in her stead, but she didn't think it wanted him. She couldn't explain it, didn't know how she knew, but she did. It wanted *her*, would only work for *her*.

And she could only hope her instinct was right.

She slipped the mirror into her reticule, put on her pelisse and bonnet, picked up her warm gloves, and went back down the stairs.

A short time later, Grace found herself in the modiste's shop. The footman and driver were huddled inside the carriage for warmth.

"You will look ravishing in this," the modiste said as she adjusted a pin in the heavy silk. "Blue is wonderful with your fair hair and skin. Your husband will be most pleased."

"Thank you. I did need something warmer, now that the weather has gone so cold."

"Yes. If you wish, I am getting some fine wool for a pelisse, and furs for trim." Grace opened her mouth to protest, but the modiste hurried on. "I know you do not approve of the fur, but it is most warm in this weather."

"I will check with my husband." She wasn't going to order anything new until the threat was over. "When can this gown be done?"

"There is little left to do. I can have it delivered tomorrow. Will that be sufficient?"

"That is perfect. Thank you." As she turned toward the fitting room, a telephone rang from the back of the shop. A secretary answered in brisk, if muffled, tones. Grace stopped in mid-step.

"Madame? Are you well?" The modiste looked at her with worried eyes.

Grace couldn't speak. She only nodded. The shaking didn't start until she was safely in the fitting room. She had to get to Grandfather's today. Now.

"Take me to my grandfather's," she told the driver as he scrambled out of the carriage box where he had been keeping warm.

"Yes, m'lady."

Thank goodness for servants who would not dream of arguing, she thought as she pulled the carriage blanket up over herself. A shiver shook her.

Hurry, hurry, hurry, she chanted silently as the carriage clopped along the street. She wished for a car and a clear road, and scolded herself for the traitorous thought. *Hurry, hurry, hurry,* as they passed The Green Park. *Hurry, hurry, hurry* as the townhouses passed slowly by. Her feet were cold, and even the carriage blanket didn't seem to hold in warmth, maybe because she had none left to give off.

The reticule felt heavy as it hung on her wrist. It dragged her arm down, or was it just the carriage blanket on top?

They rocked to a stop at last, and she hurled the heavy blanket off. The steps weren't down yet, and Grace began to leap, but the coachman gave a shout. "Don't you dare, m'lady, or I'll never hear the end of it iffen you slip!" She stood there, braced in the doorway, and waited for the steps to be put in place.

The walk was slightly slippery, but her Minnesota winter walking skills held strong.

Grandfather's butler recognized her. "Where is my grandfather? Is he back?" Grace asked without preamble as she walked through into the chilly foyer.

"Yes. He is resting in the parlor, Lady Fairfax."

She didn't wait for him to lead the way. No one was moving fast enough for her.

Resting, thank goodness, did not equal sleep. Grandfather was reading the newspaper as she walked in. "Grandfather. Please, I need your help." She knelt before him, their eyes almost level. "You are the only one who knows my tale. You saw the mirror before. I need you to look at this." Grace pulled out the mirror and held it up for him to see. "Can you explain the change? In six months?"

Grandfather's eyes grew big. "Is this the same one?" He didn't even reach out to touch it, as if—at last—what he saw frightened him.

He just looked at her. "What do you want me to do?"

"Grandfather, I don't want to go back. I don't know how this mirror works any more than you. It didn't come with instructions." Grace didn't know why her eyes were still dry; something inside was screaming sobs. "All I can think of is getting away from it, but even that might not be a guarantee. Will you keep it here?"

He looked at it as she held it in her hand. "I don't hold with witchcraft or magic. If you say this brought you here, I will have to take your word. I admit, I have never seen a mirror alter this much so quickly. If this is the key that brought you here and it stays with me, the worst that can happen is that it takes me instead of you."

His eyes were sad. "I'm an old man. If I go, I won't have missed much." His lips trembled as if he finally realized the impact of what he was taking on.

"It won't take you," Grace said, even more positive than when she slipped it into the reticule. The mirror only wanted her. *No one had seen the taxi, no one had heard the phone.* "My one hope is that maybe I need to be within the range of its power to work."

With both the taxi and the phone, the mirror had been halfway across the city. She hadn't gone back yet, despite all the future flashes.

Perhaps both places were out of its reach. It was all the guarantee she had. "I'm in the house with it most of the time, well within its grasp."

Grandfather straightened his shoulders, looking like a convicted man bravely willing to be shot. "Very well, leave it with me."

"Thank you, Grandfather." She hesitated, doubt assailing her, but put it in his hand, not letting go yet as if she needed to hold it there lest it jump back to her. "Whatever you do, don't let anyone break it. I have this awful certainty that if it breaks, I will disappear from both times."

His hand tightened on the mirror, she felt it secure, and let go. "You have my utmost promise."

Grace gave him a quick kiss on the cheek and got briskly to her feet, feeling lighter. "Well, I have to go back home. I don't want him to worry." She paused, then asked hesitantly, "Garrett wants to take us to the theater tomorrow. Are you two planning on coming?"

He smiled, a pale shadow of the enthusiastic ones from before. "As long as I am still here, I promise."

36

Grace was being laced in back when Garrett tapped on the connecting door and walked in. He smiled at her. "You look lovely. I shall have to get you another necklace to match that gown."

Grace glanced down at the blue silk. When her gaze came back up, she smiled at him, but he knew it didn't come at the mention of jewelry. Her eyes lit up as they always did when she saw him, and the very room seemed brighter. One smile—Grace smiled often—and his whole chest felt fuller, his body relaxed into a peace unlike anything he'd ever known.

Could he be falling in love with his wife?

Her maid stepped back. Grace heard the door shut, and held out her gown at the sides. "It's new. Do you like it?"

"Very much." He thought again of jewelry. Sapphire would match the gown, but those brown eyes needed something other than blue. Pearls, perhaps?

The pelisse waited on the bed. Garrett picked it up. In the dressing-table mirror, he could see her face and part of his as he stood behind her.

They looked . . . complete. Husband and wife together, a tableau of a happy family.

Were they happy? Grace seemed to be. She promised him she was glad they wed. She even said that she loved him.

Something was missing though, and he could not quite figure out what. Women seemed much better at this than men.

He didn't like problems of this nature. Give him tenants disputes, legal discussions, even a good argument in Parliament. Or a duel. He'd rather stand opposite another man with a gun than try to unravel this nebulous area of . . . *feelings*.

"Garrett?" Grace's face in the mirror tilted up toward him. He looked down at her, trapped by this quandary, this urgent need to do —something, the *right* something.

He knew how to clothe her, house her, feed her. He was generous with her allowance. It never left his mind that she had once supported herself. He knew she missed her old occupation, could see a longing in the way she occasionally touched his furniture as she passed.

He made love to her at every opportunity, couldn't seem to stop. Now was not the time to think of that, however. There would be time tonight. He would stay in her bed when they were done, not go back to his own.

Yes. That was it. That would show how he valued her.

Maybe there would be no need for uncomfortable words.

He slipped Grace's pelisse over her shoulders, turned her around and leaned down to fasten it, hoping his face wasn't clearly visible. A man didn't show this confusion. It was up to him to be strong.

At the theatre, Grandfather gave her an extra-long hug and a piercing look. "Are you feeling well?"

Only the two of them knew the meaning behind the question.

She smiled, and it was easy to do. "Yes, Grandfather, I feel quite well. What about you?"

"If you feel well, I feel well."

Grace's heart swelled. What an amazing man he was, open-minded and willing to take terrifying risks for those he loved. She went up on tiptoe and kissed his cheek, not caring who saw.

Grandfather cleared his throat. "Yes, yes, enough of that." Then he extended his arm to Grandmother. "Shall we follow the young people in, my dear?"

"Certainly." Grandmother slipped her hand through his elbow and turned to Grace. "Do you mind being with two old people?"

"No. I'm so proud of both of you."

The opera's costumes were ornate and elegant; the singers seemed at their best. Even the peanut gallery down on the floor, as Grace still liked to think of it, couldn't find any excuse to throw things in the first half.

She went down during intermission with the men, and looked out the window at the sparkling clear night. The moon was so perfect the edges seemed drawn in.

It struck her with a jolt that there was no space debris on it at this time. No lunar lander, no rover, not even the plaque that the Apollo 11 crew left behind. In fact, now that she thought of it, the heavens were clearer too. No satellites floated by out of sight, no weather balloons.

Just her, the only thing out of place and time.

Grace shivered. *No more thoughts like that.* She deliberately turned away from the window.

"Are you cold?" Garrett's sharp eyes must have caught that little shiver. He scanned her face and picked up her hand with the one that didn't hold a drink. His own felt large and warm. He set his glass on a window ledge and rubbed her fingers. "Should we go back to our seats?"

"Yes." *Oh, yes. Leave the night sky and all its memories and shadows behind.*

Back in the theater box, Grace couldn't seem to get rid of that shiver. She wrapped her arms tight around herself, but the chill had settled in her bones. She must be getting sick. Oh, well, she could stay in bed tomorrow.

One of the perks of being the lady of the house in this time. If she wanted to stay in bed, the house would still get clean, the dishes would still get washed, and the meals would still get made.

She applauded vigorously at the play's end, but she hadn't absorbed anything after the intermission. As the applause faded and the audience rose to leave, Garrett sat in the box and waited.

"Aren't we leaving?"

"You're obviously not feeling well." Those pale eyes of his fixed on her face. "I won't have you fighting through the crowds."

The shiver seemed to get worse as they waited. The funny thing was, it was just a shiver. Grace didn't feel sick to her stomach, didn't have a headache, wasn't even dizzy.

She refused to think of any other possibility.

Grandfather gave her another hug as they parted. In a low tone, too quiet for Grandmother to hear, he said, "I'll send a note around in a day and see how you are doing."

"I actually feel fine," she reassured him. "I just can't stop shivering."

"A chill is nothing to dismiss," Garrett said in the pontificating voice that always made her smile. He did it so well.

They climbed into the carriage, and Garrett wrapped the carriage blanket around her. It was, of course, cold as ice, but he gave off as much heat as a furnace and the little pocket underneath became warm quickly.

Grace leaned against him and waited for the shivers to subside. His arms tightened around her, and she tried to find the perfect place to rest her head.

She couldn't find one. That special curve where her head always fit as they lay together in bed was covered in shirt, and vest, and coat, and greatcoat.

And gone.

Garrett was gone.

No, *she* was gone. He sat bolt upright, his eyes suddenly wild, his hands flailing at the carriage blanket where she had been a moment ago, and yelled her name. "Grace!" She had never heard such utter terror in anyone's voice.

Unless it was in her own as she screamed his name back. "Garrett!" How could he be pounding and pulling at the very space she sat, and she could not feel him? His hands went right through her, but she was still there.

The mirror had found her. So where was the tunnel? What happened to the wind? *Please let it hold off*, Grace prayed, *just long enough to say goodbye.*

He cried her name again, and the carriage slowed. The coachman called down, "What be the matter, sir?"

His voice raw, Garrett said, "Just stop the carriage. Stay here. Don't let it move."

He climbed out, and slammed the door behind him. Grace reached for the handle, but her hand passed right over it. She could see it, her mind remembered the feel of it, but even though her hand was right there, there was nothing to touch.

Garrett's terrified voice hollered her name into the still night. "Grace! Grace, where are you?" His voice was raw, as if his fear had shredded it. And then came the most painful call of all, "Grace, come back. Please come back to me."

"I'm right here," she screamed against the window she couldn't feel, but he never turned his head. "Garrett! I'm still here!" Her voice echoed in her head, but the window didn't fog from her breath.

It was time to think. Grace tried to block out Garrett's anguished shouts outside the carriage. She couldn't go to him. If she was going to help—and she *was* going to help, somehow, some way—it would have to be done with brain, not brawn.

No tunnel, no wind. This time was very different. Did that mean the ending could change? She would not let herself think of another outcome. Unlike the first time, when she was pulled out of her house, the door still held her in. She could not feel it, but somehow it still confined her within its barriers.

She could still see Garrett. That was one good thing. Not just see, but hear him.

Think, Grace, think!

Garrett stood in the cold, not just the winter cold but surrounded by the cold, through his bones and into the very heart of him.

Grace was gone. How could someone disappear like that? She had been right there in his arms, her head trying to find that special place in his shoulder, and then his arms were empty. The carriage blanket had—

He stopped, trying to think through the cold in his mind, the cold coming through his coat, trying to recreate every second of those precious moments right before . . .

She had been snuggled as closely as their coats would allow, the carriage blanket over them, he could feel the warmth build and knew with satisfaction that his own body did that for her, and then—

He did not know how long he stood. The snow seeped wetly through his boots, and dampened his legs through their covering. His calls echoed back from the buildings, and she did not appear. She would have. With heavy feet, Garrett slogged back to the carriage still waiting in the darkness, terrified to leave this last place where he had seen Grace, but she wasn't out here. Wherever she had gone, it hadn't been out in the snow.

His eyes were burning. Through the lump in his throat he called Cokewell's address to the coachman, but his voice was a weak thing. The man had to know what happened, he and his granddaughter were so close, and Garrett knew they shared secrets Grace had never told him. Maybe together they could unravel this.

And find her. *Please, God, find Grace safe, wherever she was, and bring her back.* That was all he wanted, to have Grace back.

He climbed back into the carriage, his legs so heavy with shock and disbelief they hardly could make the step he normally handled so easily. He could even smell her in here, that light fresh lemony scent.

He pulled the carriage blanket up over himself. Grace had been so cold during the play, now he was the one who needed warming.

Wherever she was, was she warm?

37

Grace wanted to get under the blanket with him, but it was impossible. Anyway, was she still cold? She could not tell. Did the cold belong to this world?

She could feel Garrett's terror, sense the tears he wanted to shed, but he was too much of a man to let himself cry. Men did not cry, he would say, but Grace knew how silly that was.

Only—right now—she didn't want him to cry, either.

They were going to Grandfather's. Was that good, or bad? Grandfather had the mirror. Would her sudden proximity make it work and whisk her away? Her heart began to race as they pulled onto his street. She wanted so desperately to reach out and touch her husband, maybe for the last time. Just one more touch. Was that too much to ask?

The carriage pulled up and Garrett sat unmoving. She had no choice, she couldn't get out, so sat with him. Even that much comforted her.

No wind yet, no sudden whirling. No tunnel.

He opened the door, and Grace moved fast. If she was going to get in or out, she had to be right on his heels.

The door opened to Garrett's knock. The butler stood there

looking surprised, and Grace slipped around the two men and into the house.

She thought she brushed against Garrett when she slipped past, but neither he nor the butler gave any indication they felt a thing as her husband was ushered inside.

Cokewell was in his parlor reading with one last glass of whiskey before bed, when Garrett arrived. He took one long look, and his eyebrows raised in sudden alarm.

Garrett guessed he must look awful because the first words out of the man's mouth were, "Good Lord, Fairfax, what happened to you?"

"Grace is gone." Putting the awful event into words drained all the strength out of Garrett's legs, and he fell into the nearest chair. He couldn't bring himself to sit upright, just slumped there, his legs stretched out into the floor where anyone could trip over them, and looked at Cokewell. He hurt everywhere. His chest, his every breath, even the beating of his heart burned inside him.

Any smile was gone from Cokewell's usually merry face. "Tell me."

"Did I marry a witch?" Garrett cleared his throat. "We were in the carriage, under the blanket, trying to get her warm. She was cold, so cold." His voice broke, and he cleared his throat before he dared speak. "One minute she was there, and the next she was gone."

Oh, Garrett, I'm here. Her heart cried out to him. *I'm here, I've been here the whole time.*

She looked at her grandfather, and willed him to see her, hoping on a faint hope that his knowledge of the truth might pierce the curtain, but there was no recognition in his eyes.

An awful sound tore the air and Grace stared at Garrett.

Her strong husband was weeping.

"I need to tell you something," Cokewell said. His skin had gone as pale as Garrett felt. "I have known a long time. Perhaps I should have told you right away, perhaps Grace should have, but she was afraid of your reaction if she did. I hoped she was wrong, I thought I knew better than she what the right thing to do was, but it appears she knew more than I."

The sadness on the man's face was nearly a match for the pain in his heart. Garrett made himself sit up properly. He was not the only one grieving. How could he ignore the other man's sorrow? "What do you know?"

"You might not have believed before, but it is hard to deny when this has happened." Cokewell paused, and his gaze pierced Garrett, as though looking for something. "Grace is from another time. She came from the future."

"What?" Anger simmered beneath the sadness, and he leaned forward, pushed to the edge of his seat by the insult to his intelligence. "This is not a time for jokes. I know not where you got such a fantasy."

Cokewell appraised him for a long moment, and the quietness in the man's demeanor sent a trickle of unease down Garrett's spine. "A *joke*? You call this a *joke*? Can't you understand? Why would either of us tell you before? Tell me, can you explain her disappearance? If not, then sit and listen, because I know now that what she told me is the truth."

Garrett took a deep breath and forced himself to sit back.

"Good." Cokewell straightened in his chair, authority radiating from him. "Grace is from two hundred years in the future."

Impossible! A flash of rage rushed up Garrett's throat, but he kept his mouth shut and prayed his face did not show it for fear Cokewell would stop.

"She bought a mirror on some outdoor shopping trip, some strange market. She said she has always loved older things, something you no doubt have noticed."

Garrett nodded, finally on solid ground amidst raging uncertainty. "Yes, I have noticed that."

"She showed it to me the day we met, and it looked new, but she says when she bought the mirror, it was tarnished and the glass spoiled and foggy." Cokewell blew out a pained breath. "She believed the mirror brought her here because when she landed in your house, it was the only thing that came with her." He raised a finger to hold Garrett's attention. "Only instead of tarnished and cloudy, the mirror was new. No tarnish, the glass perfect."

Garrett could tell there was more to the story, so he waited, saying nothing even as he wished the man would hurry. Tell the tale, so they could solve this and find her. The delay made his skin prickle.

Cokewell sighed. "Yesterday she came over with the same mirror. Unlike the first time I saw it, the glass was as useless as she said, totally fogged and gray, the silver black with tarnish. The mirror is distinctive, very elaborate, quite unmistakable." He pulled himself to his feet. The man was tired, but this clearly was driving him. "Stay here." He pointed at Garrett. "Don't move."

Garrett leaned back in his chair, but he couldn't sit still. From the future? That was absurd. Ridiculous! He stood up and walked to the fireplace, leaned against the mantle, and watched the flames. They leapt with a gust of air from the chimney, and then settled down. The heat felt good, baking through his coat, but he didn't want to take it off yet, for fear the chill would come back.

Fire. He couldn't explain fire, could he? Yet he knew it worked. He couldn't explain how the sun shone, or how the wind blew, yet he couldn't deny either of them. Garrett held out his hand and felt the warmth from the fire radiating outward.

For a moment, he thought he felt Grace's hand on his back, the lightest of touches, and closed his eyes, trying to recapture that feeling, wishing . . . "Grace," he whispered, because he needed to say her name one more time.

Cokewell's footsteps came back down the stairs. He had a mirror in his hand. Garrett went back, sat down and watched.

Grace was afraid, truly, horribly afraid. She was in the same room with the mirror.

Cokewell sat down with a sigh and looked at the mirror, dark with tarnish, exactly as he had said. "This exact mirror," Cokewell said, and handed it over as if it were the crown jewels, "is the very one Grace showed me. It is the only thing to come with her. Be careful with it. Grace believes if it breaks, she will vanish from both times."

Garrett took the mirror, turned it around. The glass was so cloudy it reflected nothing. The silver was black with age. "It is very old." He was very careful as he held it. Not that he believed, of course, but . . . a little care never hurt.

"It was perfect the day I met her." Cokewell repeated, and gave him a firm look, daring him to challenge. Garrett didn't. The conviction in the man's voice made him want to listen. "She is from the future." It was a flat statement, and Cokewell's gaze never wavered. "Somehow she was brought here. She has been watching the mirror age, knowing she was being drawn back."

"She knew?" Grace knew, and she deliberately put him through this? Rage, or hurt, bubbled up from the middle of his chest. "She married me, knowing she could not stay? Why would she do that? What kind of cruelty does that take?"

Cokewell's gaze grew, if possible, even more inflexible. "What choice did she have, a woman in our time? Months went by, and still she stayed. She feared she would go back, but the longer it went, the more it looked like that would never happen."

He folded his arms, and leaned back in the chair, his brows furrowed, his dark eyes—Grace's eyes—piercing. "Would you turn the clock back and undo everything? Not meet her, not marry her?"

Garrett looked down at the mirror that reflected nothing, and thought. Would he turn the clock back? Give up the months with his wife, wipe her out of his life? He felt moisture trickle down his face, and wiped it away, too sad to be embarrassed. His throat was tight as he choked out, "No."

"She was very brave to risk this, knowing the possible future for her. And for you." Cokewell sighed. "I hoped you two would fall in love or I would not have allowed her to marry you."

"Could I have kept her here?" There it was, his odd feeling that he needed to do something. That he had forgotten something very important. "Is this my fault?" The moisture came again, his loss ripping his heart out, his pain slipping, wetly, down his face.

"I think she is gone. It is too late for that." Grandfather was weeping now, too, silently, the tears running down his face. They sat in the study for a long time, the fire began to die. The room cooled.

Suddenly Cokewell took a shuddering breath, cleared his throat, and spoke. "Were you good to my child?"

There was a reminiscence now, the wake after the death. "I think I was."

"Was she happy with you?"

His head came up. "Yes, I believe she was. She said that she loved me." But what had he said in return? His head bowed again under the weight of his guilt. How hard would it have been to return those simple words?

They had felt so uncomfortable before, yet now he wished he had said them back. Just once.

"Let that be your consolation, son. You made her happy. She wanted to stay, she didn't want to go, that's why she left the mirror with me. But we were playing with forces beyond us, and our puny efforts had no effect on the outcome."

Garrett turned the mirror around in his hand. "Let me keep the mirror. It was hers, and I want it."

Grandfather nodded. "I think she would like that."

She hadn't vanished yet. It was so hard to be so close, but . . . she hadn't vanished yet.

The fire was warm behind her. The sensation crept up on her. She was warm; she felt the heat. Grace looked down at herself and thought, wondered, hoped, she was more solid.

She wasn't sure. Even when no one else could, she had been able to see herself. "Garrett? Grandfather?"

Garrett went very still, his head lifted as though he was listening for something, but then he shook it, his hair drifting with the movement. Despite that last movement, Grace took heart. He must have suspected, wished he heard her, but how could he admit such a thing? Did that mean there might be a way out of this?

The mirror must be waiting for something.

But what was it?

He couldn't stay here forever, Garrett thought, tempting though it was. He felt like a survivor of a war, battered, wounded, and in pain. Cokewell looked like he felt the same, his skin still that worrisome shade of gray that almost matched his hair, his eyes red-rimmed and sad. The older man began to weep again, turning his face away as if ashamed of his grief.

Garrett got up and rested his hand on Cokewell's shoulder for a moment. There wasn't anything to say right now. *Goodbye* was too final.

He walked out, leaving Cokewell to his grief, and taking his own with him.

38

Grace stayed right at his heels. He didn't move with his normal lithe gait, but then, neither did she on the icy walk even in her ephemeral body, so they were about even.

The carriage steps hadn't been pulled down. Garrett rarely used them. Without steps and hampered her skirts, she barely made it, falling heavily on her side onto the floor of the carriage. The door slammed right behind her.

The ride was very somber. Garrett sat still and looked at the mirror. Grace hardly dared breathe. She couldn't resist this one last chance to sit by him. Maybe, even if he couldn't hear her, he could sense her if she was close. She crept across the small gap separating them in the jostling carriage and sat beside him, reached out and rested a hand on his.

She could feel him—almost, as if her hand only imagined the touch, the time tunnel holding her away from anything that held emotion. Grace leaned her head against Garrett's shoulder, but though she knew it was there, she could not feel it. Her neck started to get sore, the muscles tensing from the awkward position.

It was far too short a ride.

They were home. He sat after the door opened, while the coachman stood outside, confused and respectful. Taking advantage of Garrett's stillness, she quickly slid out and eased around the waiting coachman.

Garrett nodded to the driver as he got out. Grace looked back after she got halfway up the steps. He was still there, the carriage pulling away, watching it go as if he did not want to go inside. He turned around and walked up the steps to the door. Grace kept close beside him.

She wasn't gone, and as long as she was still here, she refused to quit trying to find a solution. It had to be there. "Garrett? Please see me."

The butler opened the door for him and looked behind Garrett in puzzlement, but he was too respectful to ask where she was.

Garrett held out the mirror. Grace noticed he didn't loosen his grip on the handle. Cokewell's warning had made an impression. "Have you seen this before?"

The butler frowned down at it. "No, sir. I recommend it be discarded. It isn't good for much, not in that condition."

Garrett shook his head. "No. This is your mistress's mirror."

"I could talk to her maid, but I can't see that she would find any use for it."

"No. Don't bother. Go to bed." Garrett seemed to have used up all his conversation, because he walked off without looking at the man again.

She followed Garrett to his office. Tonight it was oppressively dark, the walls of books, the rich wood, the heavy red curtains closed for the night. He sat at his desk and picked a key from a carved wooden dish, fitted it to one of the drawers and pulled it open, then slipped the mirror inside.

He poured a single splash of amber drink from the decanter on the side table. After dismissing the butler, he hadn't made so much as a sound. He didn't even raise the glass to his mouth, just held it and stared at the sparkles off the cut glass while the sharp tang of whiskey painted the air. Grace glanced down at her skirt to see if—oh, wishful thinking—she'd suddenly appeared. Garrett was so wrapped up in himself she feared her appearance would shock him into a heart attack.

He turned his glass around in his hands, as if wondering whether someone had stolen sips when he wasn't looking.

What would he think if he knew she was still here?

His arm whipped out, Grace jumped aside as the glass zinged through the air beside her to smash against the wall, with a rain of droplets and tinkle of shattered glass.

Garrett marched out the door, up the stairs and down the hallway to his bedroom, Grace right behind.

She scuttled around him before he quietly shut the bedroom door, such a contrast from the shattered glass of his office.

He walked through the bedroom and opened the connecting door to her room, almost like a zombie, lost in his thoughts. A restless breeze picked at Grace's skirts. She looked at the windows. They were closed tight, but from somewhere, the teasing wind was blowing, building, and fear swelled inside her, panic filling her chest, seemingly shoving everything else aside until there was no room for a gasp or scream. Her hair ripped free from its careful style and blew into her face, her skirts billowed out at her sides like a sail.

She fought the wind, knowing where it came from, using all her strength to stumble toward the bedpost, the wind pushing and pushing against her, her skirts flapping with more violence. The space between herself and her husband seemed to stretch like a rubber band.

Her hands wrapped around the bedpost. It was no more solid to her than the carriage door had been, but she could feel her fingers clutch at each other, holding her there. Somehow she stayed, somehow that post held. She would not question it, grateful for these moments with him.

She still had time—they still had time. But for what?

Garrett sat on the edge of her bed for a moment, then abruptly lay down, right in the small indentation her body left, grabbed her pillow, and held it tight to his chest. The wind that swirled so violently around her didn't touch him. There was nothing to warn Garrett of her desperate struggle against the force that tried to swallow her up. She was alone in a swirling bubble, being pulled away despite all her yearnings.

"Let me stay," she screamed into the whirling air, but the tunnel continued to whirl, oblivious to her plea. Garrett didn't hear her. He didn't move, didn't blink, just lay there, clutching her pillow. She thought she saw a tear slide down his cheek.

An awful sound burst from his mouth. He sat up so abruptly that Grace jumped and nearly lost her grip, and hurled her pillow across the room just as he had done to his glass, grief released as anger. "Grace," he shouted, his voice thick and rough, "come back. I love you! Come back to me, Grace, come back, please."

With such suddenness that Grace stumbled, the wind died, leaving her holding onto the bedpost—the solid bedpost—as her skirts settled about her, and her hair tumbled down to her shoulders. She must have made a sound, a real sound, not one confined to her bubble, because Garrett whirled, a scowl on his face as though to blister whoever dared to intrude.

"Grace?" His voice was the barest whisper. His eyes went wide, the color drained from his face, leaving the new lines that had appeared in the past hour starkly visible.

"Do you see me?" she whispered, afraid, despite the wind having died, wishing she dared let go of the bedpost and push her hair away for a better look at his beloved face.

"Yes." The word was barely audible, as if he was still too stunned to talk.

And then, almost as if a band holding him in place snapped, he hurtled across the room and grabbed her away from the post so fiercely her fingers stung as they slipped past, clutching her tight. His lips found her mouth, her eyes, her cheeks, even as his arms never loosened.

Grace clasped him just as tight, holding him as fiercely as she had the post, meeting his mouth every time it passed her own before moving onto something else to kiss.

"You are here, you are back. Oh, my darling, I love you." And then he found her lips again.

When they finally had to breathe, he rested his forehead against hers. "This was all my fault. I was a coward."

"No. The fault was mine. I should have trusted you, should have told you I was from another time."

He loosened one hand enough to touch her lips, muting her, then wrapped that arm back where it had been. "Would I have believed you? I think not." Another kiss. "I love you. I wanted to say that at Cokewell's. I ached to say the words, but you were not there to hear them. I will never make that mistake again. I have learned my lesson."

She smiled. Even her heart was smiling, she was certain of it. "I love you too."

"I cannot let you go yet. I need to feel you beside me." His fingers were busy behind her, working blind as they found the bow and loosed her laces. First the gown slipped off her shoulders, caught by the press of their bodies, then the corset followed.

"I must undress." He whispered the hot words into her ear. "If I let go, will you still be here?"

Grace nodded. "I think so. I believe I am here to stay."

He gave her one long promise of a kiss, then released her slowly, inch by inch, pausing with each move as if to make sure she remained, then stepped back. His eyes never left her face. When she remained, Grace saw him heave a sigh, but he made quick work of removing his clothes, his gaze still fixed on her.

She did the same, and he came back and scooped her up. Tears filled her eyes.

"What is it?" He stopped beside the bed. "What is wrong? You must not cry. You must never cry."

But she could not stop, the tears becoming sobs as her arms tightened around his neck. "I never thought I would hold you again."

His eyes grew moist as he set her on the bed and settled beside her. "I know."

It was not time for tears, she realized as the first touches came and the sobs faded into sighs, but for loving.

Garrett stroked a hand down her arm. "Where did you go? Where were you when you were missing?"

Grace touched his face. She didn't think she would ever take that for granted again. "I was right beside you the whole time. I couldn't open anything, couldn't grasp anything, so I had to stay close. You couldn't even feel me touch you. I know, because I tried at Grandfather's."

He stilled. "I think I felt you. I felt something, but I thought it was just my heart wishing for it." He paused, and the fireplace cracked, the only sound. "If you were right there all the time, why didn't you speak?"

"I did, but you couldn't hear me. It was horrible. I saw you jump out of the carriage on the street and call for me but I was trapped inside the carriage." She felt a tear slip down her face, but didn't wipe it away. "I was so afraid! I watched you suffer, and I couldn't help."

He stroked that drop away. "I still struggle to comprehend this idea of traveling through time."

"I understand. I truly do. You have no idea what I left behind. Television, telephones, a car. Electricity and running water, antibiotics and ambulances and hospital emergency rooms. My own business, my friends, my own place."

Garrett slid his fingers into her hair. "I love these curls." A quick kiss. "I don't know what those things are you mentioned. I only recognize some of your words. You will have to explain them to me." A smile started on his face. "Yet, in spite of all these things you left, you wanted to stay, did you not? When Cokewell gave me that mirror, I thought I heard your voice even though I could not see you."

"I think you did. I saw you go still. I even thought I felt the warmth of the fire and hoped I could be seen, so I said both your names. I didn't know if it would do any good, but I was desperate. I had tried and tried. At Grandfather's house, you looked up when I spoke to you, but then—nothing. I could feel time slipping away—and me with it."

She rose on one elbow. "We still have a problem. That thing is still here. A locked desk drawer won't work. We can't let it out of our sight until we have it safe. What are we going to do with it? It can't sit around, waiting for someone to pick it up."

"God, no." A quick shudder rippled across Garrett. "I won't feel safe until it's locked away where it can never ever be discovered. I can't risk going through that again." They both reached for each other again.

Some time later, Garrett sat up. The blankets fell down to his waist. "I know the perfect solution." His normal confidence accented the statement. "We'll brick it up. I have just the place. There are chimneys that run up through the attic. We'll widen one of them with another layer of brick, and tuck the mirror inside. I can have a mason here by the end of tomorrow."

He stood up and reached for his pants. "Until that mirror is safely bricked up, I'm not letting you out of my sight. Do you think you're up to a quick jaunt across town? We must tell your grandfather you are alive and well, no matter the hour. He needs to know."

Grace sat up herself, and slid out of the bed. Despite the fireplace, the room still held a bit of the winter chill. Something she would grow used to, she knew. "You are right. After what he went through tonight, I'm sure he will still be awake. We have to hurry. We can't let him tell Grandmother."

As they rode through the dark to tell the good news to the one person who had believed in her, Grace leaned back against Garrett's shoulder, in that special notch that fitted her head perfectly, as if it had been waiting for her all that time, and sighed in contentment. She had lost much, but she had Grandfather, and now a husband who loved her.

Perhaps some day there would be children, too.

She looked down at the mirror in her hand. It was clear again, the tarnish gone.

EPILOGUE

And a good life it was. They had six children, four boys first, and two girls at long last when Garrett had almost decided he would never have a daughter like Grace. The children were the perfect blend of their best selves. All the boys looked just like him, tall and strong and opinionated, fiercely protective but equally fiercely bossy with their younger sisters. That lasted only until the girls got old enough to give back as good—and usually better—than they got.

Neither of the girls were interested in upholstery or fixing things despite Grace constantly fixing the furniture the children wore out. The youngest daughter, who had more stubbornness than all the others put together, became a skilled and popular portrait painter despite Garrett's carefully planned lectures about going into trade and predictions of social doom.

Instead, all of London society flocked to her studio to be immortalized, making her the most popular and eligible lady of the time. She waited, just like her mother, until she found love, and wed a younger son of an earl who had no title but lots of money. He brought his wife along on his travels all over the world. She found another outlet for her skill, painting miniature landscapes of all the stunning natural beauties she saw, and sold them, making herself another impressive pile of money, and Grace was quite satisfied with that.

The other girl wanted nothing more than to have a happy marriage like her parents and raise just as many children, married a lord, and proceeded to do exactly as she hoped.

The oldest son, who inherited the title, took after his grandfather Cokewell and produced better crops than all his neighbors. The second son became an architect and worked alongside the famous Mr. Nash. The third son fell in love with learning and became a professor at a small university, teaching—of all things, Grace often thought—history. And the youngest of their four sons went into law, eventually becoming a judge.

Despite the antics of six very intelligent, very lively, very inquisitive children who rampaged over all their houses from top to bottom and played endless games of hide and seek and found the most unlikely places to hide until all the good ones had finally been used, and more of the same from the generations that followed, the work of the master mason Garrett hired that day in the beginning of their lives remained hidden.

So the mirror rested, in a metal box bricked in the false fireplace wall in the attic, until the family estate sold the London house to the nation as a museum, with the stipulation that the beautiful family portraits done by their daughter—of Garrett and Grace smiling, radiating contentment over their children and grandchildren—remain in their places, untouched. Those portraits were a lasting legacy of two remarkable people and the family they founded.

During the conversion into the museum, a clever architect with a specialty in restoration and a fixation for proper measurements discovered the false wall, and in the interest of architectural accuracy, removed it. He found the box with the mirror inside.

The man cared about buildings, not fussy little bits of tarnished metal, so it went into a bunch of odds and ends of interesting but hardly memorable items. A scrap dealer with a stall on Portobello

Road purchased the bits, and sold the ornate mirror to an elderly American couple there on the trip of a lifetime.

The woman put the mirror on a shelf with other antiques, and there it sat until the elderly couple died. Their children took what they wanted out of the estate, and turned the rest over to an auctioneer, who sold the mirror in a box lot of assorted junk. A strange, canny middle-aged man with odd young blue eyes bought the box. He claimed to own a business of selling odd and ends at flea markets.

This strange man knew it would find the right owner, so set it out on a hot summer day in one of the largest flea market sales in Minneapolis.

And the rest was, quite literally, history.

ABOUT THE AUTHOR

Mary Ellen Boyd is a romance author of Regency and Biblical fiction, although if the muse strikes, she will happily branch into other genres. Her special passion is building fictional stories around factual accounts.

She also raises roses. All the flower pictures on her website are from her garden.

She has been happily married since 1982, in May, the prettiest month of the year. She and her husband have one son, who is now married himself to his high school sweetheart.

ALSO BY MARY ELLEN BOYD

Temper the Wind

A captive bride, a new land, and the chance of an everlasting love.

His Brother's Wife

By law she must face her worst nightmare, and wed a total stranger.

Warrior of the Heart

A bitter war, a stolen bride, forgiveness, acceptance, and love in unexpected places.

Fortune's Flower

She might not agree, but she needs him, and he will risk everything to win her heart.

The Thief's Daughter

An audacious plea for help, and a forbidden love.

Printed in Great Britain
by Amazon